Collins

C000221462

WATERWAYS GUIDE

River Thames & the Southern Waterways

CONTENTS

Mapping sourced from Ordnance Survey

Also available:

Collins NICHOLSON
Waterways guides and maps

Grand Union, Oxford & the South East

Severn, Avon & Birmingham

Birmingham & the Heart of England

Four Counties & the Welsh Canals

North West & the Pennines

Nottingham, York & the North East

Norfolk Broads

Inland Waterways Map of Great Britain

Published by Nicholson
An imprint of HarperCollins*Publishers*
Westerhill Road, Bishopbriggs, Glasgow G64 2QT

www.collinsmaps.com

River Thames Guide first published by Nicholson 1969
Waterways guides 1 South, 2 Midlands and 3 North first published by Nicholson 1971
This edition first published by Nicholson and Ordnance Survey 1997
New edition published by Nicholson 2000, 2003, 2006, 2009, 2012
New edition 2014

Wildlife text from *Collins Complete Guide to British Wildlife* and *Collins Wild Guide*.

This product uses map data licensed from Ordnance Survey® with the permission of
the Controller of Her Majesty's Stationery Office.
© Crown copyright. Licence number 100018598.

Ordnance Survey is a registered trade mark of Ordnance Survey, the national mapping agency of Great Britain.

The representation in this publication of a road, track or path is no evidence of the existence of a right of way.

Researched and written by Jonathan Mosse, Cicely Oliver and Ann Malcolm.

The publishers gratefully acknowledge the assistance given by Canal & River Trust and
their staff in the preparation of this guide.

Grateful thanks is also due to the Environment Agency
and members of the Inland Waterways Association.

Thanks are also due to CAMRA representatives and branch members.

Photographs reproduced by kind permission of: Derek Pratt Photography, p15, 19, 30, 39, 46, 58, 108, 110, 114, 149, 174, 176, 187; Jonathan Mosse p14, 31, 38, 79, 85, 94, 100, 101, 186; Mike Lane p25; Shutterstock/Gertjan Hooijer p52 (lapwing), Alexander Chelmodeev p52 (reed warbler), David Dohnal p52 (redshank), Gertjan Hooijer p53 (black-tailed godwit), Rick Thornton p53 (curlew, goldfinch), Morozova Tatyana (Manamana) p53 (skylark), Graham De'ath p53 (avocet), PhotoBarmaley p53 (little egret), Beth Whitcomb p127, unknown p135, Milan Kryl p145, Neil Mitchell p174.

Printed in China.

ISBN 978-0-00-749381-4

Wending their quiet way through town and country, the inland navigations of Britain offer boaters, walkers and cyclists a unique insight into a fascinating, but once almost lost, world. When built this was the province of the boatmen and their families, who lived a mainly itinerant lifestyle: often colourful, to our eyes picturesque but, for them, remarkably harsh. Transporting the nation's goods during the late 1700s and early 1800s, negotiating locks, traversing aqueducts and passing through long narrow tunnels, canals were the arteries of trade during the initial part of the industrial revolution.

Then the railways came: the waterways were eclipsed in a remarkably short time by a faster and more flexible transport system, and a steady decline began. In a desperate fight for survival canal tolls were cut, crews toiled for longer hours and worked the boats with their whole family living aboard. Canal companies merged, totally uneconomic waterways were abandoned, some were modernised but it was all to no avail. Large scale commercial carrying on inland waterways had reached the finale of its short life.

At the end of World War II a few enthusiasts roamed this hidden world and harboured a vision of what it could become: a living transport museum which stretched the length and breadth of the country; a place where people could spend their leisure time and, on just a few of the wider waterways, a still modestly viable transport system.

The restoration struggle began and, from modest beginnings, Britain's inland waterways are now seen as an irreplaceable part of the fabric of the nation. Long-abandoned waterways, once seen as an eyesore and a danger, are recognised for the valuable contribution they make to our quality of life, and restoration schemes are integrating them back into the network. Let us hope that the country's network of inland waterways continues to be cherished and well-used, maintained and developed as we move through the 21st century.

If you would like to comment on any aspect of the guides, please write to Nicholson Waterways Guides, HarperCollins Publishers, Westerhill Road, Bishopbriggs, Glasgow G64 2QT or email nicholson@harpercollins.co.uk.

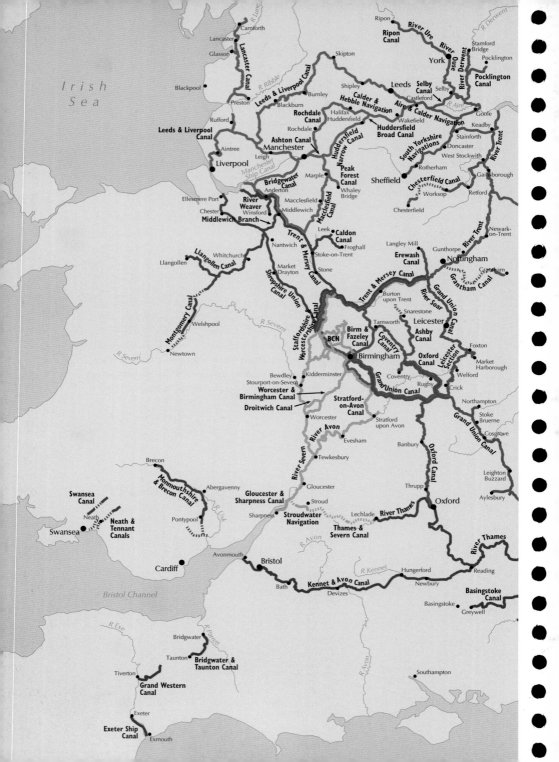

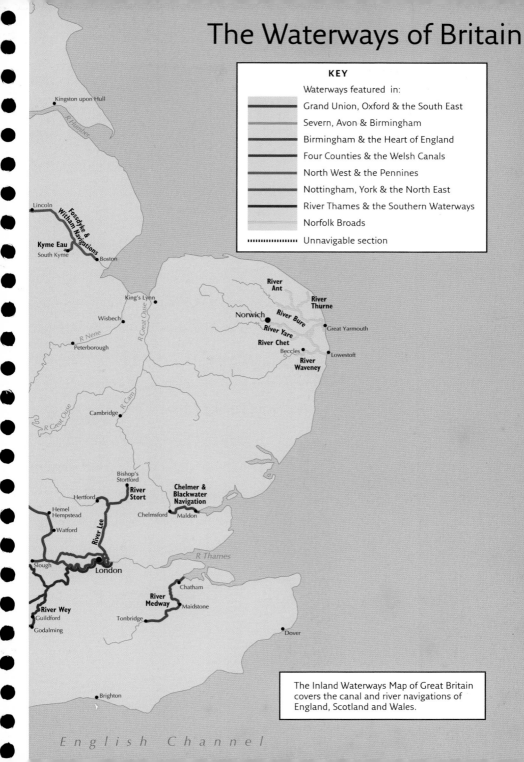

The Waterways of Britain

KEY

Waterways featured in:

- Grand Union, Oxford & the South East
- Severn, Avon & Birmingham
- Birmingham & the Heart of England
- Four Counties & the Welsh Canals
- North West & the Pennines
- Nottingham, York & the North East
- River Thames & the Southern Waterways
- Norfolk Broads
- ·············· Unnavigable section

Kingston upon Hull

R Humber

Lincoln

Fossdyke & Witham Navigations

Kyme Eau

South Kyme

Boston

King's Lynn

Wisbech

R Nene

Peterborough

R Great Ouse

River Ant

River Thurne

Norwich

River Bure

Great Yarmouth

River Yare

River Chet

Beccles

Lowestoft

River Waveney

R Cam

Cambridge

R Great Ouse

Bishop's Stortford

River Stort

Chelmer & Blackwater Navigation

Hertford

Hemel Hempstead

Watford

River Lee

Chelmsford

Maldon

Slough

London

R Thames

Chatham

River Medway

Maidstone

River Wey

Guildford

Tonbridge

Dover

Godalming

Brighton

The Inland Waterways Map of Great Britain covers the canal and river navigations of England, Scotland and Wales.

English Channel

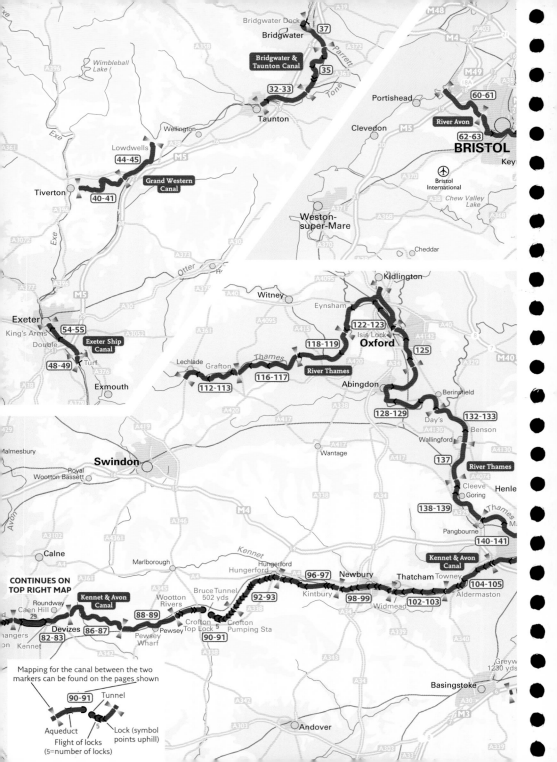

Bridgwater Dock
37
Bridgwater
35
Bridgwater &
Taunton Canal
Parrett
Tone
32-33
Taunton
Portishead
60-61
Clevedon
River Avon
62-63
BRISTOL
Key
Wimbleball Lake
A358
Lowdwells
44-45
Wellington
Exe
Grand Western Canal
Tiverton
40-41
Bristol International
Chew Valley Lake
Weston-super-Mare
Cheddar
Exe
Otter
Kidlington
Witney
Eynsham
122-123
Isis Lock
Exeter
54-55
King's Arms
Double
Exeter Ship Canal
48-49
Turf
Exmouth
Thames
Lechlade Grafton
118-119
Oxford
125
116-117
River Thames
112-113
Abingdon
Berinsfield
128-129
132-133
Day's
Benson
Wallingford
Malmesbury
Royal Wootton Bassett
Swindon
Wantage
137
River Thames
Cleeve
Goring
Henle
138-139
Calne
Marlborough
Kennet
Hungerford
Hungerford
96-97
Newbury
Thatcham
Towney
104-105
Kennet & Avon Canal
Pangbourne
140-141
Avon
CONTINUES ON TOP RIGHT MAP
Kennet & Avon Canal
Wootton Rivers
Bruce Tunnel 502 yds
92-93
Kintbury
98-99
Aldermaston
Widmead
102-103
Roundway
Caen Hill
29
Devizes
88-89
Crofton Top Lock 5
Crofton Pumping Sta
90-91
angers
82-83
86-87
Pewsey Wharf
Pewsey
Kennet
Greywell
1230 yds
Basingstoke
Andover

Mapping for the canal between the two
markers can be found on the pages shown

90-91 Tunnel

Aqueduct
5
Flight of locks
(5=number of locks)
Lock (symbol points uphill)

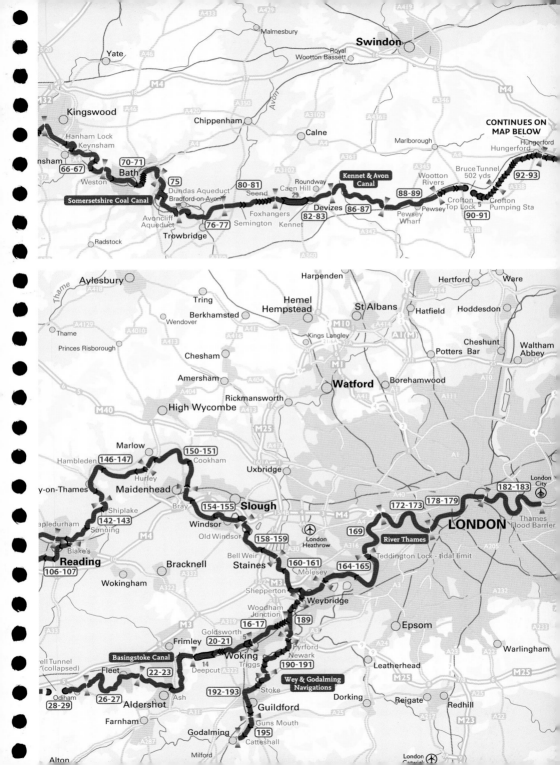

GENERAL INFORMATION FOR WATERWAYS USERS

INTRODUCTION

Boaters, walkers, fishermen, cyclists and gongoozlers (on-lookers) all share in the enjoyment of our quite amazing waterway heritage. Canal & River Trust (CRT) and the Environment Agency, along with other navigation authorities, are empowered to develop, maintain and control this resource. It is to this end that a series of guides, codes, and regulations have come into existence over the years, evolving to match a burgeoning – and occasionally conflicting – demand. Set out in this section are key points as they relate to everyone wishing to enjoy the waterways.

The *Boater's Handbook* is available from all navigation authorities. It contains a complete range of safety information, boat-handling know-how, warning symbols and illustrations, and can be downloaded from www.canalrivertrust.org. uk/boating/navigating-the-waterways/boat-handling.

CONSIDERATE BOATING

Considerate Boating gives advice and guidance to all waterway users on how to enjoy the inland waterways safely and can be downloaded from www.canalrivertrust.org.uk/boating/navigating-the-waterways/considerate-boating. It is also well worth visiting www.considerateboater.com. These publications are also available from the Customer Services Team which is staffed *Mon – Fri, 08.00 – 18.00*. The helpful staff will answer general enquiries and provide information about boat licensing, mooring, boating holidays and general activities on the waterways. They can be contacted on 0303 040 4040; customer. services@canalrivertrust.org.uk; Canal & River Trust, Head Office, First Floor North, Station House, 500 Elder Gate, Milton Keynes MK9 1BB. Visit www.canalrivertrust.org.uk for up to date information on almost every aspect of the inland waterways from news and events to moorings.

Emergency Helpline Available from Canal & River Trust outside normal office hours on weekdays and throughout weekends. If lives or property are at risk or there is danger of serious environmental contamination then contact 0800 47 999 47 immediately for emergency help.

ENVIRONMENT AGENCY

The Environment Agency (EA) manages around 600 miles of the country's rivers, including the Thames and the River Medway. For general enquiries or to obtain a copy of the *Boater's Handbook*, contact EA Customer Services on 03708 506 506; enquiries@ environment-agency.gov.uk. To find out about their work nationally (or to download a copy of the *Handbook*) and for lots of other useful information, visit www.environment-agency.gov.uk. The website www.visitthames. co.uk provides lots on information on boating, walking, fishing and events on the river.

Incident Hotline The EA maintain an Incident Hotline. To report damage or danger to the natural environment, damage to structures or water escaping, telephone 0800 80 70 60.

LICENSING – BOATS

The majority of the navigations covered in this book are controlled by CRT and the EA and are managed on a day-to-day basis by local Waterway Offices (you will find details of these in the introductions to each waterway). All craft using the inland waterways must be licenced and charges are based on the dimensions of the craft. In a few cases, these include reciprocal agreements with other waterway authorities (as indicated in the text). CRT and the EA offer an optional Gold Licence which covers unlimited navigation on the waterways of both authorities. Permits for permanent mooring on CRT waterways are issued by CRT.

Contact Canal & River Trust Boat Licensing Team on 0303 040 4040; www.canalrivertrust. org.uk/boating/licensing; Canal & River Trust Licensing Team, PO Box 162, Leeds LS9 1AX.

For the Thames and River Medway contact the EA. River Thames: 0118 953 5650; www.environment-agency.gov.uk; Environment Agency, PO Box 214, Reading RG1 8HQ. River Medway: 01732 223222 or visit the website.

BOAT SAFETY SCHEME

CRT and the EA operate the Boat Safety Scheme – boat construction standards and regular tests required by all licence holders on CRT and EA waterways. A Boat Safety Certificate (for new boats, a Declaration of Conformity), is necessary to obtain a craft licence. CRT also requires proof of insurance for Third Party Liability for a minimum of £1,000,000 for powered boats. The scheme is gradually being adopted by other waterway authorities. Contact details are: 0333 202 1000; www.boatsafetyscheme.org; Boat Safety Scheme, First Floor North, Station House, 500 Elder Gate, Milton Keynes MK9 1BB. The website offers useful advice on preventing fires and avoiding carbon monoxide poisoning.

TRAINING

The Royal Yachting Association (RYA) runs one and two day courses leading to the Inland Waters Helmsman's Certificate, specifically designed for novices and experienced boaters wishing to cruise the inland waterways. For details of RYA schools, telephone 023 8060 4100 or visit www.rya.org.uk. The practical course notes are available to buy. Contact your local boat clubs, too. The National Community Boats Association (NCBA) run courses on boat-handling and safety on the water. Telephone 0845 0510649 or visit www.national-cba.co.uk.

LICENSING – CYCLISTS

You no longer require a permit to cycle on those waterways under the control of Canal & River Trust. However, you are asked to abide by the ten point Greenway Code for Towpaths available at www.canalrivertrust.org.uk/see-and-do/cycling which also provides a wide range of advice on cycling beside the waterways. Cycling along the Thames towpath is generally accepted, although landowners have the right to request that you do not cycle. Some sections of the riverside path, however, are designated and clearly marked as official cycle ways. No permits are required but cyclists must follow London's Towpath Code on Conduct at all times.

TOWPATHS

Few, if any, artificial cuts or canals in this country are without an intact towpath accessible to the walker at least and the Thames is the only river in the country with a designated National Trail along its path from source to sea (for more information visit www.nationaltrail.co.uk). However, on some other river navigations, towpaths have on occasion fallen into disuse or, sometimes, been lost to erosion. The indication of a towpath in this guide does not necessarily imply a public right of way or mean that a right to cycle along it exists. Horse riding and motorcycling are forbidden on all towpaths.

INDIVIDUAL WATERWAY GUIDES

No national guide can cover the minutiae of detail concerning every waterway, and some CRT Waterway Managers produce guides to specific navigations under their charge. Copies of individual guides (where available) can be obtained from the relevant CRT Waterway Office or downloaded from www.canalrivertrust.org.uk/waterway-guides. Please note that times – such as operating times of bridges and locks – do change year by year and from winter to summer. For free copies of a range of helpful leaflets for all users of the River Thames – visit www.visitthames.co.uk/form/75/publications.html.

STOPPAGES

CRT and the EA both publish winter stoppage programmes which are sent out to all licence holders, boatyards and hire companies. Inevitably, emergencies occur necessitating the unexpected closure of a waterway, perhaps during the peak season. You can check for stoppages on individual waterways between specific dates on www.canalrivertrust.org.uk/boating/navigating-the-waterways/route-planning-stoppages-and-restrictions, lockside noticeboards or by telephoning 0303 040 4040; for stoppages and river conditions on the Thames, visit www.environment-agency.gov.uk/homeandleisure/recreation/131885.aspx or telephone 0845 988 1188.

NAVIGATION AUTHORITIES AND WATERWAYS SOCIETIES

Most inland navigations are managed by CRT or the EA, but there are several other navigation authorities. For details of these, contact the Association of Inland Navigation Authorities on 0113 243 3125 or visit www.aina.org.uk. The boater, conditioned perhaps by the uniformity of our national road network, should be sensitive to the need to observe different codes and operating practices.

The Canal & River Trust is a charity set up to care for England and Wales' legacy of 200-year-old waterways, holding them in trust for the nation forever, and is linked with an ombudsman. CRT has a comprehensive complaints procedure and a free explanatory leaflet is available from Customer Services. Problems and complaints should be addressed to the local Waterway Manager in the first instance. For more information, visit their website. 9

The EA is the national body, sponsored by the Department for Environment, Food and Rural Affairs, to manage the quality of air, land and water in England and Wales. For more information, visit its website.

The Inland Waterways Association (IWA) campaigns for the use, maintenance and restoration of Britain's inland waterways, through branches all over the country. For more information, contact them on 01494 783453; iwa@waterways.org.uk; www.waterways.org.uk; The Inland Waterways Association, Island House, Moor Road, Chesham HP5 1WA. Their website has a huge amount of information of interest to boaters, including comprehensive details of the many and varied waterways societies.

STARTING OUT

Extensive information and advice on booking a boating holiday is available from the Inland Waterways Association, www.visitthames.co.uk and www.canalrivertrust.org.uk/boating/boat-trips-and-holidays. Please book a waterway holiday from a licensed operator – this way you can be sure that you have proper insurance cover, service and support during your holiday. It is illegal for private boat owners to hire out their craft. If you are hiring a holiday craft for the first time, the boatyard will brief you thoroughly. Take notes, follow their instructions and do ask if there is anything you do not understand. CRT have produced a 40 min DVD which is essential viewing for newcomers to canal or river boating. Available to view free at www.canalrivertrust.org. uk/boatersdvd or obtainable (charge) from the CRT Customer Service Centre 0303 040 4040; www.canalrivertrust.org.uk/shop.

PLACES TO VISIT ALONG THE WAY

This guide contains a wealth of information, not just about the canals and rivers and navigating on them, but also on the visitor attractions and places to eat and drink close to the waterways. Opening and closing times, and other details often change; establishments close and new ones open. If you are making special plans to eat in a particular pub, or visit a certain museum it is always advisable to check in advance.

MORE INFORMATION

An internet search will reveal many websites on the inland waterways. Those listed below are just a small sample:

National Community Boats Association is a national charity and training provider, supporting community boat projects and encouraging more people to access the inland waterways. Telephone 0845 0510649; www.national-cba.co.uk.
National Association of Boat Owners is dedicated to promoting the interests of private boaters on Britain's canals and rivers. Visit www.nabo.org.uk.
www.canalplan.org.uk is an online journey-planner and gazetteer for the inland waterways.
www.canals.com is a valuable source of information for cruising the canals, with loads of links to canal and waterways related websites.
www.associationofcontinuouscruisers.org. uk is the independent organisation supporting continuous cruisers. As well as providing support and advice to its members, the Association is an advocate for the interests of all actively cruising boaters.
www.ukcanals.net lists services and useful information for all waterways users.

GENERAL CRUISING NOTES

Most canals and rivers are saucer shaped, being deepest at the middle. Few canals have more than 3-4ft of water and many have much less. Keep to the centre of the channel except on bends, where the deepest water is on the outside of the bend. When you meet another boat, keep to the right, slow down and aim to miss the approaching craft by a couple of yards. If you meet a loaded commercial boat keep right out of the way and be prepared to follow his instructions. Do not assume that you should pass on the right. If you meet a boat being towed from the bank, pass it on the outside. When overtaking, keep the other boat on your right side.

Some CRT and EA facilities are operated by pre-paid cards, obtainable from CRT and EA regional and local waterways offices, lock keepers and boatyards. Weekend visitors should purchase cards in advance. A handcuff/anti-vandal key is commonly used on locks where vandalism is a problem. A watermate/sanitary key opens sanitary stations, waterpoints and some bridges and locks. Both keys and pre-paid cards can be obtained via CRT Customer Service Centre.

Safety

Boating is a safe pastime. However, it makes sense to take simple safety precautions, particularly if you have children aboard.

- Never drink and drive a boat – it may travel slowly, but it weighs many tons.
- Be careful with naked flames and never leave the boat with the hob or oven lit. Familiarise yourself and your crew with the location and operation of the fire extinguishers.
- Never block ventilation grills. Boats are enclosed spaces and levels of carbon monoxide can build up from faulty appliances or just from using the cooker.
- Be careful along the bank and around locks. Slipping from the bank might only give you a cold-water soaking, but falling from the side of, or into a lock is more dangerous. Beware of slippery or rough ground.
- Remember that fingers and toes are precious! If a major collision is imminent, never try to fend off with your hands or feet; and always keep hands and arms inside the boat.
- Weil's disease is a particularly dangerous infection present in water which can attack the central nervous system and major organs. It is caused by bacteria entering the bloodstream through cuts and broken skin, and the eyes, nose and mouth. The flu-like symptoms occur two–four weeks after exposure. Always wash your hands thoroughly after contact with the water. Visit www.leptospirosis.org for details.

Speed

There is a general speed limit of 4 mph on most CRT canals and 5 mph on the Thames. There is no need to go any faster – the faster you go, the bigger a wave the boat creates: if your wash is breaking against the bank, causing large waves or throwing moored boats around, slow down. Slow down also when passing engineering works and anglers; when there is a lot of floating rubbish on the water (try to drift over obvious obstructions in neutral); when approaching blind corners, narrow bridges and junctions.

Mooring

Generally you may moor where you wish on CRT property, as long as you are *not causing an obstruction*. Do not moor in a winding hole or junction, the approaches to a lock or tunnel, or at a water point or sanitary station. On the Thames, generally you have a right to anchor for 24 hours in one place provided no obstruction is caused, however you will need explicit permission from the land owner to moor. There are official mooring sites along the length of the river; those provided by the EA are free, the others you will need to pay for. Your boat should carry metal mooring stakes, and these should be driven firmly into the ground with a mallet if there are no mooring rings. Do not stretch mooring lines across the towpath and take account of anyone who may walk past. Always consider the security of your boat when there is no one aboard. On tideways and commercial waterways it is advisable to moor only at recognised sites, and allow for any rise or fall of the tide.

Bridges

On narrow canals slow down well in advance and aim to miss one side (usually the towpath side) by about 9 inches. *Keep everyone inboard when passing under bridges and ensure there is nothing on the roof of the boat that will hit the bridge.* If a boat is coming the other way, the craft nearest to the bridge has priority. Take special care with moveable structures – the crew member operating the bridge should be strong and heavy enough to hold it steady as the boat passes through.

Going aground

You can sometimes go aground if the water level on a canal has dropped or you are on a particularly shallow stretch. If it does happen, try reversing *gently*, or pushing off with the boat hook. Another method is to get your crew to rock the boat from side to side using the boat hook, or move all crew to the end opposite to that which is aground. Or, have all crew leave the boat, except the helmsman, and it will often float off quite easily.

Tunnels

Again, ensure that everyone is inboard. Make sure the tunnel is clear before you enter, and use your headlight. Follow any instructions given on notice boards by the entrance.

Fuel

Hire craft usually carry fuel sufficient for the rental period.

Water

It is advisable to top up daily.

Lavatories

Hire craft usually have pump out toilets. Have these emptied *before* things become critical. Keep the receipt and your boatyard will usually reimburse you. The Green Blue, an organisation providing environmental advice for boating and watersports, has produced a series of maps locating pump out facilities within the UK. Visit www.thegreenblue.org.uk/youandyourboat for these and other advice.

Boatyards
Hire fleets are usually turned around at a weekend, making this a bad time to call in for services.

VHF Radio
The IWA recommends that all pleasure craft navigating the larger waterways used by freight carrying vessels, or any tidal navigation, should carry marine-band VHF radio and have a qualified radio operator on board. In some cases the navigation authority requires craft to carry radio and maintain a listening watch. Two examples of this are for boats on the tidal River Ouse wishing to enter Goole Docks and the Aire & Calder Navigation, and for boats on the tidal Thames, over 45ft, navigating between Teddington Lock and Limehouse Basin. VHF radio users must have a current operator's certificate. The training is not expensive and will present no problem to the average inland waterways boater. Contact the RYA (see Training) for details.

PLANNING A CRUISE
Don't try to go too far too fast. Go slowly, don't be too ambitious, and enjoy the experience. Mileages indicated on the maps are for guidance only. A *rough* calculation of time taken to cover the ground is the lock-miles system:

Add the number of *miles* to the number of *locks* on your proposed journey, and divide the resulting figure by three. This will give you an approximate guide to the number of *hours* your travel will take.

TIDAL WATERWAYS
The typical steel narrow boat found on the inland waterways is totally unsuitable for cruising on tidal estuaries. However, the adventurous will inevitably wish to add additional 'ring cruises' to the more predictable circuits of inland Britain. Passage is possible in most estuaries if careful consideration is given to the key factors of weather conditions, tides, crew experience, the condition of the boat and its equipment and, perhaps of overriding

importance, the need to take expert advice. In many cases it will be prudent to employ the skilled services of a local pilot. Within the text, where inland navigations connect with a tidal waterway, details are given of sources of advice and pilotage. It is also essential to inform your insurance company of your intention to navigate on tidal waterways as they may very well have special requirements or wish to levy an additional premium. This guide is to the inland waterways of Britain and therefore recognizes that tideways – and especially estuaries – require a different approach and many additional skills. We do not hesitate to draw the boater's attention to the appropriate source material.

LOCKS AND THEIR USE
A lock is a simple and ingenious device for transporting your craft from one water level to another. When both sets of gates are closed it may be filled or emptied using gates, or ground paddles, at the top or bottom of the lock. These are operated with a windlass. On the Thames, the locks are manned all year round, with longer hours from April to October. You may operate the locks yourself at any time.

If a lock is empty, or 'set' for you, the crew open the gates and you drive the boat in. If the lock is full of water, the crew should check first to see if any boat is waiting or coming in the other direction. If a boat is in sight, you must let them through first: do not empty or 'turn' the lock against them. This is not only discourteous, and against the rules, but wastes precious water.

In the diagrams the *plan* shows how the gates point uphill, the water pressure forcing them together. Water is flooding into the lock through the underground culverts that are operated by the ground paddles: when the lock is 'full', the top gates (on the left of the drawing) can be opened. One may imagine a boat entering, the crew closing the gates and paddles after it.

In the *elevation*, the bottom paddles have been raised (opened) so that the lock empties. A boat will, of course, float down with the water. When the lock is 'empty' the bottom gates can be opened and the descending boat can leave.

Remember that when going *up* a lock, a boat should be tied up to prevent it being thrown about by the the rush of incoming water; but when going *down* a lock, a boat should never be tied up or it will be left high and dry.

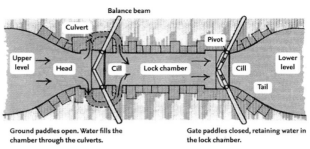

Ground paddles open. Water fills the chamber through the culverts.

Gate paddles closed, retaining water in the lock chamber.

A plan of a lock filling.

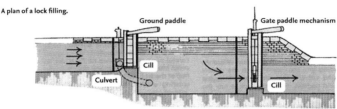

Ground paddles closed preventing water from the upper level filling the chamber.

Gate paddles open. Water flows from the chamber to the lower level.

An elevation of a lock emptying.

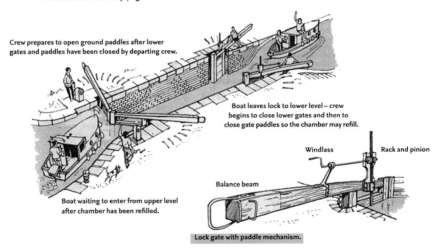

Crew prepares to open ground paddles after lower gates and paddles have been closed by departing crew.

Boat leaves lock to lower level – crew begins to close lower gates and then to close gate paddles so the chamber may refill.

Boat waiting to enter from upper level after chamber has been refilled.

Lock gate with paddle mechanism.

- Make safety your prime concern. *Keep a close eye on young children*.
- Always take your time, and do not leap about.
- Never open the paddles at one end without ensuring those at the other end are closed.
- Keep to the landward side of the balance beam when opening and closing gates.
- Never leave your windlass slotted onto the paddle spindle – it will be dangerous should anything slip.
- Keep your boat away from the top and bottom gates to prevent it getting caught on the gate or the lock cill.
- Never drop the paddles – always wind them down.
- Be wary of fierce *top gate* paddles, especially in wide locks. Operate them slowly, and close them if there is *any* adverse effect.
- Always follow the navigation authority's instructions, where given on notices or by their staff.

13

Pulteney Bridge and weir at Bath (see *page 71*)

BASINGSTOKE CANAL

MAXIMUM DIMENSIONS
Length: 72'
Beam: 13'
Headroom: 5' 10"
Draught: 3'

MILEAGES
WOODHAM JUNCTION (River Wey) to:
Woodham Top Lock: 1 mile
Goldsworth Bottom Lock: 5 miles
Pirbright Bridge: 8 miles
Deepcut Top Lock: 10 miles
Mytchett: 13 miles
Ash Lock: 16 miles
Pondtail Bridges: 20 miles
Crookham Wharf: 23 miles

Barley Mow Bridge: 27 miles
Odiham Wharf: 29 miles
Limit of navigation: 30¾ miles
Greywell Tunnel: 31 miles

29 locks

LICENCES
All craft wishing to use the canal navigation require
a licence issued by: Basingstoke Canal Authority
Canal Centre, Mytchett Place Road
Mytchett
Surrey GU16 6DD
01252 370073
info@basingstoke-canal.co.uk
www.basingstoke-canal.co.uk

An Act of Parliament for the building of this canal was passed in 1778, and the navigation opened to Basingstoke in 1794. Intended as an artery to and from London for mainly agricultural produce – timber, grain, fertilizers, chalk and malt – it was never a financial success. Built by the great canal contractor, John Pinkerton (who issued his own tokens or coins as payment to his navvies), it was originally estimated to cost £86,000. By 1796 £153,463 had been spent. Tonnages of goods carried averaged about 20,000 per annum, 10,700 tons below what was anticipated, and profit forecasts of £7,783 8s 4d proved wildly optimistic, the best figure achieved being £3,038 4s 2d in 1800.

The Napoleonic Wars, and the danger they brought to coastal shipping, benefited the Basingstoke Canal, which could transport goods bound for Portsmouth and Southampton in safety. But with the advent of peace, trade slumped – the canal managers commenting that 'some considerable injury must be sustained by the Canal'.

There was a minor boom in goods carried in 1839 to build the London & South Western Railway, but when this opened it was clear that the navigation had been instrumental in its own demise. Trade flourished for a while in 1854 with the building of the barracks at Aldershot, but this was short-lived. Plans for a revival by building a link canal from Basingstoke to the Kennet & Avon Canal at Newbury came to nothing, and the company went into liquidation in 1866. A dissolution order followed in 1878.

Purchased by new owners in 1896, and renamed the Woking, Aldershot & Basingstoke Canal, a considerable amount of money was spent on improvements, to link with the new brickworks at Up Nately, but all to no avail, and by 1904 it was once again offered for sale. In 1913, *Basingstoke*, the last narrowboat to almost reach Basingstoke, carried 5 tons of moulding sand. The canal was owned by A.J. Harmsworth between 1923 and 1947, and he did much to ensure its ultimate survival, despite the collapse of Greywell Tunnel in 1934. Munitions were transported on the canal during World War II, and the last commercial traffic, 50 tons of timber on *Gwendoline*, came to Woking in June 1949. In 1950 the canal was auctioned and sold to the Inland Waterways Association but due to insufficient funds being raised the canal was sold on to what was to become the New Basingstoke Canal Company. Now owned by the County Councils of Hampshire and Surrey, its restoration represents a magnificent achievement by both councils, the Surrey & Hampshire Canal Society and the IWA.

Woking

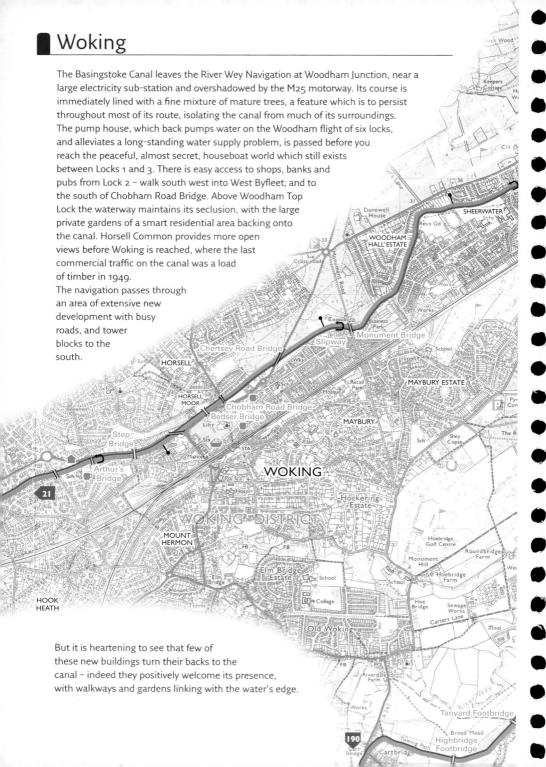

The Basingstoke Canal leaves the River Wey Navigation at Woodham Junction, near a large electricity sub-station and overshadowed by the M25 motorway. Its course is immediately lined with a fine mixture of mature trees, a feature which is to persist throughout most of its route, isolating the canal from much of its surroundings. The pump house, which back pumps water on the Woodham flight of six locks, and alleviates a long-standing water supply problem, is passed before you reach the peaceful, almost secret, houseboat world which still exists between Locks 1 and 3. There is easy access to shops, banks and pubs from Lock 2 – walk south west into West Byfleet; and to the south of Chobham Road Bridge. Above Woodham Top Lock the waterway maintains its seclusion, with the large private gardens of a smart residential area backing onto the canal. Horsell Common provides more open views before Woking is reached, where the last commercial traffic on the canal was a load of timber in 1949.

The navigation passes through an area of extensive new development with busy roads, and tower blocks to the south.

But it is heartening to see that few of these new buildings turn their backs to the canal – indeed they positively welcome its presence, with walkways and gardens linking with the water's edge.

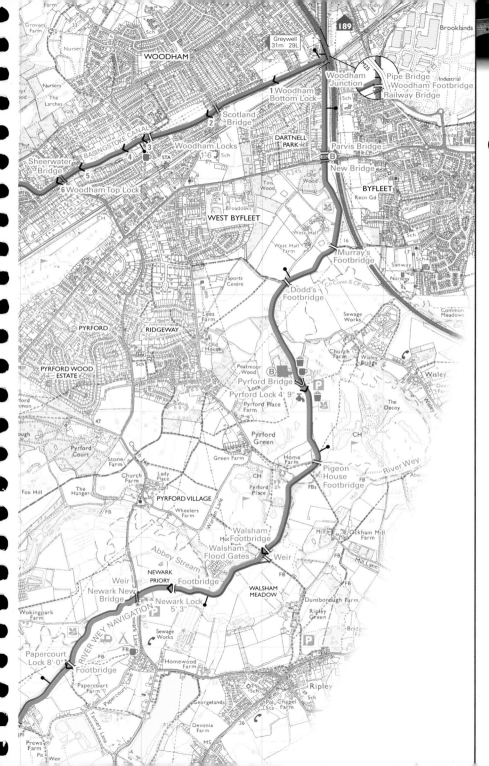

1 Facilities for boaters are fairly limited on the Basingstoke Canal. There is water available at Mytchett; Ash Lock; Barley Mow; Bridge Barn pub, Woking and Odiham (CRT Watermate key required for all sites) together with pump-out facilities at Mytchett and Galleon Marine, Odiham.

2 Slipways are available at Barley Mow Bridge, Winchfield, Farnborough Road Aldershot, and Potters Pub, Mytchett (restricted hours only).

3 Dry dock facilities are available at Frimley Lock 28 and can be booked through the Canal Centre, Mytchett.

4 Lock flights are opened by appointment between the hours set out in the table at www3.hants. gov.uk/basingstoke-canal/canal-boating/canal-navigation/locking-times.htm. To book a passage telephone 01252 370073 by 1pm on the working day before you intend to go through. Boats need to clear Thames Lock on the River Wey by 5pm (2pm in Winter) the day before the planned entry onto the Basingstoke Canal. Any boats arriving after the locking times will have to wait until the next day.

BOAT TRIPS

Woking Recreational Boating for the Handicapped offer free trips for small groups aboard *Maggie G*, a boat specially designed for wheelchair users. Trips operate from Woking. Telephone 01483 761499 or visit www.pyrford.com/wrbh for details. From *Easter–Sep*, trips are offered to disadvantaged community groups aboard *Swingbridge2*, which is also wheelchair accessible. The boat is operated by the Surrey Care Trust who work with volunteers and offenders on Community Punishment Orders, carrying out conservation work along the canal. Contact 01483 426990; www.surreycaretrust.co.uk for more information.

Woking

Surrey. All shops and services. Surrey's largest town, built around the railway, which came here in 1838. The original village, Old Woking, lies 2 miles to the south. Development carries on apace, making dormitory homes for the thousands of commuters who rush up to the city daily. It is, however, worth walking south from Monument Bridge, and taking the third turning on the right, Oriental Road, to see the Shah Jehan Mosque, built in 1889 and reminiscent of the Taj Mahal in India with its onion-shaped dome. Built by the enormously rich Begum Shah Jehan, ruler of Bhopal State in India, its design, by W. I. Chambers, is honest and dignified. A P&O captain was employed to take bearings to ensure an exact orientation towards Mecca.

Brooklands Museum Brooklands Road, Weybridge KT13 0QN (01932 857381; www. brooklandsmuseum.com). Assembled within what remains of the Brooklands race track, the world's first purpose-built motor racing circuit, constructed by wealthy landowner Hugh Locke King in 1907. Its heyday was in the 1920s and 30s, when records were being set by the likes of Malcolm Campbell and John Cobb, driving vehicles with evocative names, such as the Delage, Bentley and Bugatti. It became very fashionable, and was known as the Ascot of Motorsport. It was also an aerodrome and an aircraft factory, and it was here that A. V. Roe made the first flight in a British aeroplane. The Sopwith Pup and Camel were developed here, and later the Hawker Hurricane and the Vickers Wellington were built here – the only Wellington that saw war time service, salvaged in 1985 from Loch Ness and restored, is on display. The outbreak of war in 1939 brought an end to racing,

and aircraft production ceased in 1987. Now you can walk on part of the legendary circuit, and see historic racing cars and aircraft, including a *Concorde*, in the museum. The clubhouse is a listed building. You can also visit the Raleigh Cycle Exhibition, a reminder that cycle races were also held at Brooklands. Shop. Special events are staged throughout the year. *Open 10.00–17.00 (16.00 winter). Closed Xmas.* Charge.

Elmbridge Museum Church Street, Weybridge KT13 8DE (01932 843573; www.elmbridgemuseum.org.uk). Above the public library. A collection established in 1909 and refurbished in 1996, covering local and social history and featuring items relating to Oatlands Palace, near Weybridge, which was built by Henry VIII in 1537. Also finds from a Romano-British bathhouse near Cobham. *Open Fri 11.00–17.00; Sat 10.00–13.00 & 14.00–17.00.* Buses or train to Weybridge.

New Victoria Theatre Peacocks Centre, Woking GU21 6GQ (Box office 0870 060 6645; www. atgtickets.com/venues/new-victoria-theatre). Situated in the Peacocks Arts & Entertainments Centre and providing a 1300-seat venue for drama, musicals, opera and ballet. Also big-screen cinemas, bars, cafés and restaurants.

Woking Leisure Centre and Pool in the Park Woking Park, Kingfield Road GU22 9BA (01483 771122; www.woking.gov. uk). Three swimming pools and a cafeteria. The leisure centre includes aerobics, gym, health suite, squash, badminton, children's activities, a multisensory suite and a 1930s Wurlitzer organ, restaurant and bar.

Woking Visitor Information Visit www.woking. gov.uk/woking/visit or www.visitsurrey.com for a wide range of visitor information about the area.

- **Woodham**
  Surrey. All shops and services. A typical commuter conurbation of dull, closely packed houses, only pretty in the more expensive areas, where large, spacious houses and gardens nestle among trees.

Definitely at its best and most characterful by the canal.

- **Horsell**
  Surrey. Indistinguishable from Woking (*see above*), although if you look hard enough, you will find a few original cottages.

UPS AND DOWNS ON THE BASINGSTOKE

The Basingstoke Canal was at one time often portrayed as a restoration failure, but this was borne entirely out of a misconception. At the outset the objective of the two county councils involved was to create a 32-mile, linear country park for the benefit of a wide variety of potential users, of which boaters were to be but one (albeit significant) group.

Two barge movements a day was the average traffic when the waterway was opened and water supply was always constrained by an undertaking not to tap existing watercourses, jealously guarded by millers and landowners alike. Apart from springs and rainwater run-off – plentiful during the winter months – the only other water source is limited to two pumped supplies: one at Woking and a second at Frimley, lifting storm water from a drainage sump on the trackbed of the mainline railway. A pumping station, installed at the bottom of Woodham Locks, serves to stop water losses to the River Wey, and maintains the level in the pound above the flight. Springs work on more or less a six month cycle so a good time to visit the canal is between February and mid June when water supplies should be at their maximum.

It has aptly been described as a sleepy backwater of a canal and navigating it is more akin to boating in the 1950s: locks fill slowly and require care, and the waterway itself is not to be rushed alike. Herein lies its real charm and to appreciate it – together with the abundant wildlife and SSSIs – visitors must understand its constraints, together with the way in which it has successfully fulfilled all the aims of its restorers and delighted one-and-a-half million diverse visitors annually.

King John's Castle, Odiham (see page 29)

WALKING & CYCLING

The towpath is in excellent condition throughout the entire length of the navigation, including the disused section west of Greywell Tunnel as far as Penny Bridge. The short section across Greywell Hill, however, may be uneven and overgrown. The towpath is well used by walkers and cyclists alike and in conjunction with the numerous British Rail stations, situated at regular intervals close to the canal, it is fairly easy to plan excursions without having to double back.

Pubs and Restaurants

There are plenty of pubs and restaurants in Woking and West Byfleet but only one is adjacent to the canal.

The Catherine of Aragon Station Road, West Byfleet KT14 6DR (01932 336353; www. thecatherineofaragon.co.uk). Opposite West Byfleet station. Family-run pub, restaurant and hotel serving a wide range of home-made food and real ales. Large outdoor seating area. Children welcome *until 21.00*. B&B. *Open Mon–Sat 12.00-23.00 & Sun 12.00–22.30*. Restaurant *closes 21.30*.

O'Neills Crown Square, Woking GU21 6HR (01483 728304). A typical example of the O'Neills pub chain with wooden furniture and wall panelling throughout. Meals *L and E* until *22.00 daily*. Live music *every Fri and Sat*. Quiz *Sun*.

The Bridge Barn Bridge Barn Lane, Woking GU21 6NL (01483 763642; www.thebridgebarn. com). Beside Arthur's Bridge. Tastefully converted 17th-C timbered barn housing 'Beefeater' restaurant. Meals *L and E*. Real ale. Children welcome. Canalside garden with play area. Moorings outside. Venue for the Basingstoke Canal Festival, held *each Easter*.

The Herbert Wells 51-57 Chertsey Road, Woking GU21 5AJ (01483 722818; www. jdwetherspoon.co.uk/home/pubs/the-herbert-wells). Popular, town centre Wetherspoon's pub. Real ale. Meals *all day*. Children welcome *daily 08.00-18.00*. Outside seating. *Open 08.00-00.00 (Fri 01.00)* with food *available until 22.00*.

Brookwood

Woking is gradually left behind as the canal rises through the five St John's Locks (where back-pumping is now installed) to Kiln Bridge, where there are good moorings above the bridge. Here there is easy access to shops, Indian and Chinese restaurants, and a laundrette. The railway, which accompanies the canal to Frimley Green, comes very close at Knaphill, and is then replaced by the trees of Brookwood Lye. Houseboats moored here, by Hermitage Bridge, add a picturesque touch. Brookwood Locks are pleasantly situated and once again the trees reappear. An old overgrown pill box still guards Pirbright Bridge – beyond the bridge is the first of the Deepcut, or Frimley, flight of locks. The canal now climbs steadily up the 14 locks in a superb, tree-lined, setting.

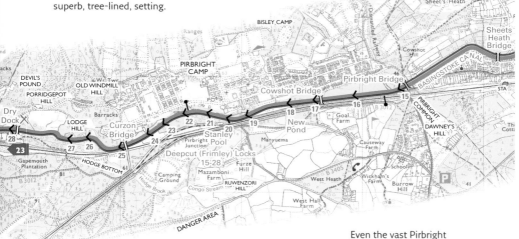

Even the vast Pirbright Army Camp to the north hardly intrudes, although you may hear the odd burst of practice gunfire. Between many of the locks there are wide pools – check the depth of these carefully if you dare to stray off the direct course (not recommended). Each of the locks has a footbridge, and a ladder in the chamber, but not all have an easy means of landing below the bottom gates, so it is a good idea for a member of the crew to walk ahead to open the gates while ascending. Above the top lock is a dry dock, rebuilt in 1984, and available for hire. (see Navigational Note 3, page 18). The building here was once a workshop and forge.

● **St John's**
Surrey. PO, stores, takeaways, chemist, laundrette.
Swallowed up by Woking, the area around Kiln Bridge somehow, against all odds, manages to retain the feel of a village centre. Notice the well-restored building topped by a clock tower, right by the bridge.

● **Knaphill**
Surrey. Basically a large Victorian village around the barracks and the site of the gaunt Brookwood Mental Hospital, a mid 19th-C asylum which was once entirely self-sufficient, generating its own electricity and running its own farm in the grounds. To the west is Bisley, famous for its annual rifle shooting competitions.

● **Brookwood Bridge**
Surrey. Adjacent to Brookwood Locks. Shop, garage, cashpoint.
Brookwood Cemetery Four miles west of Woking GU24 0BL (01344 891041; www.tbcs.org.uk) Superbly landscaped expanse of heathland covering 2,400 acres, to the south of Brookwood Station, where mature trees and eccentric mausoleums coexist harmoniously. Founded by the London Necropolis Company in 1854, when the numbers of dead Londoners were becoming increasingly difficult to accommodate, it was once served by a railway – indeed one of the station buildings still survives. There is a military cemetery in the south west corner, where British and American soldiers are buried.

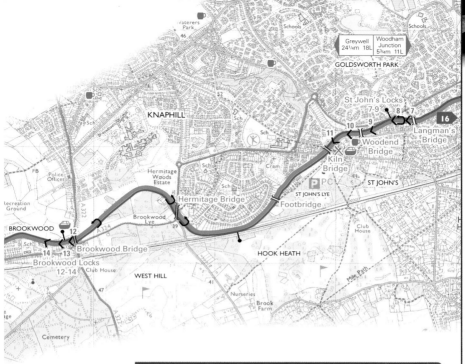

Greywell 24¼m 18L | Woodham Junction 5¾m 11L

NAVIGATIONAL NOTES

1 St John's and Brookwood Locks are *open 09.00-14.00 daily*. Boats must clear the flight *by 15.00*. (See also Navigational Note 4 on page 18).
2 Do not stray from the direct course of the canal without first checking the depth. Many of the wide pools are quite shallow.

Pubs and Restaurants

The Rowbarge 39 St John's Road, St John's GU21 7SA (01483 761618; www.rowbarge.co.uk). Friendly, family-run hotel, restaurant and pub serving home-cooked food daily *L and E*. – anything from snacks to a three course dinner. Real ales. Children's menu. Large garden. B&B.

The Robin Hood 88 Robin Hood Road, Knaphill GU21 2LY (01483 472173; www.robinhoodknaphill. com). Comfortable, newly refurbished pub serving real ale and food *L Mon-Sat 12.00-14.00 & Sun 12.00-16.00*. Children welcome. Large garden. Pub games. Quiz night *Wed* and music night *Fri*.

Tiger Tuu 1 St John's Road, St John's, Woking GU21 7SE (01483 721173; www.tigertu.co.uk). Beside Kiln Bridge. Specialists in Thai, Peking and Vietnamese cuisine. *Open Mon–Sun 12.00-14.30 (Sun 15.00) & 18.00-23.00. Sun* Buffet. Takeaway.

Spice Village Restaurant & Takeaway 3 St John's Road, St John's, Woking (01483 715611; www.spicevillagewoking.com). 50 yds south of Kiln Bridge. Excellent Indian food *L & E*. For takeaways telephone 01483 722822.

The Hunter's Lodge Bagshott Road, Knaphill, Woking GU21 2RP (01483 474602; www. vintageinn.co.uk/thehunterslodgewoking). North of Brookwood Bridge. Attractive and welcoming pub. Real ale. Traditional English bar food *all day*. Free from loud music – and it has a *silent* fruit machine. Children welcome. Garden. *Open all day*.

The Garibaldi 134 High Street, Knaphill, Woking GU21 2QH (01483 473374; www. thegaribaldi-knaphill.co.uk). Ten minute walk along Bagshot Road. A traditional pub, describing itself as a 'pub for the village', rather than a village pub. Home-cooked food prepared from local ingredients *available daily 12.00-21.30 (21.00 Sun)*. Large garden and family room. Curry night *Tue* and quiz *Sun*. Occasional live music.

21

Mytchett

Having climbed 90ft, the navigation now enters the dramatic Deepcut cutting, 1,000yds long and up to 70ft deep. Lined with large, mature, deciduous trees, it is pleasantly shady and remote. Beyond Wharfenden Lake, now part of a country club, and the supposedly lead-lined aqueduct over the railway, the canal turns sharply south towards Mytchett, with woods and heathland rising to the east. Mytchett Lake, owned by the army and renowned amongst anglers for the size of its pike, adjoins the canal, but is closed to navigation. The canal continues south, enclosed by the railway and thick woods on one side, and leafy gardens on the other. Just beyond the railway bridge at Ash Vale is the corrugated iron boathouse, dated 1896, where 15 barges were built between 1918 and 1935, and repairs were undertaken until 1947. There is a takeaway and a stores here (by the station), an off-licence and easy access to shops. Great Bottom Flash, which contains the sunken remains of *Basingstoke*, the last narrowboat to almost reach Basingstoke, is surrounded by trees. It was here that Samuel F. Cody came to test his early seaplanes, prior to World War I. It is now a Danger Area, used by the army. Large houses with gardens landscaped to the water's edge face a busy road at Ash Vale before the navigation resumes its general westerly course. There is a post office and a good range of shops and takeaways in the local shopping centre at Ash Wharf Bridge. It then crosses Spring Lake on an embankment and the Blackwater Valley Road on an aqueduct, leaving Surrey and entering Hampshire. There are good moorings above Ash Lock, opposite the Canal Depot (slipway). The reappearance of army property – barrack blocks behind high wire fences – announces the approach to Aldershot. The canal has now climbed 195ft since leaving Woodham Junction. Queen's Avenue Bridge is notable for its modestly ornate iron balustrades, bringing a little light relief from the army camps which now completely enclose the waterway. Beyond Eelmoor Bridge, the canal widens at Eelmoor Flash, a Site of Special Scientific Interest (SSSI) due to its exceptional dragonfly population.

The canal continues its westward course eventually to reveal the low buildings of Farnborough airfield, which still hosts the world-famous Farnborough Air Show.

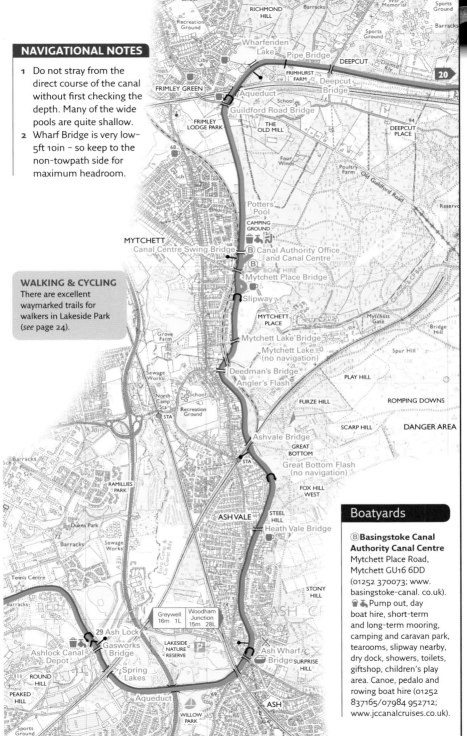

NAVIGATIONAL NOTES

1. Do not stray from the direct course of the canal without first checking the depth. Many of the wide pools are quite shallow.
2. Wharf Bridge is very low– 5ft 10in – so keep to the non-towpath side for maximum headroom.

WALKING & CYCLING

There are excellent waymarked trails for walkers in Lakeside Park (*see page 24*).

Boatyards

Ⓑ **Basingstoke Canal Authority Canal Centre**
Mytchett Place Road, Mytchett GU16 6DD (01252 370073; www. basingstoke-canal. co.uk). Pump out, day boat hire, short-term and long-term mooring, camping and caravan park, tearooms, slipway nearby, dry dock, showers, toilets, giftshop, children's play area. Canoe, pedalo and rowing boat hire (01252 837165/07984 952712; www.jccanalcruises.co.uk).

Royal Logistic Corps Museum Princess Royal
Baracks, Deepcut, Camberley GU16 6RW
(01252 833371; www.rlcmuseum.co.uk). North of
the canal, on the B3015. This collection depicts the
last 500 years of history of the Royal Corps
of Transport, the Royal Pioneer Corps and the
Army Catering Corps. *Mon–Fri 09.00–16.00;
Sat 12.00–16.00. Closed Sun.* Museum shop. Free.

Frimley Lodge Park Sturt Road, Frimley Green
GU16 6HY (01276 707338; www.surreyheath.gov.uk).
Playing fields, café, pitch & putt, play areas together
with miniature railway, canalside and woodland
walks. *Closes at dusk.*

Basingstoke Canal Visitor Centre Mytchett Place
Road, Mytchett GU16 6DD (01252 370073;
www.basingstoke-canal.co.uk). Overlooking the
canal, also the location of the boating facilities.
Picnic and play area, information centre, gift shop,
tearoom and campsite. The information centre
contains a detailed map, historical references,
interactive lock model and a replica barge cabin.
Summer boat trips *(Easter–Sep, weekends 11.30–17.00
and Tue–Sun during school holidays).* For contact
information, *see* Boat Trips page 25. Visitor Centre
*open Easter to Sep Tue–Sun 10.30–16.45 & October to
March Tue–Thu, 10.30–16.00; Fri, 10.30–13.45.* Charge

● **Ash and Ash Vale**
Surrey. PO, stores. Villages which are now enclosed
by the sprawl of Aldershot. St Peter's Church, Ash,
is early medieval and retains a Norman window,
a finely detailed south door, c.1200 and a 17th-C
wooden font.

Army Medical Services Museum Keogh Barracks,
Ash Vale, Aldershot GU12 5RQ
(01252 868612; www.ams-museum.org.uk/
museum). Tells the contribution the Army Medical
Services have made in the history of medicine,
nursing, dentistry and veterinary science. Shop. Free.
*Open Mon–Fri 09.30–15.30; weekends and evenings
by appointment.*

Lakeside Park (01252 331353; www.blackwater-
valley.org.uk). Access by foot from Blackwater Valley
Path, between the canal and Lakeside Road Railway
Bridge. Gravel extraction during the 1950s created
the fine landscape of lakes and woods we see today.
Remnants of the original field system still remain,
and common spotted and bee orchids flower
annually. Dragonflies are prolific during the summer
months. On warm evenings bats can be seen.
Network of footpaths and children's natural play
area.

● **Farnborough**
*Hants. All shops and services (but they are some
distance north of the canal).* A name synonymous
with the famous biennial air show *(see below)*,
Farnborough is now just a northerly extension of
Aldershot, the original village having been engulfed
by light industry, housing and the military. Almost
2 miles north of Wharf Bridge is St Peter's Church,
dating from around 1200, with a wooden porch
and weatherboarded tower. A short walk further
north of this is Farnborough Hill, the former home

of the Empress Eugenie, wife of Napoleon III of
France, from the time of her exile to England in
1871 until her death in 1920. The building is now
a convent school but is occasionally open to the
public. The Empress built an extravagantly French
mausoleum for her husband, her son and herself
in 1871, as well as an abbey, known as
St Michael's, now occupied by English
Benedictine monks.

Farnborough Airport Farnborough. This
aerodrome was set up in 1905 as His Majesty's
Balloon Factory. The American showman,
Samuel Cody, and a Red Indian friend, made the
first powered flight in Britain at Laffan's Plain,
Farnborough, in 1908, when Cody was Chief
Kiting Instructor at the Balloon School here.
Cody died in an air crash in 1913. During the two
World Wars extensive research into developing
military aircraft was carried out at the airfield.
Much of the design and development work on
Concorde was executed here. The world-famous
Farnborough Air Show is held here biennially in
July, and attracts over 200,000 visitors with its
static exhibitions and dramatic flying displays.
Considering the orientation of the main runway,
you should get a good view from the canal.

● **Aldershot**
*Hants. All shops and services, cinema and theatre
(but some distance south of the canal).* In 1854
the army bought 10,000 acres of heathland
surrounding the rural hamlet of Aldershot,
bringing building materials on the Basingstoke
Canal and descending upon the area in force. It
has never been the same since. In spite of a great
deal of redevelopment it is still, for the most part,
an uninspiring place, with the military being all
pervasive. What is left of the original village, and
it is not much, is to the south east of the station.
The spectacular biennial army display has
become a free one-day celebration of Armed
Forces Day.

Aldershot Military Museum Queen's Avenue,
Aldershot GU11 2LG (0845 603 5635;
www3.hants.gov.uk/museum/aldershot-
museum.htm). North of Queen's Avenue Bridge.
The story of Aldershot Military Town and the
civil towns of Aldershot, Farnborough and Cove,
housed in the only surviving brick-built barrack
blocks left in Aldershot. Visitors can learn about
daily life for both soldier and civilian since 1854.
Open Wed–Fri 10.00–17.00, Sat–Sun 11.00–16.00.
Shop. Charge.

Army Physical Training Corps Museum Army
School of Physical Training, Queen's Avenue,
Aldershot GU11 2LB (01252 347168; www.army.
mod.uk/raptc/6427.aspx). Records, equipment,
medals and history of the corps. *Open Mon–
Thu 9.30–16.30, Fri 9.30–12.30, weekends by
appointment only.* Free.

Princes Hall Princes Way, Aldershot GU11 1NX
(01252 329155; www.princeshall.com). Theatre,
concerts and other events.

West End Centre 48 Queens Road, Aldershot GU11 3JD (01252 330040; www.westendcentre.co.uk). Licensed bar, comedy, music, jazz, theatre, classes in pottery and art, and other events.

Tourist Information Centre Princes Hall, Princes Way, Aldershot GU11 1BH (01252 320968; www. rushmoor.gov.uk). *Open Mon–Fri 10.00–17.30, Sat 10.00–15.00 (closed Sun).*

BOAT TRIPS
Merlin lunch and dinner cruises, cream tea cruises and private charter for up to 35 passengers, operating from the Canal Centre, Mytchett. *Daydream* provides 45-minute public trips. *Astra* self-drive hire for small groups. All these trips operate from the Canal Visitor Centre. For details telephone 01252 837165/07984 952712 or visit www.jccanalcruises.co.uk.

WILDLIFE
Daubenton's Bat is a medium-sized bat (wingspan 23–27cm) with comparatively short ears. Frequently associated with water and seen flying low over lakes, ponds and canals just as dusk is falling. Also feeds along woodland rides. Chirps can be heard by those with good hearing. In summer, roosts, sometimes in colonies, in hollow trees and tunnel entrances. In winter, hibernates in caves, mines and cellars. Widespread and fairly common in Britain. Daubenton's Bat is one of the species found in Greywell Tunnel. The Basingstoke Canal Authority run bat walks along the canal in the autumn. Visit www.basingstoke-canal.co.uk for information.

Pubs and Restaurants

⬛✕**The King's Head** Old Guildford Road, Frimley Green, Camberley GU16 6NR (01252 835431; www.harvester.co.uk/thekingsheadcamberley). By King's Head Bridge, Frimley Green. A Harvester restaurant with a large garden. Food *L and E, daily.*

⬛**The Rose & Thistle** 1 Sturt Road, Frimley Green GU16 6HT (01252 834942; www.theroseandthistlefrimleygreen.co.uk). West of the King's Head overlooking the village green. Real ale, good choice of wine and Belgian beers. Meals *L and E.* Garden and patio. Children welcome until *20.30.* Quiz *Sun. Open 12.00–00.00 (01.00 Sat & Sun)*

⬛✕**The Old Wheatsheaf** 205 Frimley Green Road, Frimley Green GU16 6LA (01252 835074; www.theoldwheatsheaf.co.uk). South of the Rose & Thistle along A321. Traditional village local with panelled alcoves. Real ale. Home-made food and à la carte restaurant *Tue–Sat 18.30–21.30;* bar meals *L and E;* traditional *Sun* roasts *12.00–18.00.* Outside patio area and traditional pub games. *Open Mon–Thur 11.00–15.00 & 17.00–23.00; Fri & Sat 11.00–23.00 & Sun 12.00–22.30.*

✕**Canal Centre Tearooms** Canal Centre, Mytchett Place Road, Mytchett GU16 6DD (01252 370073). Friendly, welcoming establishment.

Inexpensive and enticing array of home-baked cakes and light meals. Tea, coffee, soft drinks and ice creams. Garden with children's play area. *Open Easter–Sep Tue–Sun 10.30–16.45 & Oct–Mar 10.30–15.45.*

⬛✕**Potters Inn** Mytchett Place Road, Camberley GU16 6DD (01252 513934; www.pottersinn.co.uk). Above Mytchett Place Bridge. Large pub with garden overlooking the canal. Real ale. Breakfast, lunch, *afternoon* teas and dinner. B&B. *Open 07.00–23.00.* Public slipway in garden and good off-line moorings. Slipway users must park their cars at the Canal Centre opposite.

⬛✕**The Swan** 2 Hutton Road, Ash Vale, Aldershot GU12 5HA (01252 758172; www.chefandbrewer.com/pub/swan-ash-vale-aldershot/c2187). Beside Heath Vale Bridge. Large pub with garden overlooking the canal. Children welcome. *Open Mon–Sat 11.00–23.00 & Sun 12.00–22.00.* Food served *Mon–Sat 12.00–22.00 & Sun 12.00–21.30.*

✕🍷**Spice of India** 2 Wharf Road, Ash Vale, Aldershot GU12 5AZ (01252 313638/325163). By Ash Wharf Bridge. Locally recommended Indian restaurant with friendly service and generous portions. *Open daily 17.30–23.30.*

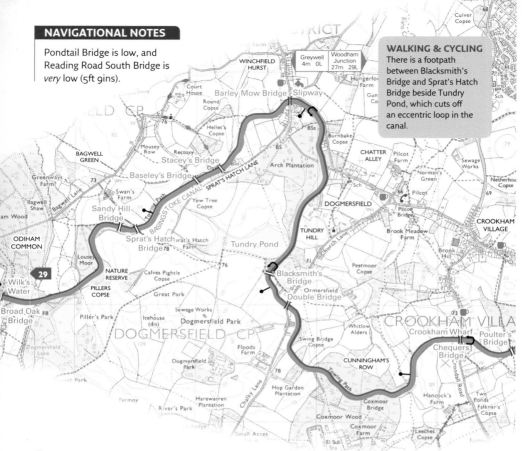

NAVIGATIONAL NOTES

Pondtail Bridge is low, and Reading Road South Bridge is *very* low (5ft 9ins).

WALKING & CYCLING
There is a footpath between Blacksmith's Bridge and Sprat's Hatch Bridge beside Tundry Pond, which cuts off an eccentric loop in the canal.

Crookham

The course of the navigation is now rural and isolated and, notwithstanding all the military presence, approaches Fleet in a richly wooded cutting through Pyestock Hill. There is an excellent licensed supermarket at Pondtail Bridges, selling fresh meat and vegetables as well as the usual things – this marks the eastern extremity of Fleet. Houses and gardens back on to the canal and generally seem to appreciate it being there. A canoe slalom course is marked out (slow down and take care) and there are some moored craft. Shops are close at hand to the north west of Reading Road South Bridge. Between Chequers and Double Bridges old World War II anti-tank barriers still stand by the waterway, and pill-box defences can be seen gently crumbling away in the undergrowth.

● **Fleet**
Hants. All services. Useful for its shops and services, but little else of interest.
● **Crookham Village**
Hants. PO, stores.
● **Dogmersfield**
Hants. A well-preserved village with pretty thatched and timbered houses.

● **Winchfield**
Hants. Walk north from Barley Mow Bridge to see the church of St Mary, a Norman building dating from c.1170. There are three original windows in the tower, and boldly decorated doorways.

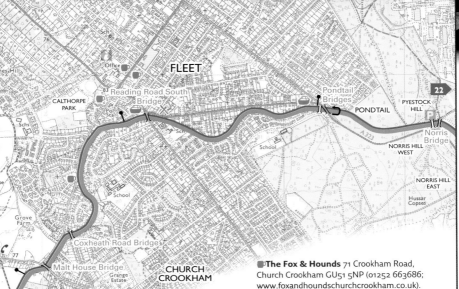

Pubs and Restaurants

♪ Propaganda Music Canteen
317-321 Fleet Road, Fleet GU51 3BU
(01252 620198; www.musiccanteen.co.uk).
Formerly the Hogs Head. Now described as a
casual, fun and relaxing approach to food and drink
with excellent service in stylish surroundings. Large
variety of lager and ciders, cocktails, soft drinks and
coffee. Inexpensive food available *all day*. Outside
seating and patio. *Open Mon–Wed 11.00–23.00;
Thur 11.00–00.30; Fri 11.00–01.00 & Sat 11.00–01.30.
Closed Sun.* Live music *Thur from 21.00*.

Old Emporium 271 Fleet Road, Fleet GU51 3QW
(01252 816797). Trendy, young persons' pub,
described as an Ale Café. Real ale. Interesting
selection of snacks and bar meals *all day*. Garden
and patio seating. DJs *Thu, Fri and Sat evenings*.

✕ The Oat Sheaf 2 Crookham Road, Fleet GU51
5DR (01252 819508; www.theoatsheaf.co.uk). Large
main road pub at the Oatsheaf crossroads, north of
Reading Road South Bridge. Real ale and meals *all
day* including prix fixe menu for *L and early E*. Range
of daily culinary attractions. Large garden. *Open daily
11.00–23.00 (Sun 22.30); food available Mon–Sat
12.00–22.00 (22.30 Fri & Sat) & Sun 12.00–21.00.*

The Fox & Hounds 71 Crookham Road,
Church Crookham GU51 5NP (01252 663686;
www.foxandhoundschurchcrookham.co.uk).
Friendly pub with large canalside garden. Real ale.
Homemade, freshly prepared meals *Mon–Fri L and
E, Sat–Sun throughout day until early evening*. Food
service times may alter if a special event is being
held, so please telephone and book in advance.
Children welcome (under 10s until *20.00*). Dogs
welcome. Boat rally *mid-Sep*. Live music *Fri*. Quiz
night *Tue*.

✕ The Exchequer Cromdall Road, Crookham
Village GU51 5SU (01252 615336; www.
theexchequer.co.uk). North of Crookham Wharf.
Described as a 21st-century local and recently
refurbished. Good range of real ales and wide-
ranging menu *Mon–Thur L and E; all day Fri–Sun*.

The Black Horse The Street, Crookham Village
GU51 5SJ (01252 616434). Beamy village local. Real
ale. Inexpensive bar meals *L Mon–Sat, and Sunday
lunch*. Children welcome *L*, dogs welcome outside.
Garden. Live sport, pool and darts. Poker monthly.

The Queen's Head Pilcot, Dogmersfield
RG27 8SY (01252 613531; www.queensheadpub.
co.uk). Fine 17th-C country pub, where Catherine
of Aragon met Arthur, Henry VIII's brother. Real
ale. Extensive range of meals *L and E*. Children
welcome. Patio and large garden.

✕ The Barley Mow The Hurst, Winchfield RG27
8DE (01252 617490; www.barley-mow.com). Large
country pub, with an intriguing central fireplace.
Meals *L and E (not Sun or Mon E)*. Garden. Dogs and
children welcome. BBQ facility and function room.
The home of the local cricket team.

BOAT TRIPS

Canoeing: Basingstoke Canal Canoe Club (www.b3c.org.uk/). A type of boating very popular on
this canal.

North East Hants Water Activity Centre Fleet (www.blackwater-valley.org.uk/nehwaca.htm).
Canoeing for the able-bodied and disabled with specially adapted boats and hoists as required.
Details of both the above from the Basingstoke Canal Visitor Centre, Mytchett Place Road, Mytchett
GU16 6DD (01252 370073; www.basingstoke-canal.co.uk).

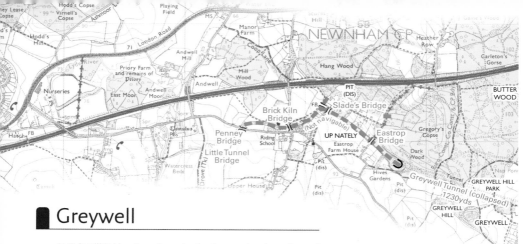

Greywell

At Colt Hill Bridge there is a wharf, a boatyard and good moorings.
The course of the canal now becomes more open as it makes its approach to Greywell
Tunnel. The few houses and gardens of North Warnborough are followed by a mechanised lift
bridge, beyond which is the limit of navigation for cruisers, by Odiham Castle. The last commercial
boat reached Odiham in 1916. It is then just a short walk to the eastern portal of the collapsed
Greywell Tunnel (1,230yds), passing the remains of Lock 30. This was built to raise the water
level above here by 12ins, to give increased draught and aid navigation. A footpath leads over the
tunnel portal to Greywell village, and the Fox & Goose pub. It is possible to follow rough paths over
Greywell Hill to see what remains of the western entrance to the tunnel and a short isolated stretch
of the canal passing the village of Up Nately. Greywell Tunnel is well known for its colony of some
12,500 bats, including the largest known colony of Natterer's bats in the UK.

NAVIGATIONAL NOTES

1 The mechanised lift bridge at North Warnborough is operated with a Watermate key.
2 The limit of navigation is a few yards beyond Odiham Castle. Do not attempt to take your boat
   any further than this. *Turn here.*

BOAT TRIPS

John Pinkerton This is a 50-seater boat operated by the Surrey &
Hampshire Canal Society for public trips and private charter. Telephone
(01962) 713564 or visit www.johnpinkerton.co.uk/ for details.
Accessible Boating operate two boats (*Dawn* and *Madam Butterfly*) for
self-steer hiring or skippered trips. Both craft have been especially designed
to provide facilities for disabled passengers. Bookings and further details
on (01252) 622520 or visit www.accessibleboating.org.uk.

WALKING & CYCLING

The path over Greywell
Hill connects with other
footpaths through Butter
Wood. You can, if you wish,
make a circular route back to
Warnborough Green, where
there are a couple of pubs.

Boatyards

Ⓑ**Galleon Marine** Colt Hill Bridge, Odiham
RG29 1AL (01256 703691; www.galleonmarine.
co.uk). ⚓ Pump out, gas, narrowboat hire, day hire
craft, overnight mooring (by arrangement), winter
storage, slipway, used boat sales, chandlery, books,
maps and gifts, ice cream. Hire of rowing boats,
canoes, kayaks and punts by the hour, or longer.
Picnic area.

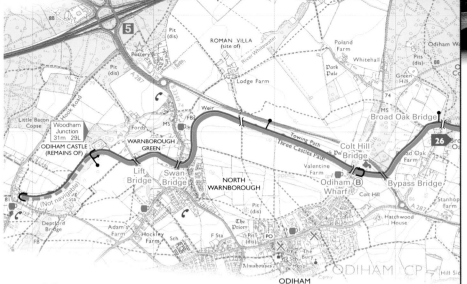

ODIHAM

- **Odiham**

Hants. PO, stores, banks, butcher, off-licence, takeaways, chemist, bakery. It is a pleasant walk up the road from Colt Hill Bridge, past May's Model Cottages (1862) and a pub to the broad High Street, rich with 17th- and 18th-C buildings.

- **North Warnborough**

Hants. A group of attractive houses, some thatched and dating from the 15th C. There is no church, the village being virtually an extension of Odiham.

Odiham (King John's) Castle (RG29 1HQ) Dating from 1207, this picturesque pile of flint is all that remains of the only octagonal keep in England, a three-storeyed building used by King John as a stopping place between Windsor and Winchester.

- **Greywell**

Hants. A village of charming red-brick houses around the pub and tunnel entrance.

Pubs and Restaurants

The Water Witch Colt Hill Bridge, London Road, Odiham RG29 1AL (01256 702778; www. chefandbrewer.com/pub/waterwitch-odiham-hook/c3350). Comfortable beamed pub with rustic bar decorated with canal artefacts. Vast waterside garden. Real ale together with food *available all day, everyday 12.00–22.00 (Sun 21.30).* Children welcome.

The Kings 65 High Street, Odiham RG29 1LF (01256 702559/703811; www.kingschineseodiham.co.uk). Smart restaurant in converted pub, serving Peking and Szechuan cuisine – not cheap, but good value *Open Mon 18.00–23.00; Tue–Thur 12.00–14.00 & 18.00–23.00; Fri & Sat 12.00–14.00 & 18.00–00.00. Closed Sun.* Takeaway service.

The George Hotel 100–102 High Street, Odiham RG29 1LP (01256 702081; www.georgehotelodiham.com). Handsome 16th-C hotel with a Georgian façade. Inside are beams and an Elizabethan fireplace taken from Old Basing House. Bar food and real ale. A la carte restaurant *L and E.* Patio garden and orchard. Café/bar next door.

Grapevine Bistro 121 High Street, Odiham RG29 1LA (01256 701122; www.grapevine-gourmet.co.uk). Family owned bistro, established for over 15 years. Seasonal menus offering fresh, locally sourced produce. *Open daily from 10.00* for tea, coffee and patisserie. Value for money light meals *L and E until 20.00,* as well as à la carte menu. *Open L Tue–Sat 12.00–14.00; E Tue–Sat 18.00–22.00.* Children welcome and those under 10 eat free *18.00–19.00 Sat.*

El Castello 83 High Street, Odiham RG29 1LB (01256 704281; www.elcastello.co.uk). Friendly, attentive staff. An ideal place for informal eating. Children welcome. *Open all day, every day.*

The Anchor The Street, North Warnborough RG29 1BE (01256 702740). Cheerful 18th-C village pub. Real ale. Inexpensive meals *L and E* every other *Sun.* Quiz welcome.

The Fox & Goose The Street, Greywell RG29 1BY (01256 702062; www.foxandgoosegreywell. co.uk). Comfortable 16th-C country pub with two open fires. Real ale. Meals, including game in season, *L and E.* Large garden with play area. Children welcome.

BRIDGWATER & TAUNTON CANAL

MAXIMUM DIMENSIONS
Length: 51' 10"
Beam: 10'
Headroom: 7' 1"
Draught: 2' 6"

MANAGER
0303 040 4040
enquiries.kennetavon@canalrivertrust.org.uk

MILEAGE
TAUNTON Firepool Lock to:
Creech St Michael: 3 miles
Durston: 6 miles
North Newton: 8 miles
BRIDGWATER DOCK: 14 miles

6 locks

The Bridgwater & Taunton Canal represents a small part of a far more ambitious scheme, the Bristol & Taunton Canal Navigation, for which Rennie gave a quotation in 1811 of no less than £429,990. This was to be part of a ship canal from Bristol to Exeter where it would join up with the long-established Exeter Ship Canal. However, although this sum was forthcoming, very little work seems to have been undertaken and instead, in 1824, an Act of Parliament was obtained to 'abridge, vary, extend and improve the Bristol & Taunton Canal Navigation', which resulted in the much briefer line between the River Parrett at Huntworth (just south of Bridgwater) and Taunton being adopted. The ship canal scheme was abandoned. Although the total cost of the canal on its opening was £71,000, toll receipts in the early days averaged £7,000 per year; most of this, however, was drawn from traffic passing to and from the Chard and Grand Western canals which the Bridgwater & Taunton Canal joined at Creech St Michael and Taunton respectively.

The size of the locks was unorthodox at 54'x 13' with a theoretical draught of 3' 0", which meant a normal craft load of 22 tons. The distance as originally constituted from Firepool Lock, Taunton, to Huntworth was 13½ miles. Prior to the building of the Bridgwater & Taunton Canal, there already existed a navigation of sorts on the rivers Parrett and Tone (i.e. an alternative route between Taunton and Bridgwater). This route suffered from drought in summer and floods in winter and so was not particularly reliable; but it was good enough to cause the shareholders of the Bridgwater & Taunton Canal great embarrassment and they were forced to purchase the river navigation in 1832, five years after their own opening.

In 1837 a further Act was obtained authorising the extension from Huntworth to Bridgwater and the building of the dock and its entrance lock from the River Parrett. This led to the curious anomaly of there being two sets of milestones in close juxtaposition. At the time of its jubilant opening on 25 March 1841, this extension had cost fully £175,000, leaving the proprietors badly out of pocket when the whole waterway and dock complex was sold to the Bristol and Exeter Railway Company for £64,000 in 1866. When control of the waterway eventually passed to the Great Western Railway, little attempt was made to maintain commercial traffic and the last barge tolls were collected in 1907.

In 1940, at the behest of the War Office, the Bridgwater & Taunton Canal, like the Kennet & Avon, was turned into a line of defence against the possibility of enemy invasion and pill boxes were erected at strategic points along it. The bridges were fixed and strengthened to carry military vehicles.

Little interest was shown in the waterway after nationalisation in 1947, although the Bridgwater Docks continued to operate under the Railway Executive of the British Transport Commission. In 1958 the Bowes Committee Report on waterways put the canal into category 'C', i.e. suitable for redevelopment, and various surveys were carried out, seemingly without any concrete results. The canal passed to the British Waterways Board (as was) in 1963 but Bridgwater Docks remained in Railways Board ownership. In the meantime the south western branch of the Inland Waterways Association had begun to consider the canal in terms of restoration and in 1965 the Bridgwater & Taunton Canal Restoration Group was formed. A year later this group became the Somerset Inland Waterways Society, which was formed to work towards restoration of the canal for amenity purposes. A subsequent arrangement negotiated by BWB allowed for the extraction of 3 million gallons of water a day from the canal, to provide much needed revenue. Eventually a partnership between Somerset County Council and British Waterways, encouraged by the Somerset Inland Waterways Society, saw full restoration of the navigation and it was opened throughout in 1994. Bridgwater Docks have been developed into a marina, surrounded by new housing, shops and a pub.

The Sun on the Somerset Space Walk (see page 35)

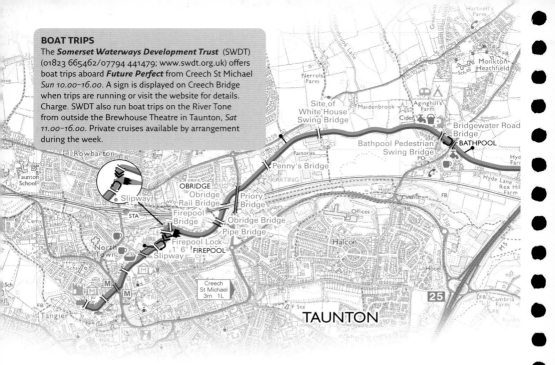

Taunton

The Bridgwater & Taunton Canal runs through attractive rolling scenery, typical of rural Somerset.
It starts at Firepool Lock, at a junction with the River Tone. In the 18th- and 19th-C the Tone, which
passes through Taunton before meeting the canal, was navigable from Taunton to its junction
with the River Parrett. Firepool Lock, pleasantly situated beside the Tone weir, is the first stage of
the canal's north easterly journey towards Bridgwater and the estuary of the Parrett. The lock is
reached from Taunton by following signs to the cattle market, or by crossing the footbridge over
the Tone from the town's Firepool district, on the river's south bank. The canal curves past the
railway station, passing under the main Bristol to Exeter line, which follows it closely to Bridgwater.
The tall railway warehouse is built on the site of the old junction with the Grand Western Canal.
Taunton is quickly left behind as the waterway continues through flat pasture land to Bathpool,
where the towpath runs briefly through the churchyard of a small corrugated iron church.
Bathpool Swing Bridge used to be the first obstacle to restoring the navigation east of Taunton,
being one of the structures fixed closed during the invasion scare of 1940, when the War Office
destroyed the swinging mechanisms on all the navigation's swing bridges. Today it operates as
a pedestrian bridge only. Contrary to popular opinion, this measure was not so much to prevent
navigation by German forces, as to create lines of defence along natural barriers. The Bridgwater &
Taunton, like the Kennet & Avon and Basingstoke Canals, was hastily turned into a fortified line of
resistance. Leaving Bathpool the country becomes hilly and more wooded and a modern housing
estate accompanies the canal into Creech St Michael. Before the village is the site of the junction
with the Chard Canal. There is little to be seen of the junction itself but to the south the long
embankment crossing the Tone flood plain is still visible.

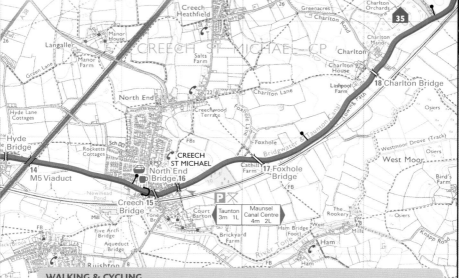

WALKING & CYCLING

This detached and often isolated waterway, just 14½ miles in length, is ideal for walking and cycling. Railway stations at each end make one-way trips possible and well sign-posted car parks along its entire length mean that 'bite-sized' chunks can be tackled by the less energetic. The Somerset Space Walk adds a unique dimension to the experience (*see* page 35 for details). In Taunton there are walkers' trails (available from the TIC) covering the town's heritage and its wealth of non-conformist chapels. For the cyclist, a range of trail guides take one further afield on a variety of interesting quests. The towpath forms part of the West Country Way, National Cycle Network Route 3, from Padstow to Bristol. Route 33 links Taunton to the South Coast Route 2 at Axminster and Seaton. The South Somerset Cycle Ride is a waymarked route around the byways of South Somerset, centred on Taunton.

NAVIGATIONAL NOTES

1. When using the locks please leave bottom gates open after use.
2. Do not tamper with the settings of the paddle gear.
3. Report any problems to CRT on 0303 040 4040 or telephone the emergency helpline on 0800 47 999 47.
4. Slipways for the use of visiting trail boaters are located at: Bridgwater YMCA HQ (01278 422511), Bathpool Car Park, Firepool Lock, Taunton.
5. Boat licenses may be obtained from CRT. Contact CRT Customer Services on 0303 040 4040; enquiries.kennetavon@canalrivertrust.org.uk or visit www.canalrivertrust.org.uk/boating.
6. Beware of reduced headroom at the following bridges: O'Bridge, Whites, Dairy and Huntworth.
7. Canal wardens can be contacted on 01278 662188.

● Bathpool
Somerset. Tel, garage. A straggling village, running into the outskirts of Taunton, much improved by severe traffic calming measures.

● Creech St Michael
Somerset. Tel, PO, stores, garage, cashpoint. Although now surrounded by modern housing, the old part of the village still survives. The largely 13th-C church is a sturdy and attractive building; inside there are fine waggon roofs.

● Chard Canal
The Chard Canal was one of the last to be built in England and was one of the shortest-lived of all canals. Work began in 1835 and the 13½ mile line to Chard from Creech St Michael on the Bridgwater & Taunton Canal was opened in 1842. The canal included three tunnels, two major aqueducts, two locks and four inclined planes. It suffered from immediate railway competition and never made any money. Bought by the Bristol and Exeter Railway Company in 1867, it closed down the next year. It is possible to follow the line of the canal on foot, although there are few rights of way that correspond with its original bed.

- **Taunton**

Somerset. All services. Taunton has long been a rich agricultural market town and an important point on the old trunk route to the West Country. The skyline is dominated by the towers of the churches of St Mary Magdalene and St James. The first, rebuilt in 1862, is 163ft high; its ornamental splendour rather dwarfs the double aisled church. In Middle Street there is an octagonal 18th-C Methodist chapel. Wesley preached here when it was opened. The centre of the town contains an interesting mixture of buildings; 15th-C municipal buildings, the 18th-C Market House, the Victorian Shire Hall and the 20th-C County Hall. Remains of the medieval town can be seen, including fragments of the 13th-C priory.

Brewhouse Theatre and Arts Centre Coal Orchard, Taunton TA1 1JL (01823 283244; www.thebrewhouse. net). Entertainment including folk, comedy, classical music, dance and drama. Box office *open Mon–Sat 10.00–20.00 (18.00 on non-performance nights).*

Chapels in Taunton It was observed in the 17th C that Taunton was 'the vineyard of the Lord of Hosts and the inhabitants his precious plants'. A trail around the town's chapels has been laid out and a leaflet is available from the TIC in Paul Street, where non-conformity was founded in 1662. Less local trails are also available from the TIC and depict such oddities as Towers & Hunkypunks and Bench Ends & Pulpits.

Ian's Cycle Centre 3A Roman Road, Taunton TA1 2BD (01823 365917; www.ianscyclecentre.co.uk).

Bicycle and bicycle parts retailer and cycle hire. *Open Tue–Fri 09.00–17.00 & Sat 09.00–16.00.*

Farmers Market Taunton (01823 336344). Held *every Thu 09.00–15.00,* in the centre of the town.

The Museum of Somerset Taunton Castle, Castle Green, Taunton TA1 4AA (01823 255088; www. visitsomerset.co.uk/things-to-do/visitor-attractions/ the-museum-of-somerset-p138493). The museum re-opened in 2011 following extensive restoration. Many galleries to explore and objects to discover, including the Frome Hoard, the second largest collection of Roman coins discovered in Britain. Shop and café. *Open Tue–Sat and B Hols 10.00–17.00.* Free.

Somerset Cricket Museum 7 Priory Avenue, Taunton TA1 1XX (01823 275893; www.somersetcricketmuseum.co.uk). Memorabilia from the Somerset County Cricket Club, bat-making demonstrations, cricket shop, refreshments. *Open Apr–Oct, Tue–Fri 10.30–16.00. Access is restricted on match days. Charge.*

Tacchi-Morris Arts Centre School Road, Taunton TA2 8PD (01823 414141; www.tacchi-morris.com). Theatre venue offering a range of shows, workshops and classes for adults and children. Box office *open Mon–Fri 10.00–16.00 and and an hour before curtain up on performance nights. Bar open on performance nights 19.00–23.00.* Café.

Tourist Information Centre Library, Paul Street, Taunton TA1 3XZ (01823 336344; www.tauntontowncentre.co.uk). *Open Mon–Sat 09.30–16.30. Closed Sun and B Hols.*

Pubs and Restaurants

The Plough 75 Station Road, Taunton TA1 1PB (01823 324404; www.theploughtaunton.co.uk). Real ales and local ciders. Bar snacks including pies, filled rolls, soup, nachos and chips available *all day, every day.* Occasional live music and events.

Crown & Sceptre 74-76 Station Road, Taunton TA1 1NX (01823 252143). Large, welcoming town pub serving food *Mon–Sat L and E (no food Sun).* Beer garden. Regular bands. Sports TV. *Open all day.*

The O'bridge Massingham Park, Taunton (01823 422340; www.brewersfayre.co.uk/ brewersfayre/our-pubs/bristol/theobridge.html). Real ales and food available all day, every day including breakfast *served from 06.30–10.30 (Sun 07.00 – 11.00).* Indoor children's play area. B&B.

Tramontes Restaurant & Pizzeria Heron Gate, Riverside, Taunton TA1 2LP (01823 323377; www.tramontesrestaurant.co.uk). Appetising and inexpensive Italian fayre described by locals as a friendly, welcoming 'little corner of Italy.' Children welcome. *Open 18.00–21.30 daily.* B&B.

The Bathpool Inn 102 Bridgwater Road, Taunton (01823 272545; www.thebathpool.co.uk). Low beamed, comfortable family pub. Real ales. Home-made food *available Mon–Fri 12.00–14.30 & 17.00–21.00; Sat 11.00–21.00 & Sun 12.00–20.00. Carvery Tue–Fri 12.00–14.00; Fri & Sun 18.00–20.00 & Sun 12.00–15.30.* Garden and children's play area. *Regular* events. *Closed Mon.*

The Bell Inn St Michael's Road, Creech St Michael, Taunton TA3 5DP (01823 444566). Village local, family-friendly pub. Real ales. *Meals L and E.* Sports TV, skittle alley. Children and dogs welcome. Pleasant, fully enclosed garden.

North Newton

This section is typical of the quiet agricultural nature of the whole canal. The canal is slightly raised above the land on a low embankment, with views to the north across farmland and to the south across the low-lying flood plain of the River Tone. The canal leaves the river to the south, passing through marsh and moorland. Several small agricultural hamlets flank the waterway. At Durston, where the CRT maintenance yard is located, the busy A361 crosses. Beyond, the canal reaches the first lock which starts the descent to Bridgwater. The paddle gear is quite unique, composed of ball-shaped weights and chains to form a counter-balance mechanism.

North Newton

Somerset. Tel. An irregular farming village. The eccentric-looking church was rebuilt first in the 17thC and then again in the late 19th. Nothing remains of the original Saxon church, where the Alfred Jewel was found in 1693. This Saxon ornament, the oldest surviving Crown jewel, is now displayed in the Ashmolean Museum, Oxford.

Maunsel Lock Canal Centre Bankland, North Newton, Bridgwater TA7 0DH (01278 663160; www.maunsellock.co.uk). The proprietors are a fund of information about the canal. Events include music, canal art painting demonstrations and art and photographic exhibitions and charity fundraisers. Tea garden. Toilets (including disabled) and showers (Watermate key holders only) 🚻. *See* Pubs and Restaurants for more details.

Somerset Space Walk
The brainchild of Pip Youngman, this unique portrayal of our Solar System has been set out to scale along the towpath using one scale for both the planets and the distances between them. There are no figures to conjure with, just the experience of a journey through space as you walk, cycle or boat the waterway.

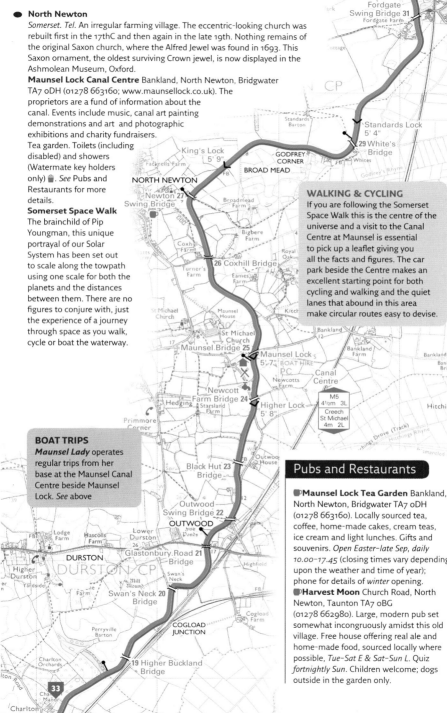

WALKING & CYCLING

If you are following the Somerset Space Walk this is the centre of the universe and a visit to the Canal Centre at Maunsel is essential to pick up a leaflet giving you all the facts and figures. The car park beside the Centre makes an excellent starting point for both cycling and walking and the quiet lanes that abound in this area make circular routes easy to devise.

BOAT TRIPS

Maunsel Lady operates regular trips from her base at the Maunsel Canal Centre beside Maunsel Lock. *See above*

Pubs and Restaurants

🍺**Maunsel Lock Tea Garden** Bankland, North Newton, Bridgwater TA7 0DH (01278 663160). Locally sourced tea, coffee, home-made cakes, cream teas, ice cream and light lunches. Gifts and souvenirs. *Open Easter–late Sep, daily 10.00–17.45* (closing times vary depending upon the weather and time of year); phone for details of *winter* opening.

🍺**Harvest Moon** Church Road, North Newton, Taunton TA7 0BG (01278 662980). Large, modern pub set somewhat incongruously amidst this old village. Free house offering real ale and home-made food, sourced locally where possible, *Tue–Sat E & Sat–Sun L*. Quiz *fortnightly Sun*. Children welcome; dogs outside in the garden only.

Bridgwater

Following the contours of the land, the waterway continues northwards towards Bridgwater. To the west, low hills rise gradually away from the canal; to the east low-lying farm and marsh land separates the navigation from the River Parrett. This tidal river, a vital drain for the whole area, swings ever nearer to the canal as they approach Bridgwater. To the east the railway line stays close to the navigation until just before Bridgwater, when it turns away to pass east of the town. The course of the waterway is quiet and isolated. There are no villages near the canal, although there is easy access for Fordgate and Huntworth. Standard's Lock drops the navigation to the Bridgwater level. Nearing the town civilisation returns with a vengeance as traffic roars overhead on the M5 viaduct. After the motorway the towpath crosses to the west and the canal enters Bridgwater. South of Taunton Road Bridge there is a useful *parade of shops, including a laundrette, stores, takeaways and a toilet,* while to the north there is a large supermarket and a garage. The waterway passes through the town in a cutting, swinging in a wide arc to the west before turning back to the docks and the junction with the Parrett estuary. Access to the town is easy from the many bridges. The canal enters the dock through a stop lock which passes it into the large inner basin, laid out marina-fashion with floating pontoons. *Toilets and showers* are available in the Bonded Warehouse, now converted into flats. The smaller outer basin is entered through a twin-bascular lift bridge and then a ship lock and a canal lock used to allow access to the River Parrett and thus the sea. The river locks have been blocked off with concrete barriers and so the Bridgwater & Taunton Canal remains just that: an isolated navigation linking its two eponymous towns and nothing else.

Bridgwater

Somerset. All services. Bridgwater is an old market town straddling the River Parrett. Formerly the town was an important centre for the cloth trade, which encouraged development of the port from the Middle Ages onwards. The old quay, despite redevelopment, still has an attractive 18th-C flavour. It suffered severely during the Civil War and, in an artillery bombardment in July 1645, lost the greater part of its commercial and domestic buildings, many of which were of timber-frame construction. Elsewhere in the town are signs of 18th-C wealth: the handsome houses in Castle Street, built c.1725, were sponsored by James Bridges, first Duke of Chances. Little of the medieval town survives. The 13th-C castle was destroyed by the Roundheads as a reprisal for the town's resistance. The watergate, on the west quay, is the only remaining relic of the castle and has a wall 12ft thick. Glass-making briefly flourished in the town when, in 1725, James Bridges built the 125ft Chandos Glass Cone. The venture failed within nine years and the cone, built from rubble from the derelict castle, was converted first to brick making and then to tile manufacture, only closing down during World War II.
Battle of Sedgemoor, 6 July 1685 When Charles II died, he was succeeded by his brother, James II, unpopular due to his Catholic faith. The Duke of Monmouth, an illegitimate son of Charles II, declared himself king in 1685 in Bridgwater. He landed at Lyme with a few supporters and soon raised an army 4000 strong, including 800 horsemen under Lord Grey. They moved to Bridgwater, while a Royalist army commanded by Lord Feversham and John Churchill (later the Duke of Marlborough) camped

near Westonzoyland, 3 miles east of the town. Monmouth decided on a night attack but lost the element of surprise when caught crossing the Langmoor Rhine, one of the many drainage ditches in the area. A fierce battle broke out in which the artillery played a dominant part. Grey's cavalry tried to outflank Feversham but were prevented by the Bussex Rhine, another deep ditch. Although firing continued all night, Monmouth's cause was already lost. The leaders of the rebellion escaped for a while but the ill-armed rebel army was rounded up, many to be transported or executed on the orders of Judge Jeffreys. To find the site of the battle take the A372 east from Bridgwater; turn left in Westonzoyland. There are signs to the Sedgemoor Memorial Stone.
Blake Museum Blake Street, Bridgwater TA6 3NB (01278 456127; www.blakemuseum.org). Robert Blake was born in Bridgwater in 1598 and represented the town as a Member of Parliament. After a distinguished army career he was appointed by Cromwell as one of his first Generals at Sea and went on to destroy the Dutch fleet in a battle of 1653 and to achieve a resounding victory over the Spaniards in 1657. He is recognised as one of the major influences in establishing the reputation of the Navy – later to become the Royal Navy. The museum houses a collection of Blake memorabilia; depicts the drama of the Monmouth Rebellion and the humour of an 18th-C artist; and presents a fascinating selection of local history and archaeology. Shop. *Open Apr–Nov; Tue–Sat 10.00– 16.00.* Telephone for other times. Entrance by donation.

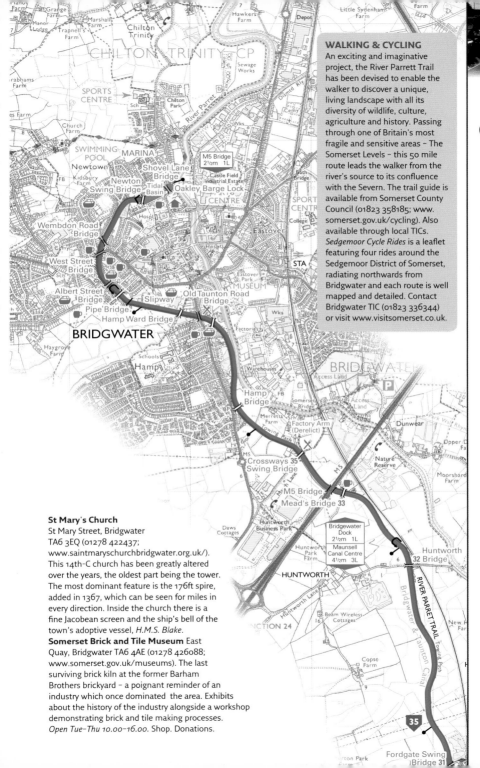

WALKING & CYCLING

An exciting and imaginative project, the River Parrett Trail has been devised to enable the walker to discover a unique, living landscape with all its diversity of wildlife, culture, agriculture and history. Passing through one of Britain's most fragile and sensitive areas – The Somerset Levels – this 50 mile route leads the walker from the river's source to its confluence with the Severn. The trail guide is available from Somerset County Council (01823 358185; www. somerset.gov.uk/cycling). Also available through local TICs. *Sedgemoor Cycle Rides* is a leaflet featuring four rides around the Sedgemoor District of Somerset, radiating northwards from Bridgwater and each route is well mapped and detailed. Contact Bridgwater TIC (01823 336344) or visit www.visitsomerset.co.uk.

St Mary's Church

St Mary Street, Bridgwater
TA6 3EQ (01278 422437;
www.saintmaryschurchbridgwater.org.uk/).
This 14th-C church has been greatly altered
over the years, the oldest part being the tower.
The most dominant feature is the 176ft spire,
added in 1367, which can be seen for miles in
every direction. Inside the church there is a
fine Jacobean screen and the ship's bell of the
town's adoptive vessel, *H.M.S. Blake*.

Somerset Brick and Tile Museum East

Quay, Bridgwater TA6 4AE (01278 426088;
www.somerset.gov.uk/museums). The last
surviving brick kiln at the former Barham
Brothers brickyard – a poignant reminder of an
industry which once dominated the area. Exhibits
about the history of the industry alongside a workshop
demonstrating brick and tile making processes.
Open Tue–Thu 10.00–16.00. Shop. Donations.

BRIDGWATER

Westonzoyland Pumping Station Museum of Steam Power and Land Drainage Hoopers Lane, Westonzoyland, Bridgwater TA7 0LS (www.wzlet.org). A display of pumping engines, both static and in steam, housed in old pumping station buildings dating from the 1830s. Even without steam there is plenty to enjoy, including a Crossley engine, a Lister and a waterwheel. *Open as a static display 13.00–17.00. In steam first Sun and B Hols Sun–Mon (except Xmas and Boxing Day).* Shop and tearoom. Charge.

Pubs and Restaurants

Boat & Anchor Meads Crossing, Huntworth, Bridgwater TA7 0AQ (01278 662473; www.theboatandanchor.co.uk). Six separate cottages, now all knocked into one. Home-cooked food *L and E daily.* Real ales and *Sunday* Carvery. Children welcome. Canalside garden and orangery. B&B and holiday cottages.

The Hope Inn 80–82 Taunton Road, Bridgwater TA6 6AF (01278 424239; www.thehopeinn.ndo.co.uk). Home made pub grub *L and E (not Tue)* and real ales served in a town pub. Children and dogs welcome. Outside courtyard. Pool, darts and skittles. *Monthly* music/disco. B&B.

Horse and Jockey 1 Durleigh Road, Bridgwater TA6 7HU (01278 424283). Situated beside the racecourse, serving real ale. Regular live music *Fri.*

Green Dragon 84 Friarn Street, Bridgwater TA6 3LJ (01278 446936). Reputed to be the oldest pub in town, and has the friendliest landlord and locals you are ever likely to meet. Dogs and children welcome. Pool and juke box.

Maltshovel 2 Wembdon Road, Bridgwater TA6 7DN (01278 422496). Real ale. Children welcome. Beer garden with play area. Live music *every Fri evening.* Darts, pool and skittles.

Old Vicarage Hotel and Restaurant 45–51 St Mary Street, Bridgwater TA6 3EQ (01278 458891; www.theoldvicaragebridgwater.com). Charming old establishment opposite the church serving fresh, locally grown food *L and E Tue–Sat.* There is also an integral café *open Mon–Sat 10.30–15.00.* B&B.

Admiral's Landing Admiral's Court, The Marina, Bridgwater TA6 3EX (01278 422515). Real ales and food served *L and E (not Sun E)* in an old warehouse. Children welcome. Dockside seating.

British Flag 77–83 Chilton Street, Bridgwater TA6 3HX (01278 422537). Real ales. Children and dogs welcome. Large enclosed garden. Pool, darts, skittles and large-screen TV.

The Wharf, Tiverton (see page 40)

GRAND WESTERN CANAL

MAXIMUM DIMENSIONS

As there are no locks on this navigation the following measurements refer to the overall canal dimensions.

Length: Unlimited
Width: 40' except Waytown Tunnel: 12'
Draught: 4'
Headroom: 7' 3"

Realistically boats with a beam greater than 7' should not try to navigate throughout this waterway: Dudley Weatherley Jubilee Bridge being the constraining structure.

Permits are required for all boat use and are available from the Tiverton Canal Co., Mid-Devon Moorings and the Best-One Convenience Store, Canal Hill, Tiverton (see page 41), Minnows Touring Park (see page 44) and Holcombe Rogus Village Shop (approximately ½ mile east of Waytown Tunnel). Permits may also be bought in person from the Canal Ranger Service:

The Moorings, Canal Hill,
Tiverton, Devon
EH16 4HX
01884 254072; www.devon.gov.uk/grand_western_canal; gwcanal@devon.gov.uk.

MILEAGE

Tiverton to:
Halberton: 4½ miles
Sampford Peverell: 6½ miles
Ayshford: 7½ miles
Lowdwells: 11¼ miles

Originally conceived as part of a proposal to link the English and Bristol Channels, the Grand Western Canal was to run from Taunton to Exeter, with branches to Tiverton and Cullompton. Subsequently an expanded scheme was floated to include a canal from Bristol to Taunton, linking in with the Kennet & Avon, to give a through navigation from London to Exeter.

After much delay and conflicting advice from many engineers, including William Jessop and John Rennie, work started in 1810, on an 11-mile section which included the Tiverton branch and a small portion of the main line from Lowdwells to Burlescombe. This was completed four years later at a cost – for an entirely lock-free length – of £224,505; more than the original estimate for the entire canal. During the course of construction it had been decided to lower the planned level at Holcombe, necessitating an additional 16ft cutting, thereby setting the Tiverton branch on the summit level as a lock-free, contour canal. This was largely responsible for the considerable escalation in cost but subsequently proved beneficial to the large tonnages of limestone transported into Tiverton.

After another delay, work started on the main line in 1827. The section from Taunton to the Tiverton branch was finally opened in 1838 and included seven vertical lifts and one inclined plane: the site of the incline, at Wellisford, ½ a mile north of Thorne St Margaret, can still be seen. The construction of the lifts and the inclined plane was in the hands of James Green who, at the time, was engaged in enlarging the Exeter Canal and building a terminal basin in the city. However, his work on this navigation was less than satisfactory, and he was eventually replaced by Captain John Twisden, Royal Navy retired. The canal was never completed to Exeter. It was a financial disaster, suffering from its over-ambitious engineering, together with railway competition almost from its opening day. The canal was leased to the Great Western Railway in 1854, and they gradually absorbed most of the canal traffic. The predictable pattern of minimal maintenance, coupled with an inevitable decline ensued and the main line was closed in 1867. It has largely disappeared.

However, the trade in limestone persisted and boats continued to ply between Burlescombe and Tiverton until 1924, when a major leak developed, severing the navigation into two separate sections. At this point the canal was finally abandoned as a commercial carrying enterprise.

Some 50 years later, in a joint venture with Mid Devon District Council, Devon County Council purchased the waterway and set about restoration. Today it offers an attractive, linear country park, well patronised by boaters, walkers, anglers and cyclists alike.

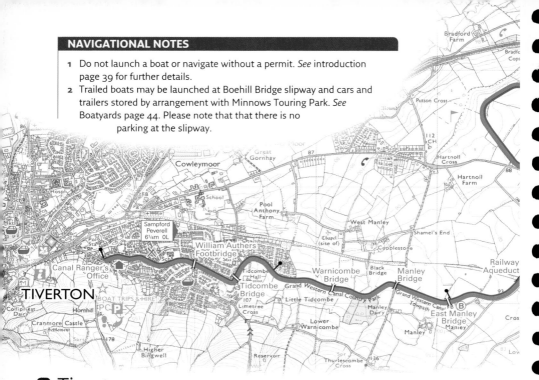

NAVIGATIONAL NOTES

1 Do not launch a boat or navigate without a permit. *See* introduction page 39 for further details.
2 Trailed boats may be launched at Boehill Bridge slipway and cars and trailers stored by arrangement with Minnows Touring Park. *See* Boatyards page 44. Please note that that there is no parking at the slipway.

Tiverton

The canal occupies an elevated position above Tiverton and is set some way out of the town. The terminal basin is cut into the hill on the south side while to the north, limekilns form a sturdy embankment, squatting solidly beside the towpath. Positioned thus, they serve the function of retaining wall and are also ergonomically placed for direct loading from arriving tub boats. These were towed in chains of three, carrying the waterway's dominant cargo of limestone and coal; the former being burnt in the kilns to produce a soil conditioner-cum-fertiliser for the local acid soils. Nearby is a pretty thatched cottage, now a tearoom but originally the lime-burner's dwelling. Heading west out of the basin, the waterway soon wanders beyond Tiverton's suburbs before bending sharply to the north under Tidcombe Bridge. Here it skirts Tidcombe Hall, originally called Rectory House and once the home of the Bishop of Exeter. In 1810 the then incumbent refused to allow the navigation to come any nearer to the house than 100yds, hence its exaggerated course at this point. At Manley Bridge the canal passes East Manley Farm, which is mentioned in the Domesday Book. More recently it was home to the Victorian Jesuit priest, Gerard Manley Hopkins. Following the road round to the north, the waterway crosses an aqueduct 40ft above the disused trackbed of the old Tiverton Junction to Tiverton line. It consists of a cast iron trough, supported by brick-encased cast iron arches, the structure being wide enough to span the original broad gauge line. At Crownhill Bridge the towpath changes over to the east side of the navigation where it remains, almost to Lowdwells. Tiverton Road Bridge heralds an old wharf, now a car park; another sharp bend and mile marker number three. Alongside the road bridge is the lift bridge, Dudley Weatherley Jubilee Bridge. It is named for a well-known local artist and canal restoration campaigner who sadly died in 2004, aged 92. The combination for the bridge is given to boaters when they purchase their permit. The next mile of the canal bed, running over badly fissured rock, was a constant source of leakage during the waterway's commercial usage and has now been sealed with an artificial membrane. Beyond, the navigation comes suddenly upon a delightful side

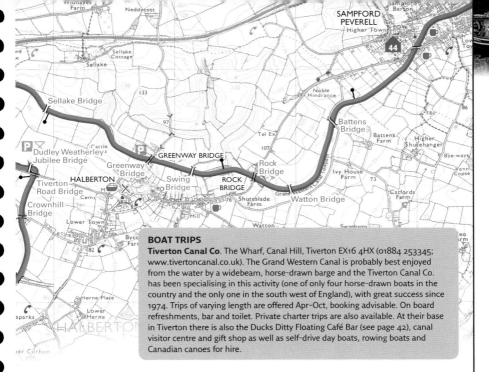

BOAT TRIPS

Tiverton Canal Co. The Wharf, Canal Hill, Tiverton EX16 4HX (01884 253345; www.tivertoncanal.co.uk). The Grand Western Canal is probably best enjoyed from the water by a widebeam, horse-drawn barge and the Tiverton Canal Co. has been specialising in this activity (one of only four horse-drawn boats in the country and the only one in the south west of England), with great success since 1974. Trips of varying length are offered Apr–Oct, booking advisable. On board refreshments, bar and toilet. Private charter trips are also available. At their base in Tiverton there is also the Ducks Ditty Floating Café Bar (see page 42), canal visitor centre and gift shop as well as self-drive day boats, rowing boats and Canadian canoes for hire.

cutting. Then Greenway Bridge is approached, providing the best access to Halberton village (cycle hire here). Crossing another diminutive valley, the canal runs through old sandstone quarries; these were the source of much of the material used to build the attractive bridges seen throughout the navigation. Standing beside Rock Bridge is an intriguing house built for Captain John Twisden, who completed the main line of the canal to Taunton. Complete with Doric columns and somewhat eccentric detailing, Rock House is thought to have been constructed to a design of the Captain's. Leading out of the cutting, the waterway now heads for Sampford Peverell. There are fine views to the east over the Blackdown Hills.

Boatyards

Ⓑ **Mid Devon Moorings** Orchard Farm, East Manley, Tiverton EX16 4NJ (01884 252178/0774 9001631; www.middevonhireboats.co.uk) 🛁🏠🔧D Narrowboat moorings (short- and long-term), on-site car park, BBQ area, gas, fuel and trailer storage, boat-handling tuition.

● Tiverton

Devon. All services (station at Tiverton Parkway 5 miles away). The town grew up on a narrow spit of land between the Rivers Exe and Lowman; its name derived from Twyford, meaning two fords. The oldest part of the settlement is probably around the castle and church and the main street pattern, as seen today, would have developed beside the Exe bridge in the 14th C. By the beginning of the 13th C the town was recorded as having a market and three fairs. Throughout the Middle Ages it quietly prospered, its wealth based on the local cloth trade, becoming one of the key centres in the county by the 16th C. Few buildings from before this time remain due to a series of disastrous fires spanning a period 1598–1731, after which legislation was enacted decreeing that all roofs were to be of a tile, slate or lead construction. Surviving houses from the 18th and 19th C testify to the town's wealth and the Industrial Revolution was heralded by the arrival of John Heathcoat's lace factory in the town. This arrested the decline that was setting into other cloth towns in the area and brought Tiverton renewed prosperity. In the 100 years

41

between 1790 and 1891, the population more than doubled as Heathcoat's new bobbin net lace machine placed the town at the forefront of the country's lace production. He had attempted to install this machine in a factory in Loughborough, in 1816, whereupon it was destroyed by a mob from Nottingham. His response was to move to Tiverton where, with a few skilled workers recruited from the Midlands, he established production in a closed cloth- weaving factory. Here, for the first time, water power was harnessed to lace-making machinery. Heathcoat went on to become a significant benefactor to the town, providing housing and community facilities.

Knightshayes Court Bolham, Tiverton EX16 7RQ (01884 257381; www.nationaltrust.org.uk/knightshayes-court). A house designed by William Burges combining medieval romanticism with lavish Victorian decoration in a series of rich interiors. The well-known garden features rare shrubs, fine specimen trees, a water lily pond and topiary. Woodland walks. Shop and plant centre. Licensed restaurant. House *open Mar–Oct, daily (except Fri) 11.00–17.00 ; Nov–Dec, daily (except Fri) 11.00–16.30.* Garden *open Mar–Oct, daily 11.00–17.00.* Charge. Located 2 miles north of Tiverton.

Mid Devon Bus Information Traveline (0871 200 22 33; www.journeydevon.info/).
Pannier Market Tiverton (01884 243351; www.tiverton-market.co.uk). Friendly local market operating *Tue, Fri & Sat 08.30–16.00 (Sat 15.00).* Café
Tiverton Castle Park Hill, Near Tiverton EX16 6RP (01884 255200; www.tivertoncastle.com). Originally built in 1106 by Richard de Redvers, later the home of the Courtnays and besieged by Fairfax in 1645 during the Civil War. It fell to him after a chance shot hit a drawbridge chain. It was subsequently modernised by a rich Tiverton merchant, Peter West, although the early gatehouse remains one of its most striking features. Walled, kitchen and woodland gardens. *Open Easter Sun to end of Oct on Sun, Thur and B Hol Mon 14.30–17.30. Last admission 17.00.* Charge.
Tiverton Mid Devon Museum of Life Beck's Square, Tiverton EX16 6PJ (01884 256295; www. tivertonmuseum.org.uk). Reputed to contain the largest social history collection in the south west, housed in a listed building that was once the National School. The collection is displayed in a variety of galleries on a site covering half an acre. *Open Feb–Xmas, Mon–Fri 10.30–16.30 and Sat 10.00 – 13.00. Extended Sat opening times in summer.* Charge.

Pubs and Restaurants

✗**Canal Tearooms** Lime Kiln Road, Canal Hill, Tiverton EX16 4AQ (01884 252291). Once the lime-burner's dwelling, this 18th-C thatched cottage serves cream teas, home-made cakes, coffee and light lunches. Covered seating area and canalside gardens. *Open Easter–Oct, daily 10.00–18.00.*
✗**Duck's Ditty Floating Café Bar** The Wharf, Canal Hill, Tiverton EX16 4HX (01884 253345; www.tivertoncanal.co.uk). Teas, coffees, soft drinks, real ales, wines and cider. Also sweet and savoury snacks. *Open daily, Easter–Oct.*
🍺**Racehorse** Wellbrook Street, Tiverton EX16 6AA (01884 252606). Busy local serving real ales and food *L*. Children welcome. Garden. *Open all day.*

✗**Halberton Court Tearooms** Halberton, Tiverton EX16 7EH (01884 821458). Leave the canal at Greenway Bridge and walk downhill towards the village of Halberton, turning right at the foot of the hill. A bright, airy, welcoming establishment serving a wide range of home-made delights including breakfasts, lunches, delicious cakes and afternoon teas. Child and dog friendly. *Open May–Sep, 7 days a week & Thur–Sat during winter.* Farm shop adjacent selling wide range of fresh produce including meat. Also PYO.
🍺 **Barge** 93 High Street, Halberton, Tiverton EX16 7AG (01884 820316). Friendly locals pub. Real ale. Food available *Wed–Mon L & E*. Children welcome if eating. Pool, skittles and darts. Patio garden, dogs welcome. *Open Mon–Sat 12.00–14.00 & 17.30–00.00. Sun 12.00–22.30.*

WALKING & CYCLING
National Cycle Route 3, otherwise known as The West Country Way, makes use of the towpath throughout. Whilst the route can be entirely off-road (by remaining on the towpath) the official route diverts through villages along the way. It links in with the 1-mile Tiverton Parkway Station to Grand Western Canal route, a combination of off- and on-road tracks. It also connects with the 3-mile Tiverton Parkway to Culm Valley route. Other connected (or nearby) routes include the Exe Valley Cycle Route, Lowman Valley Cycle Route and eight routes in the Blackdown Hills. Detailed leaflets (charge) are available from local TICs.
Mid Devon Country Walks and Villages are a series of walks detailed in leaflets produced by Mid Devon District Council and available from local TICs. Leaflet No 4 covers walks based on the canal.
On a more local level, the District Council also publish a Tiverton Town Trail, available from the TIC.
See Burlescombe, page 45 for further information.

Burlescombe

The village of Sampford Peverell was bisected by the newly-dug canal with the loss of several buildings and the re-alignment of the main road. It also cut through land belonging to the old Rectory and, in 1841, a new Rectory was constructed by the Canal Company in Regency Gothic style with stone mullioned windows, as recompense. This was again replaced in 1993 by a modern building. An attractive skew brick bridge crosses the waterway in the village centre, close to the old wharf situated on the north bank. Beyond Buckland Bridge there is an example of a syphon culvert, not uncommon on this navigation, which carries a stream beneath the canal bed. Where an intersecting water course 'crosses' a canal at a similar level, the more usual culvert is unworkable and the water has to be dropped vertically to a point below the canal bed. It is then led up the other side, via a curved masonry tube, to resume its course across the adjoining fields; the water being effectively syphoned under the navigation. On the offside, just beyond Boehill Bridge, lies the overgrown 'Engineers Clay Pit': in past times a source of the clay puddle material used to seal the canal bed against leaks. At Ayshford, one of the waterway's architectural gems appears in the form of Ayshford Court and Chapel. The rendered front of the house conceals a medieval manor, dating from the 17th C, complete with two-bay hall and evidence of its central open fire witnessed by the smoke-blackened ridge purlin supported on jointed cruck trusses. On the chimney stack is the inscription 'Built 1607, restored 1910'. The adjoining chapel is a small, freestanding, Perpendicular construction complete with tiny pierced quatrefoils, set into its side walls. The plain roof is topped with a pleasing, simple belfry. The building was restored in 1847 and contains some striking Victorian stained glass. The navigation continues, bounded by open countryside but with higher ground beyond. Soon the main Bristol to Exeter railway line is approached and the waterway bends sharply to the north. This marks the point at which it was originally intended that the Tiverton branch would meet the main line. It was to have continued southwards to meet the River Exe at Topsham, running down the Clyst valley and with a branch to Cullompton. Ahead is the tramway bridge that used to lead from the limestone quarries at Westleigh to the main line railway, now swinging away to the east. In the bed of the canal, just before Fenacre Bridge, there was a spring which provided a feed for the canal; two others remain, in the vicinity of Whipcott and near Waytown Tunnel. The discovery of these natural water sources, when plans were modified and the navigation was 'dropped' into a 16ft deep cutting, eliminated the need to construct storage reservoirs in the Lowdwells area. It also did away with the proposed locks on the Tiverton branch, making it the contour canal we see today. Beyond Whipcott Bridge is a quarry which, during the early 20th C, was an important source of roadstone for the area, the material being regularly transported along the waterway to wharves at Tiverton Road Bridge and Halberton. There are also limekilns in the area so that limestone could be burnt for local use. At Waytown Tunnel the towpath crosses on the south portal and ducks into the trees. A length of chain attached to an iron ring was the means of propulsion through the tunnel and probably an improvement on the alternative of legging. The navigation terminates at Lowdswell lock, beside the restored lock keeper's cottage, from whence it would have continued to the first lift, crossing the nearby lane on an aqueduct.

Pubs and Restaurants

■✕Globe Inn 16 Lower Town, Sampford Peverell, Tiverton EX16 7BJ (01884 821214; www.the-globeinn.co.uk). Traditional country pub with two comfortable bars and a restaurant serving an appetising range of home-made food *L and E daily*. Cream teas served *11.30–18.00*. Bar and restaurant menus and a range of real ales. Beer garden and children's play area. Dogs welcome. Canalside seating and moorings. Quiz *monthly*. B&B. *Open all day, every day*.

■✕Merriemeade Lower Town, Sampford Peverell, Tiverton EX16 7BJ (01884 820270). Restaurant, close to the canal, serving meals and snacks *L and E (not Mon L)*. Children and dogs welcome. Garden.

■Ayshford Arms Station Road, Burlescombe, near Tiverton EX16 7JN (01823 672418). Country pub serving real ales and traditional, home-cooked bar meals, including *Sunday* roasts. Children and dogs welcome. Garden. Darts, pool and skittles. *Open daily 19.00–00.00*.

■Prince of Wales Inn Holcombe Rogus, near Tiverton TA21 0PN (01823 672070). Delightful 17th-C country pub serving real ales and home-cooked food *L and E*. Log fires in winter. Garden. Darts. Worth the additional walk or ride from the canal. Children and dogs welcome. *Closed Mon L. Open all day Sat & Sun*.

● **Halberton**
Devon. Tel, stores, farm shop and café open May–Sep. A village strung out along the Tiverton road, set a little way away from the canal, containing a mix of old and new housing.

● **Sampford Peverell**
Devon. PO, tel, stores, farmshop, station (1 mile away). A village of character ranged around the canal which clearly led to the demolition of some properties and a diversion to the approach from Tiverton. The church was founded in the 13th C by Sir Hugh Peverell, with later work on the tower and nave and the addition of the porch and south aisle in 1498. Restored in Victorian times, there remains a Norman font and a 17th-C brass. The PO is located in the village store.

● **Holcombe Rogus**
Devon. Tel, PO, stores, garage. Very much the focus of the village, Holcombe Court is a rebuilt medieval manor house constructed by Sir Roger Bluett in the early part of the 16th century, making it one of the grandest Tudor houses in Devon. Today it is generally considered to be the finest house of that period still surviving in the county. Although not open to the public, a good view of the main south elevation, with its four-storey entrance porch, can be seen from the gateway.
The grounds are beautifully landscaped and include a fine walled garden.

● **Westleigh**
Devon. Tel. A quarry village.

Boatyards

Ⓑ**Minnows Touring Park** Sampford Peverell, Tiverton EX16 7EN (01884 821770; www.ukparks.co.uk/minnows). 🚾🎣 Boating and fishing permits, parking for cars and trailers.

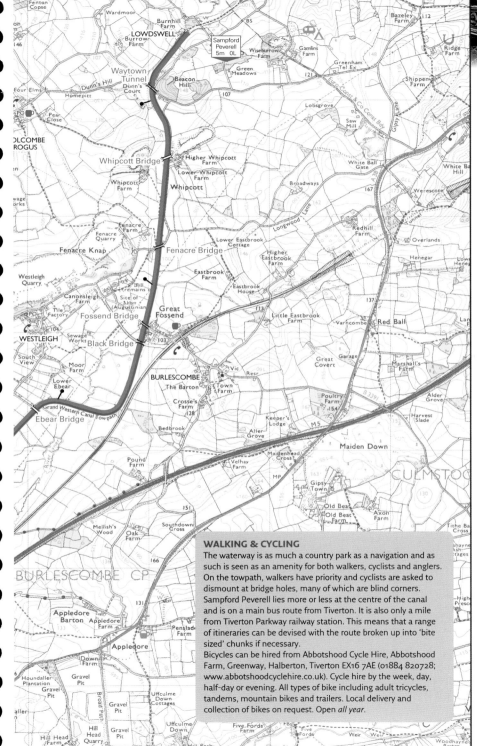

WALKING & CYCLING

The waterway is as much a country park as a navigation and as such is seen as an amenity for both walkers, cyclists and anglers. On the towpath, walkers have priority and cyclists are asked to dismount at bridge holes, many of which are blind corners. Sampford Peverell lies more or less at the centre of the canal and is on a main bus route from Tiverton. It is also only a mile from Tiverton Parkway railway station. This means that a range of itineraries can be devised with the route broken up into 'bite sized' chunks if necessary.

Bicycles can be hired from Abbotshood Cycle Hire, Abbotshood Farm, Greenway, Halberton, Tiverton EX16 7AE (01884 820728; www.abbotshoodcyclehire.co.uk). Cycle hire by the week, day, half-day or evening. All types of bike including adult tricycles, tandems, mountain bikes and trailers. Local delivery and collection of bikes on request. Open *all year*.

EXETER SHIP CANAL

MAXIMUM DIMENSIONS

Length: 122'
Beam: 26' 3"
Headroom: 32' 9"
Draught: 9' 9"

MANAGER

01392 274306; river_canal@exeter.gov.uk

Operating Authority
Exeter City Council
River and Canal Office
Haven Road
Exeter EX2 8DU
www.exeter.gov.uk

MILEAGE

Turf Lock to:
Topsham Lock (closed): 1½ miles
Double Locks: 3½ miles
Kings Arms: 4½ miles
St David's Station: 6½ miles

Locks: 2

The Exe estuary is up to 1½ miles wide, although it narrows considerably between Exmouth and Dawlish Warren. Its deep water channel can be tortuous and it has proved difficult for shipping since vessels first traded to Topsham and Exeter. Seaborne trade with the city was further constrained by the construction of a weir – by Isabella de Fortibus, Countess of Devon – during the reign of Edward I. This was built above Topsham and ensured that all craft had to unload downstream of the city until an Inquisition, held in 1290, decreed that a 30ft gap be formed in the obstruction. Thirty years later the Earl of Devon, whose successors went on to establish a thriving quay at Topsham, blocked the hole and all goods to Exeter passed through the town, attracting considerable shipping dues in the process.

Towards the middle of 16th C, Exeter Corporation obtained an Act of Parliament to remove what were now three weirs across the river and in 1539 unsuccessfully attempted to remove a series of shoals which had built up in the river and estuary. Passage into the city remained all but impossible so John Trew, of Glamorgan, was engaged to dig a canal, parallel to the river on its west bank. This opened in 1566, at a cost of £5000. For this he received £225 and a percentage of the tolls. This original navigation ran from just below the city walls to a connection with the Exe at Matford Brook, and shipping still had to pass Topsham, attracting dues, despite the quays not being used. The navigation was 16ft wide, 3ft deep and enabled vessels to carry 16 tons. It is reputed to be the first navigation constructed in this country with pound locks; three in total, with guillotine gates. Boats loaded direct from sea-going craft anchored in the estuary but had to contend with an awkward entrance into the canal that was only possible at high tide. Silting in both the estuary and the canal remained an additional problem, as did opposition from quay owners in Topsham who still collected dues from passing barges. This was temporarily overcome when Exeter Corporation bought the Topsham Quay lease, but this was not renewed when it expired in 1614.

After the Civil War the waterway was in poor condition, suffering water shortages from unauthorised mill abstraction, silting and continuing rivalry with Topsham. In 1676 the Corporation decided on improvements, dredging the canal and extending it south by half a mile thereby eliminating one mile of awkward river navigation. They built a larger entrance lock and an adjoining transhipment basin able to handle 60-ton craft.

Exeter was becoming an increasingly prosperous city, its wealth founded on the cloth-making industry and again it found the need to enlarge its waterway. In 1698, the Corporation put in hand a scheme to improve the navigation but the engineer in charge absconded with the city funds, leaving an unnavigable canal and the Corporation to complete the task on its own. Completed in 1701, the enlarged waterway measured 50ft wide, 10ft deep and could carry coasters up to 150 tons. The three old locks were removed and replaced by Double Locks, and flood gates were installed at King's Arms. However, it was still approached up a narrow, winding side channel and was only accessible to larger vessels on spring tides.

In the first part of 18th C an average of 310 craft used the canal per year; by the end of the century this had risen to 448. Notwithstanding this modest increase, the decision was taken in 1825 to further improve and extend the canal and under the direction of James Green, work commenced. He had previously dredged and straightened the navigation and his new strategy was a two mile extension to Turf; raised banks to allow passage by vessels of 14ft draught and the construction of a deep-water basin in Exeter. The old entrance lock was blocked up and as a result of representations from Topsham, a new side lock opposite the port was built in 1829. The total cost was £113,355, more than a fifth being absorbed by Turf Lock which was built on piles driven through clay and bog to the underlying bedrock. Although silting continued to be a problem, the largest ship recorded as using the improved navigation was of 350 tons, drawing 13ft 6ins. The new basin, measuring 900 x 120ft, came into its own – handling paper, leather, wheat, oats and manganese.

In the 1840s steam-driven vessels appeared on the canal but because their speed exceeded the 5 mph limit and their wash threatened the banks, they were prohibited from using their own power and had to be towed by horses. This unpopular move was a turning point for the navigation and the tonnage handled began to decline, as shipping unloaded at nearby coastal ports for onward carriage by rail. In the first half of 20th C traffic stabilised but then steadily dropped off with a single sludge tanker the only vessel finally left. With an end to the estuarine dumping of raw sewerage, this tanker is now no longer visible from the elevated section of the M5, berthed beside the city's sewerage works. Today Exeter is working hard to exploit the leisure potential of the navigation and her once commercially vibrant and historic quays.

WALKING & CYCLING

To make the most of this section you will need to use a combination of bike/hike on the canal towpath, ferry and train. It is straightforward to start at Dawlish Warren or Starcross and travel north – you can then bike or hike all the way to Exeter St David's.

From here you can either retrace your journey to Topsham lock and then use the ferry over to Topsham and catch the train to Lympstone, or you can catch a train from Exeter St David's to Lympstone. In March 2008, the first part of the Exeter to Exmouth cycleway was opened from Lympstone to Exmouth. From Exmouth catch the ferry over the river to Starcross (see page 50) to complete your route. Alternatively you can start at Exeter St David's, Exmouth, Lympstone or Topsham, which all have car parks.

At the Countess Weir Road Bridges National Cycle Route 2 – The South Coast Route – joins the Ship Canal and follows it into Exeter on the east bank. Plans are in hand to extend southwards, along the estuary, but routing through the SSSI may take some time to finalise.

In Exmouth there is the Exmouth to Budleigh Salterton Cyclepath along the old railway line; a quiet and almost level route. For the keen off-roader there is the challenging terrain of Woodbury Common. Details of both these possibilities can be obtained from Knobblies Bike Hire (see page 50), who will also help you plan a route.

Running south from Exeter, along the estuary and around Torbay, is the South West Coast Path, a challenging walk that can be followed all the way to Lands End.

The 40-mile East Devon Way starts at Lympstone and runs to the county border at Lyme Regis. There are four circular linking paths that tie in with it and detailed leaflets are available from TICs.

Powderham

At Starcross the road is set somewhat below the level of the railway track, separating it from the Exe estuary. Motorists are thus initially greeted with a view of grubby carriage bogies as trains race backwards and forwards to and from the West Country. The railway is very much a central feature of the village, as it was here that Brunel built a pumping station to create vacuum for his ill-fated atmospheric railway. The Italianate building survives today and now houses the local yacht club. The route north closely follows the trackbed, which from the road interrupts views out across the river into east Devon, 1½ miles away at this point. The ferry operates from a pier in the village and is accessible by crossing the railway. Soon a minor road leaves the main A379 and walkers and cyclists can proceed in relative peace, broken only by the passing trains: a mix of the new, futuristic Voyagers; the still elegant High Speed 125s and a regular procession of local, stopping DMUs. Pre-Beeching there were two routes into Cornwall; a more northerly one via Okehampton and this route, perched precariously on the sea wall, prone to the vagaries of foul weather and high tide. The most spectacular section, to the south of Dawlish, is also the most vulnerable, and services can be interrupted during storms; the cost of its upkeep is particularly high. Powderham Castle nestles, immediately to the west on raised ground, looking out across the estuary. It is passed not long before the route leaves the road for good, crossing over the railway to join the foreshore. After a mile Turf Lock and its attendant and very isolated hotel are approached: this is the beginning of the Exeter Ship Canal. It is an excellent spot to linger, to enjoy the views and the wildlife and to wonder at this unusual location (more solitary in winter than in summer). The railway finally diverges from the towpath and makes a beeline for the distant suburbs of Exeter, to ultimately follow the river to St David's as it loops round the city's western boundary. The path leads through Exminster Marshes, an SSSI and nature reserve administered by the RSPB; home to geese, curlew and widgeon in winter and lapwings, redshank and warblers in summer. River and canal run now in close partnership, only separated (in varying degrees according to the state of the tide) by mudflats as walker and cyclist approach Topsham which is spread out along the river's east bank.

Walkers setting out from Exminster are confronted by a mix of track, road, footpath and foreshore and are accompanied throughout by the bustling, single-track railway line. Views across the estuary are at all times uninterrupted and the sea and mudflats, in a continuous state of flux, can be constantly enjoyed. Cockle Sand provides a rich feeding ground for a variety of birds and the area is important for its abundance of eel grass, a favourite food of the Brent goose. In Lympstone, keeping north along the metalled road, walkers round a corner leading to the inlet to be confronted with a charming range of seaside cottages and the delightful Peters Tower. The station is but a short walk up the diminutive Strand.

BOAT TRIPS
Stuart Line River Cruises Exmouth (summer 01395 222144; winter 01395 279693; www.stuartlinecruises.co.uk). A wide-ranging selection of river and sea cruises, fishing trips and private charter. All-weather, all year round sailings in fully covered, heated boats. Bar and toilets. Telephone for further details or collect brochure from TIC.

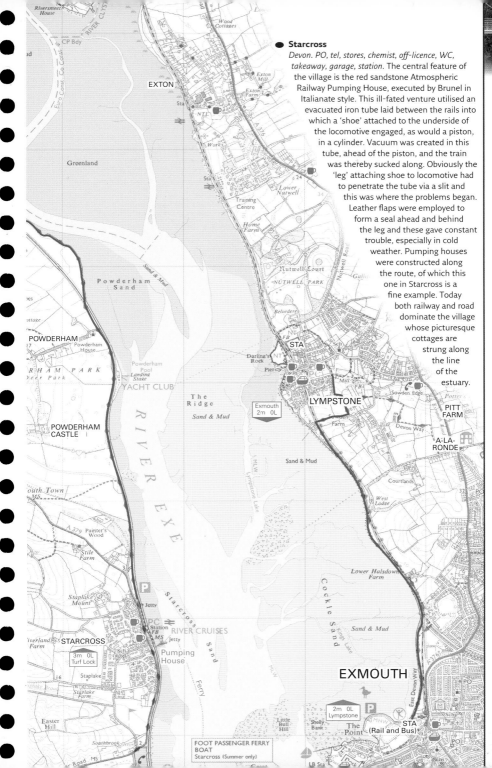

● **Starcross**

Devon. PO, tel, stores, chemist, off-licence, WC, takeaway, garage, station. The central feature of the village is the red sandstone Atmospheric Railway Pumping House, executed by Brunel in Italianate style. This ill-fated venture utilised an evacuated iron tube laid between the rails into which a 'shoe' attached to the underside of the locomotive engaged, as would a piston, in a cylinder. Vacuum was created in this tube, ahead of the piston, and the train was thereby sucked along. Obviously the 'leg' attaching shoe to locomotive had to penetrate the tube via a slit and this was where the problems began. Leather flaps were employed to form a seal ahead and behind the leg and these gave constant trouble, especially in cold weather. Pumping houses were constructed along the route, of which this one in Starcross is a fine example. Today both railway and road dominate the village whose picturesque cottages are strung along the line of the estuary.

Starcross Ferry Starcross, Dawlish EX6 8PA (01626 774770/07974 772681; www.exe2sea.co.uk). Operates *Apr–Oct* from the pier beside the Atmospheric Railway Pumping House. *First crossing 10.00 and thence hourly, on the hour. Last crossing Easter–mid May and mid Sep–Oct, 16.00; mid May–mid July and 1 Sep–mid Sep, 17.00; and mid July–31 Aug, 18.00.* Also various cruises. Cycles carried. Charge. *See* Exmouth for return crossing details.

- **Kenton**
Devon. PO, tel, stores, garage. Set a little way off from the estuary, the village provides the access point for Powderham Castle. It is a pretty village, especially the streets behind the main road, with a striking Perpendicular church. The ashlar tower is 120ft high; there are elaborate porches and carvings, and the mullions are in Beer stone. In contrast, the remaining stonework is red sandstone, much patched with grey and white. The pulpit is 15th-C and there is considerable Victorian restoration. Opposite stands a charming row of late 19th-C almshouses.

Powderham Castle Kenton EX6 8JQ (01626 890243; www.powderham.co.uk). Medieval castle with beautiful gardens and grounds, miniature steam railway, children's secret garden and fort, picnic area. Tea room, farm shop and plant centre. Castle and grounds *open Apr–Oct, Sun–Fri 10.00–16.30 (17.30 during summer hols).* Last guided tour *1 hour before closing.* Charge. Sometimes closed for private functions: telephone in advance of visit.

- **Cockwood**
Devon. Estuary village, 1 mile south of Starcross. Well worth a diversion to the pubs here.

- **Exminster**
Devon. PO, tel, stores, takeaway, garage. Again a little way from the navigation. The old village centre is now almost totally submerged in prolific dormitory housing for Exeter.

- **Exmouth**
Devon. All services. Exmouth probably first attracted attention when the Danes landed in 1001; the town became of consequence by the beginning of 13th C, by which time a castle had been built to guard the entrance to its sheltered harbour. During the Civil War it was alternately held by Parliamentarians and Royalists, finally falling to the former in March 1646. After a lengthy period of decline, the benefit of its balmy sea air, together with the sheltering hills to the east, was finally recognised and Exmouth became a celebrated seaside resort in Victorian times. The town developed in an irregular pattern with fine Georgian housing on Beacon Hill overlooking the sea and later building occupying the flat ground, at the base of the Beacon and facing the estuary. Further change was initiated by the Hon. Mark Rolle, during the second half of the 19th C, in an attempt to capitalise on the town's popularity – in its heyday it vied with Torquay in its importance as a seaside destination – but this has produced little of architectural importance. The docks were constructed on the south west point in 1867 and proved to be financially unsuccessful. Notwithstanding, they were rebuilt in 1882 and today, somewhat incongruously, have been developed into a marina, totally encased with upmarket 'New England' style housing.

A la Ronde *NT.* Summer Lane, Exmouth EX8 5BD (01395 265514; www.nationaltrust.org.uk). sixteen-sided cottage built in 1798 by Miss Jane Parmiter and her cousin, Mary Parmiter. It was inspired by San Vitale in Ravenna, which they visited as part of their ten year Grand Tour. Built of stone, with lozenge-shaped windows, the central hall – from which rooms radiate – is top-lit by a lantern roof. The gallery is reached by a narrow, grotto-like, shell-lined staircase. The tiled roof was originally thatched. Coffee, teas and light lunches. Shop. *Open Mar–Oct, daily except Thu and Fri (open Fri Jul–Aug) 11.00–17.00.* Charge. Timed tickets operate during busy periods.

Bicton Park Botanical Gardens East Budleigh, Buddleigh Salterton EX9 7BJ (01395 568465; www.bictongardens.co.uk).Sixty acres of beautiful gardens, a magnificent 19th-C palm house, an arboretum and a house of shells. An indoor exhibition hall packed with nostalgic delights for all ages. Miniature train, nature trail and children's play areas. Restaurant, shop and plant centre. *Open summer 10.00–18.00 and winter 10.00–17.00. Closed Xmas day and boxing day.* Charge.

Knobblies Bike Hire 107 Exeter Road, Exmouth EX8 1QE (01395 270182). Adult, children and toddler cycle hire. Repairs, spares and free safety checks. Good advice on local cycle routes. *Open Mon–Sat 09.00–17.30.*

Starcross Ferry Starcross, DawlishEX6 8PA (01626 862452; www.exe2sea.co.uk). Operates *Apr–Oct on the half hour* from Exmouth Docks. *Easter–mid May and mid Sep– Oct, first crossing 10.30, last crossing 16.30; mid May–mid Jul and 1st Sep–mid Sep 17.30; and mid Jul–Aug 18.15.* Cycles carried. Charge.

World of Country Life Sandy Bay, Exmouth EX8 5BU (01395 274533; www.worldofcountrylife.co.uk). Hall of transport, exhibition hall, pets centre and children's play areas, falconry centre, adventure playground, quad bikes. *Open Apr–Oct, 10.00–17.00 daily.* Shop.

Tourist Information Centre Alexandra Terrace, Exmouth EX8 1NZ (01395 222299; www.exmouth-guide.co.uk).

- **Lympstone**
Devon. PO, tel, stores, butcher, station. A charming village set out around the inlet. Winding, narrow cobbled streets, little more than passages, tightly flanked by irregular rows of cottages, rambling down to the water. The village is best approached on foot or by train.

Peters Tower Lympstone. Delightful red and yellow brick-built clock tower, with a short spire, erected in 1885 by W.H. Peters in memory of his wife. The clock was designed to face seawards to tell the fishermen the time of the tides. There are two stone limekilns nearby.

- **Exton**
Devon. Tel, station (request stop). Just a few houses, sandwiched between the river and main road, lining the estuary and with splendid views. The Royal Marines training camp, complete with its own railway station, lies a little way to the south. The excellent pub is well worth a visit, justifying a break in the train journey!

Pubs and Restaurants

Galleon Inn The Strand, Starcross, Dawlish EX6 8PR (01626 890412). Reputedly the ghost of a child can be heard bouncing a ball along the landing, whilst bottles are knocked off shelves in the bar by a more mature, female spirit. Food *L and E (except Mon and Tue in winter)*. Real ale. Children and dogs welcome. Patio garden. *Monthly* live bands and regular karaoke. B&B.

Atmospheric Railway Inn The Strand, Starcross, Dawlish EX6 8PA (01626 890335). A striking inn sign, although somewhat strangely depicting a train hauled by a steam locomotive. Real ales and bar meals *L and E*. Pub games. Patio seating and family garden with swings and slides.

Dolphin Inn Fore Street, Kenton, Dawlish EX6 8LD (01626 891371). Something of the Tardis about this establishment – its diminutive appearance from the outside belies the never-ending, rambling array of bars and eating spaces inside. Excellent selection of home-made bar snacks and meals served *L and E*. Real ales and a pleasant ambience, enhanced by two old kitchen ranges that are lit throughout the winter months. Children welcome, beer garden.

Chi Restaurant & Bar Fore Street, Kenton, Dawlish EX6 8LD (01626 890213; www.chi-restaurant.co.uk). Fine oriental cuisine and fresh seafood served *L and E* in this restaurant with several dining rooms, a landscaped garden and comfortable, modern hotel rooms.

Rodean Restaurant The Triangle, Kenton, Dawlish EX6 8LS (01626 890195). Attractive, village-centre restaurant serving a tasty range of British cuisine, prepared from local produce. À la carte and house menus available *L and E*. Telephone for opening times out of season.

Anchor Inn Church Road, Cockwood, Starcross EX6 8RA (01626 890203; www. anchorinncockwood.com). Overlooking the old harbour, this charming inn is over 465 years old and is reputedly haunted by a friendly ghost and his dog. A la carte restaurant and bar snacks, fish dishes a speciality. Real ales, outside sitting area. Children and dogs welcome. Live music occasionally.

Ship Inn Cockwood, Starcross EX6 8NU (01626 890373). Open fires, real ales, homemade meals available *all day in the summer*. Beer garden.

Turf Exminster, Exeter EX6 8EE (01392 833128; www.turfpub.net). Only accessible by boat, bike or on foot, this establishment enjoys a unique position in the Exe estuary at the entrance to the Ship Canal. Real ales and food served *L and E*. Camping. *Summer* barbecues in the large lockside/estuary garden. *Open Mar–Nov; sometimes open outside this period.* Opening times vary so please telephone to confirm, or visit the website.

Swan's Nest Station Road, Exminster, Exeter EX6 8DZ (01392 832371; www.swans-nest.co.uk). Elton John's 1941 Wurlitzer occupies pride of place in this large pub-cum-restaurant with an extensive menu serving traditional English food *L and E (not Boxing Day)*. Carvery, salad bar and live music at *weekends*. Real ales and a large selection of country wines. Children and dogs welcome. Garden and patio.

Royal Oak Main Road, Exminster, Exeter EX6 8DX (01392 832332). Traditional village local offering real ales and food *L and E; Sun* carvery. Children welcome. Beer garden and children's play area.

Stowey Arms Main Road, Exminster, Exeter EX6 8AT (01392 824216). Comfortable establishment created from a terrace of three cottages, originally belonging to the Stowey Estate. Traditional English à la carte menu *L and E*. Real ales. Children and dogs welcome. Garden. B&B.

Beach Hotel Victoria Road, Exmouth EX8 1DR (01395 272090; www.thebeachpub.co.uk). Overlooking the harbour and the estuary. Real ales and food available *L and E*. No children under fourteen. Dogs welcome. Outside patio seating. Live bands at *weekends*.

The Grove The Esplanade, Exmouth EX8 1BJ (01395 272101). Overlooking the seafront, large garden at the front of the pub. Homemade food served *all day*. Children and dogs welcome. Quiz every *Thu evening*.

Strand Inn 1 The Parade, Exmouth EX8 1RS (01395 263649). A long, low establishment with wooden panelling and floors and a friendly, local trade. Food available *L*. Children's menus, 'meal deals' and a *Sunday* roast. Real ales.

Powder Monkey 2–2A The Parade, Exmouth EX8 1RJ (01395 280090). A Wetherspoon pub dispensing an ambitious range of real ales, including at least two from local breweries at any time. Open from *08.00* for breakfast. Food available *all day until 22.00*. Patio seating.

Globe Inn The Strand, Lympstone, Exmouth EX8 5EY (01395 263166). This pub offers open fires. A previous landlady fell down the stairs to her death, and is reputed to be still in residence. A reputation for excellent food, majoring on fresh, locally caught fish served *L and E*, together with real ales. *Sunday* roasts. Traditional fish & chips *Thu E*. Children and dogs welcome. Quiz *Tue* and occasional music. Outside seating.

Swan Inn The Strand, Lympstone, Exmouth EX8 5ET (01395 270403). Traditional, friendly village local serving bistro style food *L and E*. Real ales. Children and dogs welcome Patio seating and regular *summer* barbecues. Live music at *weekends*.

Redwing Inn Church Road, Lympstone, Exmouth EX8 5JT (01395 222156; www.redwingbar-dining.co.uk). Cosy pub/restaurant serving continental beers and fresh food, locally sourced and cooked to order. Booking recommended. Children welcome. No dogs.

Puffing Billy Inn Station Road, Exton, Exeter EX3 0PR (01392 877888). Excellent food in spacious modern surroundings. Friendly, courteous and attentive staff. Meals available *L and E, daily, Sunday lunch*. Real ales. Children welcome; dogs in the large garden only.

BIRD LIFE

The Exe Estuary The estuary is internationally important for wildlife, with sandbanks, mud flats, salt marshes and extensive reed beds. It is recognised as a Site of Special Scientific Interest and an important habitat for wading and migrating birds. Route 2 of the National Cycle Network runs alongside Exminster Marshes and Bowling Green Marsh, and links both sides of the estuary. Exminster Marshes are also accessible on foot via the canal towpath from Exeter and a footpath from Powderham Village, along the estuary seawall and onto the towpath. During spring, among many different species, you are likely to see lapwings and redshanks, warblers, swifts and swallows. The estuary is the only place in Devon where both lapwing and redshank breed. Summer time is when you'll see damselflies and dragonflies and, later in the summer, waders, including black-tailed godwits returning south from their northern breeding grounds. During autumn ospreys are regularly seen hunting over the estuary or roosting in trees. The estuary is well-known for flocks of avocets during winter, together with large numbers of ducks and waders, feeding on the mudflats at low tide. Other birds seen during winter include large flocks of brent geese, golden plovers and red-breasted mergansers. You may also see peregrines hunting in the skies above the estuary and occasionally short-eared owls.

RSPB Nature Reserve (01392 824614; www.rspb. org.uk). The reserve comprises two areas of coastal grazing marsh on opposite sides of the estuary. There is a hide and viewing platform at Bowling Green. Powderham Marshes (part of Exminster Marshes) has a nature trail and viewing platform. Also toilets, picnic area, guided walks and a regular programme of events for all the family. The local RSPB group run Avocet Cruises on the River Exe.

Darts Farm just outside Topsham, Exeter EX3 0QH (01392 878200; www.dartsfarm.co.uk). As well as lots of different shops, Darts Farm is the location of the RSPB shop, the Exe Estuary Visitor Centre and a tea-room. *Open Mon–Sat 08.00–17.30, Sun 09.30–16.30.*

Devon Wildlife Trust (01392 279244; www. devonwildlifetrust.org) has nature reserves within the Exe Estuary, at the Exe Reed Beds and the adjacent Old Sludge Beds. There is no public access to the reserves, but great views can be had from the canal towpath. The reeds are an important nesting site for swallows and martins as well as other migrants and wintering birds.

Lapwing Formerly more numerous but are still common in many parts of Britain and Ireland and can be seen on the Exe Estuary particularly in spring. They breed in open, flat country, including undisturbed farmland and coastal marshes, and nest on the ground. After nesting, flocks form and travel to find suitable feeding areas free of frost. In winter the British population is boosted by an influx of continental birds. The lapwing looks black and white at a distance but in good light has a green, oily sheen on the back; winter birds have buffish fringes to their feathers on the back. The spiky crest feathers are longer in male birds that the females. In flight the lapwing has rounded, black and white wings and a flapping flight. Their call is a loud 'peewit'.

Reed warbler As the name suggests, these birds are almost always associated with reedbeds around lakes or along rivers. Dense, wet reedbeds may be home to large numbers of reed warblers: a summer visitor, usually seen between May and August. Singing birds clamber up reeds or occasionally use bushes to deliver a grating, chattering song that includes some mimetic elements. The birds have rather nondescript sandy-brown upperparts, paler underparts and dark legs. They construct woven, cup-shaped nests, attached to upright reed stems, usually over water. They feed on insects and spiders. In autumn reed warblers return to central Africa.

Redshank A fairly common resident breeding species, numbers being boosted by an influx of continental birds in winter. A nervous bird, the loud, piping alarm call alerts observers to its presence. It is easily recognised by its red legs and long, red-based bill. Plumage is mostly grey-brown above and pale below with streaks and barring; plumage is more heavily marked in the breeding season. In flight the redshank shows a characteristic broad, white trailing margin to the wing. During the breeding season, the bird favours flood meadows, salt marshes and moors, nesting among grasses; in winter, coastal habitats, especially mudflats and estuaries. Its food includes shrimps, snails and worms. The redshank has an even-paced, jerky walk as it hunts its prey.

Black-tailed godwit A rare breeding species favouring flood meadows. As a winter visitor, they are more widespread, forming flocks on mudflats and estuaries. The black-tailed godwit is a large, long-legged wader with an incredibly long, very slightly upturned bill which is pinkish at the base. In all plumages, it is recognised in flight by a black tail, white rump and conspicuous white wingbar. In winter plumage, the bird has rather uniformly grey-brown upperparts and pale underparts. In breeding plumage, it acquires an orange-red wash to its head and neck, with feathers on its back having black centres. The juveniles have a buffish wash on neck and breast.

Curlew Widespread year-round, with numbers boosted by an influx of continental birds in the winter months: the commonest large wader with a long, downcurved bill. Plumage is mainly grey-brown with streaked and spotted underparts and a pale belly. In flight, the wings are uniformly dark brown but show a white rump and wedge on the lower back; the tip of the tail has dark, narrow barring. The curlew breeds on damp grassland and moors, building its nest on the ground among short vegetation. In winter, it is usually found on coasts, preferring estuaries and mudflats. The curlew uses its long, blue-grey legs to wade in deep water, probing for worms, crabs and other crustaceans. Its call is 'curlew', with a bubbling song.

Goldfinch A beautiful, small finch, with bright yellow wingbars and a white rump. The adult has red and white on face, a black cap extending down the sides of the neck, buffish back and white underparts with buff flanks. The juvenile has brown, streaked plumage but yellow wingbars as in the adult. A common and widespread resident in Britain and Ireland (except northern Scotland). Favours wasteground and meadows where the narrow, pointed bill is used to feed on seeds of thistles and teasel in particular. The goldfinch builds a neat, deep nest towards the end of a branch. They are usually seen in small flocks which take to the wing with a tinkling flight call. The male's song is twittering but contains call-like elements.

Skylark Its call, an incessant trilling and fluty song, delivered in flight, can be heard over areas of grassland as the bird hangs in the air, almost too high to see. Its plumage is rather nondescript with streaked, sandy-brown upperparts and paler underparts; it has a short crest. Northern populations migrate; in autumn flocks fly south and west to feed on arable fields. It eats insects and seeds and nests on the ground.

Avocet An elegant wader of pools and marshes near the coast. In winter northern birds move to sheltered estuaries in western Europe, while others migrate to northern Africa. It is easily recognised by its black and white plumage, long, blue legs and long, upcurved bill swept from side-to-side through water when feeding. Avocets feed on invertebrates in shallow water. The avocet is the RSPB's symbol.

Little egret A common and conspicuous year-round resident on many estuaries and coastal waterways, roosting in colonies. An unmistakable, pure white, heron-like bird with a black, dagger-like bill and a long neck. The legs are long and black, with plastic-yellow feet, often not visible if the bird is wading. In the breeding season the little egret acquires head plumes and trailing plumes on its back. In flight, the trailing legs and yellow feet are conspicuous; the neck held in a hunched 's' shape. An active feeder, often chasing after fish in shallow water and stabbing with great accuracy. At other times, the bird may rest in a hunched-up posture with the head and bill hidden, when it can be confused with a mute swan.

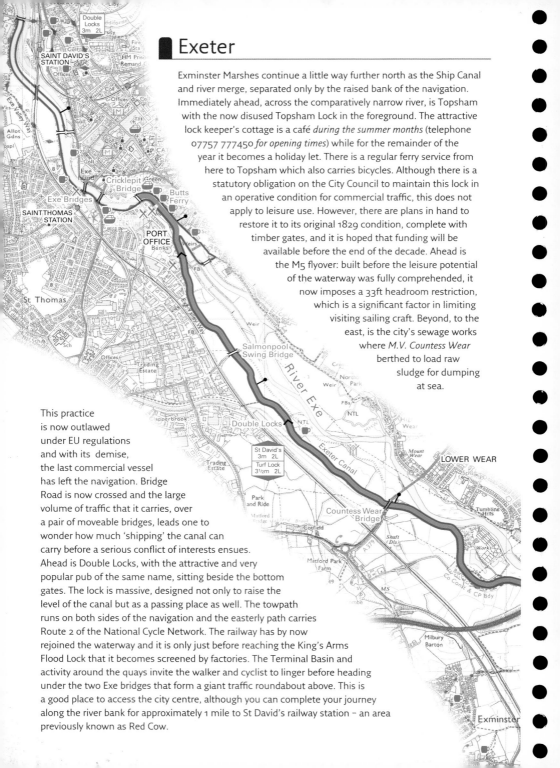

Exeter

Exminster Marshes continue a little way further north as the Ship Canal and river merge, separated only by the raised bank of the navigation. Immediately ahead, across the comparatively narrow river, is Topsham with the now disused Topsham Lock in the foreground. The attractive lock keeper's cottage is a café *during the summer months* (telephone 07757 777450 *for opening times*) while for the remainder of the year it becomes a holiday let. There is a regular ferry service from here to Topsham which also carries bicycles. Although there is a statutory obligation on the City Council to maintain this lock in an operative condition for commercial traffic, this does not apply to leisure use. However, there are plans in hand to restore it to its original 1829 condition, complete with timber gates, and it is hoped that funding will be available before the end of the decade. Ahead is the M5 flyover: built before the leisure potential of the waterway was fully comprehended, it now imposes a 33ft headroom restriction, which is a significant factor in limiting visiting sailing craft. Beyond, to the east, is the city's sewage works where *M.V. Countess Wear* berthed to load raw sludge for dumping at sea.

This practice is now outlawed under EU regulations and with its demise, the last commercial vessel has left the navigation. Bridge Road is now crossed and the large volume of traffic that it carries, over a pair of moveable bridges, leads one to wonder how much 'shipping' the canal can carry before a serious conflict of interests ensues. Ahead is Double Locks, with the attractive and very popular pub of the same name, sitting beside the bottom gates. The lock is massive, designed not only to raise the level of the canal but as a passing place as well. The towpath runs on both sides of the navigation and the easterly path carries Route 2 of the National Cycle Network. The railway has by now rejoined the waterway and it is only just before reaching the King's Arms Flood Lock that it becomes screened by factories. The Terminal Basin and activity around the quays invite the walker and cyclist to linger before heading under the two Exe bridges that form a giant traffic roundabout above. This is a good place to access the city centre, although you can complete your journey along the river bank for approximately 1 mile to St David's railway station – an area previously known as Red Cow.

● **Topsham**

Devon. All services. Delightfully unspoilt, it is not hard to imagine the Topsham of 500 years ago when, as a port and centre for ship building, it was more important than Exeter. Its unique architectural heritage, with shops and housing dating from as early as the 14th C, can be enjoyed on foot. Take a stroll along The Strand to view some exquisite examples of 17th- and 18th-C merchant housing, with their characteristic Dutch gables. The nearby Goat Walk is equally charming; with its tiny beach it has been a walking and meeting place over many centuries. In spite of the bustle brought on by the tourist season, the locals remain tolerant, friendly and hospitable. There is a heated, open-air pool and a small museum.

Topsham Ferry Boat Topsham, Exeter (07801 203338). Plying between Ferry Road Causeway, Topsham and Topsham Lock on the Ship Canal, carrying pedestrians, dogs and cycles. *Operates 09.30-17.30 Apr hols & late May-3 Oct daily (except Tue). Otherwise Sat & Sun & most B hols.* Telephone for times or check with Exeter Visitor Information (see below).

● **Exeter**

Devon. All services. Early records for the city mention the construction of a fort, between AD55 and AD60, as headquarters for the 2nd Augustan Legion and located at the centre of the present city, overlooking the lowest possible crossing of the Exe. It was surrounded by a timber and earth rampart and a ditch; the foundation was exposed during an excavation in 1971, but was subsequently covered over again. The burgeoning Roman town took over much of the plan area of the fortress and spread beyond to be enclosed by a stone wall in the 2nd C. This is the basis of the present city wall which has been extensively rebuilt over the years. Urban life continued to flourish through the following centuries, with the withdrawal of the Roman garrison and the building of a monastery at which St Boniface was educated in the 7th C. The present High Street follows the line of the Roman main road and the four main medieval gates are sited on Roman gateways. Exeter was occupied by the Danes in AD877 when the chief religious establishment was St Mary Major, which survived in its Victorian

form, in the cathedral close, into the 1970s. The city became a See in 1050 and the Norman cathedral was built in the 12th C; later to be much remodelled in medieval times. From the 15th C onwards, Exeter was the chief cloth marketing town in the south west and by the 17th C had become one of the richest cities in England. It was a significant port, although imports greatly outweighed exports and it was prey to serious and sustained competition from Topsham, downstream on the Exe estuary. However, the eventual confirmation of its customs rights over the entire estuary during the 17th C, together with the relative success of the canal, restored much of its prosperity and resulted in the construction of the delightful Custom House and development of the City Quays. Over the 19th C the population almost trebled, aided by the appearance of the railway in 1844. Some 130 years later, the arrival of the M5 was a further improvement in the city's communication links with the rest of the country and a variety of light industries thrive. Exeter lost much of its rich architectural heritage during the pernicious bombings of the 1942 air raids and this has been replaced, in varying degrees, by insensitive redevelopment dating from the 1950s.

Barnfield Theatre Barnfield Road, Exeter EX1 1SN (01392 270891; www.barnfieldtheatre.org.uk). Mix of amateur and professional theatre, dance and music. Coffee, snacks and bar.

Exeter Visitor Information & Tickets Dixsfield, Exeter EX1 1GF (01392 665700; www.heartofdevon. com). Source of walking and cycling leaflets and times for the Topsham Ferry Boat. Also bookings for a range of accommodation in the area, from hotels to camping barns. *Open Mon-Fri 09.30-16.30 & B Hols 10.00-16.00.*

Devon Wildlife Trust Cricklepit Mill, Commercial Road, Exeter EX2 4AB (01392 279244; www.devonwildlifetrust.org). The trust cares for some 40 nature reserves around the county, totalling more than 3,000 acres in all. Most are *open to the public at all times*. The Old Sludge Beds lie between the Ship Canal and the Exe, just upstream from the M5 flyover, and are maintained as an area of reed bed which is home to a wide variety of wetland birds. There are two further reserves within reach of Exmouth.

Exeter Cathedral Cathedral Close, Exeter EX1 1HS (01392 285983; www.exeter-cathedral.org.uk). Although completed in the 14th C by Bishop Grandisson, the two Norman transept towers date from the building's foundation. It was extensively remodelled by Bishop Bronescombe in the 13th C and the pepperpot roofs replaced the traditional

TOPSHAM

Newport Park
Boatyard
The Retreat
M5 Bridge
Topsham Lock (disused)
Ferry
FIRE STATION
48
Works
Rivermeet

Norman pyramids during further work in the 15th C. There is much original glass in the late 14thC east window and Sir Gilbert Scott's canopied choir stalls incorporate the oldest set of misericords that survive complete; they were carved 1260–80. The bishop's throne, carved from oak in 1312, is quite exquisite. Restrictions to general visiting during services, otherwise *open Mon–Sat 09.00–17.00*. Charge. Tours, shop and café.

Royal Albert Memorial Museum & Art Gallery Queen Street, Exeter EX4 3RX (01392 665858; www.rammuseum.org.uk). Extensively enhanced and refurbished during 2011. A wealth of interesting items in a Victorian treasure house. Exhibitions include world cultures, local history and archaeology, exotic birds and butterflies, glassware and West Country silver, clocks and watches. Temporary visiting art exhibitions alongside a rotating permanent collection. Workshops and activities for children and adults throughout the year. Shop and licensed café. *Open Tue–Sun 10.00–17.00. Closed Mon & B Hols.*

Exeter Picture House 51 Bartholomew Street West, Exeter EX4 3AJ (0871 902 5730; www.picturehouses. co.uk/cinema/exeter_picturehouse). Award-winning, purpose-built, two-screen cinema showing the best in contemporary film. Bar, coffee and tea.

Killerton House Broadclyst, Exeter EX5 3LE (01392 881345; www.nationaltrust.org.uk/killerton). Elegant 18th-C house containing treasures from the renowned Killerton dress collection, revealing the secrets of a woman's wardrobe in days gone by. Large hillside garden, Victorian rock garden, ice house and woodland walks. Gift shop, plant centre and licensed restaurant. House open *Feb–Dec at varying times. Garden open daily throughout year, 10.00–19.00.* Charge. Seven miles north of Exeter.

Exeter Northcott Theatre Stocker Road, Exeter EX4 4QB (01392 493493; www.exeternorthcott.co.uk). Venue for professional visiting theatre companies and the theatre's resident company. Backstage tours, theatre talks and visiting musicians. Restaurant serving tea, coffee and light meals. Licensed bar.

Phoenix Arts Centre Bradninch Place, Gandy Street, Exeter EX4 3LS (01392 667080; www. exeterphoenix. org.uk). High calibre, eclectic mix of varied material on offer, including galleries, workshops and courses. Excellent café and bar. Worth a visit just to see the automaton phoenix in action as the hour strikes.

Exeter Quay Striking example of an inland port that has developed over the ages to reflect the city's prosperity, founded on the production of serge cloth. Today it is given over solely to leisure use but this does nothing to detract from the wealth and diversity of the buildings, some dating back to the late 17th C. The Custom House, completed in 1681, was designed by Richard Allen and enabled Exeter to re-establish its dominance as a port over its long-time rival, Topsham, situated downstream in the tidal estuary. The building is brick-fronted, with two storeys and five bays and white painted stone quoins. The stairhall, together with some of the downstairs rooms, have superb plasterwork ceilings and the staircase incorporates bulbous, urn-shaped balusters. The warehouses north of the Custom House date from a similar period; cut into the cliffs, they provided a bonded stores. The two five-storey warehouses fronting the cliffs date from 1835, and the open fish market is also 19th-C. It incorporated a King's Beam, used for weighing dutiable goods. There are also two further warehouses nearby, built in the late 19th C, and used for storing wine. Further west, Cricklepit Mill (which gives its name to the nearby pedestrian bridge) dates from the end of the 17th C and encloses a large waterwheel. It was variously used for fulling, grist production and malting. On the other side of the water, set beside the basin constructed by James Green in 1830, is a large warehouse from the same period. The Quay House Interpretation Centre displays models, artefacts and pictures relating to the historic dock area, together with an audio-visual history of Exeter.

Rail Travel (National Rail Enquiries 08457 484950; www.nationalrail.co.uk). Exeter is served by five railway lines and has eight railway stations, two of which are on the mainline. On the east side of the Exe services run from both Exeter St David's and Exeter Central, having originated in Barnstaple. The run north is well worthwhile as an extension to activities around the estuary. On the west side of the Exe stopping services depart from both Exeter stations (many also stop at Exeter St Thomas) and may have originated from Bristol or South Wales. A few are from Exmouth. For cyclists, advanced bookings are essential on some services, usually the long distance routes. The *Cycling by Train* leaflet can be downloaded from the website.

Saddles & Paddles 4 King's Wharf, The Quay, Exeter EX2 4AN (01392 424241; www.saddlepaddle.co.uk). Bike and canoe hire on the quayside. Sales, spares and repairs. Canoeing group nights out.

WALKING & CYCLING
There are two valuable leaflets produced by Devon County Council entitled *Making Tracks – Cycle Routes in Devon* and *Making Tracks – Walking Trails in Devon*. The first features over 70 cycle routes while the second covers over 700 miles of walks. *See* Exeter Visitor Information amongst the Exeter attractions on page 55 for further details. Exeter City Council's Countryside Service publish a series of walks leaflets under the heading *Countryside Walks in Exeter*. Telephone (01392) 265890 or visit www.exeter.gov.uk. They also manage the Riverside Valley Park which extends for 7 miles through the city forming part of a major wildlife highway linking Exmoor to the sea. This offers additional walking and cycling opportunities and is supported by further leaflets. *See also* Walking & Cycling on page 47.

Pubs and Restaurants

Double Locks Hotel Canal Banks, Marsh Barton, Exeter EX2 6LT (01392 256947; www.doublelocks.com). A popular family pub overlooking the canal and serving food *all day* together with a selection of real ales. Dogs welcome. Lockside seating. Open fires and regular events and live music.

✕**Welcome Café** Haven Banks, Exeter EX2 8DU (01392 279003). Beside King's Arms Lock. Friendly, welcoming establishment where the proprietors have time to converse with their customers. Teas, coffees, home-made cakes and light meals using local produce wherever possible. Very child and baby friendly. *Open Tue–Sun 10.00–17.00.* Cash only.

✕♀ **Bar Venezia Piazza Terracina** 61 Waterside, The Quay, Exeter EX2 8GY (01392 423688; www.barvenezia.co.uk). Ristorante and café bar beside the quay. Traditional Italian menu, pizzas and Italian-style snacks *all day*. Hot and cold drinks. Children welcome. Quayside seating. Also Turkish café. Salsa on *Sun E.*

Port Royal Weirfield Path, Exeter EX2 4DR (01392 272360; www.theportroyal.co.uk). Reputed to be the longest pub in Exeter, its low ceilings serve only to substantiate this claim. It incorporates the old boathouse and serves an à la carte menu and bar snacks *L and E (not Sun E)*, together with real ales. Children and dogs welcome. Patio seating. *Closed Mon in winter and open all day in summer.*

Prospect Inn The Quay, Exeter EX2 4AN (01392 273152; www.heavitreebrewery.co.uk). Set in an attractive old building with exposed beams, panelled walls and multi-level seating areas, this establishment is *open all day in summer*, serving food *daily*, together with real ales. Children welcome. Beer garden. Live music *Fri and Sat E.*

On the Waterfront 4–9 The Quay, Exeter EX2 4AP (01392 210590; www.waterfrontexeter. co.uk). Occupying the bottom floor of a converted warehouse with vaulted brick ceilings, this establishment serves real ale and restaurant meals *L and E daily*. Bar meals *available daily 12.00–21.00*. Children's menu. Quayside seating.

Harvesters Malthouse 7 Haven Road, Haven Bank, Exeter EX2 8BP (01392 490555; www.harvester.co.uk/themalthouseexeter). Old riverside malthouse, tastefully restored with exposed brickwork and lots of beams. Alongside a range of old malting paraphernalia it serves real ales and food *all day*. Fun Factory and soft toy area – a child's paradise.

✕**Exebridge Café** 180 Cowick Street, Exeter EX4 1AA (01392 203183). Excellent and inexpensive home-cooked café meals. Children welcome, friendly service. *Open Mon–Sat 08.45–15.30.*

Mill on the Exe Bonhay Road, Exeter EX4 3AB (01392 214464; www.millontheexe.co.uk). Converted paper mill. Real ales and an extensive international selection of food in atmospheric surroundings. Children and dogs welcome. Upstairs river balcony overlooking the weir and downstairs garden contribute towards making this a unique building. *Open 11.00–23.00 daily*; food *available 12.00–21.00.*

Imperial New North Road, Exeter EX4 4HF (01392 434050; www.jdwetherspoon.co.uk). This 'pub' makes use of all the downstairs rooms in a Georgian country house which is now a grade II listed structure. It includes a stunning orangery, the roof supported on cast-iron bow trusses and possibly originally built by Brunel on a site at Streatham Hall. Popular with the nearby university, it dispenses an ever changing array of real ales and a range of snacks and light meals *all day until 22.00*. Garden.

Great Western Hotel St David's Station Approach, Exeter EX4 4NU (01392 274039; www. greatwesternhotel.co.uk). This unlikely venue dispenses a wide selection of cask beer. Food available at the bar and in the restaurant *L and E*. B&B.

Jolly Porter Imperial Lodge, St David's Hill, Exeter EX4 4BB (01392 254848). Real ales served in an atmospheric, panelled bar. Selection of wines by the glass in this popular local. Also incorporates a Chinese restaurant and takeaway.

Route 2 1–2 Monmouth Hill, Topsham, Exeter EX3 0JQ (01392 875085; www.route2topsham. co.uk). Formerly the Steam Packet and now transformed into a café bar. This licensed eco-café, situated on the Exe Estuary Trail, part of NCN 2, also offers cycle hire and repair. *Open Mon–Wed 08.00–18.00, Thu–Sun 08.00–20.00.*

Lighter Pub Restaurant The Quay, Topsham, Exeter EX3 0HZ (01392 875439; www.lighterinn.co.uk). Once the custom house, now dispensing real ales and an appetising selection of food *L and E (not Sun E)*. Children welcome. Quayside seating.

✕♀ **Galley** 41 Fore Street, Topsham EX3 0HU (01392 876078; www.galleyrestaurant.co.uk). Wherever possible only local, organic and seasonal produce is used in the preparation of a range of appetising food served *L and E* in this charmingly located restaurant. Booking recommended. Children welcome.

Passage House Inn Ferry Road, Topsham, Exeter EX3 0JN (01392 873653; www.passagehouseinntopsham.co.uk). One of the oldest pubs in Topham. Fresh fish is a speciality. Good collection of real ales. Food served *daily until 21.00*. Riverside seating, next to ferry.

KENNET & AVON CANAL

MAXIMUM DIMENSIONS

Avonmouth to Bristol Harbour
Length: 325'
Beam: 50'
Draught: 18'
Air Draught: 90'

Bristol Harbour to Hanham Lock
Length: 80'
Beam: 18'
Draught: 6' 3"
Air Draught: 10' 3"

DOCK MASTER
0117 927 3633

Hanham Lock to Bath
Length: 75'
Beam: 16'
Headroom: 8' 9"

Bath to Newbury
Length: 70'
Beam: 13' 6"
Headroom: 8'
or
Length: 72'
Beam: 7'
Headroom: 7'

Newbury to Reading
Length: 70'
Beam: 14'
Headroom: 7' 8"

MANAGER
0303 040 4040
enquiries.kennetavon@canalrivertrust.org.uk

MILEAGE
AVONMOUTH entrance to Severn Estuary to:
Bristol Docks: 7¾ miles
HANHAM Lock (start of tidal section): 14¼ miles
Bath, junction with River Avon: 25½ miles
Dundas Aqueduct: 30¾ miles
Bradford-on-Avon: 35¼ miles
Devizes Top Lock: 47¼ miles
Pewsey Wharf: 59¼ miles
Crofton Top Lock: 65¾ miles
Hungerford: 73¼ miles
Kintbury: 76¼ miles
Newbury Lock: 82¼ miles
Aldermaston Wharf: 90¾ miles
Tyle Mill Lock: 92¾ miles
READING: 100¾ miles

Locks: 104

The Kennet & Avon Canal is one of the most splendid lengths of artificial waterway in Britain, a fitting memorial to the canal age as a whole. It is a broad canal, cutting across southern England from Reading to Bristol (shown in this guide from Avonmouth to Reading). Its generous dimensions and handsome architecture blend well with the rolling downs and open plains that it passes through, and are a good reminder of the instinctive feeling for scale that characterised most 18th- and early 19th-C civil engineering.

The canal was built in three sections. The first two were river navigations, the Kennet from Reading to Newbury, and the Avon from Bath to Bristol, both being canalised. Among early 18th-C river navigations the Kennet was one of the most ambitious, owing to the steep fall of the river. Between Reading and Newbury 20 locks were necessary in almost as many miles, as the difference in level is 138ft. John Hore was the engineer for the Kennet Navigation, which was built between 1718 and 1723 and included 11 miles of new cut. Subsequently Hore was in charge of the Bristol Avon Navigation, carried out between 1725 and 1727. These river navigations were interesting in many ways, often because of the varied nature of the country they passed through. The steep-sided Avon Gorge meant that a fast-flowing river had to be brought under control. Elsewhere the engineering was unusual: for example the turf-sided locks on the Kennet, now partially replaced with brick structures.

For the third stage, a canal from Newbury to Bath was authorised in 1794. Rennie was appointed engineer, and after a long struggle the canal was opened in 1810, completing a through route from London to Bristol. The canal is 57 miles long, and included 79 broad locks, a summit level at Savernake 452ft above sea level and one short tunnel, also at Savernake. Rennie was both engineer and architect, anticipating the role played by Brunel in the creation of the Great Western Railway; in some ways his architecture is the more noteworthy aspect of his work. The architectural quality of the whole canal is exceptional, from the straightforward stone bridges to the magnificent neo-classical aqueducts at Avoncliffe and Limpley Stoke.

Rennie's solution to the anticipated water supply problems on the top pound was to build a 4312yd tunnel, thereby providing a reservoir 15 miles long. The company called in William Jessop to offer a second – and hopefully cheaper solution – and it was he who suggested a shorter tunnel in conjunction with a steam pumping engine. This resulted in a saving of £41,000 and a completion date two years earlier. In some places the canal bed was built over porous rock, and so leaked constantly, necessitating further regular pumping. Nevertheless, the canal as a whole was a striking achievement. West of Devizes the waterway descends Caen Hill in a straight flight of 16 locks. In total 29 locks are navigated within 2 miles of Devizes. The many swing bridges were designed to run on ball bearings, one of the first applications of the principle. The bold entry of the canal into Bath, a sweeping descent round the south of the city, is a firm expression of the belief that major engineering works should contribute to the landscape, whether urban or rural, instead of imposing themselves upon it as so often happens nowadays.

Later the Kennet & Avon Canal Company took over the two river navigations, thus gaining control of the whole through route. However traffic was never as heavy as the promoters had expected, and so the canal declined steadily throughout the 19th C. It suffered from early railway competition as the Great Western Railway duplicated its route, and was eventually bought by that railway company. Maintenance standards slipped, and this, combined with a rapidly declining traffic, meant that navigation was difficult in places by the end of World War I. The last regular traffic left the canal in the 1930s, but still it remained open, and the last through passage was made in 1951 by *nb Queen*, with the West Country artist P. Ballance on board. Subsequently the canal was closed, and for a long time its future was in jeopardy. However, great interest in the canal had resulted in the formation of a Canal Association shortly after World War II, to fight for restoration.

In 1962 the Kennet & Avon Canal Trust was formed out of the Association, and practical steps towards restoration were under way. Using volunteers to raise funds from all sources, and with steadily increasing inputs from what was then British Waterways, the trust has catalysed the reopening of the entire navigation as a through route from Reading to Bristol. This achievement was commemorated on 8 August 1990, with HM The Queen navigating through Lock 43, at the summit of the Caen Hill flight, which now bears her name.

NAVIGATIONAL NOTES

1 Do not navigate in tidal waters without charts, tide tables, anchor, and all the other essential safety equipment. Ensure that your craft is suitable and well maintained. Seek expert advice if in any doubt. Inland waterways craft do navigate the Severn Estuary to Sharpness (and vice versa) but this is a foolish practice without suitable weather conditions and the services of a river pilot. For further details about pilotage telephone Gloucester Pilots Partnership on 07774 226143. *Safety Guidance for Small Boat Passage of Severn Estuary* is available free from www.gloucesterpilots.co.uk/services/leisure or by sending a large SAE to: The Harbourmaster, Sharpness Port Authority, Severnside House, Berkeley, Glos. GL13 9UD. See also *Nicholson Waterways Guide Severn, Avon and Birmingham*.

2 Note that most insurance policies covering inland craft do not include cover for tidal waters for which there are often special requirements to be met and usually an additional charge. Contact your insurance company before planning your trip below Hanham Lock.

3 Bristol City Council publish the comprehensive *Bristol Harbour Information for Boat Owners*, available free by telephoning the Dock Master on 0117 927 3633. This covers everything from locking procedures into the floating harbour through to details relating to exiting the feeder canal at Nether Lock. There is also information relating to use of the Floating Harbour and its environs available at www.bristol.gov.uk/page/arrival-and-departure-bristol-harbour.

Avonmouth

The Severn Estuary, with its
two dramatic road crossings,
must be well known to all
who travel the motorway
system into Wales and the
West Country. Equally well
known is its extreme range of
tides – giving rise to the Severn
Bore – which in the world record
books come third, surpassed
only by those in the Bay of Fundy
(bordered by Nova Scotia and New
Brunswick) and in Ungava Bay, Quebec.
The inland boater is, therefore, only likely to
venture along the River Avon between Bristol and
Avonmouth and thence out onto the Severn when
making passage north to Sharpness on the Gloucester
& Sharpness Canal (or of course, in reverse). This provides a
means, for the intrepid navigator, to access the non-tidal river
beyond Gloucester, avoiding a lengthy easterly detour. It is not
something that will be undertaken lightly as the Navigational Notes make
only too clear. For every boater who passes under the elevated section of the
M5 at Avonmouth there will, no doubt, be hundreds of thousands of walkers and
cyclists anxious to enjoy the beauties of the Avon Gorge from a slightly less exciting
(though equally dramatic) vantage point. From Pill, on the south bank of the river, there
is a combined cycleway and pedestrian path running the 5 miles to Bristol's Floating Harbour,
so-called to differentiate it from its predecessor, a series of mud berths along the old course of The
Avon through the city. On the north bank, the busy A4 heads for the city accompanied for some of
the way by the Severn Beach railway line which terminates close to the Second Severn Crossing.
Running through Pill and close companion to the cycleway is another, newly re-opened, freight
line connecting Bristol to the docks at Portishead. Beyond Pill the river bends north, around a steep
promontory as the gorge begins to close in from both sides. Initially the sides are rocky and free
from trees and walkers and cyclists alike have uninterrupted views across the river to Shirehampton
Park on the north bank. Then the river curls round to head in an almost southerly direction past a
disused quarry and the old Roman settlement of Abona. Soon the bare rock becomes cloaked by the
dense foliage of Leigh Woods. Further quarries are followed by The Avon Gorge Nature Reserve and
then path and river head for the graceful Clifton Suspension Bridge.

WALKING & CYCLING

Bristol is the home of Sustrans whose vision spawned the National Cycle Network, and it would be very
surprising indeed if the cyclist was not well catered for in this area. The Pill Riverside Path runs from the
Harbour, along Cumberland Road to follow the river through to Pill. There is also a linking route into Leigh
Woods and to Ashton. Further west the cycleway crosses the river by way of the M5 bridge and connects (at
both ends) with the Avon Cycleway; an 85-mile signposted route along a mixture of traffic-free paths and
quiet lanes around Bristol. The routes mentioned are, of course, available to both walker and cyclist alike. On
the north bank of the river, in Shirehampton Park, there are excellent walks, offering spectacular open views
to the south, along the river and beyond. A free *Bristol Cycling Map* is available from Sustrans (0845 1130065;
www.sustrans.org.uk). Visit the Better by Bike website (www.betterbybike.info/), for comprehensive cycling
information about Bristol, Bath, North Somerset and South Gloucestershire: you can download free cycle
maps or order paper copies.

● **Easton-in-Gordano**
Somerset. Tel, garage. Largely a dormitory village for Bristol running into, and indistinguishable from, its neighbour, Pill. The western end, around the Kings Arms, is the more interesting part.

● **Pill**
Somerset. PO, tel, stores, chemist, takeaway, garage. A continuation of Easton-in-Gordano, only with some shops. Beyond the Railway Inn there are views across the River Avon.

● **Avonmouth Dock**
In the 19th C, with the construction of increasingly larger ships such as the *SS Great Britain* in 1843, it was recognised that there was a need for an expansion of the deep-water docking facilities in the Port of Bristol. The more far-sighted realised that in order to compete with other large British ports (with their own seaboard) a new facility had to be built at the mouth of the Avon and not as an extension

to the City Docks. Whilst this radical concept amounted to heresy in the eyes of many prosperous Bristol merchants, the construction of Avonmouth Dock was commenced in 1868 and completed in 1877.

● **Portishead Dock**
This was opened in 1879, covering an area of 76 acres, largely to make up for the deficiencies in size and lock capacity of Avonmouth Dock on the other side of the river mouth. Again absorbed by Bristol Docks Committee in 1884 to make one unified port, it too soon proved itself woefully inadequate in the face of rapidly increasing shipping tonnage.

● **Royal Edward Dock**
Opened by Edward VII in 1908 and interconnected with Avonmouth Dock, the Royal Edward Dock had an entrance lock measuring 875' x 100' thereby allowing the revitalised dock complex the chance to again become competitive.

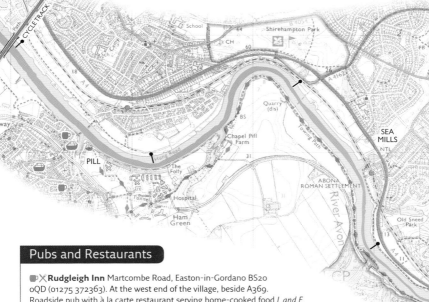

Pubs and Restaurants

● ✕ **Rudgleigh Inn** Martcombe Road, Easton-in-Gordano BS20 0QD (01275 372363). At the west end of the village, beside A369. Roadside pub with à la carte restaurant serving home-cooked food *L and E* and bar meals *all day, every day.* Real ale and *Sunday* roasts. Children and dogs welcome. Garden.

● **Kings Arms** 12 St Georges Hill, Easton-in-Gordano BS20 0PS (01275 372208; www.kingsarms.co.uk). At the west end of the village. Cheerful, village local serving real ales, traditional cider and traditional home-cooked pub food *L and E (not Sun E).* Children welcome. Beer garden and skittle alley. *Open all day.*

● **Anchor Inn** Ham Green, Pill BS20 0HB (01275 372253). Real ale and meals served *all day, every day.* Children and dogs welcome.

● **Star Inn** 13 Bank Place, Pill BS20 0AQ (01275 374926). Village local serving real ale and pub meals.

● ✕ **George Inn** Manor Road, Abbots Leigh, Bristol BS8 3RP (01275 372467; www.thegeorgeinn.uk.com). On A369 south of Leigh Wood. A friendly, welcoming pub serving home-made food *L and E* in both bar and à la carte restaurant. Also an excellent range of real ales available. Children welcome, as are dogs, in the large garden.

Bristol

River and cycleway now pass under the spectacular shadow of the Clifton Suspension Bridge, poised some 230ft above. This 700ft-long crossing into the elevated Clifton district of Bristol is breathtaking in both its concept and execution. Designed by Brunel, when he was only 23, it was not in fact completed until 1864, nearly five years after his death. Half a mile eastwards the navigation reaches the Entrance Lock and divides. The northerly channel leads into the Floating Harbour through the Entrance Lock, Cumberland Basin and Junction Lock while the river skirts round to the south, along an artificial cut constructed in 1804 when the harbour was built.

Boatyards

Ⓑ **Bristol Marina**
Hanover Place, Bristol BS1 6TZ
(0117 921 3198; www.bristolmarina.co.uk).
🛥🚿⚓D Pump out, overnight mooring, long-term mooring, slipway, gas, boat repairs, wet dock, DIY facilities, telephone, toilets, showers, laundrette, chandlery. Free Wi-Fi.
Ⓑ **Force 4 Chandlery** Albion Dockyard, Hanover Place, Bristol BS1 6UT (0117 926 8396; www.force4.co.uk). Chandlery, books and charts. *Open Mon–Sat 08.30–17.30.*
Ⓑ **Underfall Boatyard** Cumberland Road, Bristol BS1 6XG (0117 929 3250; www.underfallboatyard.co.uk). Winter storage, slipway, boat building, facilities for large vessels to 180 tonnes, all boatyard trades available on site.

BOAT TRIPS

Bristol Ferry Boat Co No 1 Harbourside, Bristol BS1 5UH (0117 927 3416; www.bristolferry.com). The company operates their distinctive yellow and blue round-trip waterbus services on the historic harbour *every day Apr – Sep & at weekends Oct–Mar*. A selection of boats, each with an individual character, plying the harbour. Also available for private charter and public trips *throughout the year.*
Bristol Packet Boat Wapping Wharf, Gas Ferry Road, Bristol BS1 6UN 0117 926 8157; www.bristolpacket.co.uk). Award-winning cruises around the Floating Harbour and up and down the River Avon. Also available for private parties. Telephone or visit the website for timetables.
Number Seven Boat Trips nb *Excalibur*, Welshback, Bristol BS1 4SB (0117 929 3659/07976 554024; www.numbersevenboattrips.com). Operators of the distinctive 'animal' boats running Floating Harbour ferry services and excursions from all points between Avonmouth and Bath running all the year round. Telephone or visit the website for timetables.
Waverley Excursions (0845 130 4647; www.waverleyexcursions.co.uk). *Waverley* and *Balmoral* operate an exciting and varied selection of trips departing from a host of locations up and down the Bristol Channel. Telephone or visit the website for a timetable.

There is a pleasing combination of old and new quays – some dating back to the 13th C – and a contrasting selection of bridges all adding variety to what is now an entirely leisure- orientated dock complex. In the main harbour, before Redcliffe Bascule Bridge is reached, the navigation passes the 'Mud Dock', which dates from 1625 and provided a soft mud berth for shipping when the quays were still subject to the tidal fluctuations of the two rivers. It is now the site of a café and cycle hire centre. Turning through a right-angled bend, the waterway now makes a beeline for Netham Lock (0117 977 6590) in concert with a busy main road along its south bank. On the apex of the bend is the site of Totterdown Basin and Old Totterdown Lock, which once provided an access into the tidal Avon. This has now become a wildlife area. Also at this point, the Avon Walkway crosses over Marsh Lane Bridge and for most of the way to Nether Lock follows the river. Meanwhile the feeder canal leads the navigation past a series of factories, some with attractively landscaped grounds, to be finally reunited with the river which curls away through the cities' suburbs.

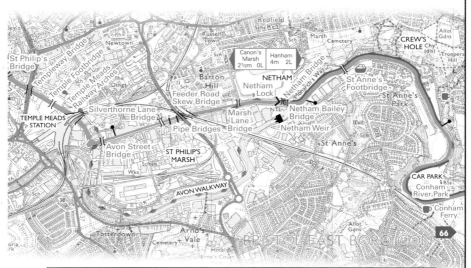

NAVIGATIONAL NOTES

1. Mooring – aim to moor either at recognised points in the Floating Harbour or on the feeder canal as set out in the *Bristol Harbour Information for Boat Owners* guide as there is no suitable overnight mooring between Netham and Hanham Locks. Also consult the guide for all facilities and their availability within the harbour complex.
2. Below Hanham Lock the river comes under the jurisdiction of Bristol City Council to whom a licence fee is payable. Visitors may purchase a licence – the cost of which is based on length of stay and length of craft – from the lock keeper at Netham Lock or from the Harbour Office (0117 903 1484; www.bristol.gov.uk/page/arrival-and-departure-bristol-harbour) Underfall Yard, Cumberland Road, Bristol – located at the western end of the Floating Harbour.
3. Visitor moorings are available in the Floating Harbour and are allocated by the Harbour Master (0117 903 1484; harbour-reception@bristol-city.gov.uk).
4. To contact bridge operators for a bridge swing within the Floating Harbour telephone 0117 929 9338 or the Harbour Master as above.
5. When navigating under Redcliffe Bridge do not use east and west arches. For Bristol Bridge use centre of arches and do not use east arch.

Bristol

Bristol. Daily markets. All services. Bristol grew up on the confluence of the Rivers Avon and Frome and was one of two cities prominent at the end of the Saxon period; the other being Norwich. It was probably established in the late 10th C beside a bridge over the Avon from which it derived the name Bridge-Stow: the place of the bridge. It developed on an easily defended site between the Avon and its tributary, the River Frome and initially built up trading links with South Wales and Ireland. By the 14th C Bristol had outgrown the small Saxon burgh of its origins and additional walls were built to enclose the newly populated areas to the south of the Avon. However, still left outside the walls were the church of St Mary Redcliffe, the Monastery of St Augustine, as well as three major friaries. The monastery and cathedral were by now one and the same. As a port Bristol was dominant along the coasts of the Severn Estuary and its local trade extended from Ireland to the Midlands where goods were transhipped into barges at Bewdley. That Bristol prospered as a port throughout the medieval period is somewhat surprising, given its location up the severely tidal River Avon and its unsatisfactory mud berthing arrangements. Yet it went on to dominate a burgeoning world trade as is witnessed by its rich legacy of Renaissance buildings – from brick classical merchants' town houses to country houses and suburban villas – and to embark on the Industrial Revolution second only to Liverpool as Britain's major transatlantic port. As a pivotal part of the slave trade, Bristol imported tobacco, timber, rum, cotton and sugar and together with its human cargoes, exported finished cotton goods, glass, brassware and soap. Its decline as a port, in the face of increasingly successful competition from Liverpool, lay as much in the Lancashire port's advantageous relationship to the expanding canal network, as to Bristol's position up a difficult tidal river in the face of the increasing size of 19th-C shipping. Today Bristol has an immense water-bound leisure facility in place of its once proud docks; home to a wealth of activity, maritime and otherwise. As a contemporary city, its prosperity is founded upon a range of financial institutions from insurance to banking; on the aerospace industry and on high technology electronic research and production.

Bristol Cathedral College Green, Bristol BS1 5TJ (0117 926 4879; www.bristol-cathedral.co.uk). Major example of a 'hall' church, one of the finest in the world; the nave, choir and aisles are all of the same height. Founded in the middle of the 12th C as the Abbey of St Augustine, the Chapter House and Abbey Gatehouse clearly remain to be seen. In 1539 the Abbey was closed and the unfinished nave demolished. However in 1868 the architect G. E. Street drew up plans to complete the nave founded on the original pillar bases. Book shop and coffee shop.

Bristol Zoo Gardens Guthrie Road, Clifton, Bristol BS8 3HA (0117 974 7399; www.bristolzoo.org.uk). They breed endangered species, aim to raise awareness of the threat to a wide range of habitats, and support conservation projects worldwide. Restaurant, café and covered picnic area. *Open daily 09.00-17.30 summer and 09.00-17.00 winter. Closed Xmas.* Charge. Buses 8 and 9 from city centre.

City Museum & Art Gallery Queen's Road, Bristol BS8 1RL (0117 922 3571; www.bristol.gov.uk/page/museums-and-galleries). Temporary exhibitions, fascinating objects and artworks from all over the world. Family activities include 'fundays' on *first Sun of month* and workshops linked to displays. *Open daily 10.00-17.00.* Shop and licensed café serving a variety of meals and snacks.

Clifton Suspension Bridge Visitor Centre Leigh Woods, Bristol BS8 3PA (0117 974 4664; www.cliftonbridge.org.uk). This potent symbol of the City of Bristol, from a design by I. K. Brunel, led a chequered career from its inception in 1754 to final completion in 1864. The centre explains all the ups and downs of the structure with the aid of models and interactive exhibitions. Photographic archive. *Open daily 10.00-17.00* Free guided tours *Easter-Oct, Sat-Sun 15.00* from the toll booth at the Clifton end of the bridge. Shop. Charge.

Floating Harbour (www.bristolfloatingharbour.org.uk). Towards the end of the 18th C Bristol's importance as a port started to slip, largely on account of the large rise and fall in the tides and the difficulties encountered by ships berthing on the river mud, placing considerable stress on a vessel's hull. In 1802 William Jessop was invited to submit plans for a 'floating harbour'. Work began in 1804 and was completed some five years later. For a while the port thrived but, to a greater or lesser extent, was always handicapped by its position up the river. The last steamships used the docks in the 1950s. Today the harbour is primarily a focus for recreational activity with a walking trail around the harbour area and a wealth of interpretation boards describing the harbour and its history.

Georgian House 7 Great George Street, Bristol BS1 5RR (0117 921 1362; www.bristol.gov.uk/page/museums-and-galleries). An 18th-C West India merchant's house furnished in the style of the period and owned by John Piny, a sugar trader who owned both land and slaves in the Caribbean. 'Living history days' when actors bring the house to life. *Open Apr-Oct Wed-Sun (not Fri) and B Hols 10.30-16.00; Jul-Aug also open Tue.*

M Shed Princes Wharf, Wapping Road, Bristol BS1 4RN (0117 352 6600; www.mshed.org). Exciting and innovative new museum telling the story of Bristol. Three galleries, train, boat and crane rides and lots of exhibitions and events. *Open Tue-Fri 10.00-17.00; weekends & B Hols 10.00-18.00.* Café and shop. Free.

St George's Bristol Great George Street, off Park Street, Bristol BS1 5RR (0845 4024001; www.stgeorgesbristol.co.uk). Music to suit all tastes in marvellously acoustic surroundings. Bar and gallery in beautifully restored crypt area.

St Mary Redcliffe Redcliffe Parade West, Bristol BS1 6SP (0117 929 1487; www.stmaryredcliffe.co.uk). Described by Elizabeth I as 'The fairest, goodliest and most famous Parish Church in England'. Coffee and light lunches served *Mon-Fri 10.00-16.00*. *Shop. Open daily*. Download the fascinating free guide.

SS Great Britain Great Western Dockyard, Gas Ferry Road, Bristol BS1 6TY (0117 926 0680; www.ssgreatbritain.org). Sea travel took a great leap forward when the famous Victorian engineer Isambard Kingdom Brunel applied his skills to the construction of an iron, steam-driven passenger ship capable of maintaining a schedule on voyages to America and the antipodes. *Open daily 10.00-17.30 Apr-Oct and 10.00-16.30 Nov-Mar.* Gift and coffee shops. Charge.

Watershed 1 Canon's Road, Harbourside, Bristol BS1 5TX (0117 927 5100; www.watershed.co.uk). Bristol's arts centre with a wide mix of entertainment that is well up to expectation. Café/bar.

Tourist Information Centre E Shed, 1 Canons Road, Bristol BS1 5TX (0906 711 2191; www.visitbristol.co.uk).

WALKING & CYCLING

The Avon Walkway-cum-Cycleway can be seen as the spinal route following the River from Pill to Bath and thence to Limpley Stoke and beyond. As such it forms the basis for a series of superb expeditions which can be linked into the extensive collection of routes radiating out from the Bristol City centre, accessed from the Floating Harbour, just north of St Augustine's Reach. This also provides a direct link to the Bristol & Bath Railway Path which in turn interconnects with the Avon Cycleway – *see* previous notes for further details. Any permutation can provide circular routes with widely contrasting scenery. Many combinations are both flat and traffic-free. LifeCycleUk, a charity that promotes cycling throughout the former Avon area, can be contacted for a range of free maps and detailed route advice (0117 353 4580; www.lifecycleuk.org.uk). Bicycles are available for hire from The Bristol Bike Project Hamilton House, 80 Stokes Croft, Bristol BS1 3QY (07983 417231; www.thebristolbikeproject.org.uk); Blackboy Cycles, 180 Whiteladies Road, Clifton, Bristol BS8 2XU (0117 973 1420 www.blackboycycles.co.uk). *See* page 60 for more information.

Pubs and Restaurants

There are a wide range of pubs, bars, cafes, clubs and eating houses thronging the Floating Harbour. These represent a small selection of them.

Merchants Arms Merchants Road, Hotwells, Bristol BS8 4PZ (0117 904 0037). Friendly traditional local with wood panelling. Real ale, bar snacks and pub meals. Children welcome. Quiz *every Thu*.

Pump House Merchants Road, Hotwells, Bristol BS8 4PZ (0117 927 2229; www.the-pumphouse.com). Old pumping station supplying water to the docks, turned chapel, turned slaughterhouse. Pub offering real ale, local cider, à la carte and traditional pub meals. Seasonal menus and *Sun* lunch. Telephone or visit website to confirm restaurant opening times. Children welcome. Dockside patio seating.

Arnolfini Café Bar 16 Narrow Quay, St Augustine's Reach, Bristol BS1 4QA (0117 917 2305; www.arnolfini.org.uk). Situated within the well-known art gallery. Superb quality and value food served *all day* in comfortably relaxed surroundings. Everyone welcome. Real ale. Quayside location. *Open daily 10.00-22.00.* Food served *until 20.00*.

Severnshed The Grove, Harbourside, Bristol BS1 4RB (0117 925 1212; www.shed-restaurants. co.uk). A versatile establishment with a wealth of food, drinks and entertainment all corralled within a 'hoverbar'. Tasty restaurant meals and cocktails. Live jazz *Sun*.

Under the Stars Narrow Quay, Harbourside, Bristol (0117 929 8392; www.underthestarsbar.co.uk). Coffee and cake, tapas and drinks in this friendly, though somewhat quirky, setting afloat. Tapas Menu available *Apr-Sep 12.00-15.00 & 18.00-21.00 (12.00-18.00 Sun); Oct-Mar 18.00-21.00 Tue-Fri; 12.00-15.00 & 18.00-21.00; Sat & 12.00-18.00 Sun.*

Riverstation The Grove Harbourside, Bristol BS1 4RB (0117 914 4434; www.riverstation.co.uk). This is an old river police building, right in the heart of Bristol's dockside, with excellent views out over the Floating Harbour serving a wide range of bar snacks *(09.00-22.00)* and an a la Carte menu *L and E* from a largely modern, European menu. Excellent service combined with a warm welcome. Breakfast, teas, coffees and pastries. Al fresco, terrace dining on two levels.

Glassboat Restaurant Welsh Back, Bristol BS1 4SB (0117 929 0704; www.glassboat.co.uk). Beside Bristol Bridge. Imaginative and varied menu, served in unusual surroundings with uninterupted views over the floating harbour. *Open L and E.*

Beeses Riverside Bar & Tea Gardens Wyndham Crescent, Bristol BS4 4SX (0117 977 7412; www.beeses.co.uk). Waterside café set in the wooded Avon Valley serving buffet food, teas and barbecues. Bar with real ales. Mooring, large garden, children and dogs welcome. Ferry service from towpath. *Open Easter-Sep, varying times.*

65

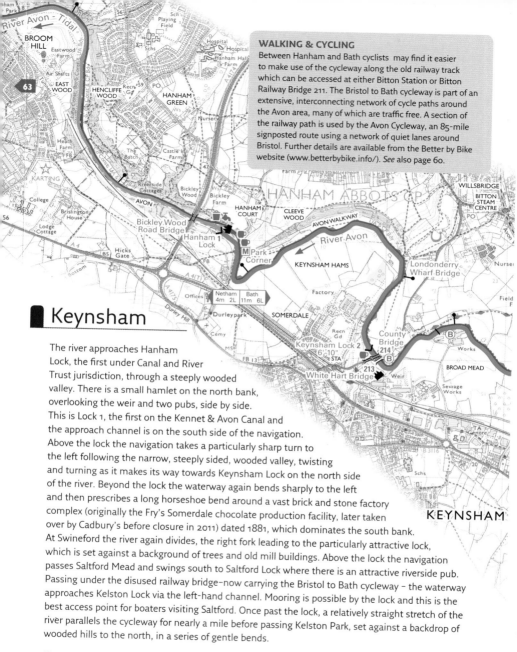

WALKING & CYCLING

Between Hanham and Bath cyclists may find it easier to make use of the cycleway along the old railway track which can be accessed at either Bitton Station or Bitton Railway Bridge 211. The Bristol to Bath cycleway is part of an extensive, interconnecting network of cycle paths around the Avon area, many of which are traffic free. A section of the railway path is used by the Avon Cycleway, an 85-mile signposted route using a network of quiet lanes around Bristol. Further details are available from the Better by Bike website (www.betterbybike.info/). See also page 60.

Keynsham

The river approaches Hanham Lock, the first under Canal and River Trust jurisdiction, through a steeply wooded valley. There is a small hamlet on the north bank, overlooking the weir and two pubs, side by side. This is Lock 1, the first on the Kennet & Avon Canal and the approach channel is on the south side of the navigation. Above the lock the navigation takes a particularly sharp turn to the left following the narrow, steeply sided, wooded valley, twisting and turning as it makes its way towards Keynsham Lock on the north side of the river. Beyond the lock the waterway again bends sharply to the left and then prescribes a long horseshoe bend around a vast brick and stone factory complex (originally the Fry's Somerdale chocolate production facility, later taken over by Cadbury's before closure in 2011) dated 1881, which dominates the south bank. At Swineford the river again divides, the right fork leading to the particularly attractive lock, which is set against a background of trees and old mill buildings. Above the lock the navigation passes Saltford Mead and swings south to Saltford Lock where there is an attractive riverside pub. Passing under the disused railway bridge–now carrying the Bristol to Bath cycleway – the waterway approaches Kelston Lock via the left-hand channel. Mooring is possible by the lock and this is the best access point for boaters visiting Saltford. Once past the lock, a relatively straight stretch of the river parallels the cycleway for nearly a mile before passing Kelston Park, set against a backdrop of wooded hills to the north, in a series of gentle bends.

KEYNSHAM

● Keynsham
Somerset. All services. Keynsham has grown steadily along the Bristol road, and so is now a vast shapeless suburb. However, the centre still retains a feeling of independence, and has many traces of Keynsham's past.

● Bitton
Somerset. Tel, stores (open late inc. Sun) garage Although a main road village, Bitton's heart survives intact south of the road. Here is a fine group formed by the church, the grange and the 18th-C vicarage, all built around the churchyard. The church has a long Saxon nave with Norman details, a 14th-C chancel, and a magnificently decorative late 14th-C tower.

Avon Valley Railway Bitton Station, Bath Road, Bitton, Bristol BS30 6HD (0117 932 5538; www.avonvalleyrailway.org). Short length of preserved steam railway offering steam trips *Apr–Oct, Sun; Jun–Jul also Wed, plus many days during school holidays and special events at other times of the year.* The railway is operated by an enthusiastic bunch of dedicated volunteers and plans are in hand to progressively extend the line to the outskirts of Bath. See the excellent website for more information. Cream teas, snacks and light refreshments.

- **Swineford**
Somerset. Tel. Although bisected by the A431, the settlement by the river is still attractive. The old mill buildings constructed in 1840 overlook the long weir.

- **Saltford**
Somerset. PO, tel, stores, takeaway, chemist, garage. Although Saltford has been developed as a large-scale dormitory suburb, the older parts by the river are still pretty and secluded.

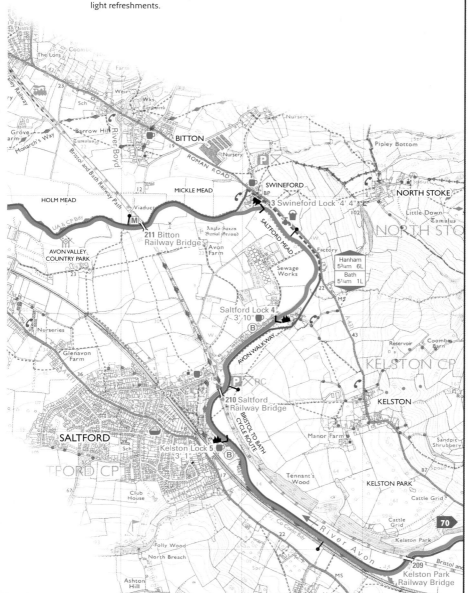

NAVIGATIONAL NOTES

1 The River Avon is usually only tidal to Hanham, however high spring tides can reach as far as Keynsham Lock.
2 Upstream craft should give way to downstream craft on fast-flowing sections of the river.
3 Downstream craft should approach the bend at Keynsham with caution and sound their horn to warn craft leaving Portavon Marina of their approach. Approach the lock cut entrance with care as it can be obscured by trees.
4 Visitor moorings are very limited on the river below Bath so boaters should plan their itinerary accordingly.
5 Bath Locks are padlocked when the river is in spate so at times of high water levels boaters should not embark on a journey upstream without first ensuring that they can leave the navigation for the safe haven of the canal.
6 *See also* Navigational Note **1** on page 59.

Pubs and Restaurants

The Chequers Hanham Mill, Hanham BS15 3NU (0117 967 6906; www.chequerspub.net). Comfortable, well appointed, riverside pub serving real ales. Food available *all day* in bar and in restaurant *L and E*. Children and dogs welcome. Riverside garden and patio. Moorings for patrons. Pool, darts and *regular* live music.

Old Lock and Weir Ferry Road, Hanham BS15 3NU (0117 967 3793; www.lockandweir.com). Riverside pub serving real ales and food *L and E (not Sun E)*. Booking advisable *Fri, Sat and Sun E*. Barbecues *in summer*. Overnight moorings available for boaters eating at the pub. Dogs on leads welcome. Special events including beer festival.

Lock Keeper Keynsham Lock, Keynsham BS31 2DD (0117 986 2383). Unpredictable flood waters forced many a crew to stay the night at the Lock Keeper. Real ales and food available *all day*. Children and dogs welcome. Garden. Occasional live music. Petanque pitch.

White Hart 140 High Street, Bitton, Bristol BS30 6HG (0117 329 0494). Village local serving real ales and food *Tue–Sat L and E; Sun 10.00–16.00*. Beer garden.

Swan Bath Road, Swineford BS30 6LN (0117 932 3101; www.bathales.com). Near Swineford Lock. 200-year-old stone-built cottage pub. Real ales on offer, drawn from the 'wood'. Home-cooked food *available daily 12.00–21.00 (Sun 20.00)*. Children welcome if dining *before 21.00*. Garden. *Open all day*.

Jolly Sailor Mead Lane, Saltford BS31 3ER (01225 873002; www.jollysailorpub.com). By Saltford Lock. A popular pub dating back to 1727. Real ale and guest ales. Food in bar and gazebo restaurant *L and E*. Children and dogs welcome.

Bird in Hand High Street, Saltford BS31 3EJ (01225 873335; www.birdinhandsaltford.co.uk). A beautifully kept village local offering locally brewed real ales and superb country views. Good food *L and E*. Large conservatory, garden and terrace. Children welcome. Family room. *Open all day Sat & Sun*.

Riverside Inn The Shallows, Saltford BS31 3EZ (01225 873862; www.theriversideinnsaltford.co.uk). Next to Kelston Lock. Smart bar, café and restaurant overlooking the river. Real ales. A wide range of food is *available all day*. Respectably dressed, over 21s only in the café *after 19.00*. Children welcome. Outside seating. B&B.

Boatyards

Ⓑ**Port Avon Marina** Keynsham Road, Keynsham BS31 2DD (01225 424301; www.bwml.co.uk). 🛒🏠♿ Overnight mooring, long-term mooring, winter storage, slipway, boat sales and repairs, engine sales and repairs (including outboards), toilets, showers.

Ⓑ**Bristol Boats Ltd** Sheppards Boatyard, Mead Lane, Saltford BS31 3ER (01225 872032; www.bristolboatsltd.co.uk). Near Saltford Lock. ♿Gas, long-term mooring, slipway, gantry, boat sales and repairs, outboard engine sales and repairs, chandlery, toilets, boat building. *Closed Tue and Sun*.

Ⓑ**Saltford Marina** The Shallows, Saltford BS31 3EZ (01225 872226; www.saltfordmarina.co.uk) Family run marina beside Kelston Lock. Overnight and long-term mooring. Restaurant and bar.

Ⓑ**R.L.L. Boats** Unit 1 Broadmead Industrial Estate, Broadmead Lane, Bristol BS31 1ST (0117 986 9860; www.rllboats.co.uk). Boat building–narrow and wide-beam, repairs and modifications, hardstanding, painting, crane.

Bath

The river, on passing Kelston Park, prepares to leave its wide, wandering course and the pastures flanking both banks in favour of the urban sprawl of Bath. It soon passes under the elegant single stone arch of New Bridge carrying the A4 and again ducks through another disused railway bridge, now the Bristol to Bath cycleway. The main line from London to South Wales closely follows the south bank, vanishing at one point into a tunnel. Soon the River Avon approaches the industrial suburbs of Bath and enters a wooded section. Ahead is Weston Lock and the lock cut is the northern channel. Beyond the lock the navigation meanders into the city in long, gentle curves flanked by roads, the railway and areas of light industry. There are several footbridges across the river and the cycleway makes two further crossings. There are good moorings east of Churchill Road bridges, convenient for a supermarket. The canal joins the Avon immediately below Bath Bottom Lock No 7 in the middle of the industrial quarter of the city. The railway station is opposite the junction of canal and river and the fine Georgian city surrounds the unnavigable river to the north and east. The junction (and moorings to the north) are the best points of access for Bath as a whole. The Widcombe flight of six locks lifts the waterway swiftly above the city allowing magnificent views in all directions. There was once a seventh lock in the flight but locks 8 and 9 were merged as part of a road building scheme, making one new lock with a fall of over 19ft. This now vies with Tuel Deep Lock, on the Rochdale Canal, for deepest lock on the navigable waterways system. Above the flight the navigation enters a cutting and passes through an ornamental tunnel that carries housing and Cleveland House, the old canal company's headquarters. Beyond the tunnel another cutting carries the waterway past two pretty cast iron bridges, both dated 1800 and houses seem almost to hang out over the water. There is another tunnel with fine Adamesque portals as the canal leaves the confines of Sydney Gardens and passes the last of the Georgian buildings lining its banks. On the south bank there are gardens running down to the water which accompany the navigation into Bath. There are useful *parades of shops* both to the south of the Widcombe Flight (including a *laundrette*) and to the west of Bridge 188. The navigation makes a magnificent exit from the city, cut into the hill, sweeping round to the south to join the river as they begin to follow the same route towards Bathampton. There are extensive views across Bath and from this point it is possible to pick out many of the features of the city; the Georgian terraces can be seen spread out over the far side of the valley. The railway is now accompanied by the new stretch of the A4 whose traffic drones continuously. The canal continues on a straight course, closely flanked by the railway, which is in a cutting below and then passes through Bathampton, on a low embankment above the school and church. Following the course of the River Avon the waterway swings sharply to the south, towards Bathford church on the opposite side of the valley, leaving behind the groups of houses that heralded the suburbs of Bath.

WALKING & CYCLING

The towpath between Bath and Devizes is in good condition. The remainder of the towpath varies in surface; generally good through urban areas, rural sections are dependent on weather conditions. Eastern sections bordering the river navigation can become very overgrown in the height of the summer. It is a very popular long distance route for walkers and cyclists alike and the latter are asked to exercise care and to give way to people on foot. The Bristol & Bath Railway Path and the riverside walk give direct, safe access into the centre of Bath. East of Bath the National Cycle Network Route 4 follows the towpath to Devizes. An audio trail has been installed on the Widcombe Lock Flight in Bath providing an interesting, historical insight into the area

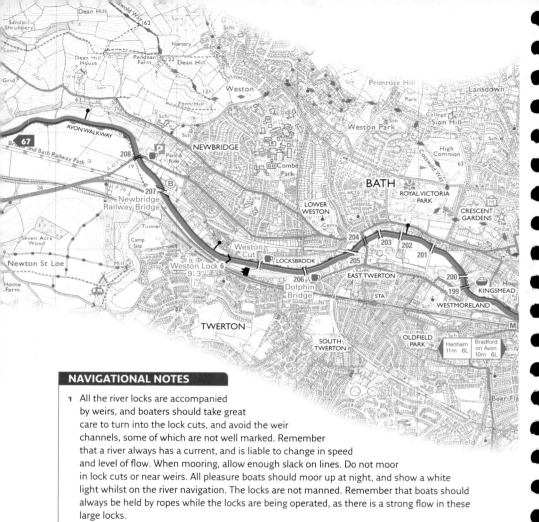

NAVIGATIONAL NOTES

1 All the river locks are accompanied
   by weirs, and boaters should take great
   care to turn into the lock cuts, and avoid the weir
   channels, some of which are not well marked. Remember
   that a river always has a current, and is liable to change in speed
   and level of flow. When mooring, allow enough slack on lines. Do not moor
   in lock cuts or near weirs. All pleasure boats should moor up at night, and show a white
   light whilst on the river navigation. The locks are not manned. Remember that boats should
   always be held by ropes while the locks are being operated, as there is a strong flow in these
   large locks.

2 Do not moor in the Widcombe Lock flight as the levels of intermediate pounds are subject to
   considerable fluctuations.

3 *See also* Navigational Notes on page 68.

BOAT TRIPS

Bath Boating Station Forester Road, Bathwick, Bath BA2 6QE (01225 312900; www.bathboating.co.uk). A
unique surviving Victorian boating station with a licensed restaurant. Traditional skiffs, punts and canoes,
for hire by the hour or the day. Free instruction for those new to punting. *Open Apr–Sep, daily 10.00–18.00*
for boating. Restaurant (01225 428844; www.bathwickboatman.com) *open Tue–Sun L and E (not Sun E).* Self-
catering accommodation also available.

Bath Narrowboats Sydney Wharf, Bathwick, Bath BA2 4EL (01225 447276; www.bath-narrowboats.co.uk).
John Rennie 64-seater restaurant boat available for private charter. On-board catering with a wide selection
of menus. Dayboat hire, Anglo-Welsh holiday boats, all usual wharf services. *Open all year 09.00-1700 (except
Xmas and New Year). See also* Boatyards page 72.

The Penny Lane North Parade Bridge, Bath BA2 4EU (01225 303434; prideofbath.com). Large, cruise boat
available for charter. Telephone or visit website for further details.

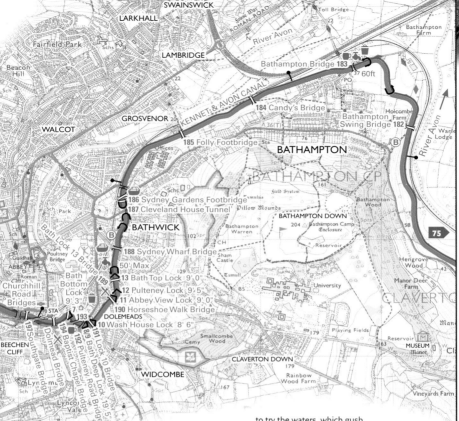

Bath

Somerset. All services. Bath was first developed by the Romans as a spa town and resort because of its natural warm springs. They started the trend of bathing and taking the waters which survives today. There are extensive Roman remains to be seen in the city, not least the baths themselves. The city grew further during the medieval period, when it was a centre of the wool trade; the fine abbey dates from this time. But the true splendour of Bath is the 18th-C development, when the city grew as a resort and watering place that was frequented by all levels of English society, from royalty downwards. Despite heavy bombing in World War II, Bath is still a magnificent memorial to the 18th C and Neo-classicism generally. The terraces that adorn the steep northern slope of the Avon valley contain some of the best Georgian architecture in Britain. Much of the city was designed by John Wood the Younger, who was responsible for the great sweeping Royal Crescent. Other architects included Thomas Baldwin, who built the Guildhall, 1766–75, and the Pump Room, 1789–99, and Robert Adam, whose Pulteney Bridge carries terraces of shops across the Avon. Bath is best seen on foot, for its glories and riches are far too numerous to list. Visitors should not fail to try the waters, which gush continuously from a fountain outside the Pump Room.

Bath Abbey 12 Kingston Buildings, Bath BA1 1LT (01225 422462; www.bathabbey. org) Set in an attractive piazza, the abbey is a pleasingly uniform Perpendicular building, founded in 1499. Twin towers crown the west front, decorated with carved angels ascending and descending ladders. Inside, the abbey is justly famous for its fan vaulting, which covers the whole roof of the building but is not all of the same date. Inside also is a wealth of memorials of all periods, an interesting indication of the vast range of people who, over the ages, have come to die in Bath. In addition to services, the abbey is *open Mon–Sat 09.00 (09.30 Mon)–18.00, Sun 13.00–14.30 and 16.30–17.30.* Tours and shop.

Holburne Museum Great Pulteney Street, Bath BA2 4DB. (01225 388588; www.holburne.org). Housed in a recently restored 18th-C Palladian building that was designed as part of the Sydney pleasure gardens, and a spectacular modern extension. The remarkably varied collection includes silver, ceramics, 18th-C paintings and furniture, 20th-C art and craft work. Lots for families and children of all ages. *Open Mon–Sat 10.00–17.00, Sun and B hols 11.00–17.00.* Garden café. Free (charge for temporary exhibitions).

Jane Austen Centre 40 Gay Street, Bath BA1 2NT (01225 443000; www.janeausten.co.uk). Enjoy the pleasure of Bath as Jane Austen knew it. A Georgian town house in the heart of the city where the visitor can find out more about the importance of Bath in her life and work. *Open daily, Apr–Oct 09.45–17.30 (Jul–Aug, Thur–Sat closes 19.00); Nov–Mar, Sun–Fri 11.00–16.30, Sat 09.45–17.30. Charge.* Tearooms (free access).

Fashion Museum Assembly Rooms, Bennett Street, Bath BA1 2QH (01225 477789; www.museumofcostume.co.uk). Display of fashion from the 17th C to the present day; one of the largest collections of costume in the world. *Open all year from 10.30; Nov–Feb closes 16.00; Mar–Oct closes 17.00.*

Postal Museum 27 Northgate Street, Bath BA1 1AJ (01225 460333; www.bathpostalmuseum.co.uk). The place from which the first postage stamp was sent on 2 May 1840. The history of the postal service and the development of the written word. *Open Mon–Sat 11.00–16.30, Mon & Sun by request for large groups.* Charge.

Roman Baths Museum Stall Street, Bath BA1 1LZ (01225 477785; www.romanbaths.co.uk). The great bath buildings with their dependent temple were the centre of Roman Bath. Much of these survive, incorporated into the 18th-C Pump Room. The museum, attached to the bath buildings, contains finds excavated from the site. *Open daily all year, Jan–Feb and Nov–Dec 09.30–16.30; Mar–Jun and Sep–Oct 09.00–17.00; Jul–Aug 09.00–21.00. Charge.*

1 Royal Crescent Bath BA1 2LR (01225 428126; www. bath-preservation-trust.org.uk). The first house of this magnificent crescent built by John Wood the Younger between 1767–74. Complete with original furniture and fittings. *Open Tue–Sun (inc B Hols) 10.30–16.30. Charge.*

Thermae Bath Spa Hetling Pump Room, Hot Bath Street, Bath BA1 1SJ (0844 888 0844; www.thermaebathspa.com). Five historic buildings plus a contemporary addition by Nicholas Grimshaw & Partners allow all-year bathing in natural thermal waters. Full range of spa treatments and complementary therapies, plus views from a roof-top pool! *Open daily 09.00–22.00 (last entry 20.00). Closed Xmas Day, New Year's Eve and New Year's Day. Charge.* Shop, visitor centre, restaurant.

Victoria Art Gallery Corner of Pulteney Bridge and Grand Parade, Bridge Street, Bath BA2 4AT (01225 477233; www.victoriagal.org.uk). Collection of 18th-C and modern paintings, prints and ceramics. Visiting exhibitions. Gallery shop and refreshments. *Open Tue–Sat 10.00–17.30, Sun 13.30–17.00. Closed B Hols.*

Tourist Information Centre Abbey Chambers, Abbey Churchyard, Bath BA1 1LY (0906 711 2000; www.visitbath.co.uk).

● **Bathampton**
Somerset. PO, tel, stores, chemist. The centre of the village surrounds the canal and is still compact and undeveloped, but new housing around the edges has turned it into a suburb of Bath. The church is mostly 19th-C.

Pubs and Restaurants

Bath is well-endowed with distinguished restaurants, lively wine bars and excellent pubs. The following is a selection of pubs close to the canal.

🍺✕**The Boathouse** Newbridge, Bath BA1 3NB (01225 482584; www.boathousebath.com). Just west of New Bridge. Pub and restaurant beside the River Avon. Real ale. Food available *daily*. Children welcome. Riverside garden and moorings for patrons.

🍺**Dolphin** 103 Locksbrook Road, Bath BA1 3EN (01225 445048; www.dolphininn.org.uk). On the Weston Cut. Real ales and bar meals available *L and E* with separate menus for each. Garden and moorings. Children welcome. Darts, dominoes and crib. *Open all day.*

🍺**Golden Fleece** 1–3 Avon Buildings, Lower Bristol Road, Bath BA2 1ES (01225 429572). One-bar local 50yds south of the river, serving a selection of real ales. Traditional pub games.

✕**Kindling Coffee** 9A Claverton Buildings, Widcombe, Bath BA2 4LD (01225 442125/07971 414860; www.kindlingcoffee.co.uk). Friendly, enticing café serving Fairtrade teas and coffees, together with a range of home-made snacks and light meals - made from local ingredients - in a relaxed atmosphere. Organic bread sandwiches. Unlimited coffee top-ups just £1 each! Outside seating. Children welcome.

🍺**The Ram** 20 Claverton Buildings, Widcombe, Bath BA2 4LD(01225 421938). Pleasant, traditional pub, serving real ales and ciders, which encourages you to bring your own food from local takeaways. The landlord provides complimentary crockery, cutlery and condiments. Dogs welcome. Open fires and outside seating. *Regular* quiz nights. *Open all day.*

Boatyards

Ⓑ**Bath Marina and Caravan Pak** Brass Mill Lane, Bath BA1 3JT (01225 424301; www.bwml.co.uk). 👕 D Pump out, long-term mooring, toilets, showers, telephone, gas, solid fuel, shop selling snacks, basic groceries and small amount of chandlery.

Ⓑ**Bath Narrowboats** Sydney Wharf, Bathwick Hill, Bath BA2 4EL (01225 447276;

www.bath-narrowboats.co.uk). 👕🛠D Pump out, narrowboat hire, day boat hire, gas, engine sales, boat repairs, chandlery, books, maps, gifts, bike hire. *Emergency call out. See also* Boat Trips page 70.

✕**Digger's Yard** Warminster Road, Bath (07790 872705; digger@diggersyard.co.uk). Beside bridge 197. Long-term mooring and caravan rental.

Claverton

Open country continues, allowing views across the valley to Bathford church and Warleigh Manor. The navigation follows the contours of the land as it leaves Bath, maintaining the level of the nine mile pound that runs from Bath Top Lock to Bradford. The waterway approaches a thickly wooded stretch passing Claverton to the west. Although the village flanks the canal it is all but hidden by the folds of the land. Access is easy and both the village and Claverton Manor are worth a visit. Claverton Pumping Station houses a water-powered pump which lifts water from the Avon to feed the canal. The pump was restored by the Kennet and Avon Canal Trust, with help from engineering students from Bath University. Now a side-cutting takes the canal towards Dundas Aqueduct preceded by the turnover bridge and a basin complete with a small wharf and crane standing over the water. Here is the junction with The Somerset Coal Canal which, until its closure in 1904, ran south from the Kennet & Avon Canal towards Paulton. At the wharf the waterway turns suddenly onto the aqueduct – perhaps the best-known feature of the Kennet & Avon Canal – which carries it across the railway and the Avon valley to the east side. Passing the village of Limpley Stoke, scattered over the valley side, the navigation runs through thick woods clinging to steep banks until the countryside again opens out on the approach to Avoncliff Aqueduct.

Boatyards

Ⓑ **Bath & Dundas Canal Co**. Brassknocker Basin, Monkton Combe BA2 7JD (01225 722292; www.bathcanal.com). At the end of the Somersetshire Coal Canal, where boats up to 60ft can turn, BUT do not bring your boat in without first walking along the main road to the office to check if space is available.

🛢 **DE** Pump out, gas, electric, day-hire craft (including canoes), long-term mooring, dry dock, boat sales and repairs, dry dock, wet dock, cycle hire, historical display of Somerset Coal Canal, café, toilets. Provisions are available at the garage above Dundas Wharf.

● **Claverton**
Somerset. Tel. Although devoid of all facilities, Claverton is well worth a visit. It is a manorial village of stone houses, surrounding the 17th-C farm, and in early days was clearly dependent upon Claverton Manor. The main road misses the village, increasing the peace and seclusion.
The American Museum in Britain Claverton Manor, Bath BA2 7BD (01225 460503; www. americanmuseum.org). The manor was built in 1820 by Sir Jeffry Wyatville in the Greek revival style. It now houses a museum of American decorative arts from the late 17th C to the mid 19th C. Teas. *Open Tue–Sun, Mar–Oct 12.00–17.00 (and late Nov–Mid Dec). Also B Hol & Aug Mon).* Charge.
Claverton Pumping Station Ferry Lane, Claverton BA2 7BH (01225 483001; www.claverton.org). The waterwheel pump at Claverton is the only one of its kind on British canals. Designed by John Rennie, the pump was

built to feed the 9 mile Bradford–Bath pound, and started operating in 1813. The two undershot breast wheels, each 15ft in diameter and 11ft wide, then powered the pumping machinery until a major breakdown in 1952 prompted its closure, and replacement by a temporary diesel pump. The original machinery has now been restored, and pumping weekends are organised. Electric pumps now do the day-to-day work, raising water from the Avon 47ft below. The Pumping Station is run by Kennet & Avon Canal Trust volunteers. *Open Easter–Oct every Sat, Sun and B Hol 10.00– 17.00, Wed closes 16.00. Telephone for pumping days.* Picnic area, gift shop. Charge.
● **Limpley Stoke**
Wilts. Tel. Built on the side of the valley overlooking the river, Limpley Stoke is a quiet village, a residential outpost of Bath. The little church includes work of all periods, from Norman to the 20th C: inside is a collection of carved coffin lids.

Dundas Aqueduct Built in 1804, this three-arch classical stone aqueduct is justifiably one of the most well-known features of the canal, and stands as a fitting monument to the architectural and engineering skill of John Rennie. It is necessary to leave the canal and walk down into the valley below to appreciate the beauty of the aqueduct, and to see it in the context of the narrow Avon valley into which it fits so well. The aqueduct was named in honour of the first chairman of the Kennet and Avon Canal Company and is widely regarded as Rennie's finest architectural work. Urgent repair work had to be carried out in the early 1980s involving relining the structure with reinforced concrete.

Somersetshire Coal Canal Opened in 1805, this narrow canal was sponsored by the Somerset Coal owners, who wanted a more efficient means of moving their coal to Bath, Bristol and the rest of England. Originally surveyed by Rennie in 1793, the canal was to run from Limpley Stoke to Paulton, with a branch to Radstock. There were steep gradients to overcome at Midford and Combe Hay, and these plagued the canal throughout its life. The Radstock Arm was never completed and tramroads were built over the difficult stretches. The main line was completed throughout, but not before some remarkable solutions to the problems of the Combe Hay gradient had been tried out. First there was Robert Weldon's caisson lock; a watertight caisson, large enough to hold a narrowboat and crew, was pulled up and down an 88ft-deep water-filled cistern by means of a rack and pinion. This terrifying device was soon replaced by an inclined plane, which in turn was replaced by a conventional flight of locks. Once open, the canal carried a large tonnage of coal throughout the 19th C: it served 30 collieries more directly than the railway. However, by the end of the century the inevitable competition was taking away the traffic, which finally stopped in 1898. The canal was officially abandoned in 1904. The first ¼ mile has been restored and is used by a boatyard, and for moorings. A stop lock at the entrance restricts its use to craft of 7ft beam only.

● **Freshford**
Somerset. PO, tel, station. Although not on the canal, Freshford is well worth the ½ mile walk south from Limpley Stoke. It is a particularly attractive village, set on the side of the steep hill that flanks the confluence of the rivers Avon and Frome. At the top of the hill is the church, and terraces of handsome stone houses fall away in both directions, filling the valley below, and crowding the narrow streets. At the bottom of the hill is the river, crossed by the medieval bridge. The hills around were a rich source of Bath stone, limestone and fuller's earth and in the early 19th C the village was involved with the production of broad cloth in its extensive factory. Ruins of an old hermitage and friary, possibly connected with Hinton Abbey, were excavated locally, as were the remains of a Roman encampment.

Pubs and Restaurants

●Ⓑ**Bathampton Mill** Mill Lane, Bathampton BA2 6TS (01225 469758; www.thebathamptonmill. co.uk). 400yds north of Bathampton Bridge. Food and real ales available at the bar *all day* and in the restaurant *L and E: Mon-Fri and all day Sat and Sun*. Garden with play area and attractive riverside terrace. Moorings.

●**George Inn** Mill Lane, Bathampton, Bath BA2 6TR (01225 425079; www.chefandbrewer.com). Family pub with canalside garden and children's play area. Real ales. Extensive range of freshly prepared food available *all day, every day*. Takeaway fish and chips *Sat-Sun*.

✕♈**Angelfish Café/Restaurant** Brassknocker Basin, Monkton Combe BA2 7JD (01225 723483). Generous portions of appetising, home-made food served in an attractive setting with a distinctly continental feel. Tea, coffee, home-made cakes, filled baguettes and crêpes, hot meals, drinks and ice creams. Family orientated. Café *open daily all year 10.00–18.00 (10.00–17.00 in winter)*. Also opens for functions and pre-booked groups. Regular events.

●**Rose and Crown** Middle Stoke BA2 7GE (01225 722237). Village pub serving real ale. Focussed on serving good food *L and E Mon-Fri and all day Sat and Sun*. Children welcome. Garden and great views across the valley.

●✕**Hop Pole** Woods Hill BA2 7FS (01225 723134). Moor at Limpley Stoke Bridge, walk down to the railway bridge and turn left to find this popular traditional oak-panelled pub, featured in the film 'Remains of the Day'. The building is at least 400 years old, originally the monks' wine lodge – it is now famous for its Hop Pole pies. Real ale. Extensive bar and à la carte menu and wine list *L and E daily*. Children welcome in designated areas, as are dogs. Old English country garden.

●**The Inn at Freshford** The Hill, Freshford BA2 7WG (01225 722250; theinnatfreshford.co.uk). It is well worth the walk to this splendid, traditional pub overlooking the river. Real ales. Bar meals available *L and E daily*. Quiz *first Mon in month*. Traditional jazz *every Thu*. Garden. Dogs and children welcome.

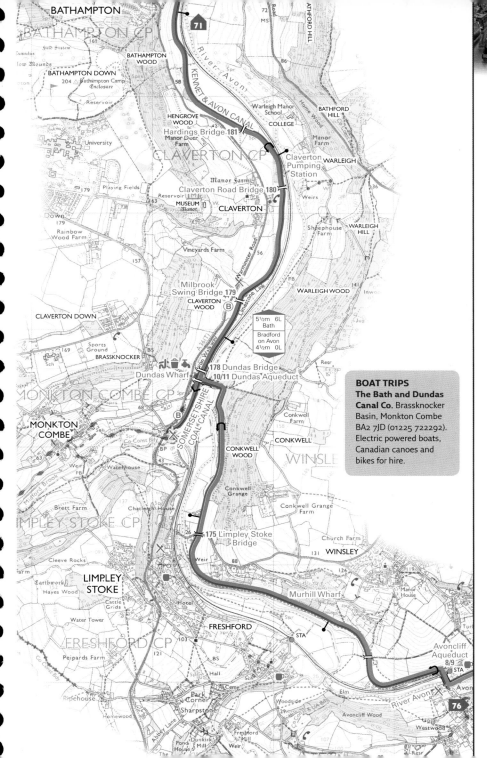

BOAT TRIPS
The Bath and Dundas Canal Co. Brassknocker Basin, Monkton Combe BA2 7JD (01225 722292). Electric powered boats, Canadian canoes and bikes for hire.

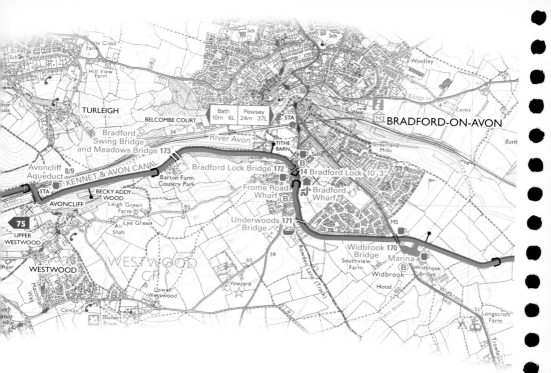

Bradford on Avon

At the aqueduct the towpath crosses under the canal to the north side and the thick woods give the canal user a feeling of total seclusion. Avoncliff makes a worthwhile stop with its tearoom and pub overlooking the river and the elegant stone arches (recently restored) of Rennie's fine aqueduct. Towards Bradford, the Avon rushes along beside the towpath and beyond it the railway appears and disappears among the trees on the far side of the valley, whilst the waterway pursues its more sedate course. Cyclists appear with great frequency since this is part of the Wiltshire Cycleway route. The town is approached through beautiful woods leading to the Tithe Barn, beyond which there are fine views of Bradford spread out above the river. Above the lock and Bradford Basin, the navigation skirts an extensive residential area and is set slightly below the surrounding area, burrowing out towards open countryside again. River and canal make their separate departures from the town to converge again with the canal high above in a side cutting, initially shielded by trees. Then fine views northwards open out over the Avon valley as the waterway crosses first the River Biss, followed by the railway on two, splendid stone aqueducts. The classical arch over the river is particularly handsome; it is necessary to walk down the side of the embankment to see it properly. To the west of Hilperton, the canal passes the grounds of Wyke House, whose Jacobean-style towers stand among the trees. Passing the boatyard and large marina basin the navigation curves around Hilperton; although the main part of the village is a mile to the south. There is a convenient pub, post office, garage and a stores beside Bridge 166. Beyond, the countryside opens out into the wide Avon valley as the canal makes a beeline for Devizes and the Caen Hill Lock Flight.

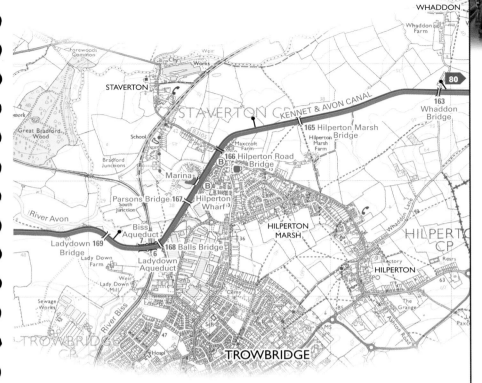

WALKING & CYCLING

Bradford on Avon is an excellent place for the cyclist to access the towpath with level rides towards Bath and bikes for hire.

Boatyards

Ⓑ**The Bike Store** 48 Frome Road, Bradford on Avon BA15 1LE (01225 867187; www. towpathtrail.co.uk). Canoe and cycle hire. Café.

Ⓑ**Wiltshire Narrowboats** Bradford, Frome Road, Bradford on Avon BA15 2EA(01225 863987/07561 096679; www.wiltshire-narrowboats). D Pump out, gas, coal, narrowboat hire, day boat hire, dry dock, chandlery, maps, books and gifts.

Ⓑ**Sally Boats** Bradford on Avon Marina, Trowbridge Road, Bradford on Avon BA15 1UD (01225 864923; www.sallynarrowboats.co.uk). Gas, narrowboat hire, dry dock, DIY facilities, laundry service.

Ⓑ**Bradford on Avon Marina** Trowbridge Road, Bradford on Avon BA15 1UD (01225 864562). D Pump out, gas, overnight mooring, long-term mooring, narrowboat hire, slipway, cranage facilities, brokerage.

Ⓑ**Hilperton Marina** Hammond Way, Trowbridge BA14 8RS (01225 765243; www.alvechurch.com). D Pump out, gas, overnight mooring, long-term mooring, chandlery (on-line), books, maps, boat sales, solid fuel, toilets, crane (22 ton), slipway, engineering, brokerage, gas safe engineer.

Ⓑ**The Boatyard** 5 Hammond Way, Hilperton Marsh, Trowbridge BA14 8RS (01225 710017/ 07790 017418; www.ukboatyard.com). D Pump out, gas, chandlery, boat sales, servicing, moorings, boat building, engineering and Gas Safe engineer.

Avoncliff

Wilts. Station. A hamlet clustered in the woods beside the canal. Originally it was a centre of weaving, and many traces of the old industry can be seen: weavers' cottages, and the old mills on the Avon, which falls noisily over a weir at this point. At one time the mills were used for flocking, a process which involved the breaking up of old woollen material to make stuffing for mattresses and chairs. The hamlet is dominated by Rennie's aqueduct, built in 1804 to take the canal across the valley to the north side. A classical stone structure, it suffered from casual repair work and patching in brick when owned by the Great Western Railways, due mainly to the inferior nature of the stone from which it was constructed. Thankfully it has been extensively and skillfully restored.

Bradford on Avon

Wilts. All services. Set in the steeply wooded Avon valley, Bradford is one of the beauty spots of Wiltshire, and one of the highlights of the canal. Rather like a miniature Bath, the town is composed of fine stone terraces rising sharply away from the river, which cuts through the centre of the town. Until the 19th C it was a prosperous centre for weaving, but a depression killed the industry and drove most of the workers away. At the time that the canal was built Bradford had no less than 30 water-powered cloth factories and some of these buildings still survive. Bradford is rich in architectural treasures from the Saxon period to the 19th C, while the abundance of fine 18th-C houses make the exploration of the town a positive pleasure. The centre is very compact, and so the walk down the hill from the canal wharf lays most of it open to inspection, including the town bridge, Holy Trinity Church, the Victorian town hall and the fine Gothic Revival factory that dominates the riverside. There is also a swimming pool near the canal.

Bradford Upper Wharf BA15 2EA The canal wharf is particularly attractive. There is a small dock with some of the original buildings still standing, plenty of mooring space, and an old canal pub beside the lock. The lock here was built to raise the canal to the same level as the Wilts and Berks Canal which joins the canal at Semington.

Kennet & Avon Canal Trust Wharf Cottage, Bradford Lock, Bradford on Avon BA15 1LE (www.katrust.co.uk). Canal shop and exhibition, range of canal books, souvenirs, gifts, light refreshments and boat trips at weekends. Tea garden. *Open Easter-Oct daily, 10.00–16.00.*

Great Tithe Barn Bradford on Avon BA15 2EF (www.english-heritage.org.uk). Standing below the canal embankment, this great stone building is one of the finest tithe barns in England. It was built in the 14th C

by the Abbess of Shaftesbury. Its cathedral-like structure (168ft long) is broken by two porches, with massive doors that open to reveal the beamed roof. The barn is part of Barton Farm, a medieval farm which was part of the monastic estate of Shaftesbury Abbey. The Granary and Cow Byres now house craft shops and galleries.

Holy Trinity Church Church Street, Bradford on Avon BA15 1LN Basically a 12th-C building with additions dating over the next three centuries. Inside are some medieval wall paintings, and fine 18th-C monuments. Many of the names that appear relate to the woollen industry.

Saxon Church of St Lawrence Mount Pleasant, Bradford on Avon BA15 1SJ Founded in AD705, this tiny church was enlarged in the 10th C. Since then it has survived essentially unchanged, having been at various times a school, a cottage and a slaughterhouse. The true origins and purpose of the building were only rediscovered in the 19th C, and so it remains one of the best-preserved Saxon churches in England.

Town Bridge The nine-arched bridge is unusual in having a chapel in the middle, one of only four still surviving in Britain. Parts of the bridge, including the chapel, are medieval, but much dates from a 17th-C rebuilding. During the 17th and 18th C the chapel fell out of use, and was turned into a small prison, serving as the town lock up.

Westwood Manor Lower Westwood BA15 2AF (01225 863374; www.nationaltrust.org.uk/westwood-manor). One mile south west of Bradford. This 15th-C stone manor house contains original Jacobean plaster and woodwork, although much was lost when the manor became a farm in the 18th C. Skilful restoration by the National Trust has returned the manor to its former glory. *Open Apr–Sep, Sun, Tue and Wed 14.00–17.00.* Charge.

Tourist Information Centre 50 St Margaret's Street, Bradford on Avon BA15 1DE (01225 865797; www.bradfordonavon.co.uk).

Staverton

Wilts. Tel. The village lies to the north of the canal, spreading down to the bank of the Avon. A small isolated part of the Avon is navigable here, and is used by a few pleasure boats. In the village are terraces of weavers' cottages, a sign of what was once the staple trade of the area.

Hilperton

Wilts. PO, tel, stores (open Mon–Sat 07.00–21.00 and Sun 08.00–20.00), garage. A scattered village that stretches away from the settlement by the canal wharf. Wyke House stands to the west of the village. This very ornate Jacobean mansion was in fact built in 1865, a replica of the original house. House *not open to the public.*

Pubs and Restaurants

◗**Cross Guns** Avoncliff Aqueduct BA15 2HB (01225 862335; www.crossguns.net). One of the most attractive pubs on the navigation with its low ceilings, stone walls and flagged floors. The terraced gardens are busy in summer with people enjoying this beautiful setting in a wooded valley. Real ales including their own brew. Good selection of imaginative, well-priced home-made food *L and E*. Children and dogs welcome. B&B. *Open all day, every day.*

✕♈**Lock Inn** 48 Frome Road, Bradford on Avon BA15 1LE (01225 867187; www.thelockinn.co.uk). A unique establishment whose proprietors openly admit to scant portion control; welcome (amongst others) 'kids, cats and dogs, muddy boots, scaffolders, bankers, plumbers (when they turn up) and old age travellers', whilst justifiably claiming to be 'suppliers of happiness and laughter'. Excellent, appetising and inexpensive food for all the family, served in the café including death-defying boatmen's breakfasts *daily 08.45–18.00*, and a tantalising restaurant menu *L and E*. Only moaners and unruly parents are banned!

◗**Canal Tavern** 49 Frome Road, Lower Wharf, Bradford on Avon BA15 1LE (01225 867426). It was outside the back door of this friendly pub that the first sod for the commencement of the canal was cut. The pub continues to benefit from its trade with an attractive terrace overlooking the navigation. Real ale. Home-made food *L and E*. Children and dogs welcome. Garden with patio.

✕♈**Maharja** 12 Frome Road, Bradford on Avon BA15 1LE (01225 866424; www.themaharajarestaurant.co.uk). Across the road from the Canal Tavern. Authentic Indian food served by friendly, attentive staff. *Open L Fri & Sat 12.00–14.00 & E daily 18.00–23.00 (Fri & Sat 23.30).*

◗**Barge Inn** 17 Frome Road, Bradford on Avon BA15 2EA (01225 863403; www.thebargeinn.co.uk). Comfortable one-bar pub. Good choice of real ale and wine list. Attractive eating area, decorated with canalware, Food served *12.00–21.00 daily*. Children and dogs welcome. Canalside garden. B&B. *Open all day.*

◗**Beef and Barge** Bradford on Avon Marina, Bradford on Avon BA15 1UD (01225 862004). Overlooking the marina this establishment serves real ales and food *L and E*. Children's play area. Garden and patio. Barbecues on *summer weekends*.

◗✕**Old Bear Inn** Staverton BA14 6PB (01225 782487; www.theoldbearinn.co.uk). 1/3 mile north west of Hilperton Bridge. Nicely kept 300-year-old inn. Real ales. Extensive menu available in the bar and restaurant *L and E*. Children and dogs welcome. Garden with covered patio. *Open L and E Mon–Fri and all day Sat & Sun.*

◗**Kings Arms** 5A Castle Street, Trowbridge BA14 8AN (01225 751310; www.thekingsarmstrowbridge.co.uk). A bit of a hike into Trowbridge but well worth taking the track south from Bridge 168. A changing selection of real ales and real cider in this cosy pub that serves home-made food *L and E Mon–Sat & Sun* roast *12.00–14.30*. Cosy, 'snug' drinking areas and an outside patio. Regular quiz and real fires. *Open all day.*

River Avon in Bath (see page 71)

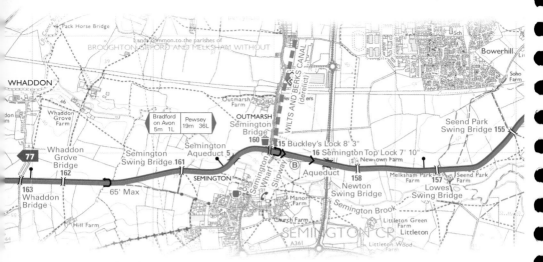

Seend Cleeve

The two Semington Locks continue the ascent towards Devizes with an attractive lock house by Lock 15. Just before the lock the canal is crossed by the A350; this is the best access point for Semington. A close examination of the north bank, just after the bridge, will reveal a bricked-up side bridge; this marks the site of the junction with the long abandoned Wiltshire & Berkshire Canal which used to go to Abingdon. The navigation continues its easterly course, maintaining a fairly straight line through open country before reaching the five Seend Locks. Beside the third lock there is a pub and a lane leading to Seend Cleeve village, although the best access is from bridge 152 below Seend Top Lock. The hills to the south climb steeply up to the village of Seend and to the north flat pasture land stretches away as the canal, passing two swing bridges, turns through Sells Green in a low cutting that hides most of the village. Gas is available 50 yds north of Bridge 148, on the right.

Boatyards

Ⓑ**Semington Dry Dock** Lock House, 545 Canal Bridge, Semington BA14 6JT (01380 870654; www.semingtondock.co.uk). Between locks 15 and 16, offering practical facilities for all aspects of canal boat maintenance and repair, 2 covered dry docks, wet dock, slipway, boat storage, DIY facilities.

Ⓑ**Wilderness Boats** Semington Dry Dock, Lock House, 545 Canal Bridge, Semington BA14 6JT (01380 870141/07973 815920; www.wildernessboats.com). GRP boat repairs and servicing, outboard repairs and servicing, wet dock, trailboat maintenance.

● **Semington**
Wilts. Tel. Semington is a pretty village. There are several large, handsome houses with fine gardens, some dating from the 18th C. The little stone church, crowned with a bellcote, is at the end of a lane to the west of the village.
● **The Wiltshire & Berkshire Canal**
Opened in 1810, the canal wound in a meandering course for 51 miles between Semington on the

Kennet & Avon Canal and Abingdon on the River Thames. A branch was opened in 1819 from Swindon to connect with Latton on the Thames & Severn Canal. Although the carriage of Somerset coal was the inspiration for the canal, its eventual role was agricultural. Profits were never high, partly because the wandering line of the canal and its 45 locks made travel very slow, and so it suffered early from railway competition. By the 1870s, moves were afoot

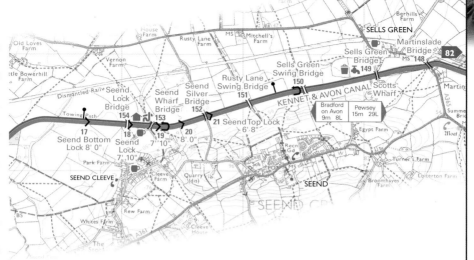

to close the canal,
and, despite various efforts
to give it a new lease of life, the situation
had become hopeless by the turn of the century.
Traffic finally stopped in 1906, and the canal
was formally abandoned in 1914. In 1977 the
Wilts & Berks Amenity Group (www.wbct.org.uk)
was formed with the aim of preserving both the
main line of the canal and the northern branch
to Latton. Twenty years later its avowed aim is
to restore the waterway to form a navigable link
between the K & A, the Thames at Abingdon and
either the Thames or the Thames & Severn Canal
at Cricklade.

● **Seend Cleeve**
Wilts. Tel. An agricultural village built on the steep
slopes of the hills that overlook the canal.

● **Seend**
Wilts. PO, tel, stores. Although the main road cuts
the village in half, Seend is still attractive. Elegant
18th-C houses flank the road, and conceal the
lane that leads to the battlemented Perpendicular
church.

● **Sells Green**
Wilts. Tel. A scattered main road village, the
houses doing their best to hide from the traffic
behind decorative gardens.

Pubs and Restaurants

■✕**Somerset Arms** High Street,
Semington BA14 6JR (01380 870067; www.
somersetarmssemington.co.uk). About ¼ mile
south of Semington Bridge 160. A traditional
village pub, more than 400 years old, serving real
ales and meals in the bar and restaurant *daily L
and E (not Sun E)*. Children and dogs welcome.
Large Garden. B&B.

■**Brewery Inn** Seend Cleeve SN12 6PX (01380
828463). 200yds south of Lock 19. A genuine,
unadulterated village local. Real ales and
traditional ciders. Appetising home-made food
available L (Wed-Sun) and E (Wed-Sat). Children
and dogs welcome. Large garden with decking
and children's play area. Traditional pub games
and a selection of board games.

■✕**Barge Inn** Seend Cleeve SN12 6QB (01380
828230; www.bargeinnseend.co.uk). By Lock
19. An extensive and extremely popular pub
occupying the former wharf house and stables,
dating back to 1805. The house was once the
home of the Wiltshire Giant, Fred Kempster,

who reached the inconvenient height of 8ft 2ins.
Real ales. Meals in the bar and restaurant *all day*.
Children and dogs welcome. Canalside garden.
Weekend barbecues *in summer*.

■✕**Bell Inn** Seend Cleeve SN12 6SA (01380
828338; www.thebellseend.co.uk). ½ mile south
of Lock 21. A conversion of an old brewhouse once
patronised by Cromwell and his troops when they
breakfasted here on their way to attack Devizes
Castle in 1645. Real ales. Food served in the
bar and restaurant *L and E (not Sun E)*. Booking
advisable *at weekends*. Function room available.
Children and dogs welcome. Outside beer garden
with panoramic views over Salisbury Plain.

■✕**Three Magpies** Sells Green, Seend,
Melksham SN12 6RN (01380 828389; www.
threemagpies.co.uk). ¼ mile north of Sells Green
Bridge 149. A comfortable pub, with converted
stables housing the restaurant. Real ale. Food
*available Mon–Thur L and E and all day Fri-Sun.
(winter times may vary).* Garden. Children's play
area and camping.

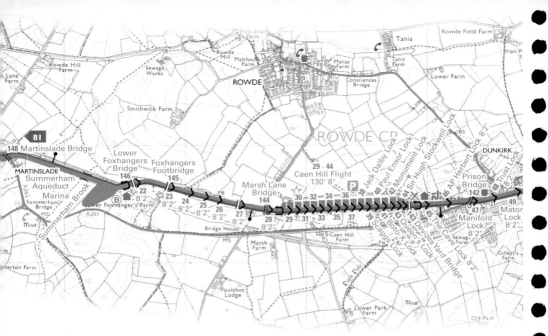

Devizes

At Lower Foxhangers the waterway swings left, under the turnover bridge, and enters Lock 22, the first of 7 locks with conventional pounds that precede the Caen Hill Flight proper. Immediately beyond Marsh Lane Bridge, carrying the B3101 to Rowde, the 16-lock Caen Hill section begins; wide lock follows wide lock up the hill, each with an enormous side pound. These were designed to hold sufficient water while permitting the locks to be close together to follow the slope. The scale of the whole flight is most impressive. The towpath is in very good condition and the whole area is obviously used for recreation by visitors and the people of Devizes alike. To the south the busy A361 accompanies the canal up the hill but it is out of sight for most of the way. Above Lock 44 the remaining locks are spaced out and finish at the generous stone bridge, with its separate towpath arch, that leads the navigation into Devizes Wharf, where the Kennet & Avon Canal Trust has a museum and shop in a converted warehouse. Twenty-nine locks have been negotiated in just $2^{1}/_{4}$ miles. The wharf is also the home of a theatre and trip boat operation. The waterway now enters a long, wooded cutting, spanned by several very elegant large stone bridges (some listed as ancient monuments) all of which offer easy access to the town. Houses appear, their gardens overlooking the cutting and running down to the water's edge. Soon the navigation passes the marina and moves out into the more remote landscape of the Wiltshire Wolds.

NAVIGATIONAL NOTES

Operating times for the Caen Hill Flight (locks 29–44) are *Apr – Sep 08.00–17.00 (clear locks by 20.00) and Oct–Mar 08.00–13.00* (lock keeper remains on duty until you have cleared the locks). No mooring on the flight.

BOAT TRIPS

Kenavon Venture (0800 028 3707; kenavonventure@ katrust.org.uk) is a wide beam boat operated by the Kennet & Avon Canal Trust from the Wharf, Devizes. Public trips *Apr–Oct, Sat, Sun, Wed and public hols*. Santa trips at *Christmas*. Available for private charter.
White Horse Boats (01380 728504; www.whitehorseboats.co.uk) are based at Devizes Wharf and operate narrowboats for self-drive hire for weekends, short breaks or by the week.

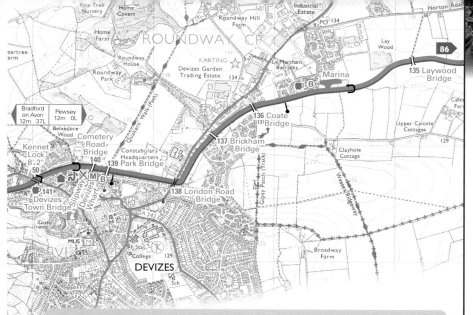

WALKING & CYCLING

The National Cycle Network route 4 joins the towpath at Devizes before heading west to South Wales via Bath. Detailed information covering the entire Cycle Network from Sustrans (08451 130065; www.nationalcyclenetwork.org.uk). Wiltshire County Council operates Connect2Wiltshire, a demand responsive bus service. Telephone Wiltshire County Council's Information Line (08456 525255) for more details or visit www.wiltshire.gov.uk.

Pubs and Restaurants

There are many good pubs and restaurants in Devizes. The following are simply a convenient selection.

George & Dragon High Street, Rowde, near Devizes SN10 2PN (01380 723053; www.thegeorgeanddragonrowde.co.uk). This pub is held in high esteem for its award-winning food, all freshly cooked to order, served *L and E*. Fresh fish is a speciality. Real ales. Traditional pub games and open fires. Children and dogs welcome. Cottage-style garden and B&B.

Caen Hill Tearooms The Locks, Devizes, SN10 1QR (01380 724880). Beside Lock 44. Local ice creams, tea, cream teas, coffee, home-made cakes, pasties and sandwiches. *Open daily, Apr–Oct 10.30–17.00; Nov–Mar, Fri–Mon 11.00–15.30.*

Black Horse Bath Road, Devizes SN10 2AU (01380 723930; www.wadworth.co.uk/devizes/black_horse). By Lock 48, on the Caen Hill section. Well placed to refresh those exhausted by the locks. Real ale and food *L and E*. Children and dogs welcome. Canalside garden. Darts, skittles and pool.

Lamb 20 St John's Street, Devizes SN10 1BT (01380 725426). Old-fashioned local drinking house dispensing real ale. Traditional pub games and enclosed yard. Children and dogs welcome.

Hare & Hounds Hare & Hounds Street, Devizes SN10 1LZ (01380 723231). A range of real ales served in traditional pub surroundings together with food *L and E*. Children and dogs welcome. Garden, open fires and pub games. *Open all day.*

British Lion 9 Estcourt Street, Devizes SN10 1LQ (01380 720665; www.britishliondevizes.co.uk). Traditional, good value, down-to-earth local, attracting a mix of customers of all ages who appreciate real ale, cider and good conversation. *Open all day.*

White Bear Monday Market Street, Devizes SN10 1DN (01380 727588). Real ale served in a popular, town local together with meals *L and E*. Open fires. B&B.

Wharfside Restaurant 13 Couch Lane, The Wharf, Devizes SN10 1EB (01380 726051). Farmhouse cooking in a canalside restaurant *open daily 09.00–16.00 in summer and 09.00–15.00 in winter.* Also morning coffee, afternoon teas and home-made snacks.

The Hourglass Horton Avenue, Devizes SN10 2RH (01380 727313; www.hourglass devizes.com). Modern bar-restaurant, serving traditional pub meals, *Sun* roasts and à la carte menu *L and E daily (not Sun E in winter)*. Large canalside terrace. Free Wi-Fi.

Boatyards

(B)**Caen Hill Marina** Lower Foxhangers, Rowde, Devizes SN10 1SS (01380 827062; www.caenhillmarina.com). 🛒🚿♿DE Pump out, gas, solid fuel, short-term moorings, long-term moorings, launderette, toilets, showers, Wi-Fi.

(B)**Foxhanger Marine** Lower Foxhangers, Devizes SN10 1SS (01380 828254; www.foxhangers.co.uk). 🛒♿Gas, narrowboat hire, long-term moorings, engine sales and repairs, boat building, toilets, showers, telephone, chandlery, camping, self-catering holidays.

(B)**White Horse Boats** Devizes Wharf SN10 1EB (01380 728504; www.whitehorseboats.co.uk). Telephone, toilets, hire boats – short and long-term.

(B)**Devizes Marina** Horton Avenue, Devizes SN10 2RH (01380 725300; www.devizesmarina.co.uk). 🛒♿ Pump out, gas, overnight mooring, long-term mooring, slipway, boat sales and repairs, boat painting, boat building and fitting out, engineering, slipway, solid fuel, chandlery, books, maps and gifts, toilets. Dayboat and canoe hire.

● **Devizes**
Wilts. Tel, PO, stores, banks, chemist, off-licence, takeaways, cinema, garage. Despite the effects of traffic, Devizes still retains the atmosphere of an old country market town. Originally the town grew up around the castle, but as this lost its significance the large marketplace became the focal point. In the early 19th C Devizes held the largest corn market in the west of England and was also a centre for the selling of hops, cattle, horses and cloth, there being many manufacturers of wool and silk in the area. The lower floor of the town hall was the site of the cheese market. Handsome 18th-C buildings now command the square, while the market cross records the sad story of Ruth Pierce. Elsewhere there are timbered buildings from the 16th C. The two fine churches, one built for the castle and the other for the parish, tend to dominate the town, and hold it well together. Only the mount and related earthworks survive of the original Norman castle; the present building is an extravagant Victorian folly. The town's own brewery, Wadworth, in Northgate Street, fills the air with the aroma of malt and hops. Wadworth still deliver their beer around the town by horse and dray.

Battle of Roundway Down, 13 July 1643 Devizes was held by a Royalist army that had already tested the Roundhead forces, who were tired, dispirited and short of supplies after their defeat at Lansdown Hill, near Bath. A Royalist cavalry charge took the Roundheads by surprise, and most of the confused and battle-weary Roundheads were killed or captured. The battlefield, off the A361 north east of Devizes, is still largely intact, and can easily be explored on foot. Mock battles are re-enacted here.

Devizes to Westminster Canoe Race The toughest and longest canoe race in the world takes place *every Easter*. The course, from Park Road Bridge, Devizes, to County Hall Steps, Westminster, includes 54 miles of the Kennet & Avon, and 71 miles of the Thames, the last 17 of which are tidal. There are 77 locks. The race grew from a background of local rivalry in Pewsey and Devizes to find the quickest way to the sea by boat; in 1948 the target was 100 hours. In 1950 the first regular annual race over the course took place; three years later the junior class was introduced.

Anyone may enter the race, but they would have difficulty in beating the highly trained army and navy teams.

Wiltshire Heritage Museum 41 Long Street, Devizes SN10 1NS (01380 727369; www.wiltshireheritage.org.uk). One of the finest prehistoric collections in Europe including finds from the Neolithic, Bronze and Iron Age sites in Wiltshire, the most famous being the Stourhead collection of relics excavated from burial mounds on Salisbury Plain. There are also Roman exhibits. *Open Mon–Sat 10.00–17.00, Sun 12.00–16.00 and B Hols.* Charge.

Kennet & Avon Canal Trust Canal Centre, Couch Lane, Devizes SN10 1EB (01380 721279; www.katrust.co.uk). The Trust's headquarters with an award-winning museum tracing the history of the canal by interactive video and exhibitions. Small charge. Meeting room and well-stocked shop with large selection of canal books, souvenirs, maps and videos. Canal information centre *open daily Feb–Dec 10.00–17.00 (16.00 in winter).* Café *open daily.*

St John's Church SN10 1NS Built by Bishop Roger of Sarum, who was also responsible for the castle, this 12th-C church with its massive crossing tower is still largely original. There are 15th-C and 19th-C additions, but they do not affect the Norman feeling of the whole.

St Mary's Church Dating from the same time as St John's, this church was more extensively rebuilt in the 15th C; plenty of Norman work still survives, however.

Wadworth Vistor Centre and Brewery New Park Street, Devizes SN10 1JW (01380 732277; www.wadworthvisitorcentre.co.uk). Interactive brewing process exhibition, working cooper, shire horses, brewery tours, tastings, shop. Telephone or visit website for times and details.

Wharf Theatre The Wharf, Devizes SN10 1EB (01380 724741; www.wharftheatre.co.uk). Small, ambient canalside theatre hosting a variety of performances throughout the year. Telephone or visit website for details.

Traveline (0871 200 2233; www.traveline.org.uk).

Tourist Information Contact the Heritage Museum or visit the Wadworth Visitor Centre.

All Cannings

At Horton Bridge, where there is a convenient canalside pub, the waterway leaves another short cutting and the tower of Bishop Canning church comes into view, half hidden by trees: a footpath from the swing bridge is the quickest way into the village. The rolling hills climb fairly steeply to the north, while the pasture falls away to the south. Beyond Horton, the lock-free pound now extends eastwards all the way to Wootton Rivers. Following the contour of the land, it swings in a series of wide arcs past All Cannings, curling around the Knoll, a major feature of the landscape to the north. Several villages are near the navigation, all visible and easily accessible from the many bridges but none actually approach the waterside. Their interests lie rather in the rich agricultural lands that flank the canal. The waterway continues to meander through the open countryside, roughly following a contour line to maintain its level. Its progress is marked by a series of shallow cuttings and low embankments. The navigation passes the delightfully named Honeystreet with its pub, boatyard and canalside café and shop. Beyond the village, to the north, can be seen the white horse cut into the hill in 1812, a copy of the one at Cherhill. Approaching Woodborough Hill, the tower of Alton Priors church comes into view as the long pound continues eastwards. To the south the land falls away while to the north the hills take on an almost sculptural quality as evidence of ancient terracing can be *seen*.

Caen Hill Locks (see *page 82*)

● **Bishops Cannings**
Wilts. Tel. Apart from one or two old cottages, the main feature of this village is the very grand church. This cruciform building, with its central tower and spire, is almost entirely Early English in style; its magnificence is unexpected in so small a village. Traces of the earlier Norman building survive. Inside is a 17th-C penitential seat, surmounted by a giant hand painted on the wall with suitable inscriptions about sin and death.

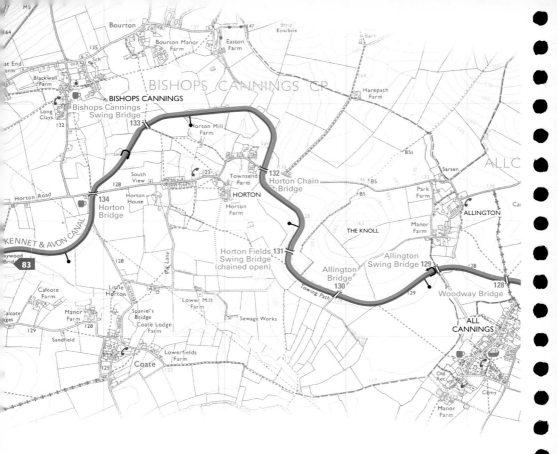

- **Allington**
  Wilts. Tel. A small agricultural village with
  picturesque cottages scattered around a Victorian
  church. East of the village is All Cannings Cross, a
  large Iron Age settlement.
- **All Cannings**
  Wilts. Tel. An attractive village built around a
  square, with houses of all periods. To the south
  there is a large green, overlooked by the church
  with its tall central tower. There is a useful shop
  selling food, beer, wine and newspapers. *Open
  Mon–Fri 07.30–13.00 and 15.00–21.00, Sat 09.00–
  17.00, Sun 09.00–13.00.*
- **Stanton St Bernard**
  Wilts. Tel. Built in a curve of the hills, the village
  has one main street, flanked by pretty gardens.
  The best building is the 19th-C manor, which
  incorporates relics of an earlier house. The
  battlemented church is Victorian.
- **Alton Priors**
  Wilts. Tel. Approached along a footpath from
  Alton Barnes churchyard, the isolated church is
  the best feature of this scattered hamlet. This
  pretty Perpendicular building with its wide,

well-lit nave contains a most
interesting monument: a big box
tomb is surmounted with a large engraved
Dutch brass plate, dated 1590, rich in extravagant
symbolism. To the east of the village the Ridgeway
runs southwards towards Salisbury; this Bronze Age
drover's road swings north east along the downs
for 50 miles, finally joining the Thames valley at
Streatley.

- **Alton Barnes**
  Wilts. Tel. The village runs along the road
  northwards from Honey Street. The best part is
  clustered around the church. Fine farm buildings
  and an 18th-C rectory are half hidden among the
  trees. The church is essentially Anglo Saxon, but has
  been heavily restored; everything is in miniature,
  the tiny gallery, pulpit and pews emphasising the
  compact scale of the whole building.
- **Honeystreet**
  Wilts. Stores, takeaway. A traditional canalside
  village, complete with sawmills, incorporating
  some new development and, arguably, one of the
  most attractively landscaped and charming on the
  waterways.

Boatyards

Ⓑ**Gibson Boat Services** Old Builders Wharf, Honey Street (01672 851232). 🛈DE Pump out, gas, overnight mooring, solid fuel, boat surveys, toilet.

Ⓑ**Honeystreet Wharf Services** Old Builders Yard, Honeystreet, Pewsey SN9 5PS (01672 851232; www.honeystreetwharf. co.uk). 🛈🛈🔧DE Pump out, gas solid fuel, narrowboat hire, day boat hire, short-term mooring, long-term mooring, DIY facilities, shop, books, maps and gifts, chandlery, café, launderette, toilets, showers. *Open Tue–Thur; Sat & Sun. Mon & Fri* by appointment only.
Ⓑ**Moonraker Canal Boats** Old Builders Yard, Honeystreet, Pewsey SN9 5PS (01672 851550; www.moonrakerboats.co.uk). Narrowboat hire.

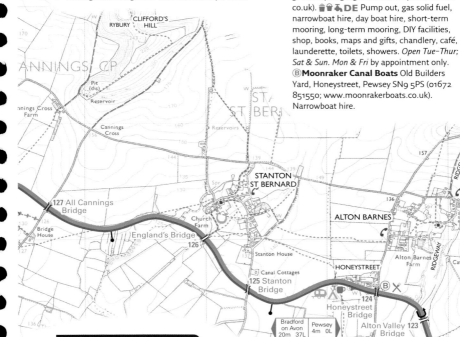

Pubs and Restaurants

🍺✕**Bridge Inn** Horton Road, Devizes SN10 2JS (01380 860273; www. thebridgeinnathorton.co.uk). Beside Horton Bridge 134. Attractive, welcoming pub with mellow brick interior. Real ales and food available in the bar and restaurant *L and E daily. Sunday* roasts and children's menu. Dogs and children welcome. Canalside garden and patio. Moorings.
🍺**Crown Inn** Chandlers Lane, Bishops Cannings SN10 2JZ (01380 860218; www. crownbishopscannings.co.uk). Friendly village pub serving real ale. Traditional pub meals *L and E Mon–Sat and all day Sun. L* carvery (sittings *12.00 & 13.30) Wed & Sun* (booking advisable). Children welcome. Spacious garden and small campsite. Quiz *Thu. Open all day Sat–Sun.*
🍺**Kings Arms** Pub Lane, All Cannings SN10 3PA (01380 860328; www.kingsarmsallcannings.co.uk). ¼ mile south of Woodway Bridge 128. Comfortable and charming village pub, serving good selection of real ale, and good value, home-made bar food *L (not Mon) and E*. Open fires. Darts, pool, dominoes and crib. Children and dogs welcome. Large garden with spectacular views over the Vale of Pewsey. *Open all day Sat and B Hol Mon.*

🍺**Barge Inn** Honeystreet, Pewsey SN9 5PS (01672 851705; www.the-barge-inn.com). An imposing canalside pub which was once a slaughterhouse, a bakehouse, a brewery and a grocers; now functioning as a community pub. Real ale and food served *L and E. Open daily.* Children and dogs welcome. Canalside beer garden. Regular live music. International crop circle centre. Temporary moorings. Camping, toilets and showers.
✕**The Honeystreet Café and Tea Gardens** Old Builders Wharf, Honeystreet, Pewsey (01672 851232; www.honeystreetcafe.co.uk). Charming canalside tea gardens, nestled in the Pewsey Vale (with views of the white horse) offering freshly made cakes, tasty sandwiches, homemade scones, tea, coffee and daily specials, together with the opportunity to indulge in a hearty breakfast!

87

Pewsey

The canal skirts Woodborough Hill giving views to the south over open countryside to the village of Woodborough itself. The equally dominant Pickled Hill now fills the north bank, giving a good view of the field terracing that is a relic of Celtic and medieval cultivation. Further east, the waterway passes through the elaborately decorated Lady's Bridge and enters the tranquil, wooded Wide Water. In 1793 this stretch was owned by Lady Susannah Wroughton who objected to the canal cutting through her land. She was appeased by £500, the building of a highly ornate bridge (dated 1808 and attributed to Rennie) and the landscaping of the marshy area around it.

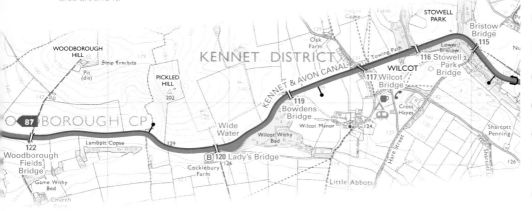

Beyond, a straight stretch leads to the first cottages of Wilcot; the rest of the village is to the south. Woods lead the waterway past Stowell Park, whose landscaped grounds extend to the north. The house, built early in the 19th-C, can be seen clearly from the canal. Closer to the navigation is a selection of delightful estate cottages built in the picturesque style. A miniature suspension bridge, the only surviving example of its kind, carries a private footpath from the park across the canal which now approaches Pewsey Wharf in a low, wooded cutting. The waterway passes well outside the town which fills the Vale to the south. Pewsey Wharf is 1 mile from the town centre and so has developed as a separate canalside settlement, with a pub, cottages and warehouse buildings. To the north, hills descend to the water's edge and to the south the land opens out, giving fine views over the Vale of Pewsey. The 15-mile-long pound continues east, now accompanied by the railway, passing New Mill – a small hamlet to the south of the canal – where there is still evidence of a small wharf.

- **Wilcot**
  Wilts. Tel. A pretty village scattered round the green; there are several thatched houses, and a converted village school with a prominent bell. Parts of the church date from the 12th C, but it was mostly rebuilt in 1876 after a fire. An important event in the village is the annual carnival dating back to 1898. Lasting for two weeks it *commences on the third Sat in Sep* – drawing large crowds – and there is at least one event every evening thereafter.
- **Pewsey**
  Wilts. All services. The little town is set compactly in the Vale of Pewsey. At its centre is a fine statue of King Alfred, erected in 1911, from where all the roads radiate. There is the usual mixture of buildings; but while many are attractive, none are noteworthy. The church is mostly 13th- and 15th-C, but parts of the nave are late Norman: the altar rails were made from timbers of the *San Josef*, captured by Nelson in 1797. The immaculate railway station harks back to the former days of GWR supremacy and is a joy to patronise.
- **New Mill**
  Wilts. Tel. A pretty hamlet scattered below the canal. The mill that gave it its name is now a house, with a fine garden.

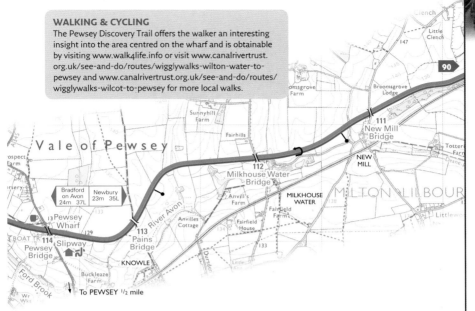

WALKING & CYCLING
The Pewsey Discovery Trail offers the walker an interesting
insight into the area centred on the wharf and is obtainable
by visiting www.walk4life.info or visit www.canalrivertrust.
org.uk/see-and-do/routes/wigglywalks-wilton-water-to-
pewsey and www.canalrivertrust.org.uk/see-and-do/routes/
wigglywalks-wilcot-to-pewsey for more local walks.

Pubs and Restaurants

Golden Swan Wilcot, Pewsey SN9 5NN
(01672 562289; www.thegoldenswan.co.uk).
A one-handed ghost is said to haunt this pub,
which stands beyond the green at the far end
of the village. However, in the flesh, there is
an affable landlord and friendly locals together
with real ale and home-made bar meals served
Tue–Sun L and E (not Sun). Open fire and garden.
Families welcome. Three cricket teams are
based at the pub. Camping. *Closed Mon L in
winter*.

Coopers Arms 37–39 Ball Road, Pewsey SN9
5BL (01672 562495; www.thecoopersarms.com).
Characterful thatched pub, tucked away up a side
street. Real ale and cider. Outside seating, open
fires in winter. Pub games, children's room. Dogs
welcome. Quiz *Sun E (winter)*, live music *Fri*. B&B
and holiday cottages.

Crown 60 Wilcot Road, Pewsey (01672
562653; www.thecrownatpewsey.co.uk). This is
a serious (and very welcoming) real ale pub
with its own micro brewery producing 4 beers.
Additional ales from local micro breweries
(together with ciders and perrys) are also
available, as are inexpensive, home-made bar
meals *Fri E* and a full roast *Sun L*. Dogs and
children welcome. Garden and play area. Pub
games and log fires.

Chequers Bistro 39-41 High Street, Pewsey
SN9 5AF (01672 564004). A bright, cheerful
establishment serving coffees, teas, snacks and
lunches *Mon-Sat* and dinner *Fri E*. Opens *Tue–Thur
E* on request.

Waterfront Pewsey Wharf, Marlborough Road,
Pewsey SN9 5NU (01672 564020). Bar and bistro.
Open 09.00–20.00 in summer; telephone to check
times in *winter*. *Closed Mon*. Everything from snacks
to steaks. Children and dogs welcome. Wharfside
seating area and garden. Also long-term mooring,
slipway, water, pump out.

Royal Oak 35 North Street, Pewsey SN9 5ES
(01672 563426). In the town centre – a family pub
with a warm welcome. Real ale and an appetising
range of inexpensive, home-made food available
L and E. Garden and children's play area. Dogs
welcome. Darts, pool, crib and dominoes. *Winter*
events. B&B.

French Horn Marlborough Road, Pewsey
SN9 5NT (01672 562443; www.frenchhornpewsey.
com). Just north of Pewsey Wharf, on the A345.
A friendly pub serving real ale together with bar
snacks and main meals, produced using local
produce where possible, *L and E, daily*. Interesting
à la carte menu (specialising in fresh fish) available
in the bar and restaurant. The emphasis is very
much on family eating. Garden overlooking canal.

Burbage Wharf

The charming, predominantly thatched, village of Wootton Rivers lies beside the eponymous bottom lock, stretching away to the north. The third lock is in the middle of Brimslade Farm, whose attractive tile-hung buildings date from the 17th C; while Wootton Top Lock sits beside a pretty cottage and garden. Above, the short summit pound leads the waterway through pasture and arable land and, as the ground rises steeply on both banks, it prepares itself for the short Bruce Tunnel. Immediately before the high brick bridge, carrying the A346, lies Burbage Wharf; several of the original brick canal buildings still stand, attractively converted to domestic use, and a restored wooden wharf crane hangs, beside the water. Woods line the approach to the tunnel's western portal, hiding the railway, which is on the south bank before crossing over the tunnel. To the north are the extensive parklands of Tottenham House and Savernake Forest itself. The towpath, passing under the railway, climbs over the top of the tunnel and descends steeply to the navigation, still secluded in a deep, wooded cutting.

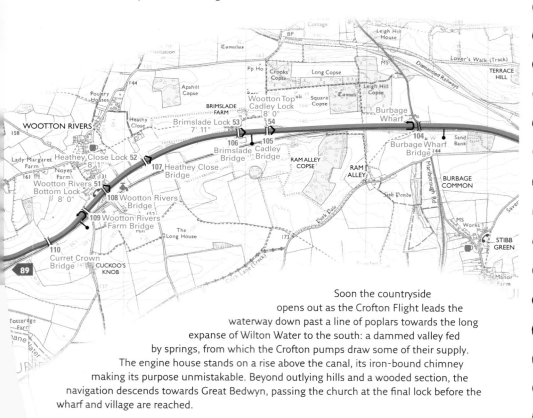

Soon the countryside opens out as the Crofton Flight leads the waterway down past a line of poplars towards the long expanse of Wilton Water to the south: a dammed valley fed by springs, from which the Crofton pumps draw some of their supply. The engine house stands on a rise above the canal, its iron-bound chimney making its purpose unmistakable. Beyond outlying hills and a wooded section, the navigation descends towards Great Bedwyn, passing the church at the final lock before the wharf and village are reached.

- **Wootton Rivers**

Wilts. Tel. A particularly pretty village composed almost entirely of timber-framed, thatched houses, climbing gently up the hill away from the waterway. The church has an unusual clock, its face having letters in place of numbers. Inside, its mechanism is equally eccentric, being assembled from a bizarre collection of cast-off agricultural implements.

- **Crofton**

Wilts. The scattered village is dominated by the brick pumping station with its separate chimney. It houses two 19th-C steam engines, one built in 1812 by Boulton and Watt, the oldest original working beam engine in the world still performing its original duties, the other in 1845 by Harvey's of Hayle, Cornwall. Both have been restored, and are steamed on several weekends in the year. The pumping station, engines and canal shop are open for viewing *Easter–Oct, daily 10.30–17.00.* For details of steaming weekends – which are *approximately once a month Easter–Aug* – telephone 01672 870300; www.croftonbeamengines.org.

Bruce Tunnel Named in honour of Thomas Bruce, Earl of Ailesbury. 502yds with the remains of the chains on the walls, which were used to pull boats through.

- **Wilton**

Wilts. Tel. A compact village at the southern end of Wilton Water, with a pretty duck pond in the centre.

Wilton Windmill Wilton (01672 870266; www.wiltonwindmill.co.uk). 1 mile south of the canal, along the footpath at Lock 60. *Open Easter–Sep, Sun and B hols 14.00–17.00.*

Pubs and Restaurants

Royal Oak Wootton Rivers SN8 4NQ (01672 810322; www.wiltshire-pubs.co.uk). North of the canal. An attractive 16th-C pub in the main street, serving real ale and a good choice of wines. Extensive range of home-cooked meals, prepared with fresh local ingredients, available *L and E, daily.* Children welcome, as are dogs on a lead. Patio. Darts, dominoes, pool and board games. B&B. *Open all day Sat and Sun.*

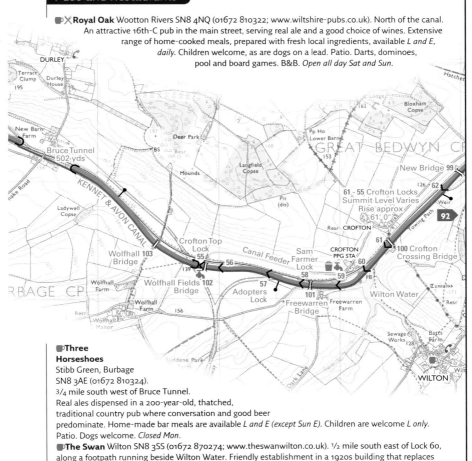

Three Horseshoes Stibb Green, Burbage SN8 3AE (01672 810324). 3/4 mile south west of Bruce Tunnel. Real ales dispensed in a 200-year-old, thatched, traditional country pub where conversation and good beer predominate. Home-made bar meals are available *L and E (except Sun E).* Children are welcome *L only.* Patio. Dogs welcome. *Closed Mon.*

The Swan Wilton SN8 3SS (01672 870274; www.theswanwilton.co.uk). 1/2 mile south east of Lock 60, along a footpath running beside Wilton Water. Friendly establishment in a 1920s building that replaces the original pub, which is now a private dwelling. Real ale. Home-made bar meals *daily L and E. Sun* roasts. Children's menu. *Open all day Sat and Sun.*

91

Froxfield

Great Bedwyn is ranged over the hillside to the north of the waterway, newer houses spilling downwards towards the canal and railway station. The navigation leaves the village, accompanied by the infant River Dunn and approaches Little Bedwyn in a shallow side-cutting. To the north is a hill fort, overlooking ridges that break up the farmland. The village is cut in half by the navigation and the railway. In the centre the lock continues the descent towards Hungerford. The spire of the village church is a prominent feature as is the Berks and Wilts main railway line that keeps constant

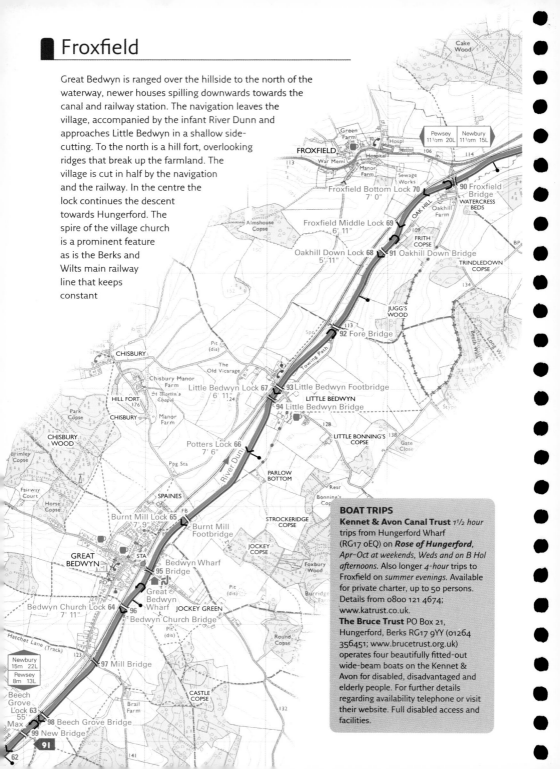

Pewsey 11½m 20L | Newbury 11½m 15L

FROXFIELD
War Memi
Hospital
Manor Farm
Sewage Works
Froxfield Bottom Lock 70
7' 0"
90 Froxfield Bridge
WATERCRESS BEDS
OAK HILL
Oakhill Farm
Almshouse Copse
Froxfield Middle Lock 69
6' 11"
FRITH COPSE
Oakhill Down Lock 68
5' 11"
91 Oakhill Down Bridge
TRINDLEDOWN COPSE
JUGG'S WOOD
92 Fore Bridge
CHISBURY
The Old Vicarage
Chisbury Manor Farm
St Martin's Chapel
Little Bedwyn Lock 67
6' 11"
93 Little Bedwyn Footbridge
LITTLE BEDWYN
94 Little Bedwyn Bridge
HILL FORT
Park Copse
CHISBURY
Manor Farm
CHISBURY WOOD
Brimley Copse
Potters Lock 66
7' 6"
River Dunn
Ppg Sta
LITTLE BONNING'S COPSE
Gate Close
PARLOW BOTTOM
Fairway Court
Horse Copse
SPAINES
STROCKERIDGE COPSE
Bonning's Cop
Resr
Burnt Mill Lock 65
7' 9"
Burnt Mill Footbridge
JOCKEY COPSE
Foxbury Wood
GREAT BEDWYN
STA
Bedwyn Wharf
95 Bridge
Great Bedwyn Wharf
JOCKEY GREEN
Burridge Fa
Bedwyn Church Lock 64
7' 11"
96
Bedwyn Church Bridge
Round Copse
Newbury 15m 22L
Pewsey 8m 13L
97 Mill Bridge
CASTLE COPSE
Beech Grove Lock 63
55'
Max
Brail Farm
98 Beech Grove Bridge
99 New Bridge

BOAT TRIPS

Kennet & Avon Canal Trust 1½ hour trips from Hungerford Wharf (RG17 0EQ) on *Rose of Hungerford*, Apr–Oct at weekends, Weds and on B Hol afternoons. Also longer 4-hour trips to Froxfield on *summer evenings*. Available for private charter, up to 50 persons. Details from 0800 121 4674; www.katrust.co.uk.

The Bruce Trust PO Box 21, Hungerford, Berks RG17 9YY (01264 356451; www.brucetrust.org.uk) operates four beautifully fitted-out wide-beam boats on the Kennet & Avon for disabled, disadvantaged and elderly people. For further details regarding availability telephone or visit their website. Full disabled access and facilities.

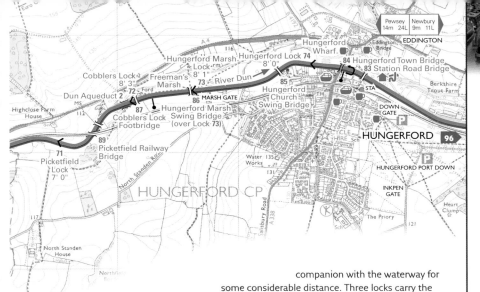

companion with the waterway for some considerable distance. Three locks carry the canal past Froxfield which lies to the north, flanked by the A4; the best access is from bridge 90. This was rebuilt in 1972 during a road improvement scheme using traditional methods and materials, even down to the correct colour of brick. To the west of the River Dunn Aqueduct the railway crosses the waterway and remains on the south bank through Hungerford. The roar of the frequent high speed trains to and from the West Country is the only interruption to the natural peace and solitude of the canal. Crossing a tree-lined embankment, beside the river, the navigation approaches the common land of Hungerford Marsh via Cobblers Lock. Water meadows and pasture, rich in buttercups, meet the water, which seems to form more of a river than a canal. On the outskirts of the town the 19th-C church is passed to the south as the waterway descends to the old wharf, flanked by an original stone warehouse. The handsome bridge gives easy access to the centre of the town set out along a wide, main street. Beyond, the waterway once again strikes off through open meadows, closely paralleled by the clear, sparkling waters of the River Kennet.

NAVIGATIONAL NOTES

1   Hungerford Marsh Swing Bridge is over Hungerford Marsh Lock. Boats over 30ft long (approx) will have to swing it clear before using the lock.
2   In spite of its benign appearance the River Kennet can make a considerable impact on the navigation when in spate. In such conditions the boater should consider carefully his own capabilities and those of his craft before proceeding east beyond Hungerford (or west beyond Reading). Hazards to be particularly aware of are: **a)** Strong pulls at the top of all draw-off weirs – look out for signs. **b)** Powerful side currents at the bottom of locks and lock cuts. **c)** Speed of craft downstream necessitated by need to maintain steerage in fast currents. **d)** Craft heading upstream, often obscured by the many blind bends on the navigation. **e)** Difficulty setting down and picking up crew at locks and moveable bridges – plan all such manoeuvres well ahead.
3   Many of the winding holes marked between Hungerford and Reading are at points where the river and lock cuts diverge and therefore should NOT be used to turn a boat when the river is flowing strongly as they lead directly to weirs.
4   Top paddles between Hungerford and Reading are a mixture of ground and gate paddles. The gate paddles can be particularly fierce, especially in the deeper locks. Secure your boat well back in the lock chamber and open gate paddles with great care.

Great Bedwyn

Wilts. PO, Tel, stores, bakery, garage, station. The main street climbs gently away from the canal and the railway. It is wide, with generous grass verges; attractive houses of all periods line the street. At the top are the pubs. The large church, with its well-balanced crossing tower, is mostly 12th- and 13th-C; inside are some interesting monuments. Relics from the old Bedwyn Stone Museum adorn the façade of the village shop. These are from a collection of stonework of all types, not without humour, and show the work of seven generations of stonemasons. There are statues, tombstones, casts, amusing plaques and even the fossilised footprint of a dinasour..

Little Bedwyn

Wilts. Tel. Divided by the canal, the village falls into two distinct parts. North is the estate village, pretty 19th-C terraces of patterned brick running eastwards to the church, half hidden among ancient yew trees. To the south is the older farming village, handsome 18th-C buildings climbing the hill away from the canal.

Froxfield

Wilts. Tel. The village is ranged along the A4, which has obviously affected its development. The main feature of the village is the Somerset Hospital, a range of almshouses founded by the Duchess of Somerset in 1694, extended in 1775 and again in 1813. Facing onto the road, the hospital is built round a courtyard, which is entered by a Gothic-style gateway, part of the 1813 extension.

Littlecote 1½ miles north of Froxfield. A Tudor building of the 16th C. Littlecote is the most important brick mansion in Wiltshire with its notable Great Hall, Armoury and Long Gallery. The formal front overlooks the gardens that run down to the Kennet. Not open to the public.

Hungerford

Berks. All services. Hungerford is built along the A338, which runs through the town southwards from the junction with the A4. The pleasant 18th- and 19th-C buildings are set back from the road, giving the spacious feeling of a traditional market town. None of the buildings are remarkable, but many are individually pretty. Note the decorative ironwork of the house by the canal bridge. The manor was given to John of Gaunt in 1366, and any monarch passing through the town is given a red rose, the Lancastrian emblem, as a token rent.

Hocktide Ceremonies On the *second Tuesday after Easter*, 99 commoners (those living within the original borough who have the rights of the common and the fishing) are called to the town hall by the blowing of a horn. Two Tuttimen are appointed, who have to visit the houses of the commoners to collect a 'head penny' from the men and a kiss from the women: they give oranges in return. All new commoners are then shod by having a nail driven into their shoes. This ceremony dates from medieval times.

WALKING & CYCLING
Great Bedwyn is a good, central point to access the Ridgeway Walk.

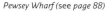

Pewsey Wharf (see page 88)

Pubs and Restaurants

Cross Keys High Street, Great Bedwyn SN8 3NU (01672 870678; www.thexkeys.com). Friendly 17th-C oak-beamed pub, run by ex-residential boaters. Real ales, log fires and home-made food served *L and E*; takeaway pizza also available. Attractive pub garden; children and dogs welcome (though please contact landlord before bringing your dog). Jazz and blues *Sat night*. Pub and children's games. Takeaway pizza service. B&B.

Three Tuns High Street, Great Bedwyn SN8 3NU (01672 870280; www.threetunsbedwyn.co.uk). This cosy, award-winning hostelry offers real ales and home-made food (sourced locally wherever possible) *L and E* together with tasty bar snacks *throughout the day*. The menu is varied and changes daily. *Sun* roasts a speciality, booking advised. Dogs and well-behaved children welcome. Garden.

Harrow Little Bedwyn SN8 3JP (01672 870871; www.harrowinn.co.uk). Upmarket restaurant serving award-winning food and listed in serious eating guides. Outstanding wine list. The menu offers an enticing range of modern British cooking served *L and E Wed–Sat*. Well behaved children welcome. Dining terrace. Chauffeur service available.

Pelican Froxfield SN8 3JY (01488 682479; www.pelicaninn.co.uk). Country pub set in an area of outstanding natural beauty, two minutes' walk from the canal. Real ales and food available *L and E (not Sun E)*. Large country garden with lake and river. Children welcome. B&B.

Bear 51 Charnham Street, Hungerford RG17 0EL (01488 682512; www.thebearhotelhungerford.co.uk). North of the canal. Hotel with 13th-C restaurant serving modern dishes using locally sourced ingredients. Also morning coffee, packed lunches, afternoon tea and bar meals *L and E*. Real ales. Visited by several illustrious visitors over the centuries – including Elizabeth I, Henry VIII and Samuel Pepys – this hotel has, today, a very relaxed atmosphere together with charming courtyard and riverside seating. Also an original Parliamentary clock used to time the mail coaches. Children and dogs welcome. B&B. *Open all day.*

John of Gaunt Inn 21 Bridge Street, Hungerford RG17 0EG (01488 683535). 16th-C pub north of the canal, serving real ale and bar meals *L and E, daily*. Children and dogs welcome in this family oriented establishment. Walled patio. Dominoes and Jenga. *Open all day.*

Plume of Feathers Inn 113 High Street, Hungerford RG17 0NB (01488 682154). South of the canal. Real ale and an extensive and appetising range of home-made food *L and E (not Sun E)*. Children and dogs welcome. Garden. *Open all day.*

Three Swans Hotel 117 High Street, Hungerford RG17 0LZ (01488 682721; www.threeswans.net). Resort hotel, south of the canal. Real ale together with Italian food and à la carte menu *L and E, daily* and bar snacks *L*. Afternoon tea. Children welcome. B&B. *Open all day.*

Railway Tavern Station Road, Hungerford RG17 0DY (01488 683100; www.railwaytavern.info). 200 yds south of Station Road footbridge. Real ale together with inexpensive bar meals available *all day Tue–Sun*. Garden. Children welcome. Darts and pool. Live music and entertainment *weekends*.

Downgate 13 Down View, Park Street, Hungerford RG17 0ED (01488 682708; www.the-downgate.co.uk). ¼ mile south east of Station Road Footbridge. Charming little pub overlooking the common and packed with memorabilia. Real ales. Home-cooked meals available *L and E*. Children and dogs welcome. Garden, open fires *in winter* and traditional pub games.

CLOSE(ISH) ENCOUNTERS

Hungerford commoners, anxious to exercise their piscatorial rights (*see* Hocktide Ceremonies, opposite), should be grateful to have been spared the experience of one Alfred Burtoo. This 78-year-old fisherman, whilst casually casting into the nearby Basingstoke Canal one night, was disturbed by the arrival of two figures in green overalls, 4 feet tall, wearing helmets with smoked visors. After pausing for several seconds they beckoned him to follow them, which he did. 'I was curious,' explained Alfred, 'They showed no sign of hostility and at 78, what had I to lose?' He was led along the towpath to a large oval object – 40–50 feet wide – and upon ascending some steps found himself inside an octagonal room. Here he stood until a voice instructed him to stand under an amber light fixed to the cabin wall. He was asked his age and, after a further pause, the voice bade him depart, stating: 'You are too old and infirm (sic) for our purpose'.

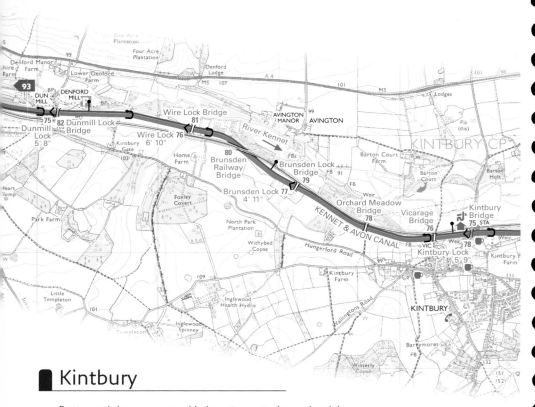

Kintbury

Pretty woods keep company with the waterway to the south as it leaves Hungerford, while to the north river and canal run side by side through water meadows and Common Portdown, an attractive common area, separated only by a narrow ridge carrying the towpath. As the diminutive River Kennet accompanies the canal past Dunmill Lock, the towpath turns over to the north bank. From the bridge there is a good view of Denford Mill. Locks 76 and 77 carry the navigation past Avington, with its Norman church visible among the trees. The railway and the River Kennet are constantly present as the waterway heads towards Kintbury through open countryside, passing the Victorian Gothic vicarage. The canal enters the village beside the railway station and the Dundas Arms, which overlooks the lock. The centre of Kintbury is up on the hill to the south of the lock. Leaving the wharf, the navigation steadily descends the locks towards Newbury, making this a particularly attractive stretch. Wooded, rolling hills flank the waterway to the south as it passes through Drewett's, Copse and Hamstead Locks and into the delightful landscape of Hamstead Park.

- **Avington**
Berks. The village is best approached along the track that runs east from Wire Lock, although the more adventurous can go directly across the water meadows, crossing the Kennet on a small footbridge. The little church is still wholly Norman, and contains a variety of original work; the chancel arch, the corbels and the font are particularly interesting.

- **Kintbury**
Berks. PO, tel, stores, butchers and bakers (closed Sun & Mon). A quiet village with attractive buildings by the canal, including a watermill and canalside pub. The church is originally 13th-C, but was restored in 1859; the railway lends excitement, and noise, to the situation.

NAVIGATIONAL NOTES

Allow for river current when winding and when approaching Copse Lock, especially after heavy rain.

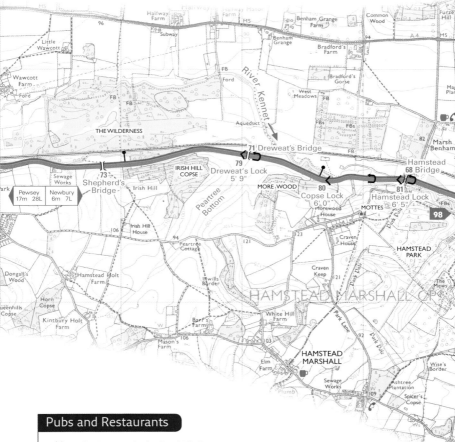

Pubs and Restaurants

Dundas Arms 53 Station Road, Kintbury RG17 9UT (01488 658263; www.dundasarms.co.uk). The River Kennet and the canal flow on either side of this pub, which was named after the Lord Dundas who opened the canal in 1810. Real ale. Restaurant has interesting menu and good wine cellar. Food available *L and E (not Sun or Mon L)*. Children welcome. Canalside garden. B&B.

Prince of Wales Newbury Street, Kintbury RG17 9UU (01488 658269). 300yds south east of Kintbury Bridge 75. Real ales served in a traditional village local. Inexpensive meals *available L and E*. Children welcome. Garden. Traditional pub games. *Occasional* quiz nights.

Blue Ball High Street, Kintbury RG17 9TJ (01488 608126; www.blueballkintbury.co.uk). 500yds south of Kintbury Bridge 75. Friendly village pub serving a range of real ales and good

value bar meals, together with an a la carte restaurant menu. Pizzas also available. Large garden. Children and dogs on leads welcome. Darts and pool. *Open Mon-Thur E and Fri-Sun all day*. Food *available L and E Fri-Sun* (pizzas *all day Sun in summer*).

White Hart Inn Hamstead Marshall, Newbury RG20 0HW (01488 657545; www.whitehartinnhamsteadmarshall.co.uk). 1 mile south of Hamstead Lock 81 (there is a footpath avoiding the road). Smart, country pub, *open all day from 10.00*, serving real ales and an appetising selection of food *daily L and E*, majoring on seasonal specialities. There is also an *all day* cold platter available together with a takeaway selection. Children welcome. Garden. B&B.

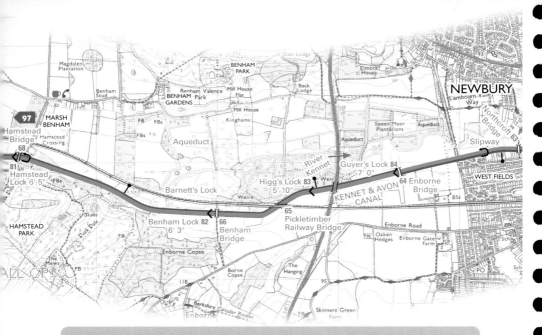

Newbury

West of Newbury the waterway again passes through extensive water meadows as the wooded hills open out to the south revealing a stretch of the controversial bypass. Above Newbury Lock is the delightful, quiet West Mills area, where rows of terraced houses face the navigation and there are extensive moorings. The river cuts right through the town and the town makes the most of it. Below the lock, where the channel gets narrower and faster, is a splendid stone balustraded bridge followed, after 500yds, by a park and an extensive wharf area opposite. This used to be the terminus of the Kennet Navigation from Reading, before the Kennet and Avon Canal Company extended it to link up with the Avon at Bath. There is also a collection of old warehouses and a stone building used by the K & A Canal Trust as an information centre, tearooms and shop. The waterway leaves Newbury Wharf under a handsome new road bridge.

NAVIGATIONAL NOTES

1   Below Newbury lock there are strong cross-flows from both sides of the navigation when the river levels are raised. Upstream boaters should prepare the lock ahead of the craft.
2   In times of fresh water there are strong flows in the narrow section below Newbury bridge and progress upstream can be very slow. Downstream craft should keep a very careful lookout.
3   All craft should keep to the north of the centre pier (i.e. towpath side) through Victoria Park Bridge 59.

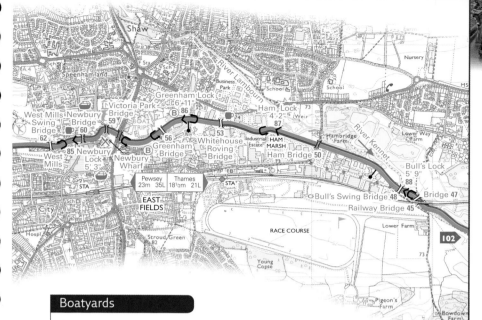

Boatyards

Ⓑ**Newbury Boat Co.** Ham Manor Marina, London Road, Newbury RG14 2BP (01635 282208; 07584 566197; www.newburymarina.com). 🚽🚿♻ Gas, overnight mooring, long-term mooring, boat and engine repairs, toilet, shower, rubbish and oil recycling.

Ⓑ**Greenham Island Boat Services** Greenham Island, Mill Lane, Newbury RG14 5SG (01635 31672/07974 088656).**D** Pump out, calor gas, coal, chandlery. Friendly service. *Open Mon by appointment.*

Newbury Marina
Greenham Island, Mill Lane, Newbury RG14 5SG (01635 282208; 07584 566197; www.newburymarina.com). 🚿 **D** Pump out, narrowboat hire, day boat hire, long and short term moorings (wide-beam and narrowboats), slipway, dry dock facilities, crane, chandlery, gas, solid fuel, toilets. Kennet and Avon trip boat *Jubilee* runs from close by.

● **Newbury**
Berks. All services. Newbury developed in the Middle Ages as a cloth town of considerable wealth, its stature indicated by the size of the church. Although the cloth trade has long vanished, the town has managed to retain much of its period charm. It is a busy shopping centre, and the shop fronts in the main streets have buried many 17th- and 18th-C houses. Elsewhere in the town the 18th C is well in evidence, especially in the West Mills area. There are fine almshouses, and a pretty ornamental stone bridge over the navigation. There are also signs of the agricultural importance of Newbury: the 19th-C Italianate Corn Exchange, for example (*see* across).

1st Battle of Newbury, 20 Sep 1643 Site of Wash Farm off A343. 1³/4 miles south of Guyer's Lock. The Royalists were defeated by the Parliamentarians in one of the bloodiest onslaughts of the Civil War. Guyer's and Higg's Locks are named after troop commanders in the battle.

2nd Battle of Newbury, 28 Oct 1644 Donnington Castle, Donnington. 1¹/2 miles north of Newbury Lock off the A34. The Royalists were in possession of Donnington Castle when the Parliamentarians attacked. Charles' army withdrew to Oxford, but a week later they returned and relieved the castle.

Corn Exchange Market Place, Newbury RG14 5BD (01635 522733; www.cornexchangenew. com). The Corn Exchange offers an extensive range of arts activities – film, theatre, dance, music, comedy and children's events. *Open all year Mon–Sat.*

The Stone Building, Kennet & Avon Canal Trust, The Wharf, Newbury RG14 5AS (01635 522609; www.kennetandavontrust.co.uk). Canal shop and exhibition. Books, gifts, souvenirs, maps and information. Picnic area, tea, coffee, light refreshments. A place for a chat and the opportunity to find out more about the canal in Newbury. *Open daily 09.00–16.30.*

Hungerford (see page 93)

Newbury Fair Northcroft Lane, Northcroft, Newbury RG14 5BT. Leave canal at Kennet Bridge. Annual Michaelmas fair held since 1215, on the *Wed following 11 Oct*.

Newbury Buses (0118 959 4000; www.reading-buses.co.uk/newbury-buses). Network of local urban and rural services.

Newbury Racecourse Newbury RG14 7NZ (01635 40015; www.newbury-racecourse.co.uk). *Midweek and weekend racing*. Flat racing *Apr–Sep* and National Hunt Racing *Oct–Mar*. Charge.

Round Barrow Cemetery Wash Common, near the site of the 1st Battle of Newbury in 1643. Memorial stones to the victims surmount the two smaller mounds.

St Nicolas Church West Mills, Newbury RG14 5HG (01635 47018; www.st-nicolas-newbury.org). Borders the canal on the south bank. A large Perpendicular church, built *c*.1500 at the height of Newbury's prosperity as a wool town. Its 17th-C pulpit is most unusual.

St Nicolas School Enborne Road, Newbury RG14 6AH. By Butterfield, 1859.

Watermill Theatre & Restaurant Bagnor, near Newbury RG20 8AE (01635 46044/45834; www.watermill.org.uk). Enterprising theatre, set in an idyllic location, staging a variety of drama, music and musicals, including world premieres. Also licensed restaurant serving snacks, meals *L and E* and cream teas. Telephone for programme. Although 2½ miles north of the town this makes a rewarding walk or taxi ride.

The Living Rainforest Hampstead Norreys, Thatcham, near Newbury RG18 0TN (01635 202444; www.livingrainforest.org). The opportunity to experience the beauty of rainforest plant life under glass. Three climates featuring different plant species and rainforest creatures. *Open daily (except Xmas Day and Boxing Day) 10.00–17.00*. Charge. Bus (Newbury–Reading route) or taxi from Newbury.

Hamstead Park Old Lane, Hampstead Marshall RG20 0JA. A very fine park bordered by the canal. There used to be a castle here and several interesting buildings adjoin the church on the side of the hill. There is an old watermill by the lock. The hamlet of Hamstead Marshall lies to the south, 1½ miles from Hamstead Lock.

Tourist Information Centre 1 The Wharf, Newbury RG14 5AS (01635 30267; www.visitnewbury.org.uk). *Open Mon – Sat 10.00 -17.00. Closed Sun & B Hol*.

Pubs and Restaurants

⬤✕**Red House** Marsh Benham RG20 8LY (01635 582017; www.theredhousepub.com). About ¼ mile north east of Hamstead Lock. Charming pub-cum-restaurant in a thatched estate village near Benham Park. Once the local bakery it now dispenses ales. Expensive, though appetising menu served in bar and restaurant *L and E, daily*. Attractive conservatory and gardens.

⬤**Snooty Fox** 148 Bartholomew Street, Newbury RG14 5HB (01635 529527). 50yds south of Newbury Bridge. Real ale and cider. Food available *L, Mon–Sat*. No Children. *Regular* live music. *Open 'til late*.

⬤**Lion** 39 West Street, Newbury RG14 1BE (01635 528468; www.the-lion-newbury.co.uk). Alcoved areas in the bar and jazz memorabilia give this pub a cosy atmosphere set off by the wooden floor. Real ales together with food *L Mon–Fri*. Quiz *Sun*. Outsideseating in summer. Large-screen sports TV.

⬤**Lock Stock & Barrel** 104 Northbrook Street, Newbury RG14 1AA (01635 580550; www.lockstockandbarrelnewbury.co.uk). Real ale served in a spacious, riverside pub with an attractive terrace. Food available *daily from 11.00*. Children welcome in garden only.

⬤**Old Waggon & Horses** 26 Market Place, Newbury RG14 5AG (01635 35081). 100yds east of Newbury Bridge. Specialises in Thai food. This comfortable pub has a pleasant terrace (with moorings) overlooking the river. Food available *daily 12.00–16.00*. No children. Live music *Sun E*.

✕**Teashop by the Canal** The Stone Building, The Wharf, Newbury RG14 5AS (01635 522609). An old fashioned delight offering teas, coffees, light meals, cakes, sandwiches, ice creams and canal gifts in a relaxed friendly atmosphere. *Open daily 09.00–16.30*.

⬤✕**Narrow Boat** London Road, Newbury RG14 2BP (01635 42614). North east of Whitehouse Bridge. Real ale together with traditional pub food *available daily*. Children welcome *until 20.00*. Large screen sports TV. Moorings and garden. *Open all day*.

⬤**Hogshead** 1-3 Wharf Street, Newbury RG14 5AN (01635 569895; www.hogsheadnewbury.co.uk). Once the local auction rooms, this spacious pub still displays posters featuring its former trade. Real ale and cider, and large range of bottled beers. Food available *daily*. Open fires and disabled access. Two riverside terraces.

BOAT TRIPS
Kennet Horse Boat Co. 1 Holt Road, Kintbury RG17 9UY (01488 658866; www.kennet-horse-boat.co.uk). Horse-drawn and motor barge. *Two hour* public trips *mid Apr–Sep* on the motor barge ***Avon*** from Newbury Wharf. Also 1½ *hour* Trips from Kintbury on the horse-drawn barge ***Kennet Valley***, of varying durations, operating *daily from Easter–Sep*. Tea, coffee, bar and catering facilities on board. Private charter. Telephone for further details. Booking advisable. Also day boat hire available aboard ***nb Cygnet***.

Woolhampton Swing Bridge (see page 103)

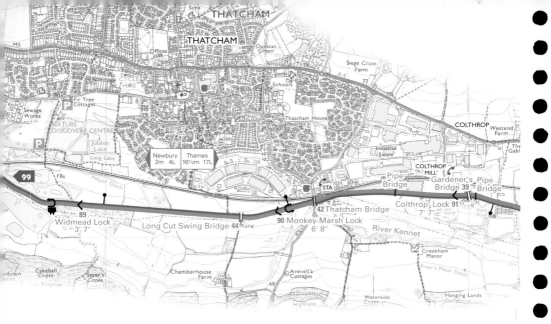

Thatcham

Beyond Bull's Lock and the railway bridge the canal now runs very straight through isolated water meadows towards Thatcham. The village itself is a mile to the north west but the station is conveniently close beside the navigation. This section of the waterway probably best serves to illustrate the wide variety of restoration work jointly undertaken by a consortium made up of county and district councils, job creation programmes, the then British Waterways and the Kennet and Avon Canal Trust, who have been at the forefront of fund raising for more than 30 years. For example, Heale's Lock to the east and Bull's Lock to the west have both been rebuilt with consortium labour, while Widmead Lock was reconstructed to a very high standard by outside contractors at a cost in excess of £385,000. The many swing bridges have either been totally rebuilt or, in some cases, replaced by a high-level structure: Colthrop Bridge being privately funded. Old Monkey Marsh Lock, one of only two remaining examples of a turf-sided lock, has been listed as an ancient monument by English Heritage. It is now restored with iron-piling to two feet above low-water level, turf-lined banks sloping to the top of the lock, together with a timber framework to delineate the actual lock chamber when full. The lock should be left empty after use.

● **Thatcham**
Berks. All services. The main square of this rapidly expanding village, now almost a suburb of Newbury, is all but dominated by sprawling housing development. Set back from the A4, it manages to retain some peace which carries over into the nearby cluster of older buildings grouped at the east end of the pretty Victorian church and churchyard.
Nature Discovery Centre Muddy Lane, Lower Way, Thatcham RG19 3FU (01635 874381;

www.rspb.org.uk/reserves/guide/t/thatcham/about.aspx). North of Widmead Lock.
A centre for the study of the unique lake and reed bed habitats of the area, rare moths and large Reed and Sedge Warbler populations. A multi-activity base where children (and adults) can make their own discoveries and have the chance to get a bird's eye view of the world. Shop and café. *Open 11.00–16.00 winter and 10.00–17.00 during summer.* The visitor centre is *closed Mon. Seasonal* adjustments – telephone for details.

- **Woolhampton**

Berks. PO, tel, stores, garage, station. A village on the A4 that owes its existence to the days of mail coaches on the old Bath road. There is a good mixture of buildings in the main street, several pubs and hotels. Up on the hill to the north of the village are the Victorian church, the Georgian buildings of Woolhampton Park and Douai Abbey and School, the latter a fine group of 19th-C buildings with more recent additions.

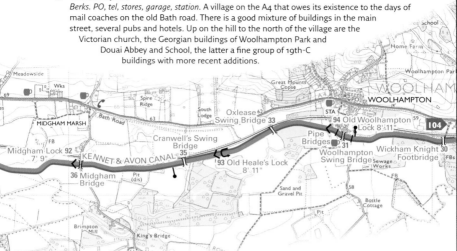

NAVIGATIONAL NOTES

1 **Woolhampton Lock** The current below the lock can cause problems, so take care! When approaching **upstream** set the lock before swinging the bridge, head into the current, turning into the lock at the last moment. When coming **downstream** swing the bridge before leaving the tail of the lock and aim straight for the skewed bridge. **Ensure that the bridge is fully open.**

Pubs and Restaurants

⬤✕Swan Station Road, Thatcham RG19 4QL (01635 862084; www.swanpubthatcham.co.uk). Food *available all day*. Real ales. Outside seating. Children and dogs welcome. B&B.

⬤Crickets 24 High Street, Thatcham RG19 3JD (01635 862113). Real ales are served in a pub that takes sport very seriously: a cricket and a football team are based at this establishment. No children or dogs. *Open all day.*

⬤✕White Hart 2 High Street, Thatcham RG19 3JD (01635 863251) Old coaching inn, dating back more than 350 years. Real ales. Excellent home-made food served *Tue–Sat L and E and Sun & Mon L*. Children welcome if eating. Patio. B&B.

⬤Kings Head 59 The Broadway, Thatcham RG19 3HP (01635 862145). Real ales. Garden and children's play area. Pool room. Darts and crib. Music *weekends*. B&B. *Open all day.*

⬤✕Angel Inn Bath Road, Woolhampton RG7 5RT (0118 971 3307; www.thea4angel.com). An imposing ivy-clad building in the centre of the village. Award-winning restaurant. Sports lounge and beer garden. *Open Mon–Thur L and E and all day Fri–Sun.*

⬤Falmouth Arms Bath Road, Woolhampton RG7 5RT (0118 971 3202). Bar meals available *L and E (except Sun E)* together with *Sun* roasts and real ale. Children welcome during eating hours and dogs welcome outside eating hours. Patio area. Darts and pool. B&B.

⬤✕Rowbarge Station Road, Woolhampton RG7 5SH (0118 971 2213; www.brunningandprice. co.uk/rowbarge). Popular canalside pub offering both restaurant and bar food *all day, every day*. Renown for its wide range of real ales and selection of malt whiskies. Children and dogs welcome. Large riverside garden. Mooring nearby.

Aldermaston

At Aldermaston Wharf there is a mechanically operated lift bridge carrying a busy road into the Village. There is also ample car parking for the attractive canal-side tearooms, shop and Information Centre (0118 971 2868; www.kennetandavonaldermaston.co.uk) which are open all the year round. The navigation remains close to the railway and A4 which have both shared its course for many miles. The canal heads north east, constantly joining and rejoining the River Kennet. The moorings at Tyle Mill are administered, together with many others on this waterway, by CRT: telephone 0303 040 4040 for further details. Beyond Tyle Mill are a series of gravel pits, excavated since 1960, which offer an undisturbed habitat for all forms of wildlife. The nature reserves of Cumber Lake to the north and Woolwich Green Lake to the south can both be reached by a short walk from Sulhamstead Lock. A pleasant, tree-lined straight cut takes the navigation through wooded fields towards Sulhamstead. Further woods and pasture land lead to Theale Swing Bridge; the village is 3/4 mile to the north. Fortunately, since the completion of the M4, this bridge has reverted to carrying relatively infrequent road vehicles, so the passage of a boat no longer causes a major traffic hold-up.

Boatyards

®**Froud's Bridge Marina** Froud's Lane, Aldermaston RG7 4LH (0118 971 4508/07831 472636; www.froudsbridge.com). 🛉🛉♨DE Pump out, gas, overnight mooring, long-term mooring, winter storage, boat sales, toilets, showers, chandlery, books, maps, gifts, solid fuel, engineering
®**ABC Leisure** Aldermaston Wharf, Padworth, Reading RG7 4JS (0118 971 4123; www.readingmarine.co.uk). 🛉🛉♨DE Pump out, gas, narrowboat hire, solid fuel, cranage facilities, hard standing, DIY facilities, short and long term mooring, shop, chandlery, books, maps and gifts, boat sales and repairs, engine sales and repairs.

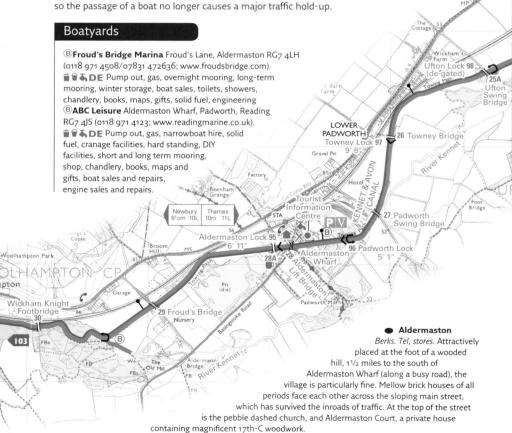

Newbury	Thames
8½m 10L	10m 11L

● **Aldermaston**
Berks. Tel, stores. Attractively placed at the foot of a wooded hill, 1½ miles to the south of Aldermaston Wharf (along a busy road), the village is particularly fine. Mellow brick houses of all periods face each other across the sloping main street, which has survived the inroads of traffic. At the top of the street is the pebble dashed church, and Aldermaston Court, a private house containing magnificent 17th-C woodwork.

● **Aldermaston Wharf**
Berks. Station. A small canalside settlement bisected by the busy A340. The old swing bridge has been replaced with a hydraulic lift bridge, push button operated with the aid of a Watermate key. It cost the local council £250,000 to build.

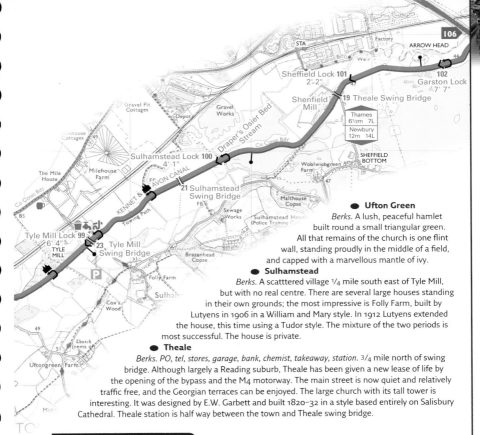

● **Ufton Green**
Berks. A lush, peaceful hamlet built round a small triangular green. All that remains of the church is one flint wall, standing proudly in the middle of a field, and capped with a marvellous mantle of ivy.

● **Sulhamstead**
Berks. A scatttered village 1/4 mile south east of Tyle Mill, but with no real centre. There are several large houses standing in their own grounds; the most impressive is Folly Farm, built by Lutyens in 1906 in a William and Mary style. In 1912 Lutyens extended the house, this time using a Tudor style. The mixture of the two periods is most successful. The house is private.

● **Theale**
Berks. PO, tel, stores, garage, bank, chemist, takeaway, station. 3/4 mile north of swing bridge. Although largely a Reading suburb, Theale has been given a new lease of life by the opening of the bypass and the M4 motorway. The main street is now quiet and relatively traffic free, and the Georgian terraces can be enjoyed. The large church with its tall tower is interesting. It was designed by E.W. Garbett and built 1820–32 in a style based entirely on Salisbury Cathedral. Theale station is half way between the town and Theale swing bridge.

Pubs and Restaurants

Hind's Head Wasing Lane, Aldermaston RG7 4LX (0118 971 2194; www.hindsheadaldermaston. co.uk). An imposing building which faces up the main street. Formerly the Congreve Arms, until it changed hands following the devastation of a great fire. The Hind's Head once brewed its own beer, selling at 2d a pint; real ales are still dispensed at the bar. Good food available in both bar and attractive dining room *L and E Mon–Fri and all day Sat & Sun (until 18.00 Sun)*. Garden. Children welcome. B&B.

Butt Inn Aldermaston Wharf, Station Road, Aldermaston RG7 4LA (0118 971 3309; www. thebuttinn.biz). 100yds walk from Aldermaston Lift Bridge 28. Serving real ales and appetising meals *L and E daily* together with *Sun* roasts. Children and dogs welcome. Large garden with patio. B&B. *Open all day (not Mon L)*. Food *available 12.00– 21.00 (Sun 18.00)*.

Spring Inn Bath Road, Sulhamstead RG7 5HP (0118 930 3440; www.thespringinn.co.uk). 1/2 mile north of Tyle Mill. Pub/restaurant serving real ale, bar meals and à la carte menu. Food

available *12.00-22.00 daily*. Children welcome. *Open all day, every day*.

Crown Inn 2 Church Street, Theale RG7 5BT (0118 930 2310; www.thecrowntheale.co.uk). A community pub serving a wide variety of real ales, some from local micro breweries. Family friendly with a quiz *alternate Thur* and live music *Wed*. There is a large, peaceful garden. Also home to the Crown Dynasty Chinese takeaway.

Falcon 31 High Street, Theale RG7 5AH (0118 930 2523). Old-fashioned 18th-C pub, sporting several friendly ghosts who appear to bar staff and customers alike from time to time. Real ales. Food *available L*. Open fires and disabled access. Children and dogs welcome. Traditional pub games. Garden. *Open all day*.

Volunteer 65 Church Street, Theale RG7 5BX (0118 930 2489; www.thevolunteertheale.co.uk). Large, friendly pub serving real ales and appetising food *L and E Mon-Fri; all day Sat & Sun L*. Attractive garden for summer and open fires for winter. *Open all day (closes 19.00 Sun)*. Large pub serving real ale and food *L and E daily*.

Reading

The M4 motorway and the railway inevitably affect the peace and quiet of this section, although almost to the outskirts of Reading the gravel pits bring a degree of serenity. The Kennet winds through water meadows, the straight stretches marking the canal sections. Continuing east, the navigation passes Burghfield Bridge, a handsome stone arch. The river gradually approaches the town, descending Fobney Lock and passing through Fobney Meadow, before beginning to wriggle its way through the outskirts. At County Lock the navigation passes over a low weir which at times of fresh water can become quite ferocious. Rows of riverside cottages and a surprising variety of bridges decorate the Kennet in Reading, High Bridge being the most central access point. The river cuts across the middle of the town and so access to all facilities is easy. However, the waterway through Reading is narrow, shallow and fast flowing, being a river navigation; also there are several sharp blind bends (now reduced as a result of the Oracle Development, *see* page 108). This section is controlled by traffic lights – boaters should not proceed until a green light is displayed. A variety of new developments complement the river's passage through this part of the town.

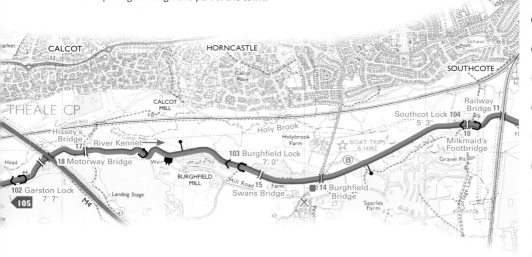

The Kennet leads north east out of the centre of Reading, passing Blake's Lock, the only lock maintained by the Environment Agency that is not actually on the Thames. Soon the Kennet approaches its junction with the Thames which is marked by a gasometer and the main railway, which runs parallel with the south bank of the river.

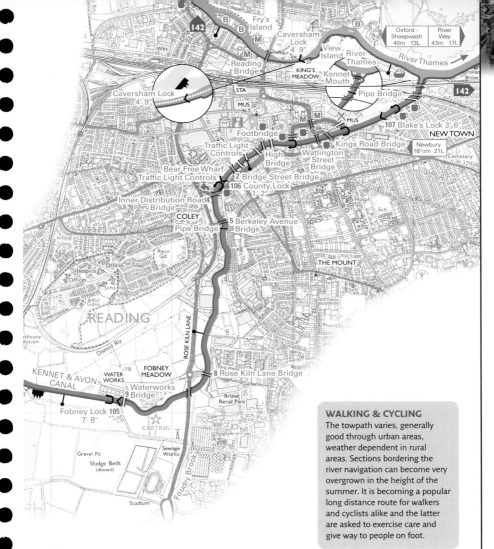

Oxford - Sheepwash	River Wey
40m 13L	43m 17L

WALKING & CYCLING

The towpath varies, generally good through urban areas, weather dependent in rural areas. Sections bordering the river navigation can become very overgrown in the height of the summer. It is becoming a popular long distance route for walkers and cyclists alike and the latter are asked to exercise care and give way to people on foot.

NAVIGATIONAL NOTES

1 See Navigational notes on page 70 before heading west from Reading.

2 **Fobney Lock** – care should be taken when using the landing stage below the lock as a strong weir stream flows at right angles.

3 To operate County Lock 106 it is advisable to first moor under the Inner Distribution Road Bridge, on the east side, to drop off crew to set the lock. Once prepared, power into the lock to avoid being swept to the west side of the river, towards the weir and away from the lock entrance.

4 River Thames licences are obtainable from the Environment Agency (*see* page 110).

5 For up-to-date information on lock closures, the Thames winter works programme and flood conditions, telephone the EA Navigation Information Line on 0845 988 1188.

Seend Cleeve (see page 80)

BOAT TRIPS

Canal & Tipi Experience Honeysuckle Cottage, Picklepythe Lane, Beenham, Reading, RG7 5NT (07713 687766/07740 492842; www.canalandtipiexperience.com). Narrowboat hire and boat handling courses. Also camping in tipis.

Kennet Cruises 14 Beech Lane, Earley, Reading RG6 5PT (0118 987 1115; www.kennetcruises.co.uk) operate public trips aboard *nb Lancing* from the Cunning Man at Burghfield Bridge, Aldermaston and Reading town centre. Also private charter, special events and short- and long-term moorings.

Reading

Berks. All services. The town lies at the extremity of the Berkshire Downs and the Chiltern Hills, where the Thames becomes a major river. It is the Victorian architecture that makes this town interesting, as the university buildings are not to everyone's taste. Since completion of the Oracle Development, in the centre of Reading, the towpath along the Kennet is continuous from the Thames throughout the town.

Abbey Ruins Abbey Street, Reading RG1 3BA Fragmentary remains of this 12th-C abbey built by Henry I lie on the edge of Forbury Park. The 13th-C gatehouse, altered by Scott in 1869, still stands.

Film Theatre Palmer Building, Whiteknights, Reading RG6 2AH (0118 378 7151; www.readingfilmtheatre.co.uk). Imaginative programme of non-mainstream cinema, showing approximately four times a week. Visit Tourist Information for up-to-date details.

Gaol Forbury Road. Designed by Scott and Moffatt in 1842–4 in the Scottish Baronial style. Oscar Wilde wrote *De Profundis* while imprisoned here.

Reading Museum The Town Hall, Blagrave Street, Reading RG1 1QH (0118 937 3400; www.readingmuseum.org.uk). Features *The Story of Reading*, tracing the town's development from a Saxon settlement on the River Kennet to the present day. Special features include a reconstructed section of the abbey and the Oracle gates entrance to the 17th-C workhouse. In the upper gallery is a full 230ft sweep of Britain's Bayeux Tapestry, Reading's faithful replica of the 11th-C original. *Open Tue–Sat 10.00-16.00; Sun & B Hol Mon 11.00–16.00.* Free. Palmers Café *open Mon–Sat 10.00–15.00.*

Museum of English Rural Life University of Reading, Redlands Road, Reading RG1 5EX (0118 378 8660; www.reading.ac.uk/merl/). All aspects of rural life in England as it was lived around 150 to

175 years ago, before the invention of the tractor. *Open Tue–Fri 09.00–17.00, Sat–Sun 14.00–16.30.* Small charge.

Riverside Museum Blakes Lock, off Kenavon Drive, Reading RG1 3DH (0118 939 9800; www.readingmuseum.org.uk). Attractive museum in the city's old sewerage pumping station, originally constructed in 1873 when the disposal of local sewerage was described as being 'very imperfect and unsatisfactory; injurious to public health'. Today the museum explores the story of Reading's two rivers and displays a gipsy caravan constructed on the banks of the Kennet. The old turbine house offers panoramic views out over the river. *Open Tue–Sat 10.00–16.00; Sun & B Hol Mon 11.00–16.00.* Free.

South Street Arts Centre 21 South Street, Reading RG1 4QU (0118 960 6060; www.readingarts.com). A wide-ranging programme of music (all types), workshops and drama in a lively arts centre which also incorporates: **Macdevitt's Bar** *Open* for drinks and light refreshments before performances. **Hexagon** Queen's Walk, Reading RG1 7UA (0118 960 6060). Mainstream theatre, pantomime, films, shows and art exhibitions. **Reading Buses** (0118 959 4000; www.reading-buses.co.uk). Information on urban and rural services.
Tourist Information Visit www.livingreading.co.uk.

Pubs and Restaurants

✗**Sally's Café** Burghfield, near Reading RG30 3RD (0118 939 4885). Opposite the Cunning Man, also known as Judges Café. *Open Mon–Sat 07.00–15.00 & Sun 07.30–14.00* for breakfasts, snacks, meals and takeaways.
🍺✗**Cunning Man** Burghfield, near Reading RG30 3RB (0118 959 8067; www.vintageinn.co.uk). Country pub and restaurant with large canalside garden. Food available *L and E, daily*.
🍺**Hook & Tackle** Kategrove Lane, Reading RG1 2ND (0118 950 0830). South east of County Lock, beyond Inner Distribution Road (via pedestrian underpass). Situated below the noise from Reading's over-zealous flirtation with the motor car, this pub offers sanctuary, together with a selection of real ales. Substantial portions of inexpensive, home-made food are available *Tue–Fri L and E and all day Sat & Sun*. Children welcome *until 19.30*. Garden. Sport TV. Traditional pub games. *Open all day*.
🍺**Sweeney & Todd** 10 Castle Street (off St Mary's Butts), Reading RG1 7RD (0118 958 6466). Something of a local institution – a pub integrated with a pie shop and dispensing real ale. Excellent, inexpensive food *L and E. Open all day, closed Sun*.
🍺**Eldon Arms** 19 Eldon Terrace, Reading RG1 4DX (0118 957 3857). Traditional town pub managed by the same landlords for more than 30 years selling real ales and cider. Food available *Mon–Sat L*. Traditional pub games and *occasional* live music. Quiz *1st Mon of month. Open L and E*. Buses 19, 22, 144.
🍺**Hop Leaf** 163–165 Southampton Street, Reading RG1 2QZ (0118 931 4700; www.hopback.co.uk). Thriving town local, serving a selection of their own real ales. Outside seating. Children's room and traditional pub games, bar billiards and darts. *Open all day*. Regular events.

🍺**Hobgoblin** 2 Broad Street, Reading RG1 2BH (0118 950 8119). Constantly changing range of real ales. Real Cider. No children. *Open all day, every day*. Outside seating.
🍺**Retreat** 8 St John's Street, Reading RG1 4EH (0118 957 1593; www.retreatpub.co.uk). Real ale along with peace and quiet in this cosy pub. Live music *Thur* and traditional pub games. Children allowed at landlord's discretion.
🍺**Zerodegrees** 9 Bridge Street, Reading RG1 2LR (0118 959 7959; www.zerodegrees.co.uk). Constructed around a micro brewery, this open plan pub serves a range of their own real ales together with pizzas from a wood-fired oven and food that compliments their beer. Customers can sit on comfy sofas and imbibe the smells from the shiny brewing vessels, admiring the exposed beams and ducting. Outside seating. *Open all day;* food available *12.00–21.30*.
🍺✗**Bel And The Dragon** Blake's Lock, Gas Works Road, Reading (0118 951 5790; www.belandthedragon-reading.co.uk). Pub and eatery housed in a former biscuit factory. Food available *Mon–Sat L and E and all day Sun*. Real ales. Beer Garden. Children and dogs welcome. *Open all day*.
🍺**Fisherman's Cottage** 224 Kennetside, Reading RG1 3DW (0118 957 1553; www.fishermanscottagereading.co.uk). Pretty 18th-C canalside pub, west of Blake's Lock. Real ale. Food available (with a Thai twist) *Mon–Fri L and E; Sat & Sun 12.00–18.00*. Children welcome. Canalside seating. Open fires. Mooring.
🍺**Jolly Anglers** 314–316 Kennetside, Reading RG1 3EA (0118 376 7823; www.thejollyanglers.com). East of Blake's Lock. There is a quaint façade to this pub which marks the last refreshment point before the Thames. Real ales, Ciders (regarded as Reading's cider centre) and Belgian beers. Fresh food available *daily 12.00–22.00 (Sun 20.00)*.

RIVER THAMES

FROM INGLESHAM TO TEDDINGTON:
The Environment Agency
03708 506 506
enquiries@environment-agency.gov.uk

Before you set out on the river your boat must be registered with the Environment Agency and be displaying a current licence.

Short-period registrations are available for boats visiting the River Thames. These can be purchased at many of the locks as you come onto the river, or in advance. Contact the Environment Agency on 03708 506 506 for further details or download an application form at www.environment-agency.gov.uk/boatregthames.

River Thames – a user's guide is a useful publication for all river users. You can download a copy of the user's guide from the Environment Agency website www.environment-agency.gov.uk.
Boats must comply with the *Boat Safety Scheme*. Telephone 0333 202 1000 or visit www.boatsafetyscheme.org for more information.

Water points Most water points have no hose connectors and are suitable for containers only.

Electric recharging Locks which have recharging points are indicated on the maps. Arrive before 16.00 to arrange use, or telephone ahead. A mooring charge is made.

Pollution If you notice any pollution, notify the relevant Waterway Office (numbers below), a lock keeper or call 0800 80 70 60.

Speed Limit This is 8 kilometres per hour (approx 5 miles per hour), the same as a brisk walking pace, or slower if your wash could cause damage to the riverbank or small craft.

BELOW TEDDINGTON:
Port of London Authority
London River House
Royal Pier Road
Gravesend
Kent DA12 2BG
01474 562200; www.pla.co.uk

All river users are governed by the *Port of London River Bye-laws*. The Port of London Authority (PLA) issues *River Thames Recreational Users Guide*. Copies of both documents can be obtained by telephoning the above number or downloaded from the website.

All river movements on the tidal section of the river covered by this guide are under the control of London VTS who can be contacted by telephone on 020 8855 0315 and VHF channel 14.

All vessels over 45ft (13.7 metres) must carry VHF radio and boat owners are reminded that they should hold an appropriate licence to operate such equipment. The only exception to this rule is for narrow boats over 45ft in transit between Teddington and Limehouse.

MAXIMUM DIMENSIONS
Below Oxford
Length: 120'
Beam: 17' 6"
Above Oxford
Length: 109' 10"
Beam: 14' 8"

MILEAGES:
INGLESHAM Junction with the Thames & Severn Canal to:
Lechlade: ½ mile
Newbridge: 17½ miles
Kings Lock *Junction with Duke's Cut, Oxford Canal*: 27½ miles
Oxford *Junction with Oxford Canal (Isis Lock)*: 30½ miles
Abingdon Lock: 39½ miles
Wallingford Bridge: 53½ miles
Reading *Junction with Kennet & Avon Canal*: 70½ miles
Marlow Lock: 87½ miles
Windsor Bridge: 100½ miles
Shepperton *Junction with River Wey*: 114 miles
Teddington Lock: 125½ miles
Brentford *Junction with Grand Union Canal*: 130½ miles
Limehouse Basin *Junction with Regent's Canal and River Lee*: 146½ miles

The Thames enjoys a special place in the hearts and minds of the English. Stretching for 215 miles from west to east and flowing past the seat of government, it links the Cotswolds, in the centre of the country, with the nation's bustling capital city. Its importance was recognised by the Romans, who built Watling Street, the Fosse Way, Ermine Street and the Icknield Way to cross the river. When the Romans left, London's population declined, and its significance diminished. It was not until the 15th C that the capital began to grow into a great trading centre, eventually becoming the largest port in the world. Goods were shipped inland from the capital – carried up-river by horse-drawn or sailing barges.

Weirs were built on the river, often in places where they hindered navigation, to power mills, and these caused constant disputes between millers and the barge men. Some weirs, known as flash locks, had movable sections to allow barges to pass through. But even then the barge men would have to wait for the fierce rush of water to subside before passing the weir, or be pulled upstream by winch. Then they would have to wait on the far side for the depth of water to build up again. Legislation tried unsuccessfully to control the building of weirs, and so allow the river to fulfil its important role as a highway, but navigation did not begin to improve until pound locks were introduced on the Thames, one of the first being built at Swift Ditch, near Abingdon, around 1620. By the end of the 18th C the Thames had been linked to the main canal network, thereby affording access to many other parts of England. However, the importance of the river as a transport artery began to diminish with the expansion of the railways.

The Thames once also supplied food, and trout and salmon could be caught readily. The latter were indeed so common they were eaten by the poor. The river was also thick with eels. These would swim up the river in such numbers that they could be caught with sieves and buckets, and were made into a form of cake.

But as the population of London grew, the amount of waste grew with it, and began to accumulate in the streets. Gradually various schemes were devised to channel this into rivers which discharged into the Thames, and these water-courses were then covered, becoming known as 'the lost rivers of London'. At this time there were still fish in the river, but from the early 19th C increasing industrial pollution drove all the salmon and eels from the lower Thames, and there were outbreaks of cholera amongst the population of London. The year 1858 was known as 'The Great Stink'. The Commission of Sewers was established in 1847, and gradually the clean-up began. Recently a vigorous campaign has restored the quality of the water: salmon have returned and amateur fishermen are now a common sight right through central London.

In the 17th and 18th C Frost Fairs were held in London whenever the river froze. There were stalls, performing bears, fairground amusements and ox roasting on the ice. The last fair was held in 1814 – the removal of the old London Bridge, which had the effect of a dam, and the building of the embankments in the 19th C, narrowed the river, and deepened and speeded the flow of water, so that it is now no longer possible for the tidal river to freeze over. Since the early 19th C the river has become the scene of regattas in summer, that at Henley being an international event.

Many Londoners are now aware that their city is sinking at the rate of about twelve inches every 100 years. As long ago as 1236 the river flooded the Palace of Westminster; in 1928 central London was flooded with the loss of 14 lives; and the disastrous surge tide of 1953 left 300 dead along the east coast and Thames estuary. To protect London from this threat the magnificent Thames Flood Barrier was built at Woolwich. Movable barriers can be raised from the river bed to hold back the tide – the four main gates having a span of 200ft and the strength to withstand a load of more than 9000 metric tons. The stainless steel shells housing the machinery are built on hardwood ribs, their design reminiscent of the Sydney Opera House.

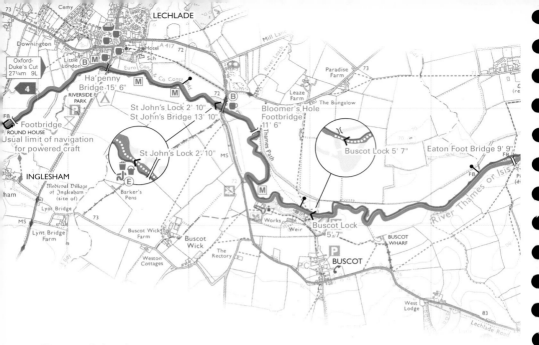

Lechlade

The navigable Thames begins at the Round House, at the junction with the presently unnavigable Thames & Severn Canal (see Nicholson Waterways Guide Severn, Avon & Birmingham) near Inglesham – an attractive group of buildings by the river's edge. Moored craft and all the activities of a riverside park are present as the Thames passes Lechlade, flowing under Ha'penny Bridge, so named because a toll was once taken. The church at Lechlade can be seen for miles around – its tall spire always visible as the river meanders to St John's Lock, the highest on the Thames. Note the modern lock house, the quaint miniature buildings in the lock gardens, and the statue of Father Thames, which once marked the river's source at Thames Head, north of Kemble, Gloucestershire. Below the lock the Thames passes under Bloomers Hole Footbridge, the final link in the Thames Path from Lechlade to London. The river's course then becomes quite extravagant – at one point even doubling back before passing the church and beautiful rectory at Buscot. Beyond Buscot Lock the river is once again in open country, delightfully rural and lonely. The church at Eaton Hastings is by the river and provides interest before reaching Grafton Lock, a remote outpost. A very isolated and rural stretch of river then follows, meandering through meadowland and having little contact with civilisation.

NAVIGATIONAL NOTES

The normal limit of navigation for powered craft on the Thames is usually at the junction with the Thames & Severn Canal, marked by the Round House below Inglesham. Here a full-length narrowboat can wind, taking care to avoid the sandbank on the north side. Those not familiar with the river are urged to proceed no further, even though the right of navigation extends to Cricklade, and craft drawing 2ft 6in may be able to proceed as far as 3 miles above Lechlade when there is plenty of water in the river. The Thames & Severn Canal is currently undergoing restoration.

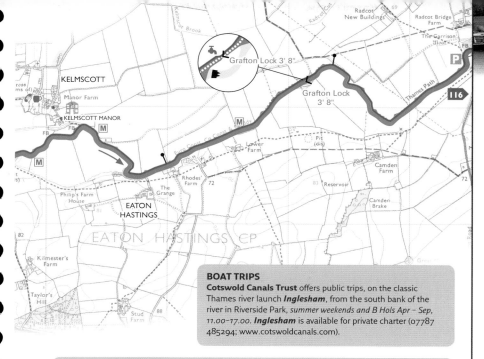

BOAT TRIPS
Cotswold Canals Trust offers public trips, on the classic Thames river launch *Inglesham*, from the south bank of the river in Riverside Park, *summer weekends and B Hols Apr – Sep, 11.00–17.00*. *Inglesham* is available for private charter (07787 485294; www.cotswoldcanals.com).

NATURAL HISTORY IN THE THAMES VALLEY
The Thames is a lowland river throughout its length with few of the striking changes in scenery or gradient that one associates with rivers of the north or west of the country. As a result its landscape is gentle and its flood plain contains woodlands, water meadows and grassland with appropriately modest plant and animal inhabitants. However, the scenery is enriched by the Goring Gap, between Goring and Reading, where during the Ice Ages the river cut a new channel through the south western end of the Chilterns, isolating the Berkshire Downs on the south bank. The river here passes through chalk hills with rich grassland and beech woods of spectacular appearance. Through most of its length the water meadows overlie river gravels; in many places these have been excavated to win gravel for roads and buildings, leaving water-filled pits in which the richest animal life of all the Thames valley can be found. As a result of these natural and man-made habitats there is a great deal of fascinating natural history interest in the Thames and its surroundings.

WALKING & CYCLING
Walking the River begins with the start of the Thames Path at Kemble and full details, including sections available to cyclists, can be downloaded at www.nationaltrail.co.uk/ThamesPath. The path is in good shape throughout the length of the river to London. The ambitious could also look to the and follow the Thames & Severn Canal towpath (and its current diversions) detailed in the Nicholson Waterways Guide: Severn, Avon & Birmingham. This will take you via Cricklade, the Cotswold Water Park, Cirencester, Stroud's Golden Valley all the way to Gloucester and the River Severn. Further details, including ideas for accommodation along the way, can be found under Walking & Cycling on page 119.

Boatyards

Ⓑ**Park End Wharf** Lechlade GL7 3AQ (general enquiries 01367 250013/252229, marina 07761 003828, boat hire 01367 253599; www.riverside-lechlade.co.uk). 🚿🏠⚓P D E Pump out at St John's Lock. Gas, day-hire boats, overnight mooring, long-term mooring, winter storage, slipway, dry dock, crane, boat building, boat and engine sales and repairs, chandlery, toilets, showers, solid fuel. *Emergency call out*. Also fishing tackle and bait, fishing permits, antiques (01367 252832) and B&B (01367 252229).

Abingdon (see pages 128–9)

Inglesham

Wilts. A marvellous architectural group around the church. Although of late Saxon origin, the present building is largely 13th-C. William Morris was responsible for the remarkably original state of the building – he loved it and saved it from 19th-C restoration. There are the remains of a rare painted 13th-C reredos, box pews, and an ancient carving of the Mother and Child. The adjoining farm was once the priory. On the north bank the Inglesham Round House is a notable landmark. It once belonged to the lock keeper on the presently unnavigable Thames & Severn Canal, which joins the river at this point.

Thames & Severn Canal Stretching almost 29 miles between Inglesham and Wallbridge, Stroud, where it joins the Stroudwater Canal and, in turn, the Goucester & Sharpness Canal. This trade link was initially closed to navigation in 1893, but remedial works were carried out and it re-opened. Taken over by Gloucestershire CC in 1901, the last laden boat crossed the summit level in 1911 and its abandonment was finally confirmed by Act of Parliament in 1933. This heavily locked canal rises to 300ft above sea level, where the Sapperton Tunnel burrows under the Cotswolds for 3808yds. Now undergoing active restoration, it is hoped that it will eventually form part of a Cotswold Ring, linking with the Gloucester & Sharpness, River Avon, Stratford-on-Avon, Grand Union, Oxford and Thames. For more information visit www.cotswoldcanals.com.

Lechlade

Glos. PO, shops. A golden grey market town dominating the river in all directions and best seen from St John's Bridge, with the tall spire of the Perpendicular wool church rising above the surrounding cluster of buildings. Shelley's Walk leads from the river to the church, where his *Stanzas in a Summer Churchyard* is quoted on a plaque in the churchyard wall. Shelley, Peacock, Mary Godwin and Charles Clairmont stayed in Lechlade in 1815, after rowing from Windsor.

Bloomers Hole Footbridge Completing the Thames Path National Trail, this bridge, although built of steel, is clad with timber. It was lowered into place by a Chinook helicopter from RAF Brize Norton.

Little Faringdon Mill (GL7 3Q) One mile outside Lechlade on the A361 to Burford. A perfect 18th-C mill in its original state, with a farm and outbuildings. Private.

Buscot

Oxon. A small village off the A417, notable for the very beautiful Queen Anne rectory (private) which stands on the riverside by the church, itself unremarkable apart from its Burne-Jones windows. The National Trust owns a picnic site by the weir pool.

Buscot Old Parsonage Buscot, Faringdon SN7 8DQ (www.nationaltrust.org.uk). A Cotswold stone building of 1703 on the river bank. *Open only by written appointment with the tenant. Please mark envelope 'NT Booking'.*

Buscot Park Faringdon SN7 8BU (0845 240932; www.buscot-park.com). Built about 1780 in the Adam style by Edward Loveden Townsend, with a park and gardens laid out by Harold Peto. In 1859 the estate was aquired by Robert Tertius Campbell, and he embarked upon a scheme to make it one of the most advanced farms of its time. His major crop was sugar beet, and he installed 6 miles of railway track to aid harvesting. He also built a distillery on Brandy Island (*see* Buscot Wharf), a gasworks and concrete farm buildings. However these works exhausted his resources, and he became bankrupt. Fine furniture and The Faringdon Collection of Paintings, including works by Rembrandt and Murillo were later bought by Sir Alexander Henderson, First Lord Faringdon. The Second Lord Faringdon continued collecting, and restored much of the original character to the house. The Italianate Water Garden was created by Harold Peto during the 20th C. Opening dates vary according to season. Telephone to confirm or check website. Groups should telephone to book. There is a tearoom on site. Charge. NT.

Buscot Wharf Little trace remains of the wharf from which brandy was shipped to France. The short arm was known as Buscot Pill.

Tourist Information Centre Corn Exchange, Gloucester Street, Faringdon SN7 7HL (01367 242191; www.faringdon.org) *Open Mon-Fri 09.00-14.00 & Sat 09.30-13.00.*

● **Kelmscott**
Oxon. A pristine village of elegant grey stone houses, firmly entrenched against development. The quiet 15th-C church has a strong medieval atmosphere.

Kelmscott Manor Kelmscott, Lechlade GL7 3HJ (01367 252486; www.kelmscottmanor.org.uk). A beautiful house behind high walls, built in 1570, and added to in 1665. It became the summer home of William Morris from 1871 until his death in 1896, and he adored it, saying it had 'quaint garrets amongst great timbers of the roof, where of old times the tillers and herdsmen slept'. He shared it with Dante Gabriel Rossetti until 1874. William Morris was buried in the churchyard at Kelmscott after his death in Hammersmith; his tomb is the work of Philip Webb. The Manor and garden are *open Apr-Oct , Wed & Sat 11.00-17.00. Last entry 16.30.* Charge.

● **Eaton Hastings**
Oxon. Quite inaccessible from the river. The 13th-C church is well situated by the water – the rest of the village is a mile away.

Pubs and Restaurants

⬤The Riverside Park End Wharf, Lechlade GL7 3AQ (01367 252534; www.riverside-lechlade.com). This pub sits amidst a pleasant mix of boats and antiques, beside Ha'penny Bridge. Food *available daily 12.00-20.00.* Real ales. Riverside terrace. B&B.

⬤✕The Swan 7 Burford Street, Lechlade GL7 3AP (01367 253571; www.swan.110mb.com). Cosy and peaceful stone-built pub, the oldest in Lechlade. Real ale. Food served *L and E (not Sun E).* Children welcome. B&B.

⬤The Crown Inn High Street, Lechlade GL7 3AE (01367 252198; www.crownlechlade.co.uk). Popular 16th-C coaching inn, with open fires and serving a choice of real ale. *Sun L only.* Children are welcome and there is a garden. Live bands *Fri and Sat.* Micro brewery in garden. B&B.

✕♀Colleys High Street, Lechlade GL7 3AE (01367 252218; www.colleyslechlade.co.uk). Restaurant/café in a 16th-C coaching inn, serving excellent meals *L and E. Booking advisable.*

⬤✕New Inn Hotel Market Place, Lechlade GL7 3AB (01367 252296; www.newinnhotel.com). Attractive pub by the church and the river. Real ale. Bar meals and à la carte restaurant from traditional dishes to the exotic, available *L and E.* Children over 5 years old are welcome and there is a large garden with a play area. There are shower facilities here. B&B.

⬤✕Pino's Italian Restaurant High Street, Lechlade GL7 3AD (01367 252373; www.arkells.com). Until recently the Red Lion, this friendly old coaching inn serves meals *Tue-Sun 12.00-14.30 & 18.00 – 22.00.* Real ales. Children welcome. Outside patio seating. B&B.

⬤✕The Trout Inn St John's Bridge, Faringdon Road, Lechlade GL7 3HA (01367 252313; www.thetroutinn.com). A justly famous 13th-C Cotswold stone pub, with plenty of wood panelling, low beams and stuffed fish. Real ale. Tasty home-made bar meals served in the bar or dining area *L and E.* Live jazz *Tue and Sun E.* Large riverside garden borders the weir stream, marquee available for special events. An intriguing old Oxfordshire game called Aunt Sally is played in the garden. Children welcome. There are fishing rights on 2 miles of the Thames. Tractor and steam rally *first weekend in June.* Music weekend *last weekend in June,* a jazz festival is usually held the following weekend (*usually first weekend in July*), and there is a folk festival *last weekend in July. Cover bands every Fri E.* Rowing boats, punts, electric boats and cruisers for hire. Mooring.

⬤✕The Plough at Kelmscott Kelmscott GL7 3HG (01367 253543; www.ploughkelmscott.co.uk). A fine 16th-C restaurant and bar with flagstone floors, serving real ale. Restaurant, with à la carte menu, and home-made bar meals served *L and E.* Children and dogs welcome, and there is a garden. Spit roasts *Sun L in summer.* Live bands *weekends.* B&B.

Tadpole

A very isolated, rural stretch of river, meandering through meadowland and having little contact with civilisation. The river divides at Radcot where two fine bridges, the ever popular Swan Hotel and a large picnic area opposite are always busy with visitors on summer afternoons. Caravans line the north bank as once more the Thames enters open meadowland around Radcot Lock and then meanders on to the splendid Rushey Lock, with its charming house and fine garden, and the handsome 18th-C Tadpole Bridge. Then again the Thames enters lonely country, passing to the south of Chimney. It is about as far away from it all as you can get on the river.

> **WALKING & CYCLING**
> There is a variety of footpaths from either Old Man's Bridge or Rushey Lock to Bampton.

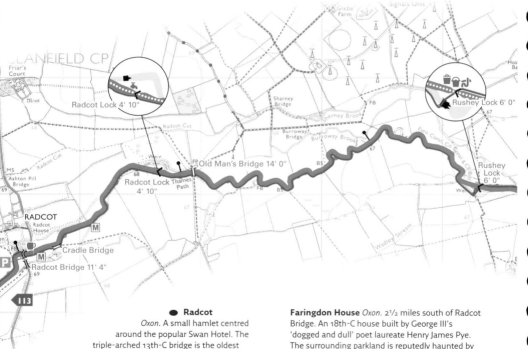

● **Radcot**
Oxon. A small hamlet centred around the popular Swan Hotel. The triple-arched 13th-C bridge is the oldest surviving on the Thames. The single-arched bridge spanning the navigation channel, an artificial cut, was built later, in 1787. The old bridge, made of Taynton stone, was the scene of a Civil War skirmish, when Prince Rupert's Royalist cavalry pounced on Cromwell's men, marching to an attack on Faringdon. Upstream caravans line the north bank – to the south picnics and tents sprawl across the meadow during the summer.

Faringdon House *Oxon*. 2½ miles south of Radcot Bridge. An 18th-C house built by George III's 'dogged and dull' poet laureate Henry James Pye. The surrounding parkland is reputedly haunted by a headless Hampden Pye, an earlier member of the family who was decapitated at sea. His story is recalled in *The Ingoldsby Legends*, 1840. The folly on Faringdon Hill, an octagonal Gothic lantern, was built by the artist and author Lord Berners in 1935.

● **Bampton**
Oxon. PO, stores, takeaway. An attractive greystone town 1½ miles from the river, easily approached by a variety of footpaths or by road north from

Pubs and Restaurants

X⅁**Biztro Wheelgate House** Market Square, Bampton OX18 2JH (01993 851151; www.biztro. co.uk). Good food, locally sourced where possible, and a comprehensive wine list make this an excellent place to eat, with its generous portions. Friendly service and B&B. *Open Tue–Sat 12.00–14.30 & 19.00–22.30.*

X**Bampton Coffee House** Temple Market Square, Bampton OX18 2JH (01993 850929). All day breakfasts, paninis and jacket potatoes, freshly made sandwiches and baguettes, coffees, teas and pastries and a variety of light meals and snacks. *Open Mon–Sat 08.00–15.00/16.00.*

The Swan Hotel Radcot Bridge, Bampton OX18 2SX (01367 810220; www.swanhotelradcot.co.uk). Comfortable and friendly old inn of great character, beside what was once a wharf. Real ale. Meals available *L and E*. Children are welcome, and there is a pleasant garden. Moorings, narrowboat hire (01793 702043; www.navigatorholidays.com), fishing permits, caravanning and camping.

X**The Trout at Tadpole Bridge** Buckland Marsh, Faringdon SN7 8RF (01367 870382; www. trout-inn.co.uk). Fine traditional riverside pub serving real ale, along with modern British food *L and E*. Excellent wine list. Children welcome, and there is a well-tended riverside garden. B&B.

Morris Clown High Street, Bampton OX18 2JW (01993 850217). Fine 12th-C pub serving real ale. Children welcome.

X**The Romany Inn** Bridge Street, Bampton OX18 2HA (01993 850237; www.theromanyinnbampton.co.uk). There are Saxon arches in the cellar of this fine old pub, which is a 19th-C listed building. Real ale. Restaurant meals available *L and E*. Children welcome. Garden B&B.

Try also **The Bampton Hotel** Bridge Street, Bampton OX18 2HA (01993 850326)

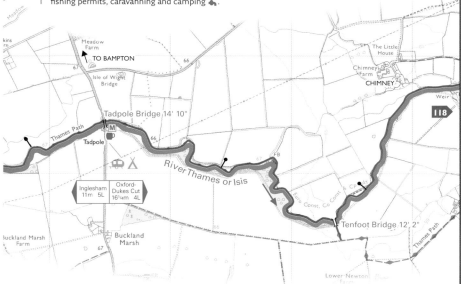

Tadpole. It has a timeless appearance in that much of the new development is built from the same materials as, and often in a style similar to, the old. The result is both unusual and pleasing. The church, largely 13th- and 14th-C, has a slightly uneasy octagonal spire. Beside the church is the old grammar school, founded in 1653. At one time the town was called Bampton in the Bush – a description dating from before the 18th C when no roads served the community. Morris dancing is reputed to have originated here.

● **Buckland**
Oxon. About a mile south of Tadpole Bridge. A village intimately connected with Buckland House, and best approached from the river, as there is a fine view over the Thames Valley. **Buckland House** Built in 1757 by Wood of Bath, it is one of the most imposing 18th-C homes in Oxfordshire, although the wings were added in 1910. There is a Gothic stable in the park. Private.

Newbridge

The navigation channel passes through a tree-lined cut to Shifford Lock, the last lock to be built on the Thames, in 1898. Again the countryside is flat, glimpsed here and there over the steep river banks which are in places heavily overgrown. Electricity pylons do little to improve the scene. Welcome relief appears at Newbridge, with a fine pub on each side of the handsome old bridge. The nearest village is Standlake, a mile to the north. As the hills close in from the east the countryside gradually loses much of the bleakness of the upper reaches and the villages come a little closer. There are attractive woods below Northmoor Lock, and Bablock Hythe, with another riverside pub, is soon reached. To the north, the grassy banks of the vast Farmoor Reservoir, much loved by anglers, come down to the river's edge.

Shifford
Oxon. A church and a few houses surrounded by lush pastureland are all that remain of what was once an important town. Alfred held a meeting of the English Parliament here in AD890. The church is situated in the middle of a field less than quarter of a mile from the river.

Hinton Waldrist and Longworth
Oxon. Two pleasant straggling villages up on a ridge overlooking the valley. Longworth church contains a good example of Arts and Crafts stained glass by Heywood Sumner, 1906. The Old Rectory, Longworth, was the birthplace of Dr John Fell, 1625–86, who participated in the early development of the Oxford University Press, especially with regard to printing types; and also Richard Doddridge Blackmore, 1825–1900, author of *Lorna Doone* (1869), who spent only the first four months of his life here – sadly his mother died shortly after his birth.

Newbridge
Oxon. A fine 13th-C stone bridge with pointed arches, one of the oldest on the river. The River Windrush joins the Thames here.

Northmoor
Oxon. The 13th-C church contains a restored bell loft, dated 1701. Behind the church is a Tudor rectory. Northmoor Lock is the only remaining example of a paddle and rymer weir on the Thames, once the most common form of water control on the river. It's continued use is somewhat contentious, as its detractors maintain that it provides a less reliable means of flood prevention than its more modern cousins. However, agreement as to its suitability for the job appears to be on the point of being reached so, hopefully, an important piece of living history will be retained on the river. For more information visit www.manorfarmappleton.co.uk/local-facilities-attractions/northmoor-lock-weir/camping-supplies

Appleton
Oxon. PO, stores, off-licence. A meandering thatch and stone village, with new development to the west. Appleton Manor, situated beside a splendid weather-boarded barn and gateway, was built at the end of the 12th C. An astonishing amount remains, including a fine doorway. The community shop stocks a wide range of produce and is open *Mon–Sat 07.00-19.00 (Sat 13.00) & Sun 08.30-12.00.* The PO opens *Mon–Thur 09.00-13.00.*

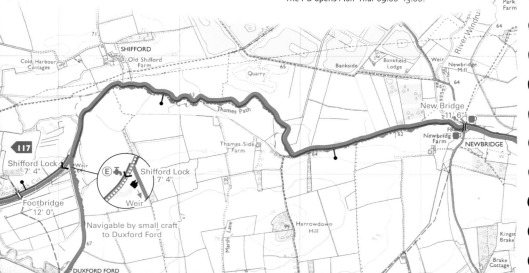

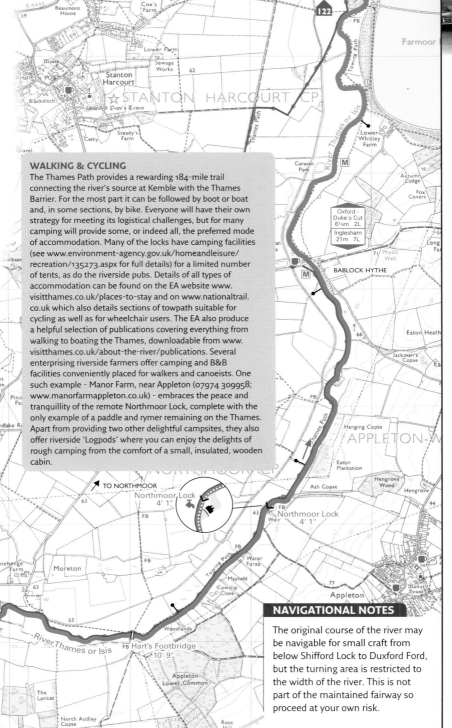

WALKING & CYCLING

The Thames Path provides a rewarding 184-mile trail connecting the river's source at Kemble with the Thames Barrier. For the most part it can be followed by boot or boat and, in some sections, by bike. Everyone will have their own strategy for meeting its logistical challenges, but for many camping will provide some, or indeed all, the preferred mode of accommodation. Many of the locks have camping facilities (see www.environment-agency.gov.uk/homeandleisure/recreation/135273.aspx for full details) for a limited number of tents, as do the riverside pubs. Details of all types of accommodation can be found on the EA website www.visitthames.co.uk/places-to-stay and on www.nationaltrail.co.uk which also details sections of towpath suitable for cycling as well as for wheelchair users. The EA also produce a helpful selection of publications covering everything from walking to boating the Thames, downloadable from www.visitthames.co.uk/about-the-river/publications. Several enterprising riverside farmers offer camping and B&B facilities conveniently placed for walkers and canoeists. One such example - Manor Farm, near Appleton (07974 309958; www.manorfarmappleton.co.uk) - embraces the peace and tranquillity of the remote Northmoor Lock, complete with the only example of a paddle and rymer remaining on the Thames. Apart from providing two other delightful campsites, they also offer riverside 'Logpods' where you can enjoy the delights of rough camping from the comfort of a small, insulated, wooden cabin.

NAVIGATIONAL NOTES

The original course of the river may be navigable for small craft from below Shifford Lock to Duxford Ford, but the turning area is restricted to the width of the river. This is not part of the maintained fairway so proceed at your own risk.

Bablock Hythe

Oxon. Mentioned by Matthew Arnold in *The Scholar Gypsy*, 1853, who was seen: 'In hat of antique shape, and cloak of grey, crossing the stripling Thames at Bab-lock-hithe'. A Roman stone altar, now in the Ashmolean, was dredged from the river here. There has been a ferry here since AD904, and it has been a little erratic in recent years. The area is surrounded by an unappealing estate of temporary homes.

Stanton Harcourt

Oxon. Stores. A superb grey stone village between the Thames and the Windrush, the waters reflecting the quiet glory of the buildings.

The grand cruciform church has fine monuments in the Harcourt Chapel. The shop can be found in the Harcourt Arms and is *open Mon–Fri 10.00–18.00 (Mon 14.00); Sat & Sun 07.30–13.00*

Stanton Harcourt Manor Main Road, Witney OX29 5RJ. The Harcourts built this manor, one of the earliest unfortified manor houses in England, between 1380–1470, with a Gatehouse being added in 1540. Now only Pope's Tower, the scene of Alexander Pope's translation of the *Iliad*, and the unique Great Kitchen, survive. The kitchen is unique in England, in that smoke escaped through vents which were opened manually – there is no chimney. Not open to the public.

WALKING & CYCLING

The prominent dome-shaped Harrowdown Hill can be approached by footpath from the river about a mile west of Newbridge. Views from the top amply repay the modest effort.

Pubs and Restaurants

Blue Boar Tucks Lane, Longworth OX13 5ET (01865 820494; www.blueboarlongworth.co.uk). Busy 16th-C country pub. Real ale. Home-cooked restaurant meals *L and E*; pizza menu, eat in or takeaway. Children welcome. Garden.

Rose Revived Inn Newbridge, Witney OX29 7QD (01865 300221; www.roserevived.com). Old Cotswold stone inn. Real ale. Bar meals and snacks served *all day. Sunday* carvery. Outside seating with children's play area. B&B.

The Plough Eaton Road, Appleton OX13 5JR (01865 863535; www.theploughappleton.com). Welcoming village pub, built in 1683, at the heart of the community serving real ales and appetising home-cooked food *Tue–Sun L and E (not Sun E)*. Takeaway fish and chips *available 18.00–21.00*. Large beer garden with children's play area.

Red Lion Northmoor, Witney OX29 5SX (01865 521033; www.redlionnorthmoor.com). Good informal village pub by the church, serving real ale. Wide range of meals available in the bar or dining area *L and E*. Children welcome *if you are eating*. Garden. *Regular* live music

The Ferryman Inn Bablock Hythe, Northmoor, Witney OX29 5AT (01865 880028; www.theferrymaninn.co.uk). A famous and welcoming pub, serving real ale. Meals available *L and E*. Children welcome. Riverside garden. B&B. Slipway, fishing. *Closed all day Tue.*

Harcourt Arms Main Road, Stanton Harcourt, Witney OX29 5RJ (01865 881931; www.harcourtarms.com). Handsome 16th-C food-oriented inn, with inglenook fire-places. Real ale. Good, interesting food, including fish and game, served *L and E*. Children welcome, and there is an all-weather terrace.

The Vine 11 Abingdon Road, Cumnor, Oxord OX2 9QN (01865 862567; www.thevineinncumnor.co.uk). Pretty pub with the aforementioned vine growing along the front wall. Real ale. Bar meals available *L and E (not Mon E)*. Booking advisable *weekends*. Children welcome. Large garden with a play area.

Bear & Ragged Staff Appleton Road, Cumnor, Oxord OX2 9QH (01865 862329; www.bearandraggedstaff.com). A large, traditional 16th-C pub close to the village pond. Real ale. Good restaurant meals from varied and imaginative menu, and bar meals *available all day, every day*. Children welcome. Garden with play area and decking area, B&B.

Eight Bells High Street, Eaton, Abingdon OX13 5PR (01865 862261; www.eightbellseaton.co.uk). About 1 mile south east of Bablock Hythe. Welcoming pub and restaurant with a log fire. Real ale. Bar meals can be selected from a large menu, and are available *L and E*. Children are welcome. Aunt Sally is played in the *summer*. Regular beer festivals and other events.

Godstow

The Thames meanders extravagantly past Farmoor Reservoir and the very pretty Pinkhill Lock, with its picnic site, towards Swinford. Below Eynsham Lock the entrance to the Wharf Stream can be seen on the east side, followed by the Cassington Cut, which bypassed the lower reaches of the Evenlode, when that river was navigable. Opposite are the dense woodlands of Wytham Great Wood, falling steeply down Wytham Hill to the river's edge. The Seacourt Stream leaves the Thames at Hagley Pool, and a short distance below is King's Lock. Access to the Oxford Canal can be gained via a backwater and the Duke's Cut, which join the weir stream. Pixey Mead lies to the west, its peace shattered by the incessant traffic of the Oxford bypass, which crosses the river above Godstow. On the weir stream is the old Trout Inn: overlooking the lock cut are the ruins of Godstow Abbey. By Port Meadow the river is now significantly wider, flowing between sandy banks to Binsey, where a small jetty indicates the presence of the village and its handsome thatched pub. The navigation channel below Binsey becomes comparatively narrow and tree-lined after Medley Footbridge. Soon a water crossroads is reached, with the unnavigable Bulstake Stream running off to the west, while to the east a short, narrow cut to the Oxford Canal branches off under a very low railway bridge. A smart terrace of railway houses stands beside the river, all with doors opening onto the towpath. The journey through Oxford proper begins at the notoriously low (7ft 6in) Osney Bridge, an obstacle which makes it impossible for larger Thames cruisers to penetrate upstream.

Pubs and Restaurants

The Talbot Oxford Road, Eynsham, Witney OX29 4BT (01865 881348; www.talbot-oxford.co.uk). North west of Swinford Bridge. Busy and attractive pub on the now unnavigable Wharf Stream, serving real ale. Meals, including fresh fish, are available *L and E daily*. Children are welcome away from the bar, and there is a garden. Dogs welcome. B&B.

Harrisons Sandwich Bar and Coffee Shop 11 High Street, Witney OX29 4HA (01865 884445). Breakfast baps, baguettes, sandwiches, panini and ciabatta – eat in or takeaway.

The Trout Inn Godstow Road, Wolvercote, Oxford OX2 8PN (01865 510930; www.thetroutoxford.co.uk). A lovely ivy-covered stone building, with a riverside terrace, built in 1138 as a hospice for Godstow Nunnery. Peacocks roam the large gardens, and the weir stream – not fished for many years – is full of shoals of large fish, swimming tamely near the surface amongst the ducks. Real ale is served, and hot and cold bar meals are available *L and E*. Children are welcome if eating.

The White Hart Wytham, Oxford OX2 8QA (01865 244372; www.whitehartwytham.co.uk). Friendly old thatched village pub with flagstone floors, a 16th-C dovecote and walled garden. Real ale. Home-cooked meals available *L and E*. Children and dogs welcome.

The Perch Inn Binsey Lane, Binsey, Oxford OX2 0NG (01865 728891; www.the-perch.co.uk). Moor at the jetty and walk 50yds along a path to this large and handsome 800-year-old thatched pub, standing in a superb large garden with willow trees. Real ale is served in the low-ceilinged bar, where the ghost of a sailor is said to appear. Food is available *L and E* including *afternoon* teas and *weekend* BBQs. Children welcome. Outside seating.

Swinford Toll Bridge A fine stone balustraded bridge and toll house, where a small toll is collected. It was built in 1777.

● **Eynsham**
Oxon. PO, tel, stores, chemist, butcher, baker, DIY shop. 3/4 mile north west of Swinford Bridge. Once a town of considerable importance, boasting a Benedictine Abbey founded in the 11th C. Today Eynsham has a good selection of shops in the Market Square, around the old town hall.

Wytham Great Wood A marvellous wood of over 600 acres, owned by Oxford University, whose field station is a good example of English vernacular architecture. A haven for birds; the hobby has nested here, nightingales and warblers sing, and teal visit in winter. There is a heronry at Wytham. Private, permit required from Wytham Sawmill Office, Keeper's Hill, Oxford OX2 8QQ.

Godstow

Oxon. A cluster of buildings around the few remains of Godstow Nunnery, founded in the 12th C by the noblewoman Evida. With many royal benefactors, the nunnery soon became prosperous, owning lands in 17 counties. Henry II's mistress Rosamund Clifford was buried here c.1176. Later, Oxford scholars were banned from the buildings in 1432 for 'junketing of every sort'. Dissolution took place in 1539, and in 1645 it was destroyed by Fairfax, commander of Cromwell's New Model Army. St Leonards, a two-storey domestic chapel and part of the abbey, was later restored, but now stands roofless. The bridge and the Trout Inn make a charming setting.

Wytham

Oxon. A very pretty small village set into the side of Wytham Hill, at its best when approached from the river. Wytham Abbey, originally 16th-C, has many later additions: the whole is pleasingly irregular.

NAVIGATIONAL NOTES

1 Access to the Oxford Canal can be gained via the weir stream above King's Lock and through Duke's Cut. Maximum dimensions on this charming rural canal are: length 70ft 0in, beam 7ft 0in, headroom 7ft 0in. The canal is described in detail in *Nicholson Waterways Guide Grand Union, Oxford & the South East.*

2 Take great care at Godstow Bridge, where the arches are narrow and low.

3 Proceeding downstream below Binsey, note that the navigation channel is under the iron footbridge on the west side, by the boatyard. Access to the Oxford Canal can be made along the channel above Osney Bridge.

4 The headroom at Osney Bridge is 7ft 6in at normal levels, less when the river is in spate. Those proceeding upstream who are in any doubt regarding the headroom should consult the lock keeper. And remember, the water levels can change very quickly, so you could get stuck *upstream*.

5 The east side of the river is shallow at Port Meadow.

119

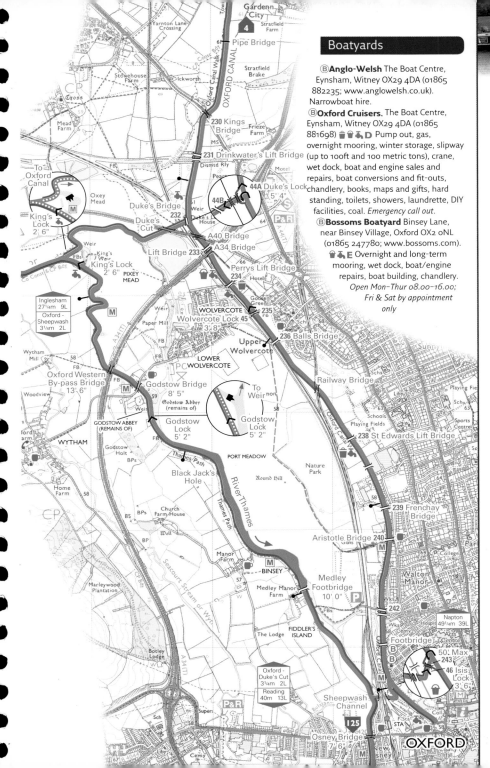

Boatyards

Ⓑ **Anglo-Welsh** The Boat Centre, Eynsham, Witney OX29 4DA (01865 882235; www.anglowelsh.co.uk). Narrowboat hire.

Ⓑ **Oxford Cruisers.** The Boat Centre, Eynsham, Witney OX29 4DA (01865 881698) 🚽🚿♨D Pump out, gas, overnight mooring, winter storage, slipway (up to 100ft and 100 metric tons), crane, wet dock, boat and engine sales and repairs, boat conversions and fit-outs, chandlery, books, maps and gifts, hard standing, toilets, showers, laundrette, DIY facilities, coal. *Emergency call out.*

Ⓑ **Bossoms Boatyard** Binsey Lane, near Binsey Village, Oxford OX2 0NL (01865 247780; www.bossoms.com). 🚽♨E Overnight and long-term mooring, wet dock, boat/engine repairs, boat building, chandlery. *Open Mon-Thur 08.00-16.00; Fri & Sat by appointment only*

OXFORD

Oxford

This section, while not particularly picturesque, provides plenty of interest, in stark contrast to the water meadows above the town. Below Osney Bridge is a lovely stretch of urban waterway, with terraced houses facing the river, a handsome pub and a lock with a new timber boathouse – an environment much appreciated by the local workers who spend their lunch-breaks here in the summer. There are many access points to the towpath, which is well used by cyclists, joggers and walkers. Just above Osney Railway Bridge stands a touching memorial to Edgar Wilson who, on 15 June 1889, saved the lives of two boys here, at the cost of his own. Folly Bridge is always a hive of activity during the summer; Salter's trip boat base is here, along with a large riverside pub. Punts are available for hire and small motor and rowing boats proceed up and down. Christ Church Meadow lies to the east, and is thronged with tourists and sunbathers when the weather is fine. Below is a long row of boathouses, facing the mock Tudor of the University Rowing Club building. Downstream of Donnington Road Bridge suburbia keeps its distance and the river proceeds along a green passage to Iffley Lock, with its pretty balustraded footbridges and fine lock house, all surrounded by trees, with a white-painted pub nearby. There is an area of parkland to the west, on an isthmus created by the Weirs Mill Stream, followed by the functional steel of Kennington Railway Bridge. As the river dog-legs past Rose Isle pylons run parallel, but still the houses and factories, for the most part, keep away. Gradually the Oxford conurbation is left behind as the river passes through a mixture of woodland, suburbia and light industry, then curves through a maze of backwaters, used as boat club moorings, to Sandford Lock, the deepest on the river above Teddington and distinguished by the presence of large mill buildings. Below here the Thames passes through open country criss-crossed by electricity pylons. An absolutely fascinating stretch.

BOAT TRIPS

Salter Bros Folly Bridge, Oxford OX1 4LA (01865 243421; www.salterssteamers.co.uk). Established in 1858, the passenger boat services were introduced in 1888. Although now diesel powered, the boats are affectionately known as 'Salter's Steamers'. Scheduled services *mid May–mid Sep, daily* from Oxford, Abingdon, Wallingford, Reading, Henley, Marlow, Windsor and Staines, with some intermediate stops. These trips are heavily booked in the main holiday season, so telephone first, don't just turn up. Boats also available for party hire. Bar on board. Also punts and self-drive for hire.

City of Oxford
Oxon. All services. The town was founded in the 10th C and has been a university city since the 13th C. Today it is a lively cosmopolitan centre of learning, tourism and industry.
Tourist Information Centre Broad Street, Oxford OX1 3AS (01865 252200; www.visitoxford.org). Here you will find a good selection of city guides and maps, and helpful and informative staff. It is, of course, the 39 **Colleges** which give Oxford its unique character – they can all be visited, but opening times vary, so check with the Tourist Information Centre. Those noted here are particularly representative of their periods.
Merton College
Merton Street OX1 4JD One of the earliest collegiate foundations, dating from 1264, the buildings are especially typical of the Perpendicular and Decorative periods. The chapel was begun in 1294 and Mob Quad was the first of the Oxford quadrangles. The library, mainly 14th-C, has a famous collection of rare books and manuscripts. During the Victorian era, the college was enlarged, and the Grove Buildings are by William Butterfield, with alterations in 1929 by T. Harold Hughes.

New College
Holywell Street OX1 3BN The college was founded by William of Wykeham, Bishop of Winchester, in 1379. The chapel, a noble example of early Perpendicular, was greatly restored by Sir George Scott in the 19th C. The great west window, after a cartoon by Reynolds, and Epstein's *Lazarus* are noteworthy. The 14th-C cloister and the workmanship of the wrought-iron screen, 1684, between the Garden Quad and the Garden, are outstanding memorials of their times.
Keble College
Parks Road OX1 3PG Built by William Butterfield in 1870, Keble is the only Oxford college entirely in the Victorian Gothic style. The frontage of red and grey patterned brickwork and the tracery windows display great self-confidence. The chapel, with its glass and mosaics, bricks, tiles and brass, contains Holman Hunt's *The Light of the World*.
St Catherine's College
Manor Road OX1 3UJ An important and interesting example of a new college, designed by the Danish architect, Arne Jacobsen in 1964. The entrance to the college is reached through an unprepossessing

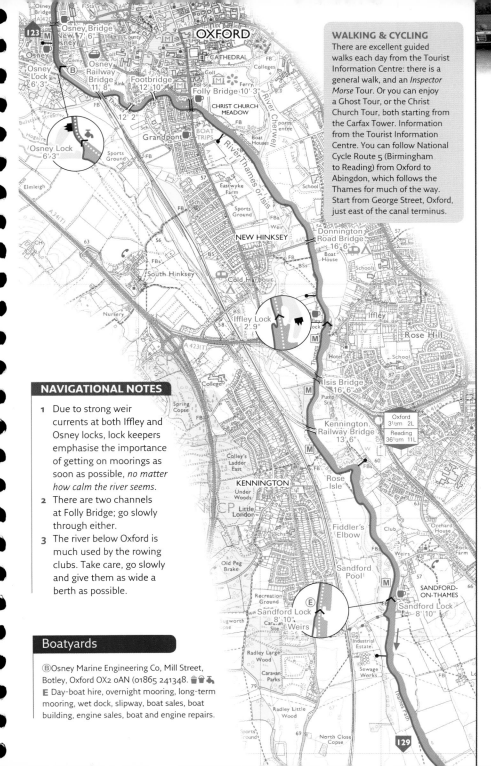

WALKING & CYCLING

There are excellent guided walks each day from the Tourist Information Centre: there is a general walk, and an *Inspector Morse* Tour. Or you can enjoy a Ghost Tour, or the Christ Church Tour, both starting from the Carfax Tower. Information from the Tourist Information Centre. You can follow National Cycle Route 5 (Birmingham to Reading) from Oxford to Abingdon, which follows the Thames for much of the way. Start from George Street, Oxford, just east of the canal terminus.

NAVIGATIONAL NOTES

1. Due to strong weir currents at both Iffley and Osney locks, lock keepers emphasise the importance of getting on moorings as soon as possible, *no matter how calm the river seems*.
2. There are two channels at Folly Bridge; go slowly through either.
3. The river below Oxford is much used by the rowing clubs. Take care, go slowly and give them as wide a berth as possible.

Boatyards

⑧Osney Marine Engineering Co, Mill Street, Botley, Oxford OX2 0AN (01865 241348. 🛒🎁⚓
E Day-boat hire, overnight mooring, long-term mooring, wet dock, slipway, boat sales, boat building, engine sales, boat and engine repairs.

car park area, but in the main quadrangle the effect is one of stark impact. The mass of glass windows with their bands of ribbed concrete stretch like concertinas on either side of the quadrangle. All is bleak but full of atmosphere. The furniture and college plate were also designed by Jacobsen.

St Anne's College

Woodstock Road OX2 6HS This college reflects some of the most exciting modern building in Oxford. The Wolfson block in the main quadrangle was designed by Howell, Killick and Partridge, 1964. With its two curving wings and square jutting windows, all of pre-cast concrete, this building is impressive and original. Facing the block is the Dining Hall by Gerald Banks, 1964, and to one side is Hartland House, mainly 1930s but with 1951 additions by Sir Giles Gilbert Scott.

Other interesting buildings include:

Radcliffe Camera

Radcliffe Square. Dr Radcliffe left £40,000 for the building of this library by James Gibbs, 1739, to house his Physic library. It is a vast domed Italianate rotunda, now a Bodleian reading room, and not open to the public. The staircase and skylight can be admired through the doorway.

Sheldonian Theatre

Broad Street OX1 3AZ (01865 277299; www.ox.ac.uk/ sheldoniantheatre). Built by Christopher Wren in 1669 under the auspices of Gilbert Sheldon, Archbishop of Canterbury, the theatre was designed to be used for university ceremonies and degrees, which are still awarded here. For many years it also housed the workshops of the University Press. The interior, with its ceiling by Robert Streeter, is delightful. *Open Mon–Sat 10.00–12.30 and 14.00–16.30 (15.30 Nov–Feb). Closed when in use for university ceremonies, meetings and concerts. Charge.*

The Old Bodleian

Broad Street OX1 3BG (01865 277162; www.bodleian. ox.ac.uk). Named after Thomas Bodley, who died in 1613 leaving a fine collection of rare manuscripts, the old Bodleian buildings, mainly 16th-C and early 17th-C, also incorporate Duke Humfrey's library, dating from the 15th C. Bodley extended Duke Humfrey's library and also financed the rebuilding of the Schools Quadrangle. Under the Copyright Act the Bodleian is entitled to claim a copy of every book published in the British Isles. It currently holds over 6½ million volumes and 160,000 manuscripts. *Open for guided tours (university ceremonies permitting) Mon–Fri 09.00–17.00; Sat 09.00–16.30 & Sun 11.00–17.00. The tour lasts 45 mins and tickets are sold in the Divinity School. Charge. Please note that children under 14 years of age are not permitted on the tours. The Divinity School is open Mon–Fri 09.00–16.45 and Sat 09.30–12.30, and the Exhibition Room is open Mon–Fri 09.30–16.45 and Sat 09.30–12.30. Free.*

Christ Church Cathedral

Broad Walk OX1 1DP (01865 276492; www.chch. ox.ac.uk). The cathedral, with its inconspicuous entrance in Tom Quad, was originally part of the Priory of St Frideswide. It is mainly 12th-C with later additions and is typically Romanesque. The most splendid feature is the 16th-C stone-vaulted fan roof of the choir. There is medieval glass and also 19th-C glass by Burne-Jones. The Chapter House is a 13th-C masterpiece.

St Mary the Virgin

High Street, Oxford OX1 4BJ (01865 279111; www. university-church.ox.ac.uk). The fine 14th-C spire is a landmark. The church is typical of the Perpendicular style, apart from the magnificent Baroque porch with its twisted columns by Nicholas Stone, 1637.

Ashmolean Museum

Beaumont Street OX1 2PH (01865 278000; www. ashmolean.org). The oldest public museum in Britain (opened in 1683) and one of the most rewarding outside London. It has an outstanding collection of Near Eastern and European archaeology, as well as the Farrer collection of 17th- and 18th-C silver. The Herberden Coin Room has a vast display of early coins, while in the Department of Fine Art, the Michelangelo and Raphael drawings are to be admired. The museum also has the bulk of the archaeological material from the Upper Thames. *Open Tue–Sun and B Hol Mon 10.00–18.00. Free. Café on site open until 18.00.*

Christ Church Gallery

Canterbury Quadrangle at the end of Merton Street, by Oriel Square OX1 1DP (01865 276172; www.chch. ox.ac.uk). Built by Powell and Moya in 1968, the gallery displays Christ Church's private collection. Exceptional Renaissance drawings by Michelangelo, Leonardo da Vinci and Rubens, as well as 14th–18th-C paintings, mainly Italian. *Open daily Jun–Sep Mon–Sat 10.30–17.00 & Sun 14.00–17.00 (closed Tue in Jun); Oct–May Mon, Wed–Sat 10.30am–13.00 & 14.00–16.30 & Sun 14.00–16.30. Charge. Shop.*

Oxford University Press Museum

Great Clarendon Street OX2 6DP (www.oup.com). Historic books, documents and presses.

University Museum

Parks Road OX1 3PW (01865 272 950; www.oum.ox.ac.uk). The building by Deane and Woodward, 1855–60, in high Victorian Gothic was much admired by Ruskin. The interior is a forest of columns and skeletons covered by a glass roof. One great rarity is the head and claw of a dodo. *Open daily 10.00– 17.00. Free.*

Christ Church Meadows

OX1 1DP The meadows lie behind Christ Church and Merton and have fine views and a path leading down to the river. The path is lined with college barges (not many remaining) and boathouses. In the afternoons you can often watch the rowing eights. Enter the Meadows from St Aldates.

University Botanic Garden

Rose Lane OX1 4AZ (01865 286690; www.botanic-garden.ox.ac.uk). The oldest botanic garden in Britain, founded by Henry Lord Danvers in 1621. The garden was originally intended for the culture of medicinal plants, but today it fosters an extensive collection of rare plants for research and teaching. The gateway is by Inigo Jones. *Open daily May–Aug 09.00–18.00; Sep, Oct, Mar, Apr 09.00–17.00 & Nov–Feb 09.00–16.00. Charge.*

Pubs and Restaurants

There are many fine pubs and restaurants in Oxford. Those listed here are on or near the river, with one notable exception.

The Punter 7 South Street, Osney OX2 0BE (01865 248832; www.thepunteroxford.com). A very fine riverside local near Osney Lock, once used by the bargees. Real ale is served along with meals *L and E*. Children and dogs welcome. Outside seating on patio area. There is also some grass to sit on by the river, in *summer*. Moorings.

The Head of the River Folly Bridge OX1 4LB (01865 721600; www.headoftheriveroxford. co.uk). A three-storey pub and dining complex built in a converted grain warehouse. Real ale and bar meals are available *all day*. Children welcome *until 21.00*. Large patio with outside seating at the front of the pub. B&B. Punts for hire close by, *Apr–Oct*.

The Folly Bridge Inn 38 Abingdon Road OX1 4PD (01865 790106). South of Folly Bridge. A pleasant pub with outside seating, serving real ale and bar meals *L and E*. Children are welcome. Quiz *Thu* and regular music.

The Chequers 131 High Street OX1 4DH (01865 727463; www.nicholsonspubs.co.uk). A 15th-C inn, with the original panelling and fireplace in the Monks bar at the front. Real ale, and meals *L and E*. Children are welcome if dining. Garden with seating.

The Mitre 17 High Street OX1 4AG (01865 244563). Parts of this building date from the 13th-C, but the majority is 17th-C. Past patrons include Peel, Gladstone and Elizabeth Taylor. Real ale. Restaurant *open all day*, bar meals are available. Children welcome *until 21.00*.

The Turf Tavern Bath Place, off Holywell Street OX1 3SU (01865 243235; www.theturftavern.co.uk). Surprisingly secluded from the bustle of the city this pub is one of the most distinctive in Oxford. Made famous through Hardy's *Jude the Obscure*, this 13th-C tavern has become popular with both students and tourists. Real ale. Bar meals available *all day until 21.00*. Three gardens, warmed by braziers *in winter*. Children welcome away from the bar.

Shanghai 30's 82 St Aldates OX1 1RA (01865 242230; www.shanghai30s.com). Fine Chinese cuisine in what used to be the Restaurant Elizabeth. *Open L and E (not Mon L) and all day Sat–Sun*. Just a short walk up from Folly Bridge.

Heroes 8 Ship Street OX1 3DA (01865 723459). Home-made soup, hot sandwiches and breakfasts. Children welcome. No dogs. *Open Mon–Fri 08.00–18.00, Sat–Sun 09.00–18.00*.

The Isis Farmhouse Riverside, Iffley Lock OX4 4EL (01865 243854). Friendly licensed riverside café, with large garden, formerly the Isis Tavern. *Summer hours vary, telephone in advance; winter open Fri–Sun*. Meals *L and E*. Telephone to confirm. With no direct road access, the beer was once delivered from the river, and during the 19th C they received 5 shillings, or 7 shillings and 6 pence for each corpse removed from the river (it depended upon which side the body was found!).

The King's Arms Church Road, Sandford Lock, Sandford-on-Thames OX4 4YB (01865 777095; www.chefandbrewer.com). A fine lockside pub serving real ale, with ceiling beams of old barge timbers. Family-style restaurant serving food *all day*. Garden with riverside seating and children's play area.

BIRD LIFE

The *Canada Goose* is a large, unmistakable goose with an upright stance and a long neck, giving it a swan-like silhouette. The goose has white cheeks on an otherwise black head and neck. Its body is mainly grey-brown except for a white under stern; the juveniles are similar but the markings less distinct. The Canada Goose nests beside wetlands and sometimes in nearby arable fields. Outside the breeding season, sizeable flocks of geese will be seen. In flight the geese utter a loud, disyllabic trumpeting call.

Abingdon

Hills close in from the east as Radley College Boathouse is passed and the landscaped grounds of Nuneham House come into view, followed by the steeply wooded slope of Lock Wood. After Nuneham Railway Bridge the river passes the entrance to the Swift Ditch – once the main navigation channel, where one of the earliest pound locks on the Thames was built about 1620. Its remains were incorporated into an overspill weir in 1967. Above Abingdon Lock a handsome river frontage faces the open fields and sports grounds of Andersey Island, in an area noted for mute swans. The River Ock enters the Thames under a bridge (dated 1824) by the Old Anchor Inn, a mellow and welcoming building. Now the river heads for open country and enters Culham Reach, passing the wooden bridge across the Swift Ditch, standing beside the old road bridge and its more modern replacement. A sharp turn east marks the entrance to Culham Cut, overlooked by the 17th-C greystone manor.

ABINGDON

Abbey Stream

ABBEY (REMS OF)

Abingdon Lock 6' 2"

Abingdon Bridge 13' 11"

ANDERSEY ISLAND

Abingdon Lock 6' 2"

Swift Ditch

Culham Brake

Industrial Estate

Barton Lane

Dismantled Railway

Thrupp House

Nuneham Railway Bridge 15' 9"

Gravel Pit

Home Farm

Resrs

Warren Farm

The Warren

Hill Pond

High Lodge

Culham Hill

Culham Bridge

The Knoll

The Toot

Sloven Copse

Thame Lane

Culham Lock 7' 11"

School

Culham Station

Govern Buildin

Marina

Sports Ground

The Burycroft

Culham Reach

Culham House

The Green

CULHAM CP

Zouch Farm

Sewage Works

Gravel Pits

CULHAM

Footbridge 12' 5"

Manor House

Culham Cut

Culham Lock 7' 11"

Sutton Bridge (dis) 14' 9"

River Thames or Isis

Sutton Pools

Appleford Railway Bridge 13' 0"

Fullamoor Plantation

THE ABBEY

Cross Tree Farm

SUTTON COURTENAY

Bridge Farm

Manor Farm

APPLEFORD

NAVIGATIONAL NOTES

1 Go slowly at west entrance to Culham Cut – blind corner.
2 Go slowly through Culham Lock Bridge – narrow.
1 Take care at Clifton Hampden Bridge – the arches are narrow and low.

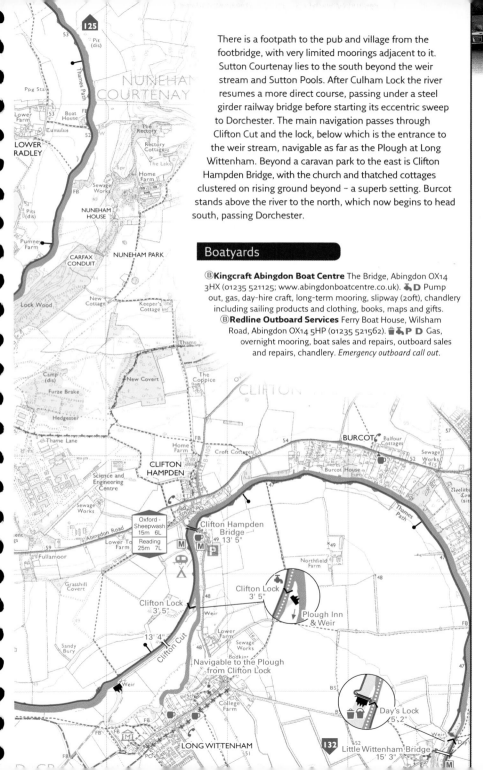

There is a footpath to the pub and village from the footbridge, with very limited moorings adjacent to it. Sutton Courtenay lies to the south beyond the weir stream and Sutton Pools. After Culham Lock the river resumes a more direct course, passing under a steel girder railway bridge before starting its eccentric sweep to Dorchester. The main navigation passes through Clifton Cut and the lock, below which is the entrance to the weir stream, navigable as far as the Plough at Long Wittenham. Beyond a caravan park to the east is Clifton Hampden Bridge, with the church and thatched cottages clustered on rising ground beyond – a superb setting. Burcot stands above the river to the north, which now begins to head south, passing Dorchester.

Boatyards

Ⓑ**Kingcraft Abingdon Boat Centre** The Bridge, Abingdon OX14 3HX (01235 521125; www.abingdonboatcentre.co.uk). 🔧D Pump out, gas, day-hire craft, long-term mooring, slipway (20ft), chandlery including sailing products and clothing, books, maps and gifts.

Ⓑ**Redline Outboard Services** Ferry Boat House, Wilsham Road, Abingdon OX14 5HP (01235 521562). 🚽🔧P D Gas, overnight mooring, boat sales and repairs, outboard sales and repairs, chandlery. *Emergency outboard call out.*

- **Radley**
  Oxon. PO, stores, station. A straggling commuter suburb.
  Radley College OX14 2HR. Founded in 1847. The college is based on Radley Hall, 1721-7, with many later additions. It is famed as a rowing school.
  Nuneham Park Nuneham Courtenay OX44 9PG. An 18th-C Palladian mansion by Leadbetter, splendidly situated in landscaped grounds (*see* Nuneham Courtenay, below) by Mason and Brown. Rousseau stayed here in 1767, and planted foreign wild flowers in the gardens. The Temple is by Athenian Stuart. Particularly noticeable from the river, standing on a wooded slope, is the Carfax Conduit, an ornamental fountain built in 1615 and once part of Oxford's water supply system. Originally situated in Carfax, it was moved here in 1786. In times of celebration wine and beer were run through it. Private, no pubic access.

- **Nuneham Courtenay**
  Oxon. Tel. An 18th-C model village of startling regularity along the main road, the result of a mass upheaval around 1760 when the 1st Earl of Harcourt required the original village site as part of his landscaped garden. Oliver Goldsmith (1730-74) wrote bitterly of this practice in *The Deserted Village* (1770):
  'The man of wealth and pride
  Takes up a space that many poor supplied'.
  However, whether the early villagers, moving from ancient clay-built cottages into far more modern houses, would have seen it that way is open to question. The site of the original village is by the estate road.

- **Abingdon**
  Oxon. All shops and services, and an extensive shopping precinct with laundrette. A busy 18th-C market town which grew up around the abbey, founded in AD695. Little of the original building now remains, except the Abbey Gate, Long Gallery and Checker, which has a 13th-C chimney, and is used as an Elizabethan-style theatre. Abbey Meadow, by the river, is a public park with a swimming pool, toilets, café and putting green. The best views of the town are from the river or the bridge, which is of medieval origin but was rebuilt in 1927. The river is dominated by the gaol, an impressive stone bastille built 1805-11 (now a leisure and sports centre) and St Helen's Church. Set among almshouses, the church has five aisles, making it broader than it is long. Long Alley Almshouses, beside the Old Anchor Inn, were built 1446-7 by the Fraternity of the Holy Cross. John Mason of Abingdon created Christ's Hospital, which has administered them since. The porches and lantern were added in 1605 and 1618. This area, around St Helen's Wharf, shows the town at its best. Each year in Abingdon, *on the Saturday closest to the summer solstice*, the people of Ock Street elect a Mayor for the day. Morris dancers perform outside each inn along the street, a custom of uncertain origin.
  Abingdon County Hall Museum Market Place, Abingdon OX14 3HG (01235 531378; www.abingdonmuseum.org.uk). What is recognised as one of the finest town halls in England stands in the Market Place. Built 1678-82 by Christopher Kempster, one of Wren's city masons, it is high and monumental with an open ground floor, once used as a market. At the time of writing, the museum was closed for redevelopment, due to reopen spring 2012.
  Swan Upping (www.royal.gov.uk) In the *third week of July*, the Queen's Swan Keeper, 19 other men (including representatives of the Vintners' and Dyers' Companies) and a supply of 'tea' (an intoxicating mixture of dark rum and milk) take to the river in double sculling skiffs, to ceremonially mark the swans. The men wear colourful uniforms, and 'round up' the swans, which are then checked, weighed and tagged with a stainless steel leg ring (beak-marking ceased a while ago). The count is carried out between Abingdon and Sunbury, and these days performs an important conservation role. This tradition dates from the 12th C, when swans were an important source of food. David Barber is currently Her Majesty's Swan Keeper - a unique appointment. Swans on the river now number around 1200.
  Tourist Information Centre 25 Bridge Street, Abingdon OX14 3HN (01235 522711). Helpful and friendly service.

- **Culham**
  Oxon. A pretty village with a fine green and replica stocks.

- **Sutton Courtenay**
  Oxon. A large village, both wealthy and rewarding, built around a green. Eric Blair (George Orwell) and Henry Asquith (Prime Minister of the Liberal government, 1908-16) are buried in the churchyard here. Overlooking the weir stream is Norman Hall, a remarkably original late 12th-C manor house. The 14th-C abbey was never used as such, but as a grange.

- **Long Wittenham**
  Oxon. Tel. Access by boat along the weir stream from Clifton Lock. A fine straggling village along the original course of the river. The 13th-C church contains choir stalls from Exeter College, Oxford.
  Pendon Museum At the far end of Long Wittenham village OX14 4QD (01865 407365; www.pendonmuseum.com). A museum of miniature landscapes and transport. The main display is an ambitious recreation of the Vale of White Horse area in the 1930s, with 25 miniature trains running automatically, controlled by a computer. There are also miniature recreations of a Great Western Railway branch on Dartmoor, John Ahern's famous Madder Valley layout, and a row of shops based upon The Shambles in York. *Open Weekends 14:00-16:45; B Hols 11:00-16:45 & selected Weds: 11:00-16:45 (museum closes at 17:30).* Telephone for details. Charge.

- **Clifton Hampden**
  Oxon. PO, store. A cluster of thatched cottages away from the brick bridge (a Norman folly built in 1864). The small church on a mound is very picturesque.

Pubs and Restaurants

There are many pubs and eating places to be found in Abingdon.

The Crown & Thistle Bridge Street, Abingdon OX14 3HS (01235 522556; www.crownandthistle.com). Bar and restaurant in old 17th-C coaching inn, with attractive cobbled courtyard. Real ales. Meals served *L and E*. Outside seating in the courtyard. Children welcome.

The Broad Face 30 Bridge Street, Abingdon OX14 3HR (01235 524516; www.thebroadface.com). Trendy pub serving excellent food and a wide range of real ales on which CAMRA members receive a discount. Also a comprehensive wine list. Regular beer festivals and live music nights, including jazz on *Sun afternoon*. Beer garden

Brasserie at the Upper Reaches Thames Street, Abingdon OX14 3JA (01235 522536; www.upperreaches-abingdon.co.uk). Relaxed restaurant in converted mill on the Abbey Stream. Meals *L and E*. Patio overlooking the river, and a working water wheel indoors. Children welcome. B&B.

The George & Dragon 4 Church Street, Sutton Courtenay OX14 4NJ (01235 848142). Traditional country pub with log fires, serving real ale and traditional home-cooked food *L and E*. Children and dogs welcome. Terrace.

The Swan The Green, Sutton Courtenay OX14 4AE (01235 847446; www.theswanfoodhouse. co.uk). A quiet, red brick local with a large garden, which has a play area. Real ale. Bar meals available *L and E*. Children welcome.

The Fish 4 Appleford Road, Sutton Courtenay OX14 4NQ (01235 848242; www.thefishatsuttoncourtenay.co.uk). A pub/ restaurant serving real ale, and a fine selection of wines. Excellent fresh food, with a wide range of fish, every *L and E* (*not Sun E or Mon all day, booking recommended*). Bistro menu at the barn, in the conservatory and in the large garden and patio *L only*. Children welcome. A short walk across fields from Culham Lock (but please leave muddy boots outside!).

Carpenters Arms Main Road, Appleford OX14 4PD (01235 848328). Real ale and bar meals *daily L and E* (*not Sun E*). Children are welcome (*but not Sat evenings*). Garden.

The Plough Inn 24 High Street, Long Wittenham OX14 4QH (01865 407738). The weir stream is navigable from Clifton Lock to this attractive pub, which serves real ale. Meals are served *L and E*. Children are welcome – they will enjoy the massive garden. The folk club meets here *every Wed*, and it is handy for the Pendon Museum.

The Vine & Spice High Street, Long Wittenham OX14 4QH (01865 409900; www. thevineandspice.co.uk). Cosy, welcoming bar/ restaurant, bedecked with flowers in the summer. Real ale. Meals served *L and E*. Children welcome. Garden.

Barley Mow Clifton Hampden (east of Clifton Hampden Bridge) OX14 3EH (01865 980350; www.chefandbrewer.com). Deservedly famous and superbly old-fashioned thatched pub built in 1350. It was described by Jerome K. Jerome as having 'quite a story book appearance'. Real ale. Bar and restaurant meals available *daily*. Children are welcome away from bar area. Dogs welcome. Pleasant garden.

The Chequers Abingdon Road, Burcot OX14 3DP (01865 407771; www.chequers-burcott.co.uk). Well worth the walk from Clifton Hampden or Dorchester to visit this handsome and totally civilised thatched pub. A large log fire is surrounded by settees, bookcases, and settles, spaciously arranged. *Open all day*, meals served *L and E*. Children are welcome and there is a garden.

The Bowyer Arms Foxborough Road, Radley OX14 3AE (01235 523452; www.bowyerarms.co.uk). Next to the station and *open all day*, this village local serves real ale and excellent, inexpensive home-made food, *daily 11.00–22.00*. Children welcome. Large beer garden. Pool.

WALKING & CYCLING
Abingdon Town Council publish a free leaflet giving details of cycling opportunities around the town. Telephone (01235) 522642 to obtain a copy. There are excellent walks across the weir at Sutton Courtenay, by Sutton Pools.

Dorchester

The river now turns south to pass Dorchester
and takes an extravagant winding route, passing
the massive 114 acres of earthworks known as the
Dyke Hills. It then takes a sharp turn to the east below
Day's Lock, where the World 'Poohsticks' Championships
are held *each March*. This unique event was the brainchild
of Lynn David, the former lock keeper, who introduced it as a
fund-raising event for the RNLI. The River Thame joins opposite Little
Wittenham Wood – very small craft can pass under the footbridge to moor
below Dorchester Bridge. Above the confluence, the Thames is sometimes
romantically known as the Isis. Open, flat farmland flanks the river on its approach
to Shillingford, marked by the smart hotel and accompanying stone bridge, which
replaced an earlier wooden structure built in 1784. A caravan park and many moored
boats then announce the presence of Benson and the lock. Below here the river makes
a beeline for Wallingford, passing Howbery Park Institute of Hydrology, once the home
of Jethro Tull (1674–1741), a pioneer of mechanised farming who conducted experiments
with seed at nearby Crowmarsh. The combine harvester underwent its first trials in Britain at
nearby Long Wittenham. There is a charge for moorings above Wallingford Bridge. The river then
passes through only a few of Wallingford Bridge's 17 arches. Flowing by some attractive Georgian
buildings, the river continues south.

Boatyards

Ⓑ ✕ **Benson Waterfront** Benson Cruiser Station, Benson OX10 6SJ (01491 838304). 🚽🚿⚓D
E Pump out, gas, boat hire, overnight and long-term mooring, winter storage, slipway, toilets, showers, shop, café.
Ⓑ**Swancraft** Benson Waterfront, Benson OX10 6SJ (0844 847 1356). 🚽⚓D E Pump out, gas, hire craft, day-boat hire, overnight and long-term mooring, winter storage, slipway, boat and engine repairs, telephone, toilets, showers, books, maps and gifts, café.

NAVIGATIONAL NOTES

1 Take care at the blind corner below Little Wittenham Bridge.
2 Wallingford Bridge – use the central arch.

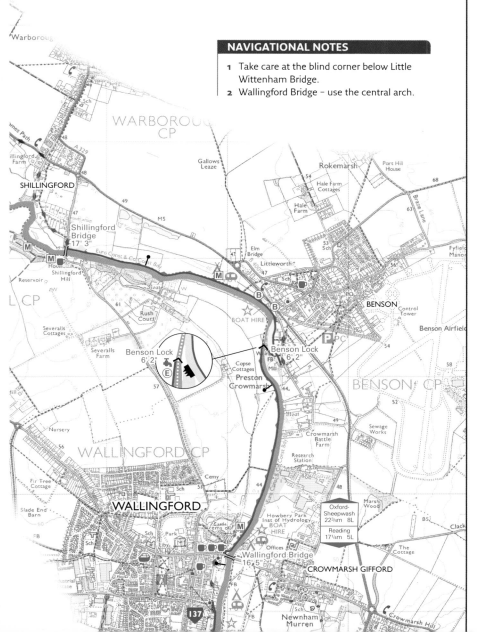

Little Wittenham

Oxon. The church here is nicely situated amongst the woods.

Dorchester

Oxon. PO, stores. This large village of antique shops and hotels was once a small Roman town sited on the River Thames. It is accessible from the river by footpath over the Dyke Hills from Day's Lock. Small craft may navigate up the River Thame to Dorchester Bridge. The town is quite quiet, now it has a bypass, and today only the abbey Church of SS Peter and Paul, founded in the 7th C, reveals that this was once the cathedral city of Wessex, then Mercia. Approached through a Butterfield lych gate, the mostly decorated abbey gives little clue to the splendid size and proportion of its interior. The most important feature is the Jesse window, with stonework imitating trees. The figures seem to grow organically from the body of Jesse. Note also the tomb of Sir John Holcombe: the realism and fluidity of the effigy has inspired many modern sculptors. The Old Monastery Guest House, built c.1400 and used in the 17th C as a grammar school, now houses the Abbey Museum, although most Roman finds are in the Ashmolean (*see* below).

Dorchester Abbey Museum The Abbey Guest House, Dorchester OX10 7HR (01865 340007; www.dorchester-abbey.org.uk). *Open Apr–Sep, daily 14.00–17.00.* Free. Shop.

Shillingford

Oxon. The extremely handsome triple-arched bridge and the hotel stand away from the village, a discreet residential area to the north.

Benson

Oxon. PO, stores, butchers, takeaways, green grocer, chemist, off-licence, garage A friendly town with a pleasant river frontage, although it is hard to believe this was once a seat of the Kings of Mercia. The church is 13th-C. The PO is in the Parish Hall, *open all day Tue; Wed & Thur morning.*

Wallingford

Oxon. All services. One of the oldest Royal Boroughs, the town received its charter in 1155. Well-preserved banks and ditches of Saxon defences still remain. From the river the town is dominated by the unusual openwork spire of St Peter's Church (key at the TIC), built by Sir Robert Taylor in 1777. At the rear of the George Hotel is the entrance to the splendid Castle Gardens, where footpaths lead to the remains of the Norman castle built on a mound by Robert D'Oilly in 1071, held for the Empress Matilda during her fight with King Stephen for the English crown, and finally destroyed by Fairfax in 1646. The town hall, built in 1670, has a typical open ground floor. The 17-arched bridge is of medieval origins (possibly as early as 1141), and was rebuilt in 1809 when the balustrade was added. It still has a Bridge Chamberlain, appointed each year by the town council. Walk up the hill from the river and turn left to enjoy the town centre, shops and market square. There is a music festival held at St Peter's Church *May–Sep,* and an illuminated river pageant in *Sep.*

Wallingford Museum Flint House, High Street, Wallingford OX10 0DB (01491 835065; www.wallingfordmuseum.org.uk). Housed in a part of a medieval hall-house. Take a walk through Saxon and Medieval Wallingford, and visit a Victorian shop. *Open Mar–Nov, Tue–Fri 14.00–17.00; Sat 10.30–17.00, Sun and B Hols 14.00–17.00.* Charge for adults.

The Corn Exchange Market Place, Wallingford OX10 0EG (01491 825000, www.cornexchange.org. uk). Theatre and cinema.

The Cholsey and Wallingford Railway Cholsey Station, Wallingford OX10 9QD, 15 minutes walk west of Wallingford (01491 835067; www.cholsey-wallingford-railway.com). This line opened in 1866 to link the Great Western Railway's main line with the Wycombe Extension Railway. The last British Rail service ran on 31 May 1981. Now 2½ miles of track have been purchased, and steam and diesel trains are run between Cholsey and St John's Road, Wallingford.

Tourist Information Centre Town Hall, Market Place, Wallingford OX10 0EG (01491 826972; www.wallingford.co.uk).

AND BABY MAKES THREE . . .

Babies who are not yet walking can be coped with fairly easily on a boating holiday. Children between the ages of one and five are probably the most difficult to deal with, and the following points may be helpful:

1. Mum, Dad and two toddlers on a heavily locked length of canal will have problems. If you cannot gather a larger crew to help, a river such as the Thames, where the locks are operated by keepers, is ideal.
2. Ensure buoyancy aids are worn by children when they are up on deck.
3. Avoid traditional style narrowboats with a small unprotected rear deck. Thames cruisers, with an enclosed cockpit, are ideal.
4. Airing cupboards are useful for drying all the washing produced by small children.
5. Pack the favourite toys and games.
6. Allow time for plenty of stops, where children can run off their excess energy.

From the age of six, children, properly supervised, can become useful crew members.

BIRD LIFE

The *Grey Heron* is a familiar large, long-legged wetland bird. The adult has a dagger-like, yellow bill and a black crest of feathers. The head, neck and underparts are otherwise whitish except for black streaks on the front of the neck and breast. The back and wings are blue-grey. In flight, the wings are broad and rounded with black flight feathers: the bird employs slow, flapping wingbeats and holds its neck folded in a hunched 's' shape close to its body. The juvenile is similar to the adult, but the markings are less distinct and the plumage more grubby in appearance. The heron is often seen standing motionless for hours on end on long, yellow legs, sometimes with the neck hunched up. It will occasionally actively stalk prey, which comprise mainly amphibians and fish, especially eels. Its call is a harsh and distinctive 'frank'.

Pubs and Restaurants

The George Hotel High Street, Dorchester OX10 7HH (01865 340404; www.thegeorgedorchester.co.uk). Built in 1495 as the brew-house of the nearby abbey, this comfortable galleried inn is one of the oldest privately owned coaching inns in the country. Real ale, along with bar meals, *L and E* and a restaurant serving English à la carte *E*. The hotel is set in pleasant grounds. Children welcome in the lounge and restaurant. Dogs welcome.

White Hart Hotel High Street, Dorchester OX10 7HN (01865 340074; www.white-hart-hotel-dorchester.co.uk). A 16th-C coaching inn serving real ale and modern European food *L and E*. Children welcome (and look for the goldfish in the well). Visit website for event calendar.

Dorchester Abbey Tearoom Abbey Guest House, High Street, Dorchester OX10 7HR (01865 340054; www.dorchester-abbey.org.uk). Next to the abbey. Delicious biscuits, cakes and scones, all home-made and including lemon drizzle cake and Dorset gooseberry cake. *Open Apr–Sep Sat, Sun & B Hols (also Wed & Thur from mid-May) 15.00–17.00 (or earlier if the cake runs out)*. Quiet enclosed garden. Children welcome. Run by the village ladies, and all the profits go to charity.

Lily's Farm Shop and Tearoom 28 High Street, Dorchester OX10 7HN (01865 340900). Cosy, welcoming establishment serving local, organic produce and cream teas, together with pork-based snacks. *Open Mon–Sat 09.00–17.00; Sun & B Hols 10.30–17.00*.

Chesters Queen Street, Dorchester OX10 7HR (01865 341467). Charming coffee shop, serving fine cakes, and *L*. Cobbled courtyard. Everything home-baked. *Open daily 10.00–17.00*.

Shillingford Bridge Near Wallingford OX10 8LZ (01865 858567; www.shillingfordbridgehotel.com). Smart riverside hotel with excellent moorings (modest fee). Patrons may use the outdoor heated swimming and paddling pools, *closed after 19.00*. Real ale. Bar and restaurant meals available *L and E*, *daily*. Children welcome. Pleasant riverside garden. B&B.

The Crown Inn 52 High Street, Benson OX10 6RP (01491 838247; www.crowninnbenson.co.uk). Welcoming, comfortable 16th-C inn with inglenooks, log fires and a ghost. Real ale, meals and takeaway pizzas *L and E (not Sun E or Mon)*. Children welcome, garden. Music at *weekends*.

The Three Horseshoes 2 Oxford Street, Benson OX10 6LX (01491 838242; www.thethreehorseshoesbenson.co.uk). Traditional 17th-C pub serving real ale. Restaurant open *L and E*, and bar meals are served. Children welcome. Large garden.

The Boathouse 103 High Street, by Wallingford Bridge OX10 0BJ (01491 834100). Lively riverside pub, with terrace and conservatory. Food *L and E*, and there is a lovely riverside terrace.

The George Hotel High Street, Wallingford OX10 0BS (01491 836665; www.peelhotels.co.uk). An attractive 15th-C inn with restaurant. The Teardrop Room recalls a Civil War story of the landlord's daughter's grief at the loss of her love, a Royalist sergeant. Real ale. Bar and restaurant meals, are available *L and E*. Children welcome. Sheltered courtyard. B&B.

The Bell 75-79 The Street, Crowmarsh Gifford, Wallingford OX10 8EF (01491 835324). Large family pub serving real ale. Meals, with steak a speciality, *L and E*. Children welcome *until 21.00*. Dogs are welcome in the garden. Regular entertainment includes quiz night *Thu*. Garden.

WALKING & CYCLING

There are great walks from either side of Little Wittenham Bridge. To the south there are paths to the hill fort at the summit of the Sinodun Hills, returning over Round Hill. To the north you can follow the riverside path to the River Thame, turning north towards Dorchester. You then return via the Dyke Hills.

Moulsford

A broad stretch of river, pleasant but unremarkable. The buildings of Carmel College stand in wooded grounds in Mongewell Park, which fronts the Thames for a mile. North Stoke lies back from the river to the east. The islands above Brunel's lovely skewed brick arched railway bridge are supposedly haunted. Gradually the hills close in as the valley narrows towards Goring. The Beetle & Wedge Hotel marks the site of the old ferry which once linked Moulsford and South Stoke. These villages face each other across the river, but they are now totally separate.

North Stoke
Oxon. An attractive red brick village among trees. The church is pleasingly original and unrestored, with notable wall paintings.

Cholsey
Oxon. PO, stores, chemist, butcher, takeaway, off-licence, station (¾ mile distant). An undistinguished village but there is a pub, a range of shops and a station nearby. The shop is *open Mon–Sat 06.00–22.00 & Sun 07.00–22.00.*

Moulsford
Oxon. Tel. A roadside village with large houses by the river. The small, secluded church was rebuilt by Gilbert Scott in 1846: his fee was reputedly £64.

South Stoke
Oxon. A pretty residential village among trees. St Andrew's Church is 13th-C. Access can be gained from the river opposite the Beetle & Wedge Hotel.

ROW, ROW, ROW YOUR BOAT . . .

In the early part of the 20th C it was not uncommon for those who were lucky enough to live by the river to own a camping boat. The Thames Gig was typical of such craft, and could have been 25ft long with a 4ft beam, constructed perhaps by Hammertons of Thames Ditton. Clinker built in mahogany and propelled by two pairs of sculls, it would have two rowing thwarts, passenger seats in the stern and bows, a camping cover and, for comfort, a carpet! A crew of two could propel such a craft at 6mph over still water for considerable distances, with the added options of a small sail on a mast stepped at the bow if the wind was favourable, or a tow line to haul from the bank when the current was adverse.

Pubs and Restaurants

The Red Lion 39 Wallingford Road, Cholsey, Wallingford OX10 9LG (01491 651295; www.theredlioncholsey.co.uk). Friendly village local serving real ales and home-cooked food *Tue–Sun L and E (not Sun E)*. Children welcome.

The Four Teas Café 2A The Pound, Cholsey OX10 9NS (01491 659026; www.fourteas.co.uk). Friendly café serving teas, coffees, snacks, sandwiches and all day breakfast. *Open Mon–Sat 09.00–17.00.*

Memories of Bengal 12 Wallingford Road, Cholsey OX10 9LQ (01491 652777; www.memoriesofbengal.co.uk). Indian restaurant serving food *L and E*. Takeaway service.

Shangki-li Peking Restaurant The Forty, Ilges Lane, Cholsey OX10 9ND (01491 652225). Popular Chinese restaurant, with a highly regarded all-you-can-eat menu, situated rather bizarrely above the local Tesco. Friendly staff and great service.

The Morning Star 98 Papist Way, Cholsey OX10 9QL (01491 659046). Village pub half a mile from the river.

Beetle & Wedge Boathouse Ferry Lane, Moulsford OX10 9JF (01491 651381; www.beetleandwedge.co.uk). A *beetle* is a mallet used to hit the *wedge* which split trees into planks for floating down river to London; a practice last recorded in 1777 but recalled in the name of this justly famous pub, where H.G. Wells stayed while writing *Mr Polly* – it features in the book as the Potwell Inn. The building is a former manor house, standing in a superb riverside situation, with a lovely garden and a jetty. The Boat House has a large open fire on which many items from the menu are cooked. Children are welcome and the large garden is a plus. Moorings. Slipway, but get prior permission to use it. B&B. Boat hire (www.hscboats.co.uk/charter).

The Perch & Pike Inn The Street, South Stoke, Reading RG8 0JS (01491 872415; www.perchandpike.co.uk). Cosy 18th-C red brick and flint pub, with low beams, open log fires, antique furniture and, perhaps, a ghost. Real ale. Extensive home-cooked menu, served *L and E*. Boaters and quiet children are welcome, and there is a pleasant garden. B&B.

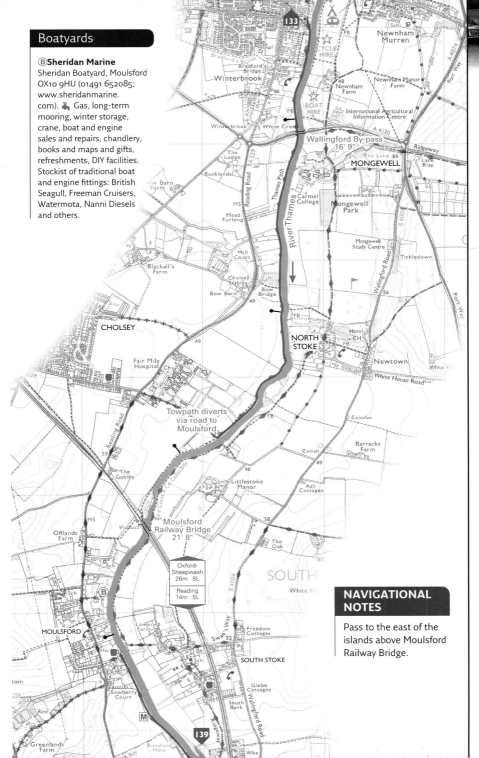

Boatyards

B Sheridan Marine
Sheridan Boatyard, Moulsford
OX10 9HU (01491 652085;
www.sheridanmarine.
com). Gas, long-term
mooring, winter storage,
crane, boat and engine
sales and repairs, chandlery,
books and maps and gifts,
refreshments, DIY facilities.
Stockist of traditional boat
and engine fittings: British
Seagull, Freeman Cruisers,
Watermota, Nanni Diesels
and others.

NAVIGATIONAL NOTES

Pass to the east of the
islands above Moulsford
Railway Bridge.

Goring

Approaching Cleeve Lock the valley narrows, with Lardon Chase rising steeply to the west behind Streatley. Little of Goring can be seen from the river – boathouses, the mill and a glimpse of the church as the river enters one of its most attractive parts. In the meadows to the east of Basildon there is a picturesque group of buildings around a church, while on the east bank beech woods rise steeply from the river's edge. The brick Gatehampton Railway Bridge was built by Brunel – beyond this Basildon House stands in wooded grounds, to the west of Beale Park.

Pubs and Restaurants

✕♇**Leatherne Bottel Restaurant** Bridle Way, Goring RG8 0HS (01491 872667; www.leathernebottel.co.uk). Riverside, above Cleeve Lock. There was a well here in Roman times which produced medicinal water. Now it is a smart riverside restaurant, serving fresh local produce *L and E*, in idyllic surroundings. Riverside terrace. Mooring.

●✕**The Swan** Streatley RG8 9HR (01491 878800; www.swanatstreatley.co.uk). Beautifully situated and very pleasant hotel/restaurant serving brasserie light lunches *all day*, with à la carte *Mon–Sat 12.00–14.00 and 19.00–22.00*. Plush interiors and fine riverside gardens. Children welcome. Moorings and boat hire. B&B.

●✕**The Bull** Reading Road, Streatley RG8 9JJ (01491 872392). Friendly 16th-C restaurant/pub at a busy crossroads. In 1895, when the Thames froze over, the pub sold water at 6d a bucket. Real ale. Bar meals available *L and E*. Children and dogs welcome, and there is a large garden, where a yew tree was planted to commemorate the 'gross misconduct' of a nun and a monk in 1440. B&B.

✕**Pierreponts Foodstore and Café** High Street, Goring RG8 9AB (01491 874464). Beside Goring Bridge and Lock. Highly regarded riverside establishment serving breakfast, brunch, lunch and afternoon tea. Also coffee, delicious cakes. All food is freshly cooked using local produce wherever possible. Pavement seating. Dog and child friendly. *Open Tue–Fri 08.00–16.00; Sat 09.00–17.00 & Sun 10.00–16.00. Later in summer months.*

●✕**The Miller of Mansfield** High Street, Goring RG8 9AW (01491 872829; www.millerofmansfield.com). Up the road from the bridge, refurbished to create a plush restaurant, bar and hotel offering a wide variety of food. B&B.

●✕**The John Barleycorn** Manor Road, Goring RG8 9DP (01491 872509; www.thejohnbarleycornpub.co.uk). A beamy 16th-C village pub serving real ale. Bar and restaurant meals available *L and E*. Children welcome in the dining area and restaurant only. Large attractive garden. Dogs welcome in garden. B&B.

●✕**Catherine Wheel** Station Road, Goring RG8 9HB (01491 872379; www.catherinewheelgoring.co.uk). This attractive 15th-C pub claims to be Goring's oldest, and has an open fire in winter. Excellent meals available *L and E (not Sun E)*. Children welcome in the restaurant, and there is a garden.

● **Goring**
Oxon. PO, tel, stores, chemist, takeaways, butcher, laundrette, station. One of the most important prehistoric fords across the river, linking the Icknield Way and the Ridgeway. The village is set in a splendid deep wooded valley by one of the most spectacular reaches on the river. A holiday paradise of indeterminate age, it retains many pretty brick and flint cottages. The church, of handsome proportions, is well situated by the river. Its bell, dating from 1290, is one of the oldest in England. Goring Mill stands below the bridge, an approximate replica (built 1923) of the earlier timber structure. Between Goring and Henley, the Thames passes through the Chilterns Area of Outstanding Natural Beauty, which covers 309 square miles.

● **Streatley**
Berks. A continuation of Goring on the west bank, but its 18th-C charm is diminished by the traffic roaring through. Of note are the old malt houses converted into a village hall by W. Ravenscroft in 1898. Lardon Chase (NT) rises to the north.

● **Lower Basildon**
Berks. An attractive group of buildings surround the church in a superb riverside situation. The 13th-C church contains a portrait group of two boys drowned in 1886. Jethro Tull (1674–1741), pioneer of agricultural mechanisation, lies buried in the churchyard.

Basildon Park Lower Basildon RG8 9NR (0118 984 3040; www.nationaltrust.org.uk). Built by John Carr of York for Sir Francis Sykes, who made his fortune in India, between 1776 and 1783, this is the most splendid Palladian mansion in Berkshire. Rescued from virtual dereliction in 1952 by Lord and Lady Iliffe, the building has been carefully restored. Octagon Room, Shell Room, Anglo-Indian objects in Nabob's Room, and many fine pictures and pieces of furniture. Exhibition of works by Graham Sutherland. 19th-C pleasure grounds. Waymarked walks. House *open late Mar–Oct, Wed–Mon 13.00–17.30; closed G Fri.* Park, gardens and woodland walks *open as house, 11.00–17.30*. Charge.

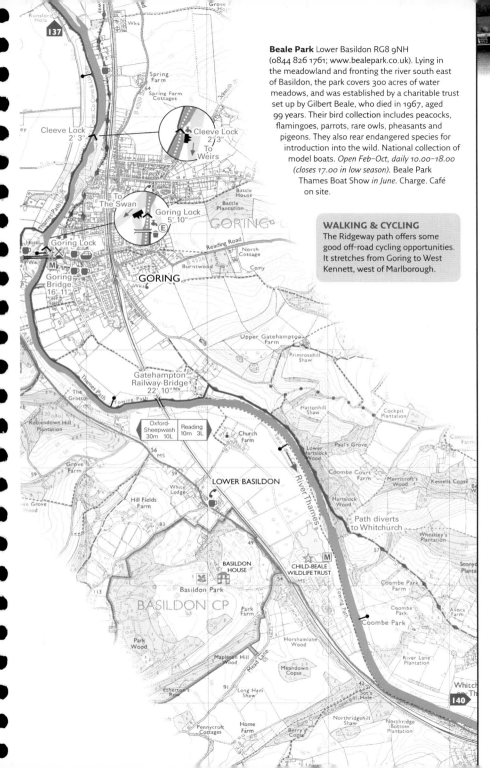

Beale Park Lower Basildon RG8 9NH
(0844 826 1761; www.bealepark.co.uk). Lying in
the meadowland and fronting the river south east
of Basildon, the park covers 300 acres of water
meadows, and was established by a charitable trust
set up by Gilbert Beale, who died in 1967, aged
99 years. Their bird collection includes peacocks,
flamingoes, parrots, rare owls, pheasants and
pigeons. They also rear endangered species for
introduction into the wild. National collection of
model boats. *Open Feb–Oct, daily 10.00–18.00
(closes 17.00 in low season).* Beale Park
Thames Boat Show *in June.* Charge. Café
on site.

WALKING & CYCLING
The Ridgeway path offers some
good off-road cycling opportunities.
It stretches from Goring to West
Kennett, west of Marlborough.

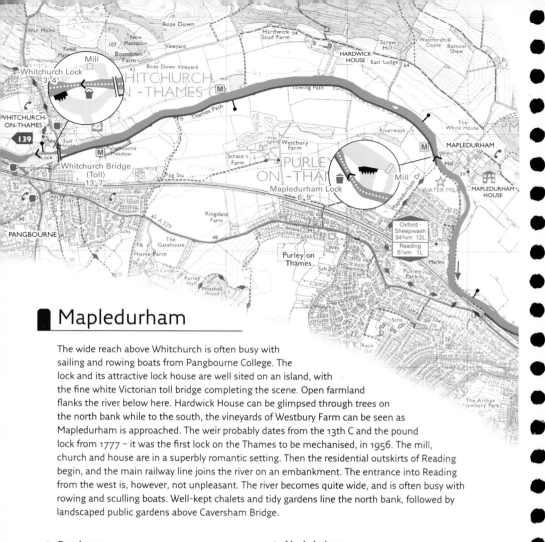

Mapledurham

The wide reach above Whitchurch is often busy with
sailing and rowing boats from Pangbourne College. The
lock and its attractive lock house are well sited on an island, with
the fine white Victorian toll bridge completing the scene. Open farmland
flanks the river below here. Hardwick House can be glimpsed through trees on
the north bank while to the south, the vineyards of Westbury Farm can be seen as
Mapledurham is approached. The weir probably dates from the 13th C and the pound
lock from 1777 – it was the first lock on the Thames to be mechanised, in 1956. The mill,
church and house are in a superbly romantic setting. Then the residential outskirts of Reading
begin, and the main railway line joins the river on an embankment. The entrance into Reading
from the west is, however, not unpleasant. The river becomes quite wide, and is often busy with
rowing and sculling boats. Well-kept chalets and tidy gardens line the north bank, followed by
landscaped public gardens above Caversham Bridge.

● **Pangbourne**
Berks. All services. A large, well-equipped commuter
town, still preserving traces of Edwardian elegance,
built at the confluence of the Thames with
the Pang, which is a famous trout stream. The
Nautical College, an imposing William and Mary
style mansion, is by Sir John Belcher, built 1897–8.
Pangbourne Meadow is now a National Trust
property of 7 acres. The Scottish author of *The Wind
in the Willows*, Kenneth Grahame (1859–1932), who
was also Secretary to the Bank of England, lived in
Church Cottage, Pangbourne, and told this story to
his four-year-old son Alastair in 1904.

● **Whitchurch**
Oxon. Quiet and attractive with a good group of mill
buildings, overlooked by the mainly Victorian church.
A small toll for motor vehicles is collected at the
Victorian iron bridge.

● **Mapledurham**
Oxon. A cluster of period houses and cottages stand
in the water meadows close to the restored and
working water mill, one of the oldest corn and grist
mills on the Thames. The scene is typical of an early
19th-C landscape painting and should be visited (but
see below).
Mapledurham House Mapledurham RG4 7TR (0118
972 3350; www.mapledurham.co.uk). Still occupied
by descendants of the Blount family, who purchased
the original manor in 1490 and built the present
Elizabethan manor house, with grounds sweeping
down to the Thames. The estate is private and there
are no rights of way from the river to the village, nor
any footpaths alongside the river on the north bank.
In 1643 the house was sacked by the Roundheads,
a year before Sir Charles Blount was killed during
the siege of Oxford. Following a period of relative

Pubs and Restaurants

The Swan Shooters Hill, Pangbourne RG8 7DU (0118 984 4494; www.theswan-pangbourne.co.uk). Above the weir. Jerome K. Jerome, his two colleagues and a 'shamed looking dog' abandoned their *Three Men in a Boat* journey here (on the way back) and took the train to London. Real ale. Food *available all day until 22.00*. Children and dogs welcome. Riverside seating.

The Elephant Hotel 3 Church Road, Pangbourne RG8 7AR (0118 984 2244; www.elephanthotel.co.uk). Old coaching inn with restaurant. Real ales. Bar meals and à la carte *available L and E (all day Sat & Sun)* Children and dogs welcome. Garden. B&B.

George Hotel Best Western The Square, Pangbourne RG8 7AJ (0118 984 2237; www.thegeorgehotelpangbourne.com). South of the bridge, under the railway. Real ale and meals *L and E*. Children welcome. B&B.

Greyhound High Street, Whitchurch RG8 7EL (www.whitchurchgreyhound.co.uk). North of Whitchurch Bridge. Real ale. Bar food *L and E (not Sun or Mon E)*. Children *over 14* welcome. Garden.

The Ferryboat Inn High Street, north of Whitchurch Bridge, RG8 7DB (0118 984 2161; www.theferryboat.eu). Real ale and food *L and E (not Sun E)*. Takeaway pizza service. Children welcome away from the bar. Covered patio. B&B. *Closed Mon.*

NAVIGATIONAL NOTES

1 You can pass either side of the island ¹/₄ mile above Mapledurham Lock.
2 Pass to the east of the island ¹/₄ mile below Mapledurham Lock.

impoverishment, the house was restored to what we see today by Michael Henry Blount (1789-1874). Mapledurham has interesting literary connections with Alexander Pope, Galsworthy's *Forsyte Saga* and Grahame's *The Wind in the Willows*. More recently it has been the setting for the film *The Eagle has Landed*, and has appeared in various television series including *Inspector Morse*.

Open Easter–Sep, Sat, Sun and B Hols 14.00–17.30. Charge. On these days a boat can be taken from Caversham Pier (0118 948 1088) to the landing stage on the Mill island. All passengers alighting must purchase an entrance ticket, as do any passengers from private boats, who are allowed to moor only for this purpose, and *only on open days.*

Reading

Caversham Bridge was built in 1926. The original bridge on this site was erected in the 13th C, and at one time had a chapel on it. Fry's Island is situated between the bridges; there are two boatyards on it. Reading lies to the south, a busy modern town which does little to welcome visitors from the river. Just below Reading Bridge is Caversham Lock, on the edge of King's Meadow. A little further down, to the east and under the railway bridge, is the entrance to the Kennet & Avon Canal (see page 107). Beyond this junction the scenery is initially uninspiring but this all changes when Sonning Lock and Mill appear amongst the willows. The 18th-C bridge and the large white hotel beside it mark the western extremity of Sonning village, which lies back from the river. About a mile below Sonning, St Patrick's Stream (unnavigable, with the River Loddon flowing in), makes its detour around Borough Marsh. The main course of the river passes numerous islands and skirts Warren Hill, a chalk ridge, before reaching Shiplake Lock. It then passes Shiplake and weaves through a group of islands to the west of Wargrave Marsh, a low-lying area enclosed by the Hennerton Backwater (navigable only by small boats).

BOAT TRIPS
Thames River Cruises Pipers Island, Bridge Street, Caversham
RG4 8AH (0118 948 1088; www.thamesrivercruise.co.uk).
Caversham Lady available for private charter. Also regular summer trips to Mapledurham, when the house is open.
Salter Bros Caversham Bridge Road, Reading (0118 957 2388; www.salterssteamers.co.uk). Scheduled summer service up and down river, with various stops.

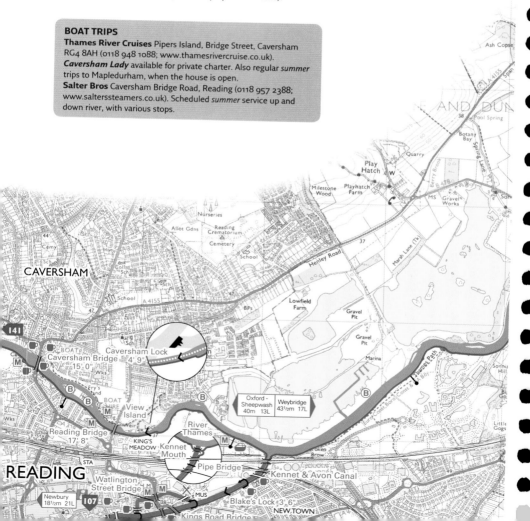

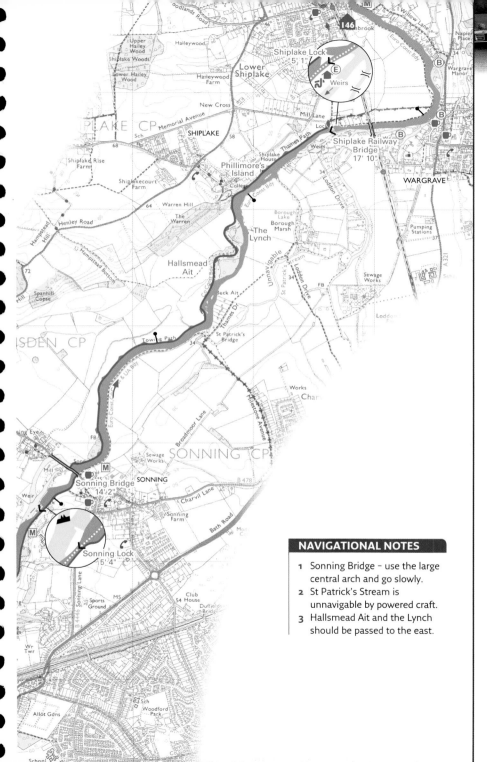

NAVIGATIONAL NOTES

1. Sonning Bridge – use the large central arch and go slowly.
2. St Patrick's Stream is unnavigable by powered craft.
3. Hallsmead Ait and the Lynch should be passed to the east.

Boatyards

Ⓑ**Caversham Boat Services** Fry's Island, De Montfort Road, Reading RG1 8DG (0118 957 4323/959 0346; www.cavershamboatservices.freeserve.co.uk). 🛥🔧D Pump out, hire craft, day-hire boats, long-term mooring, slipway, boat and engine repairs, gas, toilets, books, maps and gifts.

Ⓑ**Better Boating** Mill Green, Caversham, Reading RG4 8EX (0118 947 9536). 🛥🔧D Pump out, crane, gas, long- and short-term moorings, engine repairs, boat repairs, chandlery, toilets.

Ⓑ**Walker Outboards** (0118 947 8641; www.walkeroutboards.co.uk) are also based here.

Ⓑ**Thames & Kennet Marina** Caversham Lakes, Henley Road, Reading RG4 6LQ (0118 948 2911; www.tingdene-marinas.co.uk). 🛥🛥🔧D E

Pump out, gas, overnight and long-term mooring, winter storage, chandlery, telephone, toilets, showers, books and maps, boat sales, coal/logs, boat valeting, Wi-Fi, bar and café.

Ⓑ**Val Wyatt Marine** Willow Marina, Willow Lane, Wargrave RG10 8LH (0118 940 3211/07774 224500; www.valwyattmarine.co.uk). 🛥🔧 Pump out, gas, overnight and long-term mooring, winter storage, slipway, crane, boat & engine sales & repairs, chandlery, books, maps and gifts, DIY facilities, trailer boat parking, Wi-Fi.

Ⓑ**John Bushnell** Thameside Marina, Waterman's Way, Station Road, Wargrave RG10 8HB (0118 940 2161; www.bushnells.co.uk). Long-term mooring, winter storage, dry storage, 25 tonne travel lift, boat sales and repairs, toilets, showers.

● **Reading**
Berks. All services. A very busy town lacking a cohesive centre – it is an amalgam of university and industry with a constant stream of traffic scything through. The university buildings are uninspiring, but some of the Victorian buildings are better, and the museum houses one of the most fascinating archaeological collections in the country.

Abbey Ruins Fragmentary remains of the 12th-C abbey, built by Henry I, lie on the edge of Forbury Park. The Abbey was one of the largest in England and at one time comparable with Bury St Edmunds. The 13th-C gatehouse still stands. It was once the Abbey School where Jane Austen studied in 1785-7, although the structure was greatly altered by Gilbert Scott in 1869. The Church of St Lawrence near the Market Place was originally attached to the outer gate.

Gaol Forbury Road. Designed by Scott & Moffat, 1842-4 in Scottish Baronial style. Oscar Wilde (1854-1900) wrote *De Profundis* in 1897 while imprisoned here for homosexual practices (the *Ballad of Reading Gaol* was actually written in Paris in 1898).

Reading Museum The Town Hall, Blagrave Street RG1 1QH (0118 937 3400; www.readingmuseum. org. uk). Features *The Story of Reading*, tracing the town's development from a Saxon settlement on the River Kennet to the present day. Special features include a reconstructed section of the abbey and the Oracle gates entrance to the 17th-C workhouse. In the upper gallery is a full 230ft sweep of Britain's Bayeux Tapestry, Reading's faithful replica of the 11th-C original. Huntley & Palmers, the Reading biscuit makers, display a collection of 300 biscuit tins. *Open Tue–Sat 10.00–16.00, Sun 11.00–16.00 (open B Hol Mon).* Free. Palmers Café *open Mon–Sat 10.00–15.00.*

Museum of English Rural Life University of Reading, Redlands Road RG1 5EX (0118 378 8660; www.reading.ac.uk/merl/). The first museum in England to specialise in rural life as it was lived about 150 to 175 years ago, before the invention of the tractor. The majority of exhibits date from the period 1850-1950, and include farm equipment, beekeeping equipment, corn dollies, sewing machines and so on. *Open Tue–Fri 09.00–17.00, Sat–Sun 14.00–16.30.* Modest charge.

Tourist Information Centre Visit the website www.livingreading.co.uk.

● **Caversham**
Berks. All services – cinema and station in Reading (½ mile distant). A residential continuation of Reading, which is at its best by the river, where parks and gardens stretch alongside. The library in Church Street is worth a look – it is a jolly Edwardian building, built in 1907, with a central green copper clock supported by an angel.

● **Sonning**
Berks. Tel. A very pretty and meticulously preserved village. The largely 19th-C church has remarkable monuments, and some good 15th-C brasses. The most interesting house in the town is Lutyens' Deanery Gardens, built for Edward Hudson in 1901. To the west of Sonning is Holme Park – the Reading Blue Coat School; its wooded grounds drop steeply to the river. The railway   passes in a spectacular cutting to the south, built by Brunel.

Stanlake Park Wine Estate Stanlake Park, Twyford RG10 0BN (0118 934 0176; www.stanlakepark.com). These well-established vineyards may be visited by groups of a *minimum of 25 people.* Book in advance for a tour and wine tasting. The shop is *open Mon–Sat 11.00–17.00, Sun 12.00–17.00.* Charge for the tours.

● Wargrave

Berks. PO, stores, chemist, station. A well-situated town on rising ground among trees and overlooking the Thames. The church was burnt down in 1914 by the suffragettes – some say it was because the vicar refused to take the word 'obey' out of the marriage service. The striking Woodclyffe Hall, in the High Street, was built in 1901. Henry Kingsley (1830–76), the novelist, often stayed here. East of the town is Wargrave Manor, an early 19th-C building. The River Loddon joins St Patrick's Stream to the south west – here, in black swampy soil, the Loddon Lily (*Leucojum aestivum*) is native. Loddon Pondweed (*Potamogeton nodosus*, now a threatened species) its leaves beautifully veined, may also be found.

PLANT LIFE

The *Loddon Lily* (also known as the *Summer Snowflake*) takes its name from the River Loddon, which runs into the Thames about a mile below Sonning (*see page 143*). It resembles a snowdrop, but both the flowers and the plant are larger. The Loddon Lily is found beside rivers and in damp woodland and meadows. It flowers in April and May. The lily has drooping white-petalled flowers, with green spots on the tips of the petals.

Pubs and Restaurants

If you do not mind dodging the traffic, there are plenty of pubs in Reading (*see page 109 for a selection*) – those visiting from the Thames may wish to travel a couple of miles up- or downstream, where the surroundings are a little more congenial.

● **The Griffin** 10-12 Church Road, Caversham RG4 7AD (0118 947 5018; www.thegriffencaversham.co.uk). North of Caversham Bridge. Real ale is served in this friendly pub, along with bar meals *L and E, Sunday lunch*. Children are welcome *until 20.00*. Patio.

● **Fisherman's Cottage** 224 Kennetside, Reading RG1 3DW (0118 957 1553; www.fishermanscottagereading.co.uk). Pretty 18th-C canalside pub west of Blakes Lock. Real ale. Food available (with a Thai twist) *Mon–Fri L and E; Sat & Sun 12.00–18.00*. Children welcome. Open fires. Canalside seating. Mooring.

● **Jolly Anglers** 314 – 316 Kennetside, Reading RG1 3EA (0118 376 7823; www.thejollyanglers.com). There is a quaint façade to this pub which marks the last refreshment point before the Thames. Real ales, Ciders (regarded as Reading's cider centre) and Belgian beers. Fresh food available *daily 12.00–22.00 (Sun 20.00)*.

● ✕ **Great House Hotel** Thames Street, Sonning BridgeRG4 6UT (0118 969 2277; www.greathouseatsonning.co.uk). Beautifully situated riverside hotel and restaurant of great character, with fine gardens and lawns. One dining room is 700 years old; the main bar is a beamed room with a stone fireplace. The Ferryman's Bar has choice of real ale. Meals are served *L and E*. Children are welcome. Mooring. B&B.

● **The Bull Inn** By Sonning church,High Street, Sonning RG4 6UP (0118 969 3901; www.fullershotels.com). Lovely, old half-timbered pub in a 15th-C church house covered with wisteria. There are comfy cushioned settles, massive beams and inglenook fireplaces inside, with wooden tables in a courtyard facing the church outside. Real ale. Bar meals are served *all day*. Children welcome. Garden. B&B. In the absence of a village shop this pub will happily sell you fresh milk and eggs and similar fresh produce. In the absence of a village shop this pub will happily sell you fresh milk and eggs and similar fresh produce.

● **The Bull** High Street, Wargrave RG10 8DD (0118 940 3120; www.thebullwargrave.com). Friendly 15th-C coaching inn. Real ale. Excellent bar and restaurant meals *L and E*. Children welcome in the dining areas, and there is a garden. Look out for the 19th-C ghost of an ex-landlady. B&B.

✕ ⌂ **The Ivy of Sonning** 6 High Street, Sonning RG4 6UP (0118 969 7676; www.ivyofsonning.co.uk). Well appointed restaurant offering a fine example of Indian cuisine. Telephone for opening times.

● ✕ **The White Hart Inn** 45 High Street, Wargrave RG10 8BU (0118 940 6312; www.thewhitehartwargrave.co.uk). A fine old inn serving real ale, and bar and restaurant meals *all day Tue–Sat*. Takeaway service. Coffee and afternoon teas. Children welcome if you are eating.

● **The Greyhound** 79 High Street, Wargrave RG10 8BU (0118 940 2556). A half-timbered corner pub serving real ale. Bar lunches *L*. Children welcome away from the bar. Garden. Outside seating on patio. There is an old forge at the back of the pub. Occasional entertainment.

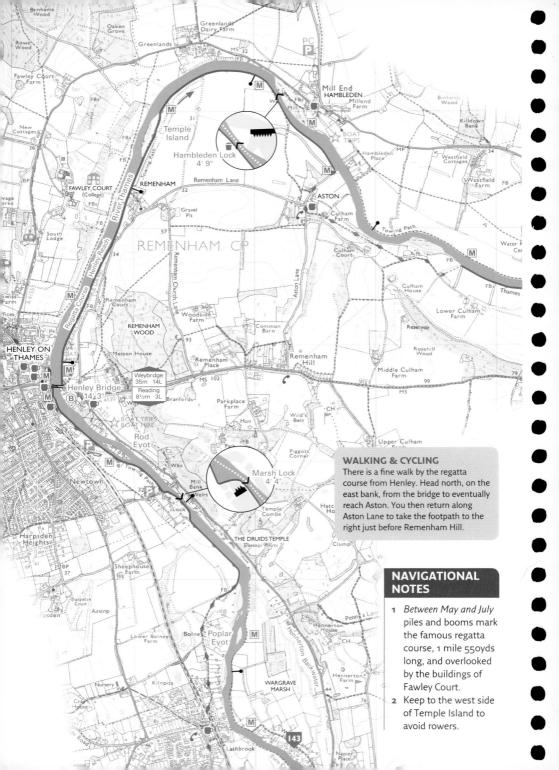

WALKING & CYCLING

There is a fine walk by the regatta course from Henley. Head north, on the east bank, from the bridge to eventually reach Aston. You then return along Aston Lane to take the footpath to the right just before Remenham Hill.

NAVIGATIONAL NOTES

1 *Between May and July* piles and booms mark the famous regatta course, 1 mile 550yds long, and overlooked by the buildings of Fawley Court.

2 Keep to the west side of Temple Island to avoid rowers.

Henley on Thames

The Thames continues north towards Temple Combe Woods, which rise steeply to the east.

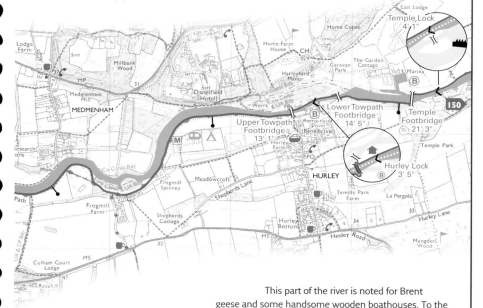

This part of the river is noted for Brent geese and some handsome wooden boathouses. To the north east of Marsh Lock is Park Place; in the grounds is part of Wren's original spire for St Bride's Church, Fleet Street. The house was once occupied by General Conway, whose daughter, Mrs Damer, sculpted the masks of Thames and Isis on Henley Bridge. The town of Henley lies to the west of the river, with an attractive waterfront, many moored boats and resident swans, facing the rise of Remenham Wood to the east. Below Temple Island the river passes the immaculate grounds of the Henley Management College before reaching Hambleden Lock, beautifully situated with an extensive weir (footpath over) and a fine weatherboarded mill, now converted into flats. The tiny village of Aston can be seen on a hillside to the south below the lock; the Thames then divides around thickly wooded islands and meanders past Medmenham and St Mary's Abbey. Beyond the next group of islands a large caravan site heralds the approach of Hurley, where the weir streams rush among more islands by the lock. To the north is Danesfield, a home built at the turn of the 20th C by a Manchester millionaire.

Boatyards

ⓑ **Hobbs & Sons** Station Road, Henley RG9 1AZ (01491 572035; www.hobbs-of-henley.com). ♿ P D Day-boat hire, passenger boat charter and river trips, long-term mooring, winter storage, crane, outboard engine repairs, telephone.
ⓑ **Peter Freebody's Boatyard** Thames Boat Houses, Mill Lane, Hurley SL6 5ND (01628 824382; www.peterfreebody.com). Overnight and long-term mooring, winter storage, crane, boat and engine sales and repairs, boat handling tuition. Established at Hurley since 1933 and before that at Caversham. Primarily a boat builder, this is a very famous yard, restoring and building many boats, including steam launches and electric boats.

Shiplake

Oxon. Stores, station. A village of desirable commuter houses climbing up into the hills that border the river. The splendidly situated Church of SS Peter and Paul contains some medieval Belgian glass of great beauty. Tennyson married Emily Sellwood here in 1850. To the north, near the station, George Orwell lived as a boy at Roselawn, Station Road. There is an award winning stores and PO at **Lower Shiplake**.

Henley on Thames

Oxon. All services. A fine market town and one of the most popular resorts on the river, described by Dickens as 'the Mecca of the rowing man'. The main street runs down to the Thames from the Victorian town hall, where, from the river, the most obvious features are the 18th-C stone bridge (note the masks of Thames and Isis) and the church, a large and gloomy building. The Red Lion Hotel, near the church, has received some notable visitors, including King Charles I (1632 and 1642), the Duke of Marlborough (early 18th C), the poet William Shenstone (1750) and Johnson and Boswell (1776). The Kenton Theatre (01491 575698) in New Street is the fourth oldest in the country, being built in 1805. The first Oxford and Cambridge boat race was rowed between Hambleden and Henley on 10 June 1829 – the race is now rowed between Putney and Mortlake. The first Henley Regatta (01491 572153) was held in 1839, becoming Royal in 1851, with Prince Albert as patron. This is now held *annually in the first week of July;* the town becomes very busy indeed, and everyone seems to be on a picnic. The epitome of an English summer (when the sun shines).

The River and Rowing Museum Mill Meadows, Henley-on-Thames RG9 1BF (01491 415600; www.rrm.co.uk). In a building clad with green oak and set upon columns in the water meadows just outside Henley, the museum has three galleries illustrating the river, the town of Henley, and rowing. Exhibits range from the world's oldest rowing boat to a state-of-the-art monocoque racing machine, and include a river gallery, with an aquarium of Thames fish. It also has a very fine painting of Henley by Jan Siberechts, dated 1698, showing the river busy with barges. *Open May–Aug 10.00–17.30; Sep–Apr 10.00–17.00.* Charge. Café, shop, library.

Fawley Court Marlow Road, Henley on Thames RG9 3AE (01491 574917; www.fawleycourt.co.uk). The court, in a fine riverside situation, was designed by Wren and built in 1684 on the arched basement of an earlier fortified manor house. It was later to be decorated by Grinling Gibbons and classicised by James Wyatt. The grounds were laid out by 'Capability' Brown in 1770. It now owned by the Marian Fathers and has a museum founded by Father Joseph Jarzebowski, consisting of a library, various documents of the Polish monarchy, including Laksi's *Code of Laws* dating from 1506, and Polish militaria, and paintings and sculpture illustrating ancient history and the Middle Ages.

Temple Island RG9 2LY The temple was built by James Wyatt in 1771 as a vista for Fawley Court, and has a set of hand-painted wall decorations by him. It is thought to be the earliest example in England of the Etruscan style. Owned by the Mackenzie family for over 130 years, the island was sold in 1988. Visited by King Edward VII and Queen Alexandra, it is very pretty, with views down the river to Henley.

Tourist Information Centre King's Arms Barn, Kings Road, Henley-on-Thames RG9 2DG (01491 578034; www.ioxfordshire.co.uk/profile/443219/Henley-on-Thames/Tourist-Information-Centre).

Hambleden

Bucks. PO, stores. Set back from the river and surrounded by heavily wooded hills, this is one of the most attractive villages – all mellow flint and brick – in Buckinghamshire, and worth the walk up from the river. The 14th-C church and the houses round the green make it a perfect village setting, with the 17th-C Manor House in the background. The mill and mill house look good by the lock.

Medmenham

Bucks. A village straggling up from the now defunct ferry into the woods behind. Medmenham Abbey (St Mary's Abbey) is a charming agglomeration of building styles:1595, 18th-C Gothic and mostly 1898. It was the house of the orgiastic Hell Fire Club, under the patronage of Sir Francis Dashwood. It was decorated in a suitably pornographic and sacrilegious style, but understandably none of this survived the 19th C.

Hurley

Berks. PO, stores. In the old part of the village the long, dark and narrow nave of the church is all that remains of Hurley Priory (St Mary's), founded before 1087 for the Benedictine Order. Opposite the church are a 14th-C tithe barn (now a dwelling) and a dovecote. The PO *is only open Tue and Thur mornings.*

Harleyford Manor Henley Road, Marlow SL7 2DX (01628 471361; www.harleyford.co.uk) On the north bank opposite Hurley. The red-brick Georgian manor was built in the late 1740s by Sir Robert Taylor for Sir William Clayton, and has been recently restored. Notable amongst visitors to The Manor have been Emperor Napoleon III, Prime Minister Disraeli and author Kenneth Grahame. The superbly landscaped grounds contain an ice house and the ruins of a Georgian temple. The whole estate is an Area of Outstanding Natural Beauty, and is now used as a leisure environment, with holiday lodges, a golf course and marina.

BOAT TRIPS

Hobbs & Sons Station Road, Henley RG9 1AZ (01491 572035; www.hobbs-of-henley.com). Skippered vessels for private charter, including Edwardian-style motor launches. Boat hire and public cruises.
Magna Carta (07836 551912; www.magna-carta.co.uk). Luxury cruises on a hotel barge, based at Henley.

Pubs and Restaurants

🍺✕**The Baskerville Arms** Station Road, Lower Shiplake, Henley RG9 3NY (0118 940 3332; www.thebaskerville.com). Real ales served. Restaurant with wide-ranging menu *L and E*. Children welcome. Garden. Barbeques in *summer*. B&B.

🍺**The Anchor Inn** 58 Friday Street, Henley RG9 1AH (01491 574753; www.lnc.net/anchor/index.cfm). Cosy and friendly 15th-C pub, haunted by a friendly cleaning lady! Real ale. Traditional English food and home-baked bread available *L and E (not Sun and Mon E)*. Children welcome. Garden and patio. No dogs.

🍺✕**The Red Lion Hotel** Hart Street, by the bridge, Henley RG9 2AR (01491 572161; www.redlionhenley.co.uk). A very auspicious and much-visited (*see* Henley, opposite) 15th-C red brick hotel with a restaurant serving meals *L and E*. Children welcome.

🍺✕**The Angel on the Bridge** Thameside, Henley Bridge RG9 1BH (01491 410678; www.theangelhenley.com). Beautiful and historic 14th-C inn adjoining the bridge. Real ale. Bar and restaurant meals available *L and E*. Well-behaved children welcome. Riverside terrace.

🍺**The Rose & Crown** New Street, Henley RG9 2BT (01491 575246; www.theroseandcrownhenley.co.uk). A traditional local with a glass-covered well inside. Real ale. Bar meals *L and E (not Sun E)*. Fish & chip specials on *Fri (19.00, book)*. Garden. B&B.

🍺✕**The Little Angel** Remenham Lane, east of Henley Bridge RG9 2LS (01491 411008; www.thelittleangel.co.uk). A 17th-C pub serving modern British food *L and E (not Sun E in winter)*. Well-behaved children welcome. Patio seating,

overlooking the cricket ground. It is haunted by Marie Blandy, who poisoned her father.

🍺**The Flower Pot Hotel** Ferry Lane, Aston, Henley RG9 3DG (01491 574721; www.brakspear.co.uk). Attractive, old-fashioned pub built about 1890. Real ale. Meals are available *L and E (not Sun E)*. Children and dogs welcome. Large garden.

🍺✕**The Stag & Huntsman Hotel** Hambleden, Henley RG9 6RP (01491 571227). Traditional brick and flint pub. Real ale. Good menu, including game in season, served *L and E (not Sun E)*. Children welcome. Large garden. B&B.

🍺✕**The Dog & Badger** Henley Road, Medmenham SL7 2HE (01491 571362; www.thedogandbadger.com). This fine old pub dates from 1390 and has historical associations with the Hell Fire Club (*see* Medmenham opposite). Real ale. Bar meals are available *L and E (not Sun E)*. Children are welcome in the front bar and restaurant. Outside seating on the terrace.

✕♀**Black Boys Inn** Henley Road, Hurley, Maindenhead SL6 5NQ (01628 824212; www.blackboysinn.co.uk). Restaurant with rooms, specialising in French home cooking.

🍺**The Rising Sun** High Street, Hurley SL6 5LT (01628 825733). Village local serving bar meals and real ale. Children and dogs welcome.

🍺✕**The Olde Bell** High Street, Hurley SL6 5LX (01628 825881; www.theoldebell.co.uk). Describing itself as a modern coaching Inn, this establishment serves bar meals *from 12.00–22.00* and offers an a la carte restaurant menu *daily*, *L and E*, using locally grown, seasonal produce wherever possible. Real ale. Children welcome and well catered for. Six acre gardens and tennis court. B&B.

Henley Regatta

Marlow

On the reach below Temple Lock you may well see canoeists and dinghy sailors from the National Sports Centre at Bisham Abbey, so take care. At the end of this long wide stretch is the elegant white Marlow suspension bridge, with the lock just beyond. The Marlow-Bisham bypass crosses below here, and this is followed by the Scouts Boating Centre, so once again the river is often full of small craft. Then the Thames turns to skirt the steep hills of Quarry Wood.

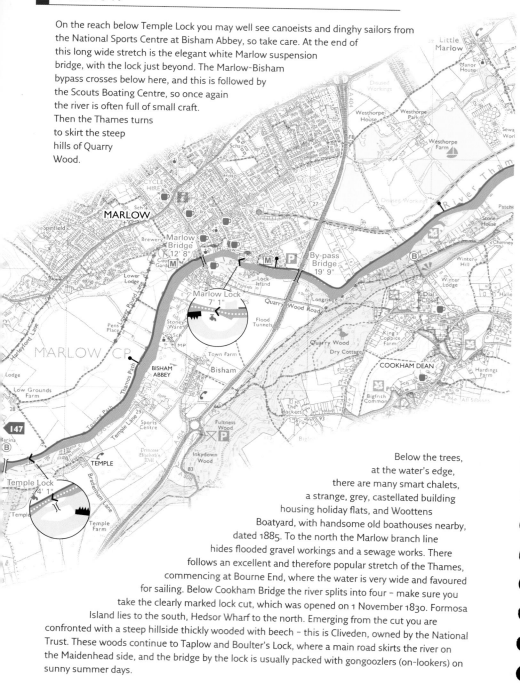

Below the trees, at the water's edge, there are many smart chalets, a strange, grey, castellated building housing holiday flats, and Woottens Boatyard, with handsome old boathouses nearby, dated 1885. To the north the Marlow branch line hides flooded gravel workings and a sewage works. There follows an excellent and therefore popular stretch of the Thames, commencing at Bourne End, where the water is very wide and favoured for sailing. Below Cookham Bridge the river splits into four – make sure you take the clearly marked lock cut, which was opened on 1 November 1830. Formosa Island lies to the south, Hedsor Wharf to the north. Emerging from the cut you are confronted with a steep hillside thickly wooded with beech – this is Cliveden, owned by the National Trust. These woods continue to Taplow and Boulter's Lock, where a main road skirts the river on the Maidenhead side, and the bridge by the lock is usually packed with gongoozlers (on-lookers) on sunny summer days.

Boatyards

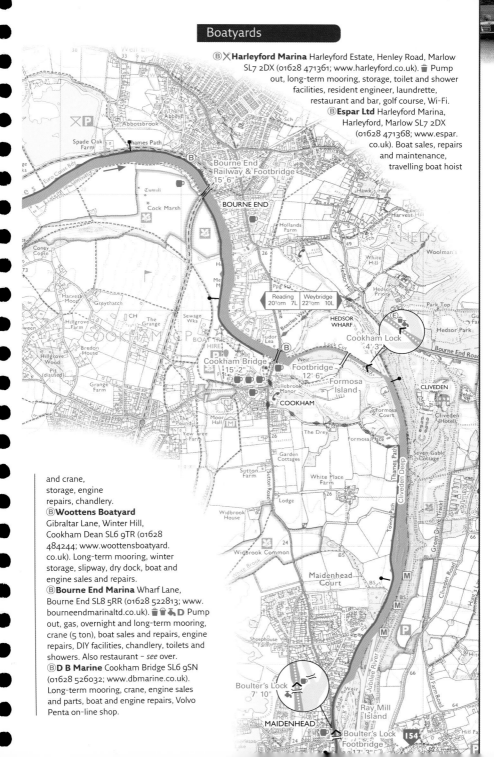

Ⓑ✕ **Harleyford Marina** Harleyford Estate, Henley Road, Marlow SL7 2DX (01628 471361; www.harleyford.co.uk). 🚿 Pump out, long-term mooring, storage, toilet and shower facilities, resident engineer, laundrette, restaurant and bar, golf course, Wi-Fi.

Ⓑ **Espar Ltd** Harleyford Marina, Harleyford, Marlow SL7 2DX (01628 471368; www.espar. co.uk). Boat sales, repairs and maintenance, travelling boat hoist

and crane, storage, engine repairs, chandlery.

Ⓑ **Woottens Boatyard** Gibraltar Lane, Winter Hill, Cookham Dean SL6 9TR (01628 484244; www.woottensboatyard. co.uk). Long-term mooring, winter storage, slipway, dry dock, boat and engine sales and repairs.

Ⓑ **Bourne End Marina** Wharf Lane, Bourne End SL8 5RR (01628 522813; www. bourneendmarinaltd.co.uk). 🚿🛢🔧D Pump out, gas, overnight and long-term mooring, crane (5 ton), boat sales and repairs, engine repairs, DIY facilities, chandlery, toilets and showers. Also restaurant – see over.

Ⓑ **D B Marine** Cookham Bridge SL6 9SN (01628 526032; www.dbmarine.co.uk). Long-term mooring, crane, engine sales and parts, boat and engine repairs, Volvo Penta on-line shop.

WALKING & CYCLING

There is good riverside walking south of Marlow Bridge – turn right just before Temple Lock, and return via Lower Pound Lane. There is also a stiff walk to the top of Winter Hill, but it is worth the effort. Walk north west from Cookham across the golf course, then along Alleyns Lane to Cookham Dean. Follow the path to Quarry Wood, turn right and walk to the summit of Winter Hill, for splendid views. Continue with the river to your left to return to Cookham, passing The Moorings pub on the way.

Pubs and Restaurants

✕♀The Compleat Angler Hotel By Marlow Bridge, Marlow SL7 1RG (0844 879 9128; www.macdonaldhotels.co.uk/compleatangler/). A restaurant and hotel with a riverside terrace, by the famous suspension bridge. It used to be the Anglers Rest; now the name commemorates Izaak Walton's famous book, published in 1653. The Riverside Restaurant serves an à la carte menu, in a romantic atmosphere *L and E* (booking preferred). Bistro *L and E, including afternoon tea*. Children welcome. Skippered boat hire available.

🍺✕The George & Dragon The Causeway, Marlow SL7 2AA (01628 814312; www.tabletable.co.uk). A restaurant/pub serving real ale. Meals *daily*. Children welcome. Patio.

🍺✕The Chequers Inn High Street, Marlow SL7 1BA (01628 482053; www.tmsteaks.co.uk). Real ale in a 16th-C inn. Restaurant and bar meals available *L and E*. Children welcome if dining. Outside seating.

✕♀The Vanilla Pod 31 West Street, Marlow SL7 2LS (01628 898101; www.thevanillapod.co.uk). Good French food, imaginatively spiced. Special evenings held throughout the year.

🍺The Prince of Wales Mill Road, Marlow SL7 1PX (01628 482970; www.the-prince-of-wales.co.uk). Locals pub serving real ale. Meals in bar or dining area *L and E*. Children welcome when eating. Outside seating. Opposite is the Tiger Club Indian restaurant. B&B.

🍺The Marlow Donkey Station Road, Marlow SL7 1NW (01628 482022). Victorian pub near the station – The Donkey was a famous local train, as the sign indicates. Real ales. Bar meals from full menu available *L and E*. Children welcome. Garden.

🍺✕The Jolly Farmer Church Road, Cookham Dean SL6 9PD (01628 482905; www.jollyfarmercookhamdean.co.uk). Opposite the local church, this friendly pub offers a varying range of real ales. Home-made meals served *L and E (not Sun and Mon E)*, with alfresco dining on the patio. Children welcome. Large garden with play area. This pub was bought by the village, for the village, in 1987. The PO is also in the pub.

🍺✕Chequers Brasserie Dean Lane, Cookham Dean SL6 9BQ (01628 481232; www.chequersbrasserie. co.uk). Historic pub/restaurant, with wooden beams

and an open fire. Good selection of wines and real ale. Meals from a daily changing menu *L and E (not Sun E)*. Children welcome. Conservatory, and seats outside.

🍺✕The Walnut Tree Hedsor Road, Bourne End SL8 5DN (01628 532417; www.walnuttree.co). A 16th-C traditional pub with a large garden. Real ale. Bar and restaurant meals *available all day, every day*. Live music *Thur*. Children welcome. Large patio garden.

🍺✕The Bounty Riverside, Cockmarsh, Bourne End SL8 5RG (01628 520056; www.thebountypub.com). Old-fashioned pub/ restaurant decorated with an array of naval flags. Real ale. Meals are served *L and E*. Children welcome. Patio overlooking the river, extensive moorings. *Open all day, every day Apr–Sep & weekends Oct–Mar, closing at dusk. Food available 12.00–20.00 in summer & 12.00–17.00 in winter.*

🍺✕The Firefly Station Approach, Bourne End SL8 5QH (01628 521197). Real ale. Bar meals served *L*. Large garden where pétanque is played. No children.

🍺✕The Ferry Sutton Road, Cookham SL6 9SN (01628 525123; www.theferry.co.uk). Relaxed, gastro-style pub by the bridge. Real ales. Meals *L and E*. Patio and river views. Children are welcome.

🍺✕Bel and The Dragon High Street, Cookham SL6 9SQ (01628 521263; www.belandthedragon-cookham.co.uk). An attractive pub dating from 1417. Real ale. Freshly prepared meals served *L and E*. Children welcome, and there is a garden with a terrace.

✕♀The King's Arms High Street, Cookham SL6 9SJ (01628 530667; www.thekingsarmscookham.co.uk). Village pub, serving real ale. Food, including classic pub dishes available *all day, every day*. Patio garden.

✕♀Malik's Royal Exchange, High Street, Cookham SL6 9SF (01628 520085; www.maliks.co.uk). Cosy, beamy and smart Indian restaurant. *L & E.*

✕♀Boulters Restaurant and Bar Boulters Island, Maidenhead SL6 8PE (01628 621291; www.boultersrestaurant.co.uk). Bar and restaurant right by the lock in the Old Ray Flour Mill, built 1726 and converted in 1950. Children welcome. *Open all day, every day. Brunch menu offered daily 10.00–11.30 and bar food available 12.00–21.30 (Sun 21.00). Brasserie open Tue–Sun L and E (not Sun E).*

Bisham

Berks. A largely Georgian village set back from the river, behind the abbey. The church is set apart from both, being superbly sited almost at the river's edge. Although rebuilt, it still has a Norman tower.

Bisham Abbey SL7 1RT The abbey, built mainly in the 14th and 16th C, was a private house from 1540. It is now a sports centre of the Central Council of Physical Recreation, a hive of activity where young players and coaches come together under the aegis of their respective governing bodies of sport. They train in the sport of their choice, ranging from archery to weight lifting. River activities feature strongly in the training programme. *The centre is not open to casual visitors.*

Marlow

Bucks. All services. A very handsome and lively Georgian town, with a wide tree-lined High Street connecting the bridge with the Market Place. A marvellous view of the weir can be had from the white suspension bridge, built by Tierny Clarke in 1831–6 and reconstructed, retaining its original width, in 1966. The town's most ancient building is the Old Parsonage, once part of a great 14th-C house and containing panelled rooms and beautifully decorated windows. West Street, at the top of the High Street, has great literary associations – Thomas Love Peacock wrote *Nightmare Abbey* at no. 47, Shelley wrote *Revolt to Islam* in Albion House, while his wife Mary Godwin created *Frankenstein* there. T. S. Eliot also lived in West Street for a while, after World War I.

Cookham Dean

Berks. PO. Large parts of Cookham Dean are owned by the National Trust. The village stands above steep beech woods by the river. Winter Hill has one of the best views over the Thames Valley, and is well worth the steep walk. Kenneth Grahame, who wrote *The Wind in the Willows,* published 1908, lived at Mayfield between 1906–10. It is thought that Quarry Wood may have been the wild wood mentioned in the story. The PO is in the Jolly Farmer pub *open Tue & Thur 15.00–17.30.*

Bourne End

Bucks. PO, stores, chemist, off-licence, takeaways, bakery, butcher, hardware, garage, station. A riverside commuter village, famous for Bourne End Sailing Week. Cock Marsh opposite, 132 acres, is owned by the National Trust. There is also a helpful cycle shop (01628 865050; www.on2wheelscycleshop.co.uk) *open Mon–Sat.*

Cookham

Berks. PO, stores, butcher, off-licence, takeaways, hardware, chemist, banks, baker, green grocer, garage, station A pretty and busy village of pubs, antique shops, restaurants and boutiques, with bijou cottages filling the gaps in between.

Cookham is famous as the home of the artist Stanley Spencer, who was born in 'Fernlea', in the High Street – the quite amazing variety of his work is splendidly exhibited in the old Wesleyan Chapel. His *Last Supper,* painted in 1920, hangs in the splendid square-towered Holy Trinity Church, built by the Normans in 1140 on the site of a Saxon building. There are fine 16th-C monuments, and the church is floodlit after dark. The bridge, an iron structure, was built in 1867.

Stanley Spencer Gallery The Kings Hall, High Street, Cookham SL6 9SJ (01628 471885; www.stanleyspencer.org.uk). Opened in 1962, this is the only gallery devoted to an artist which is situated in the village of his birth, and where he attended Sunday school. Along with his paintings, there is a collection of memorabilia associated with this remarkable man. *Open daily Apr–Oct ,10.30–17.30 & Thur–Sun Nov–Mar, 11.00–16.30.* Charge.

Odds Farm Park Wooburn Common, High Wycombe HP10 0LX (01628 520188; www. oddsfarm.co.uk). The best approach is by taxi from Maidenhead. A rare breed centre, where children (and adults) can observe the animals in close proximity. Tractor rides, log play and a calendar of special events throughout the summer. *Open daily 10.00–17.30.* Charge. Tea room, gifts.

Hedsor

Bucks. A priory and an over-restored church on the hill. It is worth the walk up for the splendid views over the beech woods. Hedsor House was rebuilt in 1862 in an Italianate style. Lord Boston's Folly, an 18th-C structure, faces the church from the opposite hill.

Hedsor Wharf An important shipping point for timber, paper and coal for over 500 years until the lock cut bypassed it in 1830. At the lower end of Hedsor Water there was once a lock – the original cottage still stands, a single room cut from the chalk and fronted with brick. Hedsor Water is private.

Cliveden Taplow, Maidenhead SL6 0JA (01494 755562; www.nationaltrust.org.uk; www.clivedenhouse.co.uk). A most marvellous stretch of beech woods from Hedsor to Taplow surrounds the house, which was built in 1851 by Charles Barry for the Duke of Sutherland. It was the home of Nancy, Lady Astor, and was the background to many 20th-C political intrigues and scandals, ending with the Profumo affair in 1963. Fine tapestries and furniture, and a theatre which heard the first performance of *Rule Britannia.* Splendid gardens. It is now a stately home/hotel, leased from the National Trust. *House open Apr–Oct, Thu and Sun 15.00–17.30. Garden open mid Mar–Oct, daily 11.00–18.00; Nov–Dec 11.00–16.00.* Charge. Restaurant. Temporary moorings (charge).

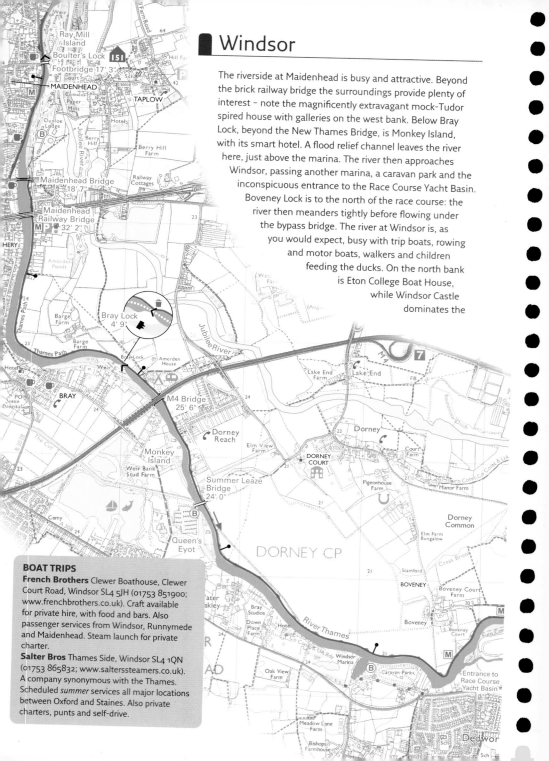

Windsor

The riverside at Maidenhead is busy and attractive. Beyond the brick railway bridge the surroundings provide plenty of interest – note the magnificently extravagant mock-Tudor spired house with galleries on the west bank. Below Bray Lock, beyond the New Thames Bridge, is Monkey Island, with its smart hotel. A flood relief channel leaves the river here, just above the marina. The river then approaches Windsor, passing another marina, a caravan park and the inconspicuous entrance to the Race Course Yacht Basin. Boveney Lock is to the north of the race course: the river then meanders tightly before flowing under the bypass bridge. The river at Windsor is, as you would expect, busy with trip boats, rowing and motor boats, walkers and children feeding the ducks. On the north bank is Eton College Boat House, while Windsor Castle dominates the

BOAT TRIPS

French Brothers Clewer Boathouse, Clewer Court Road, Windsor SL4 5JH (01753 851900; www.frenchbrothers.co.uk). Craft available for private hire, with food and bars. Also passenger services from Windsor, Runnymede and Maidenhead. Steam launch for private charter.

Salter Bros Thames Side, Windsor SL4 1QN (01753 865832; www.salterssteamers.co.uk). A company synonymous with the Thames. Scheduled *summer* services all major locations between Oxford and Staines. Also private charters, punts and self-drive.

river for miles around. Leaving Windsor, the Thames winds around Home Park, passing the famous college, on the north bank. Turbines have been installed in the weir at Romney Lock to provide a clean energy source for Windsor Castle.

Boatyards

Ⓑ **Peter Freebody** Boulters Island, Maidenhead (01628 824382; www.peterfreebody.com). Boat building and repairs. This is the Maidenhead yard of the very famous boat builders, who also construct steam launches.

Ⓑ **Bray Marina** Monkey Island Lane, Bray SL6 2EB (01628 623654; www.mdlmarinas.co.uk). 🚿🚽⚓ **D E** Gas, overnight and long-term mooring, winter storage, crane (10 ton), boat/engine sales and repairs, chandlery, toilets, showers, books, maps, restaurant, DIY facilities, hard standing.

Ⓑ **Windsor Marina** Maidenhead Road, Windsor SL4 5TZ (01753 853911; www.mdlmarinas.co.uk). 🚿🚽⚓**P D E** Pump out, gas, overnight/long-term mooring, winter storage, slipway, boat sales and repairs, engine repairs, boat hoods and upholstery, telephone, toilets, showers, DIY facilities.

Ⓑ **Racecourse Marina** Maidenhead Road, Windsor SL4 5HT (01753 851501; www.tingdene-marinas.co.uk). 🚿🚽⚓**P D** Pump out, gas, overnight and long-term mooring, winter storage, crane, boat and engine sales and repairs, small chandlery, telephone, toilets, showers, licensed club, book and maps, hard standing, yacht club, Wi-Fi.

Ⓑ **Stanley & Thomas** Tom Jones Boatyard, Romney Lock, Windsor SL4 6HU (01753 833166; www.stanleyandthomas.co.uk). Long-term mooring, winter storage, crane, boat building, boat and engine sales and repairs, restoration and repairs to historic boats, painting and varnishing.

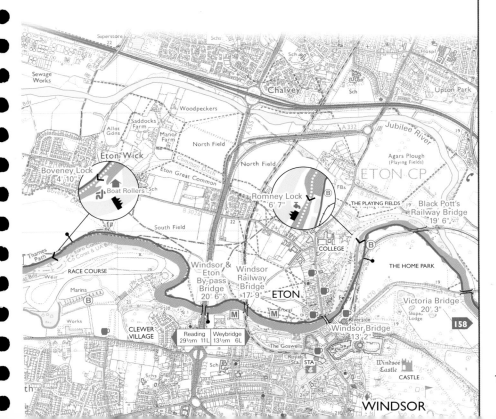

WINDSOR

Maidenhead
Berks. All services. A dormitory suburb of London, close to the M4 motorway, and with much new development.
Tourist Information Centre Central Library, St Ives Road, Maidenhead SL6 1QU (01628 796502; www. windsor.gov.uk).
The Jubilee River An imaginative solution to the ever-present threat of flooding in the Thames Valley, this newly constructed 7-mile river takes full account of environmental considerations. Built at a cost of £100 million, it passes under the main railway line from Paddington, and the M4 motorway, before rejoining the Thames near Eton College. Over 250,000 native trees have been planted – creating habitat for mandarin ducks, reed and sedge warblers, bittern, bearded tit and marsh harriers. A footpath and cycleway accompanies its course, and there are hides for birdwatchers. Boating activity is restricted to canoeing. But should a drought occur, as in 1976, this new river would be sacrificed to the more long-standing demands of the Thames, whatever the environmental cost.
Maidenhead Railway Bridge These two beautiful arches, each 123ft long, are reputedly the largest brickwork spans in the world. They were built in 1839 by Brunel.

Bray
Berks. PO, stores. Despite commuter development, Bray still retains its village centre. The largely 13th-C church is approached via a fine brick gatehouse of 1450. Simon Alwyn, the 16th-C vicar of Bray, who changed his creed three times to hold the living under Henry VIII, Edward VI, Mary and Elizabeth I, lies buried in the churchyard. Just outside the village is the Jesus Hospital, founded in 1627.
Monkey Island On the island are the fishing lodge and pavilion of the 3rd Duke of Marlborough, built in 1744 on rubble salvaged from the Great Fire of London. The Lodge was constructed from wooden blocks, cut to look like stone and still in good condition; the nearby Temple has a fine Wedgwood-style ceiling. In one of the restaurant rooms of the Pavilion there are monkey paintings on the ceiling, completed by Andie de Clermont before 1738. The name of the island, however, is a corruption of 'Monk's Eyot'. The Pavilion became an inn around 1840, and was fashionable at the start of the 20th C when Edward VII and Queen Alexandra had afternoon tea on the lawn. It is now a hotel (01628 623400; www.monkeyisland.co.uk).
Down Place A pretty 18th-C riverside mansion, once the meeting place of the Kit Kat Club. Steele, Addison, Walpole and Congreve were members. Nearby is Oakley Court, a magnificent Victorian Gothic castle of 1859.
Dorney Court and Church Near Windsor SL4 6QP (01628 604638; www.dorneycourt.co.uk). A gabled and timbered Tudor manor house, built c.1440, and occupied by the Palmer family for 400 years. Restorations have not altered the original feeling of the house which contains fine furniture and paintings.

The church contains a Norman font, 17th-C woodwork and a Garrard monument. It is reputedly haunted by a cavalier, a Turk and a young girl in white. *Open May and Jun,* check website or telephone to confirm dates and times. Charge. Garden centre and coffee shop *open daily* (01628 669999; www.walledgardencentre.co.uk).

Boveney
Bucks. A village scattered around a green, with Tudor buildings and a pretty flint and clapboard church.

Windsor
Berks. All services. The main street curves around the castle and is full of pubs, restaurants and souvenir shops. The Church of St John the Baptist in the High Street, built 1820-2, has three galleries supported by delicate cast iron piers. The town hall was built by Wren in 1689-90 after a design by Sir Thomas Fitch. The ceiling appears to be supported by four Tuscan columns which stop two inches short: a private joke of the architect's at the expense of a doubting mayor. To the west of the town there is a fine riverside park. Theatre at the Theatre Royal (01753 853888; www. theatreroyalwindsor.co.uk).
Tourist Information Centre The Old Booking Hall, Windsor Royal Shopping, Thames Street, Windsor SL4 1PJ (01753 743900; www.windsor.gov.uk). *Open daily.*

Windsor Castle
SL4 1NJ (020 7766 7304; www.royalcollection. org.uk). The largest inhabited castle in the world, established by William the Conqueror during the 1070s, the present building was started by Henry II, 1165–79. Most succeeding monarchs have left their mark, notably Charles II, and Queen Victoria who spent over £1 million on modernisation. It has been meticulously restored following the disastrous fire of 20 November 1992 (the Queen and Duke of Edinburgh's 45th wedding anniversary!) The building falls into three sections:
Lower Ward St George's Chapel, the finest example of Perpendicular architecture in the country, containing the tombs of ten sovereigns. The Albert Memorial Chapel, originally built by Henry VII and turned into a Victorian shrine.
Middle Ward The Round Tower, with a panoramic view over twelve counties.
Upper Ward The Private Apartments and the State Apartments, containing a collection of paintings. The castle is surrounded by parks. Home Park borders on the river and contains Frogmore House, built by Wyatt in 1792 out of an earlier house, and the Royal Mausoleum. The castle precincts are *open daily* – other parts of the castle are *often open to the* public but check times. Charge.
Legoland Winkfield Road, Windsor SL4 4AY (0871 2222 001; www.legoland.co.uk). A building-brick fantasy covering over 150 acres, with 40 rides, shows and attractions, including Lego Traffic, and Miniland, built from 32 million Lego bricks. *Open early Mar-Oct, daily.* Charge. Doors close if it gets crowded!

Windsor Great Park
SL4 2HT (01753 860 222; www.theroyallandscape. co.uk). A total area of 4,800 acres between the

Thames and Virginia Water. There has been a starling roost in the park for over 100 years, and a heronry at Fort Belvedere.

● **Eton**
Berks. PO, stores, bank, chemist, takeaways, garage, station (¼ mile distant). The long and rambling High Street is a pleasant place to walk.
Eton College Eton High Street, Eton SL4 6DW (01753 671177; www.etoncollege.com). Founded by Henry VI in 1440 to provide education for 70 poor scholars. The buildings date from 1441 to the present day. Now 1280 boys attend. Eighteen former British prime ministers have been educated here. Short guided tours are offered on some *Wed, Fri, Sat, Sun and daily* during Eton's holidays. Pre-booking essential. Tickets available from Royal Windsor Information Centre or Eton College Gift Shop on the High Street.

Pubs and Restaurants

Taplow House Hotel Berry Hill, Taplow SL6 0DA (01628 670056; www.taplowhouse.com). A Georgian mansion standing in 6 acres of grounds and housing a hotel, an excellent restaurant and two bars. The à la carte restaurant serves English and continental cuisine *L and E (unless there is a function)*. Children welcome.

The Thames Hotel Ray Mead Road, Maidenhead SL6 8NR (01628 628721). Cosy and relaxed riverside hotel and restaurant, built in the 1880s by a prosperous local boat builder – indeed at one time it had a telegraph office. Princess Frederika of Hanover, and many other distinguished guests, have stayed here. Real ale. Bar and restaurant meals *L and E*. Children welcome. Terrace with outside seating.

Topogigio 2 Ray Mead Road, Maidenhead SL6 8NJ (01628 777555). By the bridge. Modern Thai restaurant overlooking the river. *Open L and E.*

The Thames Riviera Hotel The Bridge, Bridge Road, Maidenhead SL6 8DW (01628 674057; www.thamesriviera.com). Residential hotel overlooking the Thames below Maidenhead Bridge. Bar meals served *L and E*. Coffee shop *09.00-17.00*. Children welcome. Garden. Maidenhead town centre, where you will find more pubs and eating places, lies about ³/₄ mile south west of the bridge.

The Waterside Inn Ferry Road, Bray SL6 2AT (01628 620691; www.waterside-inn.co.uk). Smart riverside restaurant in a beautiful setting, run by Michel Roux's son Alain – considered by some to be the best restaurant in the country. Exciting menu, attentive waiters, expensive wine. *Open L and E (closed Mon, and Tue Sep–May).* Booking essential. Children over 12 welcome.

The Crown High Street, Bray SL6 2AH (01628 621936; www.thecrownatbray.com). A beamy old pub serving real ale. Food *L and E*. Children welcome *in* the restaurant. Sheltered courtyard with vines.

Sir Christopher Wren's House Hotel Thames Street, Windsor SL4 1PX (01753 861354; www.sirchristopherwren.co.uk). A Thames-side residential hotel, built by Sir Christopher Wren as a family home, with cocktail bar and restaurant overlooking the river. Restaurant serves excellent food *L and E* plus *afternoon teas*. Children welcome. Outside seating. Windsor has many fine pubs, the following are those nearest the river:

Bel and The Dragon Thames Street, 1 Datchet, Windsor SL4 1QB (01753 866056; www.belandthedragon-windsor.co.uk). Situated in an alehouse dating from the 11th C. Fresh, seasonal food *L and E, afternoon* teas and *Sun* roasts.

The Royal Oak Datchet Road, Windsor SL4 1QD (01753 865179; www.windsorpubco.co.uk). There was a brewery here in 1539, when the building was owned by St George's Chapel and the pub was known as The Crown. On 8 March 1834 it was reported that Mrs Bitmead, of The Royal Oak, was fined ten shillings for allowing her pig to escape, and rampage around the town. Real ale is served in the bar, and there is a separate restaurant *L and E*. Children welcome. Garden.

La Taverna 2 River Street, Windsor SL4 1QT (01753 863020; www.lataverna.co.uk). Excellent Italian food and wine *L Mon–Fri and E Mon–Sat*. Booking recommended. Children welcome. River views from the first floor.

The Watermans Arms Brocas Street, Eton SL4 6BW (01753 861001; www.watermans-eton.com). Situated near the Eton College Boat House, the restaurant serves traditional English cuisine and bar meals *L and E (not Sun E)*. Real ale. Children welcome. Conservatory seating area.

The following five pubs and restaurants are easily found in Eton High Street, straight up from the bridge:

The Crown & Cushion 84 High Street, Eton SL4 6AF(01753 861531). Friendly pub serving real ale, and bar meals *L and E (not Fri–Sun E)*. Children welcome in the back bar. Garden. B&B.

The Christopher Hotel 110 High Street, Eton SL4 6AN (01753 852359; www.thechristopher.co.uk). Friendly old coaching inn. Real ales. Meals available *L and E*. Children welcome. Small patio.

Ayoush 55 High Street, Eton SL4 6BL (01753 865516; www.ayoush.com). North African and Moroccan bar and restaurant that blends unstinting hospitality with an excellent quality of service and food. Eat in the informal cushioned area around the fire; in the formal restaurant or on the terrace. Belly dancer *Fri & Sat E. Open 12.00-23.00 (weekends 00.00).*

The George Inn Eton SL4 6AF (01753 861797). Traditional pub serving real ale. Food *available all day, every day* including *Sun* roasts. Large garden. Children welcome.

The House on the Bridge 71 High Street, by Windsor Bridge, Eton SL4 6AA (01753 860914; www.house-on-the-bridge.co.uk). International restaurant with its own moorings. Meals *L and E*. Children welcome. Outside seating on riverside terrace in *summer*.

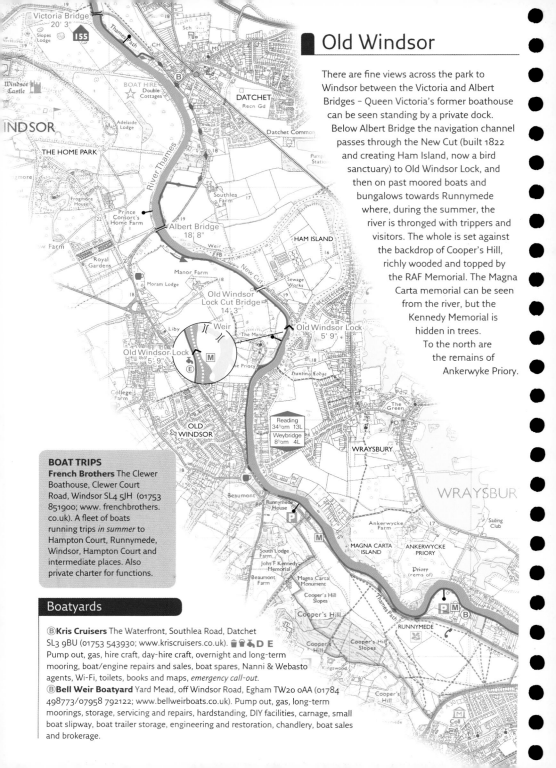

Old Windsor

There are fine views across the park to Windsor between the Victoria and Albert Bridges – Queen Victoria's former boathouse can be seen standing by a private dock. Below Albert Bridge the navigation channel passes through the New Cut (built 1822 and creating Ham Island, now a bird sanctuary) to Old Windsor Lock, and then on past moored boats and bungalows towards Runnymede where, during the summer, the river is thronged with trippers and visitors. The whole is set against the backdrop of Cooper's Hill, richly wooded and topped by the RAF Memorial. The Magna Carta memorial can be seen from the river, but the Kennedy Memorial is hidden in trees. To the north are the remains of Ankerwyke Priory.

BOAT TRIPS

French Brothers The Clewer Boathouse, Clewer Court Road, Windsor SL4 5JH (01753 851900; www. frenchbrothers. co.uk). A fleet of boats running trips *in summer* to Hampton Court, Runnymede, Windsor, Hampton Court and intermediate places. Also private charter for functions.

Boatyards

Ⓑ**Kris Cruisers** The Waterfront, Southlea Road, Datchet SL3 9BU (01753 543930; www.kriscruisers.co.uk). 🛏🛒⚓ D E Pump out, gas, hire craft, day-hire craft, overnight and long-term mooring, boat/engine repairs and sales, boat spares, Nanni & Webasto agents, Wi-Fi, toilets, books and maps, *emergency call-out*.

Ⓑ**Bell Weir Boatyard** Yard Mead, off Windsor Road, Egham TW20 0AA (01784 498773/07958 792122; www.bellweirboats.co.uk). Pump out, gas, long-term moorings, storage, servicing and repairs, hardstanding, DIY facilities, carnage, small boat slipway, boat trailer storage, engineering and restoration, chandlery, boat sales and brokerage.

Passing Holm Island, the London Stone stands by the river: this marked the former limit of the jurisdiction of the City of London over the Thames. There is some smart and mellow housing on the north bank above Staines Bridge, but for the most part the riverside is lined with a wonderful, and sometimes very eccentric, array of holiday chalets and bungalows, along with houseboats and moored craft of indiscriminate vintage.

- **Datchet**
Berks. PO, stores, chemist, off-licence, takeaways, garage, station. At its best around the green, where there is still a village feeling.
- **Old Windsor**
Berks. PO, stores, off-licence, takeaway. A great expanse of suburban houses with no sign of the 9th-C village, built around the site of a Saxon royal palace. The 13th-C church is hidden among trees. The PO is ½ mile west of the Bells of Ouzeley, along the A308 Windsor Road.
- **Runnymede**
Surrey. Beside the river on the south bank, this is a stretch of open parkland backed by the wooded slope of Cooper's Hill. The paired gatehouses, by Lutyens, introduce an area of memorials. The inspiration is the sealing of the Magna Carta in 1215. On top of the hill is the Commonwealth Air Forces Memorial. This quadrangular structure, built by Sir Edward Maufe in 1953, perfectly exploits its situation. Below are the Magna Carta Memorial and the Kennedy Memorial, the latter built on an acre of ground given to the American people. This is a popular venue in summer. There are excellent pleasure gardens with a café alongside the river.

Ankerwyke Built on the site of a Benedictine nunnery is Ankerwyke Priory, a low, early 19th-C mansion surrounded by trees, among which is the Ankerwyke Yew, whose trunk is 33ft in circumference.

- **Staines**
Surrey. All services, laundrette, fish & chips. A commuter town which has expanded hugely over the last 30 years. However, the area around the pleasantly situated church has remained virtually unchanged. Clarence Street, which culminates in Rennie's stone bridge, built 1829-32, still has the feeling of an 18th-C market town. To the north are huge reservoirs.

Pubs and Restaurants

🍺✗**The Bells of Ouzeley** Straight Road, Windsor SL4 2SH (01753 861526; www.harverster.co.uk). There has been a pub on this site for about 800 years, although it nearly all came to an end during World War II, when a V1 flying bomb destroyed part of the building. Open throughout day from 09.00 in school holidays – otherwise 10.00. Children welcome and there is a garden.

🍺✗**The Runnymede-on-Thames** Windsor Road, Egham TW20 0AG (01784 220960; www.runnymedehotel. com). Smart hotel with riverside gardens, conference facilities and the Leftbank waterfront restaurant, created by Sucha Design at a cost of £1m, and based upon an aquatic theme. Also informal restaurant, bar and conservatory. Food available all day. Children welcome. B&B.

🍺✗**Riverside Restaurant** Mercure Staines Hotel, Thames Street, Staines TW18 4SF (01784 464433; www.accorhotels.com). A Thames-side hotel, where bar meals are served all day and an a la carte menu L and E (not Sun E). Children welcome. Patio/ terrace. Mooring. B&B.

🍺**The Bells** 124 Church Street, Staines TW18 4ZB (01784 454240; www.thebellspub.co.uk). Close to the supposedly haunted churchyard. Real ale. Bar meals available L and E (Sun 12.00-18.00). Children and dogs welcome. Garden and conservatory.

WALKING & CYCLING
There are excellent walks by the river at Runnymede, where the land is owned by the National Trust.

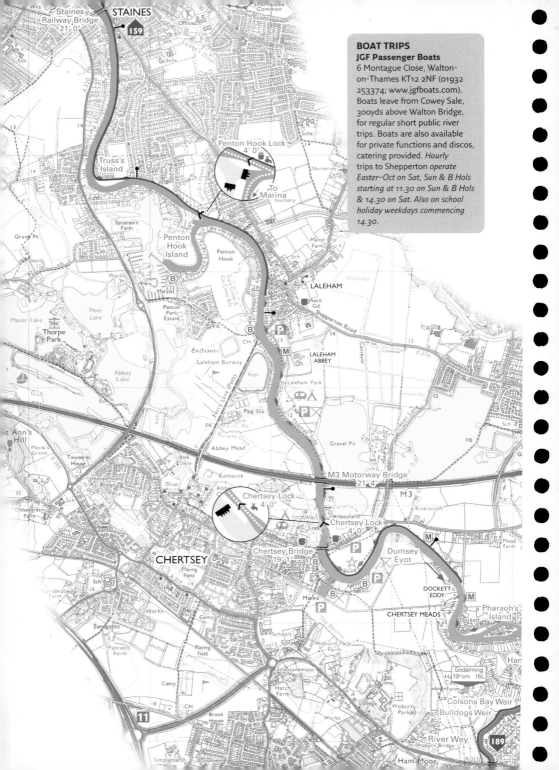

Weybridge

At Penton Hook a large marina has been established in flooded gravel pits – it is approached from below the lock. Laleham follows, and soon the bungalows disappear and Laleham Abbey and park provide a brief breathing space before Chertsey looms large. The river twists and turns on its way to Weybridge, where the River Wey (see page 187) flows in from the south joining it, and the Basingstoke Canal (see page 15) to the Thames. Desborough Cut removes two large loops from the navigable course before the river makes a direct run for Sunbury, leaving Walton-on-Thames to the east.

NAVIGATIONAL NOTES

1 Note that Penton Hook Marina is approached from *below* the lock.
2 The River Wey joins the Thames *below* Shepperton Lock.
3 The old course of the river north of Desborough Island is navigable, but it may be shallow in places.
4 *Nauticalia* runs a ferry service below Shepperton Lock for the National Trust, so walkers can enjoy this ancient crossing, noticing that 'droves of sheep will be carried at the fare of one shilling per score (shepherd to clean up afterwards)'.

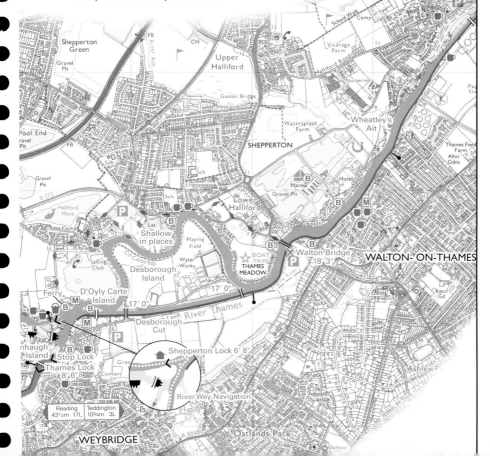

Boatyards

(B) **Penton Hook Marina** Staines Lane, Chertsey KT16 8PY (01932 568681; www.mdlmarinas.co.uk). A vast marina in flooded gravel pits. 🛒🏠♿P D Pump out, gas, overnight and long-term mooring, winter storage, slipway, crane, boat and engine sales and repairs, chandlery, telephone, toilets, DIY facilities, hoods and covers, laundrette, brokerage, Wi-Fi.

(B) **Chertsey Meads Marine** The Meads, Chertsey KT16 8LN (01932 564899; www.boatsthames.com). ♿D E Pump out, gas, day-boat hire, overnight and long-term mooring, winter storage, slipway, crane, boat and engine repairs, DIY facilities, books and maps. *Emergency call-out.*

(B) **Lindon Lewis Marine** Ferry Point, Ferry Lane, by Shepperton Lock, Shepperton TW17 9LQ (01932 254844; www.pushtheboatout.com). 🛒♿ E Gas, overnight and long-term mooring, winter storage, slipway, boat building, boat and engine repairs, chandlery, telephone, toilets, café nearby, DIY facilities, hardstanding, boat sales and brokerage, engine sales.

(B) **Eyot House** D'Oyly Carte Island, Weybridge KT13 8LX (01932 848586). 🛒🏠♿ Gas, long-term mooring, winter storage, slipway, boat and engine repairs, toilets, DIY facilities.

(B) **Walton Marina** Walton Bridge, Walton KT12 1QW (0845 293 8287; www.tingdene-marinas.co.uk). 🛒🏠♿D Pump out, gas, overnight and long-term mooring, winter storage, slipway, crane, boat and engine sales and repairs, chandlery, toilets, showers, books, maps and gifts, café, Wi-Fi.

(B) **Bridge Marine** Thames Meadow, Shepperton TW17 8LT (01932 245126; www.bridge-marine.co.uk). 🛒♿E Gas, day hire boats, winter storage, slipway, crane, boat and engine sales and repairs, chandlery, toilets, books, maps and gifts, DIY facilities. *Emergency call-out.*

(B) **Shepperton Marina** Felix Lane, Shepperton TW17 8NS (01932 247427; www.pushtheboatout.com). 🛒 🛒♿P D Pump out, gas, overnight and long-term mooring, winter storage, crane, boat and engine sales and repairs, chandlery, toilets, showers, books, maps and gifts, DIY facilities. *Emergency call out.*

(B) **W Bates & Son** Bridge Wharf, Chertsey KT16 8LG (01932 562255; www.bateswharf.co.uk). Long and short-term mooring, boat sales, chandlery.

● **Laleham**
Surrey. Stores. The first impression of Laleham is one of bungalows and houseboats. The village does not exploit the river at all, and the centre lacks the riverside feeling of some other towns hereabouts. The 18th- and 19th-C church is well placed in a wooded graveyard, which contains the tomb of Matthew Arnold (1822–88, see Bablock Hythe, on page 118). To the south of the town is Laleham Park. Formerly the grounds of Laleham House, built about 1805, it is now a wooded public park reaching down to the river.
Thorpe Park Staines Road, Chertsey KT16 8PN (0871 663 1673; www.thorpepark.com). One of the country's first theme parks, constantly being upgraded. Attractions include Colossus, which hurtles through ten loops over 2800ft long at speeds of 40 mph, along with the highest log flume ride in the UK, Rumba Rapids and the Canada Creek Railway. Treats include 'Rush' – the world's largest speed swing, and 'Slammer', the ultimate free-fall. Young visitors can enjoy Mr Monkey's Banana Ride. *Open daily Easter–Oct.* Charge.

● **Chertsey**
Surrey. All shops and services. From the river the first sight of Chertsey is James Paine's stone bridge, built 1780–2. Chertsey just manages to retain a feeling of the 18th C, especially around Windsor Street, which runs past the site of the abbey, once one of the greatest in England. Founded in AD666 and

rebuilt in the 12th C, it was finally destroyed during the Reformation. It is thought likely that materials from the abbey were used in the construction of Hampton Court.

● **Weybridge**
Surrey. All services. A commuter town in the stockbroker belt, built around the confluence of the rivers Wey and Thames – the junction is marked by a pretty iron bridge of 1865. Weybridge represents the frontier of the suburbia that now spreads almost unbroken to London.

● **Shepperton**
Surrey. All services. Recognisable from the river by the lawns of the 19th-C manor house, Shepperton is a surprising example of village survival. The square contains a number of relatively intact 18th-C inns. The church, with its fine brick tower, was built in the 17th and 18th C, and has box pews. To the north of the church is the rectory, which has a pretty Queen Anne front. The famous film studios are to the north, near the vast Queen Mary Reservoir.

● **Walton-on-Thames**
Surrey. All services.

● **Sunbury**
Surrey. PO, tel, stores, chemist, banks, off-licence, takeaways. Sunbury has a pleasant village feeling. Sunbury Court, the grand mansion of the town, was built in 1770 and is now a conference and holiday venue.

WALKING & CYCLING

National Cycle Route 4 connects Weybridge with Putney Bridge, using quiet streets and cycle paths. Follow the signs on the Thames towpath from its junction with the River Wey to pass through Kingston and Richmond Park. This is part of the Thames Valley Cycle Route, which stretches all the way to Oxford.

Pubs and Restaurants

The Three Horseshoes Shepperton Road, Laleham TW18 1SQ (01784 455014; www.3horseshoeslaleham.com). Having been a police station and a morgue, this is now a characterful, relaxed and comfortable pub, once patronised by the Prince Regent, Sir Arthur Sullivan and Marie Lloyd. Real ale. Excellent home-made food *L and E*. Children welcome *until early evening*. Dogs in garden only. Conservatory and large garden.

The Feathers The Broadway, Laleham TW18 1RZ (01784 453561; www.thefeatherslaleham.co.uk). Friendly pub serving real ale, and food *L and E*. Children welcome if eating *(until 19.00)*, and there is a garden. Large TV in bar area.

The Kingfisher Chertsey Bridge Road, Chertsey KT16 8LF (01932 579811; www.vintageinn.co.uk/thekingfisherchertsey). Cosy traditional pub, with low ceilings, timbered walls and an open fire. Real ale. Meals served *L and E*. Children welcome. On fine days you can sit by the river.

The Boat House and Bridge Lodge Hotel Chertsey Bridge Road, Chertsey KT16 8JZ (01932 565644; www.bespokehotels.com/thebridge). Busy wood and tile riverside pub and restaurant, with a nautical theme. Real ale. Food *L and E*. Children welcome. Riverside seats. Moorings.

The Thames Court Ferry Lane, The Towpath, Shepperton TW17 9LJ (01932 221957; www.vintageinn.co.uk/thethamescourtshepperton). Oak-panelled pub by Shepperton Lock. Real ale. Meals *daily*. Children welcome if eating. Large outside patio.

The Anchor Hotel Church Square, Shepperton TW17 9JZ (01932 242748; www.anchorhotel.co.uk). Friendly 400-year-old wood-panelled pub. Real ale. Bar snacks *L* and restaurant meals *E*. Children welcome, and there are seats outside. B&B.

The Old Crown 83 Thames Street, Weybridge KT13 8LP (01932 842844; www.theoldcrownweybridge.co.uk). Rambling weather-boarded pub by the old course of the River Wey, with charming nautical decor. It has been run by the same family since 1959. Real ales. Meals *L and E (not Sun, Mon or Tue E)*. Children and dogs welcome. Riverside garden, patio and landing stage.

Harrisons Hotel, Bistro and Bar Russell Road, Shepperton TW17 9HX (01932 227320; www.harrisonshotel.co.uk). Friendly riverside hotel where real ale is served, along with food *Mon–Sat E*. Traditional *Sun L 12.00 -16.00*. Children welcome in the lounge. B&B.

The Swan Manor Road, Walton KT12 2PF (01932 225964; www.swanwalton.com). Imposing and friendly riverside pub, licensed since 1770. Real ale. Meals available *L and E (all day Sat and Sun)*. Children and dogs welcome. Garden. *Summer* barbecues.

Old Manor Inn 113 Manor Road, Walton KT12 2NZ (01932 221359). Real ale in a local's pub. Bar snacks available *late E daily*. Children welcome if eating. Garden, and 14th-C manor house to the rear.

Flower Pot Hotel Thames Street, Sunbury TW16 6AA (01932 780741; www.theflowerpothotel.co.uk). A 17th-C pub/restaurant, offering real ale. Food served *L and E*. Children welcome if eating. Patio. Dog-friendly. B&B.

The Magpie 64 Thames Street, Sunbury TW16 6AF (01932 782024; www.gkpubs.co.uk/pubs-in-sunbury-on-thames/magpie-pub). Real ales. Bar meals available *L and E*. Children welcome if eating. Patio. Moorings.

The Phoenix 26-28 Thames Street, Sunbury TW16 6AF (01932 785358; www.thephoenixsunbury.co.uk). Friendly local, once two cottages. Real ale. Meals *L and E*. Garden. Log fires *in winter*.

Hampton Court

Sunbury Court Island is lined with immaculate chalets and bungalows: opposite and to the east is a vast area of reservoirs and waterworks. Platt's Eyot once supported a community of engineers and craftsmen, with boatbuilding being carried out from the 1850s. Immisch built electric launches here after 1889, in a yard later taken over by Thorneycrofts. They built 170 torpedo boats here between 1938-45, but left during the 1960s. Below Platt's Eyot is Hampton, where the ferry still survives. Hampton Church stands on the north bank opposite Garrick's Ait. Bushy Park stretches away to the north east of the river. Tagg's Island and Ash Island are lined with smart moored craft and eccentric houseboats, including a large Swiss chalet behind Tagg's Island. Below Hampton Bridge is Hampton Court Palace, standing close to the river, and separated from it by an extremely long red brick wall.

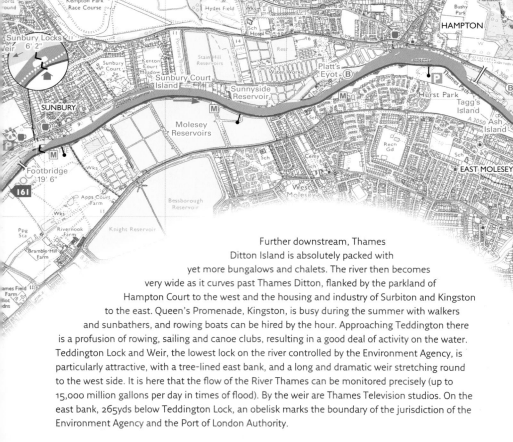

Further downstream, Thames Ditton Island is absolutely packed with yet more bungalows and chalets. The river then becomes very wide as it curves past Thames Ditton, flanked by the parkland of Hampton Court to the west and the housing and industry of Surbiton and Kingston to the east. Queen's Promenade, Kingston, is busy during the summer with walkers and sunbathers, and rowing boats can be hired by the hour. Approaching Teddington there is a profusion of rowing, sailing and canoe clubs, resulting in a good deal of activity on the water. Teddington Lock and Weir, the lowest lock on the river controlled by the Environment Agency, is particularly attractive, with a tree-lined east bank, and a long and dramatic weir stretching round to the west side. It is here that the flow of the River Thames can be monitored precisely (up to 15,000 million gallons per day in times of flood). By the weir are Thames Television studios. On the east bank, 265yds below Teddington Lock, an obelisk marks the boundary of the jurisdiction of the Environment Agency and the Port of London Authority.

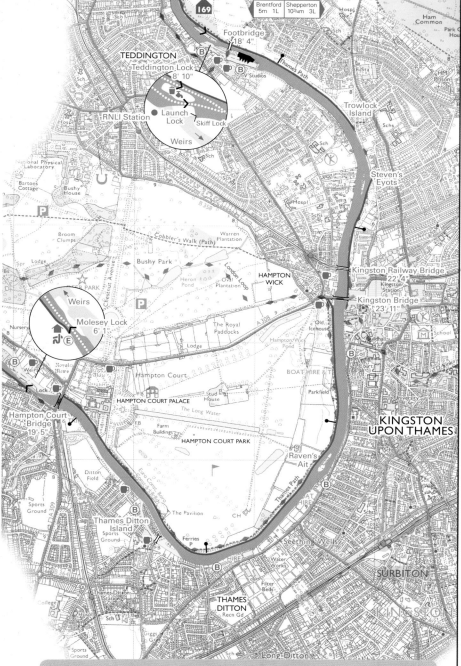

169

Brentford	Shepperton
5m 1L	10¾m 3L

BOAT TRIPS

Turk Launches Town End Pier, 68 High Street, Kingston KT1 1HN (020 8546 2434; www.turks.co.uk). Operating a public service to Hampton Court, Kingston and Richmond in *summer*. Also private charter for up to 150 people.

1 Sunbury Locks – the mechanised lock on the south side is normally used. The hand-operated lock on the north side is used only during busy periods in the summer.
2 Teddington Locks (020 8940 8723). Traffic lights are in use at these locks. Please observe the red and green light signals.
3 Those using the Skiff Lock should follow the lock keeper's instructions.
4 The river below Teddington Lock is tidal for two hours either side of high water.
5 **Teddington to Brentford** – leave Teddington 20 minutes before high water.
6 **Teddington to Limehouse** – leave Teddington 30 minutes before high water.
   Note for both 5 & 6 Arrival time must fall within normal working hours. If it will not, the passage **must** be booked 24 hours in advance with the appropriate lock keeper. *If you fail to do this, you will be left in the tideway.* Times are approximate and depend upon the speed of your boat. If in any doubt – *check before you leave.*

Boatyards

®**Port Hampton Ltd** Platts Eyot, Lower Sunbury Road, Hampton TW12 2HF (020 8979 8116). 🛏🛠 Long-term mooring, crane, toilets, DIY facilities.
®**Geo Wilson & Sons** Ferry House, Thames Street, Sunbury TW16 6AQ (01932 782067). Day-hire craft, long-term mooring, slipway, traditional boat repairs, DIY facilities, winter storage, fishing permits.
®**T.W. Allen & Son (Yachts)** Ash Island, Hampton Court, East Molesey KT8 9AN (020 8979 1997; www.twallen.co.uk). 🛠 Gas, long-term mooring, slipway, boat repairs, DIY facilities.
®**Taggs Boatyard** Summer Road, Thames Ditton KT7 0QQ (020 8398 2119; www.taggsboatyard.co.uk). 🛏🛠 E Day-hire craft, overnight and long-term mooring, winter storage, slipway, boat building, boat sales and repairs, engine repairs, toilets.

®**Thames Marina** Portsmouth Road, Thames Ditton KT6 5QD (020 8398 6159; www.thamesmarina. co.uk). D Gas, long-term mooring, slipway, crane, boat building, boat repairs, engine repairs, chandlery, toilets, books and maps.
®✕**Hart's Boats** Portsmouth Road, Surbiton KT6 4HJ (020 8399 0297; www.hartsboats.com). 🛏🛠 E Pump out, gas, electric day boats, overnight and long-term mooring, winter storage, slipway, boat building, boat sales and repairs, engine repairs, telephone, toilets, books and maps, café.
®**Turk Launches** Town End Pier, 68 High Street, Kingston KT1 1HN (020 8546 2434; www.turks.co.uk). 🛠 Pump out, long-term mooring, boat building, boat sales and repairs. *Summer* ferry to Hampton Court and Richmond.

● **Hampton**
Surrey. PO, stores, chemist, bank, takeaways, off-licence, bakery, garage, cycle shop. A lively riverside town with excellent eateries and pubs. Hampton is linked by ferry to the south bank. The church, built in 1831, is prominent on the riverside. Despite the proximity of Hampton Court, the village owes its existence to Hampton House, bought by David Garrick in 1754, and subsequently altered by Adam. By the river is Garrick's Temple, built to house Roubiliac's bust of Shakespeare. Nearby stands the large Swiss chalet which was brought over from Switzerland in 1899. There is also a useful cycle repair shop - Birdie Biles 7 Wensleydale Road (020 8941 9397).

● **Hampton Court Palace**
Surrey KT8 9AU (0844 482 7777; www.hrp.org.uk). Probably the greatest secular building in England. Cardinal Wolsey, son of an Ipswich butcher, was

graced by ambition and ability to such an extent that at the age of 40 he had an income of £50,000 a year. He was thus able to build the grandest private house in England. Work began in 1514. Henry VIII was offended by the unashamed ostentation of his lieutenant and in 1529, following Wolsey's downfall and his failure to secure the annulment of Henry VIII's first marriage, the king took over the house. Henry spent more on Hampton Court than on any other building, establishing it as a Royal Palace. Subsequently Wren added to it, but little work, other than repairs, has been done since. Visit the State Apartments, the Tudor Kitchen, the Wolsey Rooms, the King's & Queen's Apartments, the Georgian Rooms, the Courtyards and the Cloisters. In the formal gardens (at their best in *mid May*) are the Great Vine, planted in 1789, and the Maze where Harris, one of Jerome K. Jerome's *Three Men in a Boat*, got hopelessly lost, along with 20 followers and a keeper. *Open 10.00–18.00 (16.30 winter) daily. Closed Xmas. The gardens close at 21.00, or dusk*. Charge. Teas in the grounds. River launches connect with Westminster, Richmond and Kingston. Behind the palace is Bushy Park, enclosing 2000 acres. It is a formal design reminiscent of Versailles, and is famous for deer.

Hampton Green
Surrey. A fine collection of 18th-C and earlier buildings surround Hampton Green, just to the north of Hampton Court Bridge. The bridge was built by Lutyens in 1933.

Thames Ditton
Surrey. PO, stores, chemist, banks, off-licence, takeaways. The centre of this unspoilt riverside village has managed to avoid the careless development of the surrounding area. The church here has an interesting graveyard, a lovely garden and there are several good brasses inside. Pretty whitewashed houses stand close by the suspension bridge which leads to Thames Ditton Island.

Kingston-on-Thames
Surrey. All services. A Royal Borough where seven Saxon kings were crowned. The coronation stone is displayed outside the Guildhall. There is a good river frontage, centred round the stone bridge built 1825–8 by Lapidge. Away from the river the market place is the centre of the town. The Lovekyn Chapel on London Road dates largely from the Tudor period and is surrounded by many interesting 18th-C buildings. The Italianate town hall, 1838–40, is one of the most striking structures in the area. There are also the five conduit houses built by Cardinal Wolsey to supply water to Hampton Court.

Teddington
Gt London. All services. R. D. Blackmore (1825–1900), author of *Lorna Doone*, lived in Teddington from 1860. The site of his home, Gomer House, is at the end of Doone Close, near the station. The riverside, viewed from the Surrey bank, is one of Teddington's most pleasing aspects. The television studios stand in Broom Road, near the weir.

Pubs and Restaurants

The Bell 8 Thames Street, Hampton TW12 2EA (020 8941 9799; www. thebellinnhampton.co.uk). Right by the church and overlooking the river, this small, cosy pub serves real ale, and food *L and E*. Children welcome *until 17.00*. Patio and conservatory. Quiz *Sun E*; regular comedy club.

The King's Arms Lion Gate, Hampton Court Road, Hampton Court KT8 9DD (020 8977 1729; www.hamptoncourthotel.com). Superbly situated hotel and pub adjoining the palace wall. Real ale. Excellent food *L and E*. Children welcome. Outside seating.

The Crown Inn Summer Road, Thames Ditton KT7 0QQ (020 8398 4381). Friendly pub just over the river from Hampton Court. Real ale. Bar meals *L*. Children welcome. Outside seating.

The Old Swan Hotel Summer Road, Thames Ditton KT7 0QQ (020 8398 1814). Riverside pub behind Thames Ditton Island, once visited by Henry VIII. Real ale. Meals available *all day*. Children welcome. Outside seating.

The King's Head 123 High Street, Teddington TW11 8HG (020 3166 2900; www.whitebrasserie. com). Refurbished with snugs, three separate rooms, open fireplaces, walled patio and an open kitchen. Children under eight eat free. Food *available all day from 12.00*.

The Swan 22 High Street, Hampton Wick KT1 4DB (020 8943 1715; www.swanhamptonwick. co.uk). Friendly local pub serving real ale. Restaurant menu and bar snacks. Outside seating at front and rear terrace garden. Back bar has sports TV. Well-behaved children and dogs on a lead welcome. Free Wi-Fi

The Anglers 3 Broom Road, Teddington TW11 9NR (020 8977 7475; www.anglers-teddington.co.uk). Right next door to Thames Television Studios, this pleasant riverside bar and restaurant overlooking Teddington Lock offers real ale, along with food *available daily 12.00–22.00*. Children welcome away from the bar. Large garden with children's play area. Barbecues *in summer*. Mooring. Dogs welcome. Free Wi-Fi.

Tide End Cottage 8 Ferry Road, Teddington TW11 9NN (020 8977 7762). Quaint little riverside pub, offering a choice of real ale. Food *L and E (not Sun E)*. Children welcome. Pleasant patio, with a grapevine.

Richmond-upon-Thames

As the river passes Eel Pie Island and enters Horse Reach, Richmond Hill can be seen rising gently from the east bank, with the large Star and Garter Home dominating the view. To the west lies Marble Hill Park, where a ferry connects this with Ham House – the last surviving ferry on the tidal Thames. The river is the focal point of Richmond – indeed the view of the river from Richmond Hill is dramatic and much painted and photographed. Richmond Bridge is an elegant, slightly humped, 18th-C structure – one of the prettiest bridges on the river. Beyond the railway bridge is Richmond half-tide lock, movable weir and footbridge, built in 1894. Its brightly painted arches belie its more serious function of tide control. The river curves around Old Deer Park, with Isleworth Ait to the west, and the old village and church close by the river to the north. Behind wooded banks is Syon Park, and opposite are the Royal Botanic Gardens, Kew. Immediately below the park is the entrance to the Grand Union Canal, a direct link with Birmingham (see *Nicholson Waterways Guide Grand Union, Oxford & the South East*).

Boatyards

Ⓑ**Hammerton Ferry Boat House** Marble Hill Park, Orleans Road, Twickenham TW1 3BL (020 8892 9620 ; www.hammertonsferry.co.uk). Day-hire craft, overnight and long-term mooring. They run the only ferry surviving on the tidal Thames, between Ham House and Marble Hill Park – *Feb–Oct daily, Nov–Jan Sat and Sun only.*
Ⓑ**Swan Island Harbour** Strawberry Vale, Twickenham TW1 4RX (020 8892 2861). ⚓ **D E** Long-term mooring, winter storage, slipway, boat sales, boat and engine repairs, toilets, DIY facilities.

Ⓑ**Brentford Dock Marina** 2 Justin Close, Brentford Dock TW8 8QE (020 8568 7024; www.brentforddock. co.uk). ⚓⛽ **E** Overnight mooring and long-term mooring, boat sales, telephone, toilets, showers, bar.
Ⓑ**MSO Marine Construction** Dock Road, Brentford TW8 8AG (020 8560 5159; www.msomarine.co.uk). Wide range of marine services including boat building, repair and maintenance, crane, dry dock, painting and hull blacking, welding and fabrication, barge conversions.

Pubs and Restaurants

🍺**The White Swan** Riverside, Twickenham TW1 3DN (020 8744 2951; www.whiteswantwickenham.com). Startlingly attractive black and white balconied pub right by the river's edge. Fine choice of real ales. Excellent bar meals *L and E*. Children welcome, and there is riverside seating.
🍺✕**The Barmy Arms** The Embankment, Twickenham TW1 3DU (020 8892 0863; www.taylor-walker.co.uk). Lively pub serving real ale, and food *L and E*. Children welcome. Outside seating on the patio. Live music outside, and barbecues *when there are events on the river.*
🍺✕**The London Apprentice** Church Street, Isleworth TW7 6BG (020 8560 1915; www. thelondonapprentice.co.uk). A 15th-C riverside pub with Elizabethan and Georgian interiors, decorated with prints of Hogarth's *Apprentices*. Real ale. Bar meals available *L and E*. Children welcome in the conservatory, and there is a patio.

🍺**The Rose of York** Petersham Road, Richmond TW10 6UY (020 8948 5867). A Samuel Smiths pub. Large, comfortable, typically English, panelled in oak, warmed by a coal fire and decorated with reproductions of paintings of the famous turn in the river by Turner and Reynolds. Good views of the Thames from the terrace and courtyard. Food served *L and E (not Sun E)*. Children welcome. B&B.
🍺**The Waterman's Arms** Water Lane, Richmond TW9 1TJ (020 8940 2893; www.youngs.co.uk). Small cosy and popular pub, in a cobbled riverside street, which was once frequented by the watermen who trudged up from the river. Real ale. Meals available *L and E*. Children welcome away from the bar. Small garden.
🍺**The White Cross** Riverside (off Water Lane), Richmond TW9 1TJ (020 8940 6844; www.youngs.co.uk). Lively riverside pub with a garden, serving real ale. *Open from 10.00*. Meals available *all day*. Look out for the unusual fireplace. Children welcome *until 18.00*. Large patio.

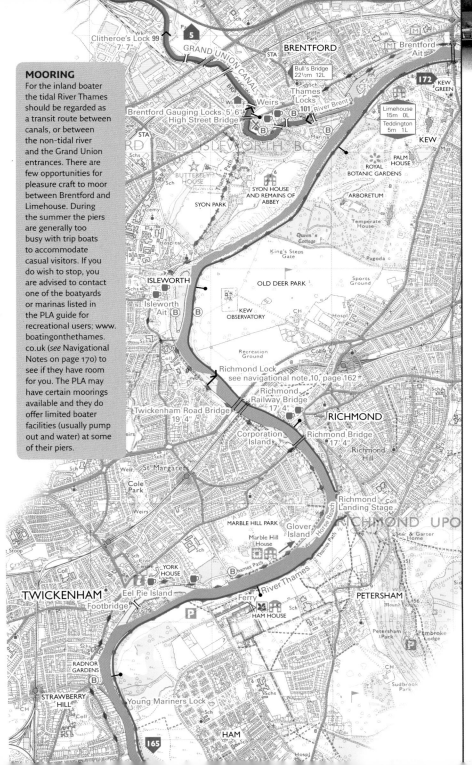

MOORING

For the inland boater the tidal River Thames should be regarded as a transit route between canals, or between the non-tidal river and the Grand Union entrances. There are few opportunities for pleasure craft to moor between Brentford and Limehouse. During the summer the piers are generally too busy with trip boats to accommodate casual visitors. If you do wish to stop, you are advised to contact one of the boatyards or marinas listed in the PLA guide for recreational users; www.boatingonthethames.co.uk (see Navigational Notes on page 170) to see if they have room for you. The PLA may have certain moorings available and they do offer limited boater facilities (usually pump out and water) at some of their piers.

Clitheroe's Lock 99
7'7"

GRAND UNION CANAL

5

BRENTFORD
STA

Griffin
Sch

Brentford
Ait

Bull's Bridge
22½m 12L

172 KEW GREEN

Thames Locks
Weirs

Brentford Gauging Locks 5'6"
High Street Bridge

101 River Brent

Limehouse
15m 0L
Teddington
5m 1L

KEW

RD AND ISLEWORTH BC

STA
Schs

BUTTERFLY HOUSE
Sch

SYON HOUSE AND REMAINS OF ABBEY

SYON PARK

Cemy

ROYAL BOTANIC GARDENS

PALM HOUSE

ARBORETUM

Temperate House

Queen's Cottage

Pagoda

King's Steps Gate

Hospital

Coll

ISLEWORTH

Isleworth Ait

KEW OBSERVATORY

OLD DEER PARK

Sports Ground

CH
Hospl

Recreation Ground

Richmond Lock
see navigational note 10, page 162

Richmond Railway Bridge
17'4"

Twickenham Road Bridge
19'4"

RICHMOND

Corporation Island

Richmond Bridge
17'4"

Richmond Hill

St Margarets

Cole Park

Weir

Richmond Landing Stage

Weirs

MARBLE HILL PARK

Marble Hill House

Glover Island

RICHMOND UPO

Star & Garter Home

Scoop

YORK HOUSE

Coll

Civic Centre

Thames Path

Petersham Park

Pembroke Lodge

TWICKENHAM

Eel Pie Island
Footbridge

Ferry

River Thames

PETERSHAM

Mound

HAM HOUSE

Petersham

CH

RADNOR GARDENS

Sudbrook Park

STRAWBERRY HILL

Young Mariners Lock

Coll

HAM

165

Hospl

NAVIGATIONAL NOTES

1   From **Brentford** to **Limehouse** navigation on the tidal Thames is far more complex than on the upper, non-tidal, reaches. The river here is a commercial waterway first and foremost and pleasure craft must take great care. The River Thames below Teddington Lock is controlled by the Port of London Authority (PLA) who produce a selection of useful information downloadable from their website: *River Thames Recreational Users Guide* is essential reading. For general navigational enquiries contact the Assistant Harbour Master, London River House, Royal Pier Road, Gravesend, Kent, DA12 2BG (01474 562200; www.pla.co.uk/notice2mariners). While hire companies do not usually allow their craft to be taken onto the tideway, owners of pleasure boats may wish to make the passage along the Thames below Teddington Locks and between the canals at Brentford and Limehouse. With proper planning this should present no particular difficulties. However, do check with your insurance company who may have special requirements.

2   **Brentford** to **Limehouse Basin** – leave Brentford *¹/₂ hour before high water* to gain the benefit of the ebb tide. Limehouse Basin is fitted with sector gates and the lock is open in line with the times published annually in the *CRT Tideway Availability Leaflet*, downloadable from www.waterscape.com/useful-downloads. This publication is also available from CRT London Unit (020 7985 7200; enquiries.london@canalrivertrust.org.uk). Always telephone Limehouse Basin (020 7308 9930) and inform them of your intentions.

3   **Limehouse Basin** to **Brentford** – pass through the entrance lock at Limehouse 2¹/₂ hours before high water London Bridge, to gain the benefit of the flood tide. Thames Lock, Brentford is manned *for a period before, and following high water (2 hours each side if this falls within normal working hours)* and you should contact the lock keeper to pre-book passage *outside the normal working hours* (which are the same as Limehouse) on 020 8568 2779. Brentford Gauging Lock is boater operated using a Watermate key.

4   **Brentford** to **Teddington** – pass through Thames Lock, Brentford, *2 hours before high water* to gain the benefit of the flood tide. Pontoon mooring is no longer available below Thames Lock, Brentford. Teddington lock keeper can be contacted on 020 8940 8723 and Richmond lock keeper can be contacted on 020 8940 0634.

5   **VHF Radio** – all vessels of 45ft (13.7 metres) or greater in length must carry a VHF radio capable of communicating with the harbourmaster at port control – channel 14. An exception is made for narrowboats over 45ft in transit between the Grand Union Canal at Brentford and the non-tidal Thames at Teddington Lock. **This is the only passage on the tideway where such a dispensation now operates.** If no radio is available such vessels must telephone the PLA duty officer (0208 855 0315) immediately before and on completion of the transit.

6   **Warning lights** – see PLA publication *River Thames Recreational Users Guide* or the three excellent colour *Tideway Handbooks* downloadable from www.canalrivertrust.org.uk. There are several short videos covering cruising on the tidal Thames downloadable from www.boatingonthethames.co.uk is also very helpful.

7   **Draught** – the depth at the centre span of Westminster Bridge is approximately 2ft 8in at chart datum (about 4ft at mean low water springs). In practice there is usually a greater depth than this. The depth at all the other bridges is greater than at Westminster.

8   **Headroom** – on the tidal river the clearance at bridges is given as the maximum at mean high water springs – this is less than the headroom at chart datum (lowest astronomical tide). In practice this means that there will usually be more headroom than that indicated.

9   **Canals** – those who wish to navigate on the adjoining Canal and River Trust canals will require a licence available from: Boat Licensing, PO Box 162, Leeds LS9 1AX (0303 040 4040; www.canalrivertrust.org.uk/boating/licensing). Details of the inland waterways encountered at Brentford and Limehouse can be found Nicholson Waterways Guide - Grand Union, Oxford and the South East - pages 40 and 26.

10 **Richmond Lock** – (020 8940 0634). The weirs are raised from approximately 2 hours before until approximately 2 hours after high water. At all other times, the lock must be used. The lock keeper can also be contacted on VHF channel 80.

- **Ham House** Ham Street, Ham TW10 7RS (020 8940 1950; www.nationaltrust.org.uk). A superb 17th-C riverside mansion, the exterior largely by Sir John Vavassour. The lavish Restoration interior has a collection of Stuart furniture, and is haunted by a ghostly dog. There are also formal gardens and an ice house. House *open Easter–Oct 12.00–17.00; shop, gardens and café open 11.00–18.00. Nov & early Dec* house *open 12.00–16.00;* shop, gardens and café *open 11.00–16.30.* Telephone for further details of opening times. Charge.

- **Twickenham**
Gt London. All services. Twickenham was one of the most elegant and desirable areas in the 18th C. The church, with its three-storey tower, dates largely from 1714. The poet Alexander Pope, 1688–1744, moved to Twickenham in 1717. Deformed at an early age by a bone disease, his most notable work was the 'Rape of the Lock', although the lock in question was associated with hair, rather than the river. Monuments to him and to his parents can be found in the church. York House, built c.1700, and now Municipal Offices, has an astonishing collection of statues in its riverside gardens.
Strawberry Hill Waldegrave Road, Twickenham TW1 4SX. The surviving glory of Twickenham is Walpole's Gothic fantasy, one of the earliest examples of the 18th-C Gothic Revival. Designed first by John Chute and Richard Bentley between 1753–63, and later by Thomas Pitt, it expresses Walpole's appreciation of Gothic forms and spirit. Strawberry Hill now houses St Mary's Training College.
Marble Hill House Richmond Road, Twickenham TW1 2NL (0870 333 1181; www.english-heritage. org.uk). A restored Palladian mansion, built in 1724–9 by George II for his mistress, Henrietta Howard. Fine collection of paintings and furniture dating from the early 18th C, plus the Lazenby Bequest Chinoiserie (chinese motifs) display. Entry to the House by guided tours only, *Apr–Oct Sat 10.30 & 12.00 and Sun 10.30, 12.00, 2.15 & 3.30. Closed Nov–Mar.* Tours *last around 1½ hours.* Charge. Free entry to the park *daily during daylight hours*
Eel Pie Island Twickenham. In Edwardian times the hotel on the island ran tea dances. In the 1960s it housed a noisy night club which featured popular rock groups.
Tourist Information Centre Civic Centre, York Street, Twickenham TW1 3BZ (020 8891 7272; www.visitrichmond.co.uk).

- **Petersham**
Surrey. But for the traffic, this would be one of the most elegant village suburbs near London. It is exceptionally rich in fine houses of the late 17th and 18th C. Captain George Vancouver, who sailed with Cook and discovered the island off the coast of Canada which is named after him, lived in River Lane and is now buried in the churchyard here.

- **Richmond-upon-Thames**
Surrey. All services. One of the prettiest riverside towns in the London area. Built up the side of the

hill, Richmond has been able to retain its Georgian elegance and still has the feeling of an 18th-C resort. Richmond Green is the centre, both aesthetically and socially; it is surrounded by early 18th-C houses. Only the brick and terracotta theatre, built in 1899, breaks the pattern; so deliberately that it is almost refreshing. The gateway of Richmond Palace is all that remains of the Royal residence built by Henry VII, out of the earlier Palace of Shene. Behind the gate, in Old Palace Yard, is the Trumpeter's House, c.1708. At the top of Richmond Hill stands Wick House, built for Joshua Reynolds in 1772. It is from here that he painted marvellous views over the Thames.
Richmond Theatre The Green, Richmond TW9 1QJ (0844 871 7651; www.atgtickets.com). Productions from London's West End and touring companies.
Richmond Park The largest of the royal parks, created by Charles I in 1637, it covers 2358 acres. The park remained a favourite hunting ground until the 18th C. Private shooting stopped in 1904 but the hunting lodges can still be seen. White Lodge, built for George II in 1727, now houses the Royal Ballet School. Park *open 07.00 – dusk (07.30 in winter).*
Old Deer Park TW9 2RA Kew Observatory was built here in 1729 (by William Chambers for George III) and was used by the Meteorological Office until 1981. The three obelisks nearby were used to measure London's official time.
Richmond Bridge This fine stone bridge with its five arches and parapet is one of the most handsome on the Thames, and was frequently the subject for paintings in the 18th–19th C. Built in the classical style by James Paine, 1777, it replaced the earlier horse ferry, and was a toll bridge until 1859.
Tourist Information Centre (020 8891 7272; www.visitrichmond.co.uk).

- **Isleworth**
Gt London. PO. The prettiest view of this village is from the stretch of river just before Syon House. The 15th-C tower of All Saints' Church, the London Apprentice Inn and a collection of fine Georgian houses all make for a delightful setting. Vincent Van Gogh taught here and used the Thames as the subject for his first attempts at painting.
Syon Park Park Road, Brentford (020 8560 0881; www.syonpark.co.uk). Set in 55 acres of parkland, landscaped by 'Capability' Brown, Syon House is built on the site of a 15th-C convent. The present square structure with its corner turrets is largely 16th-C, although the interior was remodelled by Robert Adam in 1762. The house itself is mainly of interest on account of the magnificent neo-classical rooms by Adam. Katherine Howard was confined here before her execution in 1542 and Lady Jane Grey stayed here for the nine days preceding her death in 1554. Conservatory (1827) by Charles Fowler. The Butterfly House houses a huge variety of live butterflies and insects from all over the world. House *open mid-Mar – Oct, Wed, Thur and Sun (also G Fri & Easter Sun) 11.00 – 17.00.* Gardens *open mid-Mar – Oct daily 10.30 – 17.00 (16.00 Fri & Sat).* Charge.

West London

Immediately below Brentford Dock Marina is the entrance to the Grand Union Canal, a direct link with Birmingham and places north. On the north bank opposite Kew is Strand-on-the-Green, a cluster of desirable houses and fashionable pubs facing the towpath.

The Oxford and Cambridge Boat Race finish is below Chiswick Bridge, the line being marked on both banks by wooden piles and the University Stone. The river is flanked by elegant houses at Hammersmith and Chiswick, but further downstream becomes grimy and industrial. There is, however, as always on the lower Thames, plenty of interest. Below the splendid Hammersmith Bridge, on the south bank, lies one of the most bizarre buildings on the whole riverside – the Harrods Depository – a cupolated building in the same terracotta as the main store. There is a small wharf in front where a light railway used to run directly into the building. Barn Elms Reservoir is now host to a variety of watersports and is ideal for fishing and birdwatching.

NAVIGATIONAL NOTES

Boaters joining the tidal Thames at Brentford should read the Navigational Notes on page 170, and the Mooring Note on page 169.

Boatyards

Ⓑ**Chiswick Pier** The Pier House, Corney Reach, Chiswick W4 2UG (020 8742 2713; www.chiswickpier.org.uk). Pump out, telephone, mooring (up to 14 days), showers, toilets, electrical hook-up. Visitors welcome – booking recommended.

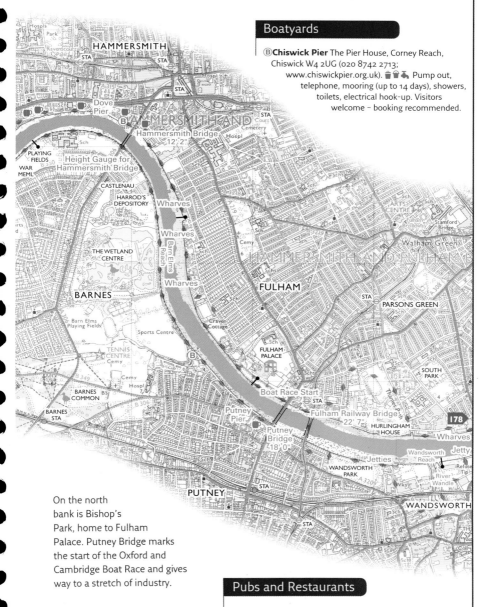

On the north bank is Bishop's Park, home to Fulham Palace. Putney Bridge marks the start of the Oxford and Cambridge Boat Race and gives way to a stretch of industry.

Pubs and Restaurants

For Pubs and Restaurants accessible to the boater entering the canal at either Brentford or Limehouse see *Nicholson Waterways Guide for Grand Union, Oxford & the South East.*

View of the London Millennium Footbridge, Shakespeare's Globe and Tate Modern from the top of St Paul's Cathedral.

WALKING & CYCLING

This is an absolutely splendid section for walking. The path keeps to the south side throughout and Kew Gardens and Kew Palace are definitely worth a visit. Across the river is Strand-on-the-Green, with its fine houses and pubs. Barnes Railway Bridge has a foot crossing, and walkers can choose which bank they take to reach Hammersmith – the scenic route is on the south bank, the pubs on the north. After the fascinating walk around Barnes to Putney, the Thames towpath terminates, giving way to road as far as Putney Bridge. The course of the river can be followed through London by paths along both sides of the river. *Collins London Street Atlases* are helpful guides when detours are necessary.

Royal Botanic Gardens Kew Road, Kew, Richmond TW9 3AB (020 8332 5000; www. kew.org). On the south bank of the Thames, opposite Brentford. (Access from the south side of the Gardens or from the Thames towpath.) One of the world's great botanic gardens, with thousands of rare outdoor and hothouse plants. Kew Palace, also worth a visit, was built in 1631 in the Dutch style. Gardens *open daily from 09.30; there are slight seasonal variations in closing times.* Telephone for current information. Charge.

Kew Bridge Opened by Edward VII in 1903 and officially called the King Edward VII Bridge. A fine stone structure designed by Sir John Wolfe Barry and Cuthbert Brereton, it replaced the earlier granite bridge of 1789.

Kew Railway Bridge When it was opened in 1869 this five-span lattice girder bridge, designed by W. R. Galbraith, was part of the London and South Western Railway extension.

● **Kew**
Surrey. Old Kew centres around the Green, the 18th-C houses built for members of the Court of George III, and the entrance to the Royal Botanic Gardens. The church of St Anne dates from 1714 but was greatly altered in the 19th C.

Musical Museum 399 High Street, Brentford TW8 0DU (020 8560 8108; www. musicalmuseum.co.uk). A fascinating collection of automatic, old and odd musical instruments and a concert hall complete with stage and a Wurlitzer console. Regular events and concerts. *Open Tue–Sun, 11.00–17.30.* Charge.

Kew Bridge Steam Museum Green Dragon Lane, Brentford TW8 0EN (020 8568 4757; www. kbsm.org). Huge Victorian building housing a large collection of steam pumping engines, restored to working order by volunteers. Also a collection of old traction engines, a working forge and steam railway. Tearoom. *Open Tue–Sun and B Hol Mon, 11.00–16.00. Steam pumping engines* run *every weekend & B Hol Mon;* railway operates *Sun & B Hol Mon, Easter – Oct.* See website for details. Charge (under 16s accompanied by adult free).

● **Chiswick**
W4. Chiswick stretches between Kew Bridge and Hammersmith Terrace and provides some of the most picturesque scenery on the London stretch of the Thames. Georgian houses extend along Strand-on-the-Green and again at Chiswick Mall. Between these points, running down to the riverside, originally stood three 18thC mansions: of the three, only Chiswick House remains. The site of Grove House has been built over, and Duke's Meadows, part of the grounds of Chiswick House, is now a recreation ground. Chiswick Cemetery backs on to St Nicholas Church where Lord Burlington and William Kent are buried.

Chiswick Bridge W4. Built in 1933, designed by Sir Herbert Baker and opened to the public by the Prince of Wales, this bridge has the longest concrete arch of any bridge on the Thames. The centre span measures 150ft.

Chiswick House Burlington Lane, Chiswick W4 2RP (020 8995 0508; www.chgt.org.uk). Lovely Palladian villa built in the grand manner by 3rd Earl of Burlington 1725–30, modelled on Palladio's Villa Capra at Vicenza. Café. *Gardens open daily, 7.00–dusk;* house *open Apr–Oct, Sun–Wed & B Hols 10.00–17.00.* Charge.

● **Mortlake**
SW14. In the 17th C Mortlake was famous for its tapestry workshop, established by James I and staffed by Flemish weavers. Some of the Mortlake Tapestries can still be seen in the Victoria & Albert Museum. The riverside here is picturesque along Thames Bank where there is a fine collection of 18th-C houses. Mortlake also marks the end of the Oxford and Cambridge Boat Race at Chiswick Bridge (although the first race took place at Henley in 1829).

Barnes Railway Bridge SW13. This light and elegant iron bridge by Locke was opened in 1849 to connect with the Richmond line. Similar in design to Richmond Railway Bridge.

Oxford v Cambridge Boat Race On a *Saturday afternoon in March or April* this famous annual event is held over a 4-mile course from Putney to Mortlake. Get to the riverside early for a good view.

● **North Bank**
Hammersmith Terrace W6. A terrace of 17 identical houses on the river bank, built c.1750. The late Sir Alan Herbert, historian of the Thames, lived in the Terrace.

Upper Mall W6. Separated from Lower Mall by Furnivall Gardens, Upper Mall boasts some fine 18th-C buildings including the Dove Inn, originally a coffee house. William Morris lived in Kelmscott House between 1878 and 1896.

Lower Mall W6. Bustling in the summer months with rowers from the number of boathouses and rowing clubs which have been established here for over a century. Lower Mall is home to the Rutland and Blue Anchor pubs, and a number of pretty 18th-C cottages.

Hammersmith Bridge W6. The first suspension bridge in London. The original, built 1824 by William T. Clarke, was replaced in 1883 by the present splendid construction by Sir Joseph Bazalgette.

Fulham SW6. In the 18th and 19th C Fulham was the 'great fruit and kitchen garden north of the Thames', a place of market and nursery gardens, attracting the more prosperous Londoners in search of purer air. Today little is left of the fertile village and the area has become quite built-up. Fulham has, however, remained an attractive area, nowadays better known for its abundance of restaurants and bars. Also home to two of London's most famous football clubs, Fulham and Chelsea. Bishop's Park and Hurlingham House can be seen from the river.

Fulham Palace SW6. The palace lies behind the long avenues of Bishop's Park, with grounds stretching to the river. The site was first acquired by Bishop Waldhere in AD704 and continued as a residence of the Bishops of London until 1973. A fascinating mixture of architectural styles, from the Tudor courtyard with its mellow red brick to the restrained elegance of the Georgian east front.

Putney Bridge W6. The wooden toll bridge of 1729 was replaced by the present bridge designed by Sir Joseph Bazalgette in 1884. Putney Bridge marks the start of the Oxford and Cambridge Boat Race.

Fulham Railway Bridge SW6. This trellis girder iron bridge was part of the Metropolitan extension to the District Railway. Designed by William Jacomb, it was opened in 1889 and connects with a footbridge running parallel to it. Part of the London Transport underground system.

Hurlingham House Ranelagh Gardens SW6. This is the only large 18th-C residence still surviving in Fulham. The house has a fine river front with Corinthian columns and is now the centre of the Hurlingham Club. Members play tennis, golf and croquet in the grounds.

● **South Bank**

Barnes Terrace SW13. The delightful village of Barnes lies behind the attractive ironwork façade of Barnes Terrace. The terrace was, and still is, a fashionable place to live, with former residents including Sheridan and Gustav Holst.

Castelnau SW13. Barnes is rich in Victorian houses and some of the most interesting are to be seen in Castelnau. Remarkably standardised, they are largely semi-detached and typical of early Victorian villa architecture with their arched windows.

Barn Elms SW13. Formerly the manor house of Barnes, the estate was later leased to Sir Francis Walsingham, Secretary of State to Elizabeth I. Today, all that remains of the former layout is part of the ornamental pond and the ice house. The Reservoir at Barn Elms now plays host to a variety of watersports, plus fishing and birdwatching.

Putney SW15. The Embankment is picturesque. The London Rowing Club and Westminster School have their boathouses here and the eights and sculls can be seen practising most afternoons.

Battersea Power Station (see page 180)

Central London

The short stretch of intrusive industry, sprawling along the south bank, is soon relieved at Battersea by the splendid St Mary's Church opposite Lots Road Power Station and Chelsea Harbour. Albert Bridge, restored in 1991, is a remarkable sight when illuminated at night by over 4,000 bulbs. From here on the River Thames curves through the heart of the capital, and has been London's lifeline for 2000 years. Indeed it was instrumental in the Roman settlement which created London as an international port. Once used as the local bypass, being cheaper and safer than travel by road, it has carried Roman galleys, Viking longships, Elizabethan barges and Victorian steamers. One of the best ways to see London is still from the Thames. The buildings and sights lining its twisting, turning path are as varied as London itself. It is fascinating by day and magical by night.

North Bank

Wandsworth Bridge SW6. In 1938 the 19th-C bridge was replaced with the existing structure by E. P. Wheeler, now painted a distinctive bright blue.

Chelsea Harbour SW11. A modern development dominated by the Belvedere tower block. The golden ball on its roof slides up and down with the level of the river. The development contains offices, restaurants, a luxury hotel, smart shops, apartments and the marina. Chelsea Wharf, just along the bank, has been transformed from old warehouses into modern business units.

Battersea Railway Bridge SW11. The West London Extension Railway, of which this bridge was a part, was opened in 1863 to connect the south of England directly with the north. Because it did not end at a London terminus, it became a target for bombing during World War II.

Lots Road Power Station SW11. This huge and dominating structure was built in 1904 to provide electricity for the new underground railway.

Battersea Bridge SW11. The original Battersea Bridge, 1772, a picturesque wooden structure by Henry Holland, has been portrayed in paintings by Whistler and Turner. The replacement iron structure, opened in 1890, was designed by Sir Joseph Bazalgette.

All Saints Church SW3. Chelsea Embankment. Rebuilt in 1964 after severe bomb damage during the war. Contains two 13th-C chapels, one restored by Sir Thomas More 1528, a Jacobean altar table and one of the best series of monuments in a London parish church. Henry VIII married Jane Seymour here before their state wedding in 1536.

Cheyne Walk SW3. Cheyne Walk, with its houseboats and its row of delightful riverside Queen Anne houses, has been home to Lloyd George, Hilaire Belloc, George Eliot, Isambard Kingdom Brunel, Turner and Whistler.

Carlyle's House 24 Cheyne Row SW3 5HL (020 7352 7087; www.nationaltrust.org.uk). Once the haunt of writers such as Dickens and Tennyson, and the home of Thomas and Jane Carlyle 1834–81.

Albert Bridge SW3. A delightful suspension bridge connecting Chelsea and Battersea, built by Ordish 1871–3. The bridge was strengthened in 1973 by a huge solid support under the main span. Illuminated by over 4,000 bulbs, the bridge is particularly beautiful at night.

Chelsea Embankment SW3. Chelsea Embankment, stretching between Albert Bridge and Chelsea Bridge, was built in 1871. The embankment is bordered on the north bank by the grounds of the Chelsea Royal Hospital where the Chelsea Flower Show is held annually in *May*. Norman Shaw's famous Old Swan House stands at No. 17 Chelsea Embankment.

Tate Britain Millbank SW1P 4RG (0207 887 8888; www.tate.org.uk). Founded in 1897 by Sir Henry Tate, the sugar magnate and by Sidney HJ Smith. Following the opening of Tate Modern, the Millbank gallery has redefined its role, concentrating on British art over the last 500 years. Five thematic displays portray historic and modern works in an imaginative and often disturbing way which, whilst adding an element of surprise, successfully demonstrates continuity over the centuries. The Clore Gallery houses the works of Turner and Constable and special displays depicting major artists range from Blake to Hockney. *Open daily*. Free (except for special exhibitions).

Millbank Tower Millbank SW1. The traditional balance of the river bank has been overturned by this 387ft-high office building by Ronald Ward and Partners, 1963.

Victoria Tower Gardens Abingdon Street SW1. A sculpture of Rodin's Burghers of Calais, 1895, stands close to the river and near the entrance to the gardens is a monument to Mrs Emmeline Pankhurst and Dame Christabel Pankhurst, champions of the women's suffragette movement in the early 1900s. Emmeline Pankhurst is reputedly the last person to have been incarcerated in the cell at the bottom of Big Ben (1902).

Houses of Parliament Parliament Square SW1A 0AA (www.parliament.uk). Originally the Palace of Westminster, and a principal royal palace until

1512. Became known as parliament or 'place to speak' in 1550. Westminster Hall, one of the few remaining parts of the original royal palace, has an impressive hammerbeam roof. The present Victorian-Gothic building was designed in 1847 by Sir Charles Barry and Augustus Pugin specifically to house Parliament and has 1100 rooms, 100 staircases and over 2 miles of passages. The Houses of Parliament and Big Ben – the bell clock housed in the adjoining St Stephen's Tower – make up London's most famous landmark.

Westminster Abbey Broad Sanctuary SW1P 3PA (www.westminster-abbey.org). Original church by Edward the Confessor 1065. Rebuilding commenced in 1245 by Henry III who was largely influenced by the new French cathedrals. Completed by Henry Yevele and others 1376–1506 (towers incomplete and finished by Hawksmoor 1734). Henry VII Chapel added 1503; fine Perpendicular with wonderful fan vaulting. The Abbey contains the Coronation Chair, and many tombs and memorials of the Kings and Queens of England.

Victoria Embankment WC2R. The Embankment was created by Joseph Bazalgette in 1868, reclaiming 37 acres of mud from the Thames banks, making the river narrower and the water faster flowing, thereby ending the skating era on the once-frozen waters. The building of the Embankment provided a wall against flooding, a riverside walk, a new west-east sewerage system and part of the District Line Railway.

It was completed in 1870, Bazalgette was knighted, and his bust incorporated into the parapet by Hungerford Bridge.

Cleopatra's Needle WC2R. Victoria Embankment SW1. A 60ft-high ancient Egyptian granite obelisk, presented to Britain by the Viceroy of Egypt, Mohammed Ali, in 1819 and brought to London by sea in 1878. When it was erected various articles were buried beneath it for posterity – the morning's newspapers, a razor, coins, four Bibles in different languages and photographs of '12 of the best-looking Englishwomen of the day'. The bronze sphinxes were added (facing the wrong way) in 1882.

Somerset House Strand WC2R 1LA (020 7836 8686; www.somersethouse.org.uk). Built in 1776 by Sir William Chambers on the site of Protector Somerset's house, this magnificent building with its arches, terrace, and river entrances decorated with lions and Tuscan columns, was intended to compete with the splendour of Adam's Adelphi. Once occupied by the General Register Office whose

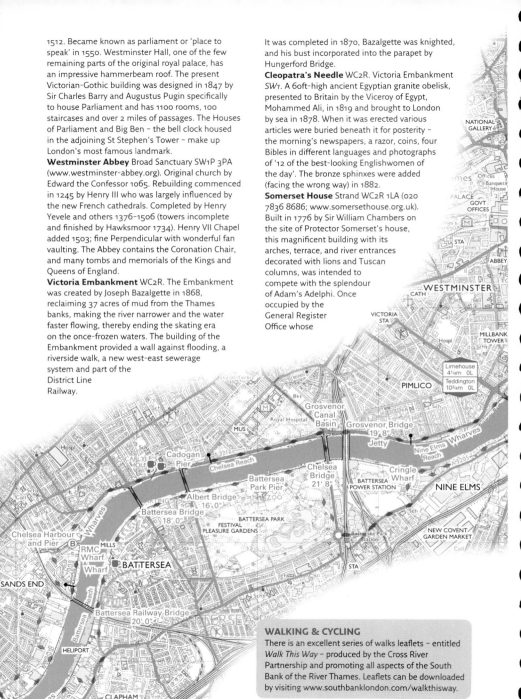

WALKING & CYCLING

There is an excellent series of walks leaflets – entitled *Walk This Way* – produced by the Cross River Partnership and promoting all aspects of the South Bank of the River Thames. Leaflets can be downloaded by visiting www.southbanklondon.com/walkthisway.

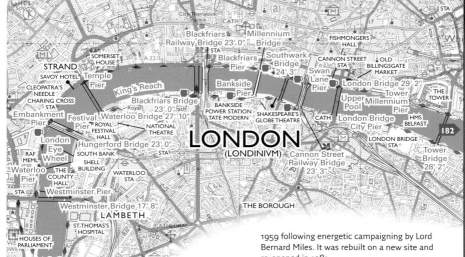

LONDON
(LONDINIVM)

records of birth and death go back to 1836, it now houses the permanent collections and special exhibitions of The Courtauld Gallery, and the Embankment Galleries. Special events and outdoor concerts and film shows are held regularly.

The Temple EC4. The name derives from the Order of Knights Templar who occupied the site from 1160–1308. In the 17th-C the Temple was leased to the benchers of the Inner and Middle Temple, two Inns of Court. These inns, together with Lincoln's Inn and Gray's Inn, hold the ancient and exclusive privilege of providing advocates in the courts of England and Wales. A visit should be made on foot, as only a few of the Temple buildings are visible from the river. On the Embankment, Sir Joseph Bazalgette's arch and stairs mark the 19th-C access to the Temple from the river.

City of London A thriving and commercial centre, stretching between Blackfriars Bridge and London Bridge, which has within its square mile such famous institutions as the Bank of England, the Stock Exchange, the Royal Courts of Justice and the Guildhall.

Mermaid Theatre Puddle Dock, Blackfriars EC4V 3DB (020 7236 1919; www.the-mermaid.co.uk). The original theatre, the first in the City since the 16th C, was opened in a converted warehouse in 1959 following energetic campaigning by Lord Bernard Miles. It was rebuilt on a new site and re-opened in 1981.

Fishmongers' Hall EC4. Built in the grand classical manner in 1831–4 by Henry Roberts to replace the original hall which was burnt down in the Great Fire of 1666. The Fishmongers' Company administers the annual Doggett's Coat and Badge Race for Thames Watermen. This race, the oldest annually contested sporting event and the longest rowing race in the world (1 furlong short of 5 miles), was introduced in 1715. Doggett, an Irish comedian and staunch Hanoverian, who used the services of the watermen to ferry him to and from the theatres, decided to mark the anniversary of the accession of George I to the throne by instituting an annual race for watermen. The race is from London Bridge to Cadogan Pier, Chelsea, and is usually held at the *end of July*. The victor is presented with a red coat, breeches and cap, and a silver arm badge bearing the words 'The Gift of the late Thomas Doggett'.

Monument EC4. A 17th-C hollow fluted column by Wren, built to commemorate the Great Fire of London. It marked the northern end of the original London Bridge and stands at 202ft, a foot in height for every foot in distance from where the fire started in Pudding Lane. Gives a magnificent view over the city.

Old Billingsgate Market Lower Thames Street EC3. The yellow-brick Victorian building with arcaded ground floor was built by Sir Horace Jones, 1875, although the first reference to a market at Billingsgate was made in AD870. A free fish market was established by statute in 1699, but until the 18th C coal, corn and provisions were also sold. The fish-porters wore leather hats with flat tops and wide brims, formerly known as bobbing hats. Bobbing was the charge made by the porter to carry fish from the wholesaler to the retailer. These hats enabled the porter to carry about a hundredweight of fish on his head.

The market moved down river to new premises on the Isle of Dogs in 1982.

The Custom House Lower Thames Street EC3. A custom house has stood beside Billingsgate since AD870. The present building is by Laing, 1813–17, but the river façade was rebuilt by Smirke in 1825. Badly bombed in the war, the building has been restored.

Tower of London Tower Hill EC3 (0844 482 7777; www.hrp.org.uk). Although greatly restored and altered over the centuries, the Tower of London is probably the most important work of military architecture in Britain and has been used as a palace, a fortress and a prison since William the Conqueror built the White Tower in 1078. *Opening times vary according to season.* Contact for details.

Tower Bridge SE1 2UP (020 7403 3761; www.towerbridge.org.uk). This spectacular bridge was built by Sir John Wolfe Barry in 1894 and the old hydraulic lifting mechanism was originally powered by steam. Exhibition, Victorian engine room and walkways with fantastic views. *Open Apr–Sep 10.00–18.00 & Oct–Mar 09.30–17.30.*

● **South Bank**

Wandsworth SW18. Until the 19th C Wandsworth was a village oasis on the River Wandle – a good fishing river – and was noted for a local silk and hat industry. The course of the Wandle can still be traced near the Church of All Saints. The Surrey Iron Railway, whose wagons were drawn by horses, ran alongside the river. Past residents include Defoe, Thackeray and Voltaire, but today little remains to point to the past.

Battersea SW11. Many of the old riverside warehouses are now gone and tall tower blocks dominate.

St Mary's Church Church Road *SW11*. The church is one of the few relics of Battersea's 18th-C village. Built in 1775 by Joseph Dixon, it is strangely Dutch in character.

Battersea Park SW11 4NJ (www.batterseapark.org). The park was laid out by Sir James Pennethorne as a public garden and opened by Queen Victoria in 1858. Re-designed in the 1950s for the Festival of Britain, there is a boating lake, a deer park, an Alpine showhouse, herb garden and greehouse, a children's zoo and sculptures by Moore, Hepworth and Epstein. The London Peace Pagoda which stands close to the river was built in 1985 by monks and nuns of the Japanese Buddhist order Nipponzan Myohoji.

Battersea Power Station SW8 4BU (www.batterseapowerstation.org.uk). This vast oblong of brick with its four chimneys was designed by Sir Giles Gilbert Scott, 1932–4. Redundant as a power station since 1980, it is now to be developed for retail and residential use.

Albert Embankment SE1. Designed as a broad footwalk by Sir Joseph Bazalgette, 1867, the Embankment stretches between Vauxhall and Westminster Bridges. The upper Embankment was once the site of the 18th-C Vauxhall Gardens, whose Chinese pavilions and walks were the envy of Europe.

Lambeth Palace Lambeth Palace Road SE1 7JU (www.bishopthorpepalace.co.uk). The London residence of the Archbishop of Canterbury since 1197. Remarkable Tudor gatehouse, fine medieval crypt.

A 14th-C Hall with a splendid roof and portraits of archbishops on its walls. The Guard Room, which houses the library, was rebuilt in medieval style in 1633. Open days and special events – visit website for details.

County Hall Westminster Bridge Road SE1 7PB (www.londoncountyhall.com). Designed by Ralph Knott in 1911, this was once the imposing headquarters of the Greater London Council. Today it houses temporary attractions and events and the London Aquarium (0871 663 1678; www.londonaquarium.co.uk), one of the largest collections of underwater life in Europe swimming in an impressive 450,000 gallons of water. Breath-taking colours abound in tanks depicting sea life from different corners of the globe. The Pacific and Atlantic tanks are spectacular in their sheer size alone, as are the sharks therein. Also touch tanks and the chance to stroke a ray. *Open daily.* Charge.

London Eye Jubilee Gardens SE1 7PB (0870 990 8883; www.londoneye.com). A gigantic ferris wheel offering a bird's eye view over London. *Opening times vary according to season.* Contact for details.

Shell Centre SE1. Part of the area known as the South Bank, the Shell Centre was designed by Sir Howard Robertson in 1962, and is of greyish white concrete with monotonous little square windows. The central 351ft-high skyscraper rises like a huge grey mountain.

South Bank Arts Centre SE1 8XX (020 7960 4200; www.southbankcentre.co.uk). Royal Festival Hall, the Queen Elizabeth Hall, the Purcell Room, the National Theatre, the National Film Theatre, the Hayward Gallery and the Museum of the Moving Image make up the complex which originated with the Festival of Britain in 1951. The Festival Hall, completed in 1951 and built by Sir Robert Matthew and Sir Leonard Martin, seats 3400. The Queen Elizabeth Hall by Hubert Bennett, 1967, is much smaller and intended for recitals. Bennett also designed the Hayward Gallery which opened in 1968. The Purcell Room is the smallest of the three concert halls; ideal for chamber music and solo concerts. The range of cultural activities on offer at the South Bank Centre is diverse and can be enjoyed by everyone.

Upper Ground SE1. The decrepit warehouses that used to line the south bank have been demolished, and replaced by the impressive London Weekend Television building and Gabriel's Wharf – South Bank's answer to Covent Garden. To the east of Gabriel's Wharf stands the fine art deco OXO tower, built in 1928 and decorated thus because advertising was forbidden on buildings.

Bankside SE1. In the 16th C the Rose Theatre, the Swan and the Globe were all situated around Bankside, and until the 19th C the area was the site of playhouses and amusement gardens. Today the area has been developed and almost all is changing apart from the few remaining 17th-C and 18th-C houses and the Anchor pub, an historic tavern with strong smuggling connections. A Tudor theatre has been reconstructed near the site of the original Globe Theatre as part of the International Shakespeare Globe Centre, and the Shakespeare

Globe Museum illustrates the theatre of the age (*see below*). From Bankside are fine views of St Paul's Cathedral and the City.

Shakespeare Globe Museum 21 New Globe Walk, Bankside SE1 9DT (020 7401 9919; www.shakespeareglobe.com). Converted 18th-C warehouse on the site of a 16th-C bear-baiting ring and the Hope Playhouse.

Tate Modern Bankside SE1 9TG (020 7887 8888; www.tate.org.uk/modern/). The Tate Gallery's international collection of 20th-C art is housed within the former Bankside Power Station, designed in 1935 by Sir Giles Gilbert Scott. Displays are themed and stylistic and historical parallels are drawn between works from different periods to challenge the viewers perception of non-representational art. Genres range from Surrealism and New Reaslism through to Pop Art and Minimal Art. Striking views from the top floor – both of the sculptures inside the building and out over the Thames. Café and restaurant with outdoor river terrace. *Open daily*. Free (except for special exhibitions).

Southwark Cathedral London Bridge SE1 9DA (020 7367 6700; cathedral.southwark.anglican. org). Built by Augustinian Canons but destroyed by fire in 1206 and greatly restored. The tower was built c.1520 and the nave, by Blomfield, 1894-7. In the Middle Ages the cathedral was part of the Augustinian Priory of St Mary Overie. Despite its 19th-C additions, it is still one of the most impressive Gothic buildings in London. Exhibitions, refectory, shop.

Kathleen & May St Mary Overy Dock, Cathedral Street SE1 (www.kathleenandmay.co.uk). Last surviving three-masted, topsail, trading schooner, beautifully restored.

● **Bridges**

Chelsea Bridge SW3. The original bridge designed by Thomas Page, 1858, was rebuilt as a suspension bridge in 1934 by Rendel, Palmer & Tritton.

Victoria Railway Bridge SW1. When it was opened in 1859, this was the widest railway bridge in the world – 132ft wide and 900ft long – and it provided 10 separate accesses to Victoria Station.

Vauxhall Bridge SW1. James Walker's Regent's Bridge which opened in 1816 was the first iron bridge to span the Thames in London. The present structure, designed by Sir Alexander Binnie, was opened in 1906. The bronze figures alongside the bridge represent Agriculture, Architecture, Engineering, Learning, the Fine Arts and Astronomy.

Lambeth Bridge SW1Y. Originally the site of a horse ferry, the first bridge was built here in 1861, designed by P. W. Barlow. This was replaced in 1932 by the present steel-arch bridge designed by George Humphreys and Sir Reginald Blomfield.

Westminster Bridge SW1Y. Built in 1750, Westminster Bridge was the second bridge to be built across the Thames in central London. The present bridge, by Thomas Page, replaced the old stone one in 1862.

Charing Cross Railway Bridge SE1. Also known as Hungerford Bridge, it has replaced the original suspension bridge which was demolished in 1864. A separate walkway and cycleway run alongside to Waterloo Station with excellent views of the City.

Waterloo Bridge SE1. John Rennie's early 19th-C bridge, a beautiful design of Greek columns and nine elliptical arches, was replaced in 1945 by Sir Giles Gilbert Scott's concrete bridge, faced with Portland stone.

Millennium Bridge EC4. Constructed in 1999 and, in conjunction with the new walkway on the upstream side of Hungerford Bridge, forms part of the City's Cross River Partnership initiative to provide an integrated transport and regeneration strategy for Thames side in central London.

Southwark Bridge EC4. Southwark Bridge was built in 1814 and was the largest bridge ever built of cast iron. Replaced 1912-21 by the present five-span steel bridge of Mott and Hay, with Sir Ernest George as architect. Southwark Causeway, the steps on the south side, were used by Wren when he travelled across the river to supervise work on St Paul's.

Cannon Street Railway Bridge EC3. Built in 1866 as part of the extension of the South Eastern Railway, the bridge's engineers were J. Hawkshaw and J. W. Barry. A prominent structure on account of the 19th-C train shed jutting out to the side of the bridge.

London Bridge EC3. Until 1749 London Bridge was the only bridge to span the Thames in London. The first recorded wooden bridge was Saxon, but it is possible that a Roman structure may have existed here. In 1176 the wooden bridge was replaced by a stone structure, with houses, shops and a church built upon it, similar in appearance to the Ponte Vecchio in Florence. The heads of traitors were displayed on the spikes of the fortified gates at either end. In 1831 this bridge was demolished and a new bridge, by John Rennie, replaced it. A granite bridge with five arches, this soon became too narrow to meet the demands of modern traffic and because of structural faults could not be widened. A new bridge, constructed under the direction of the City Engineer, was opened to traffic in 1973. Built out of concrete, it has a flat-arched profile in three spans carried on slender piers. The McCulloch Corporation of Arizona paid £2,460,000 for the facing materials of Rennie's bridge, which has been reconstructed spanning Lake Havasu.

Blackfriars Bridge SE1. Blackfriars Bridge was built in 1760. It cost £230,000 and was mainly paid for by fines which had accumulated from men refusing the post of Sheriff. Replaced by the present structure in 1860. Note the pulpits, a reminder of the religious significance of its name.

Blackfriars Railway Bridge SE1. Built in 1886 for the London, Chatham and Dover Railway, this elegant iron bridge, with its high parapet and decorative coat of arms at each end, can best be seen from the road bridge.

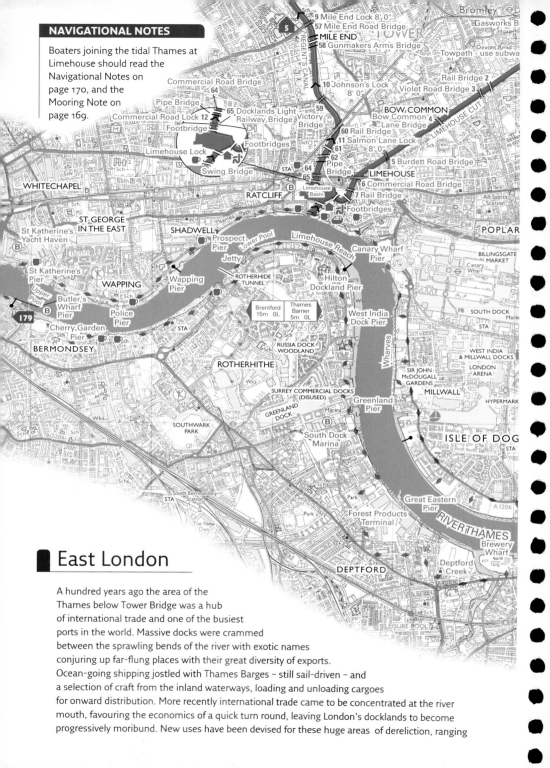

NAVIGATIONAL NOTES

Boaters joining the tidal Thames at
Limehouse should read the
Navigational Notes on
page 170, and the
Mooring Note on
page 169.

East London

A hundred years ago the area of the
Thames below Tower Bridge was a hub
of international trade and one of the busiest
ports in the world. Massive docks were crammed
between the sprawling bends of the river with exotic names
conjuring up far-flung places with their great diversity of exports.
Ocean-going shipping jostled with Thames Barges – still sail-driven – and
a selection of craft from the inland waterways, loading and unloading cargoes
for onward distribution. More recently international trade came to be concentrated at the river
mouth, favouring the economics of a quick turn round, leaving London's docklands to become
progressively moribund. New uses have been devised for these huge areas of dereliction, ranging

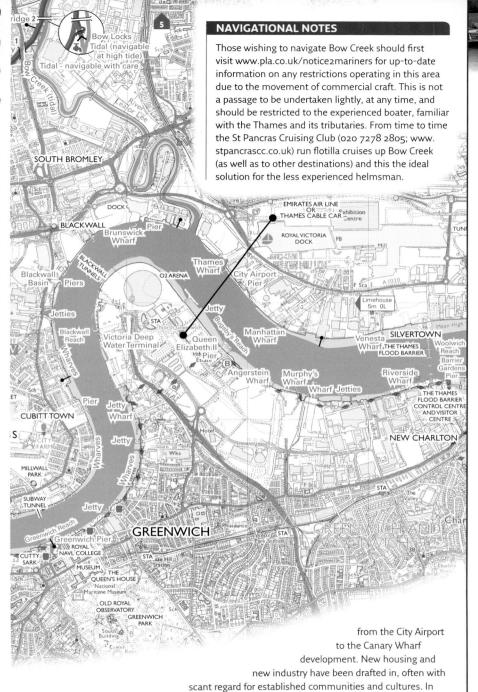

Those wishing to navigate Bow Creek should first visit www.pla.co.uk/notice2mariners for up-to-date information on any restrictions operating in this area due to the movement of commercial craft. This is not a passage to be undertaken lightly, at any time, and should be restricted to the experienced boater, familiar with the Thames and its tributaries. From time to time the St Pancras Cruising Club (020 7278 2805; www.stpancrascc.co.uk) run flotilla cruises up Bow Creek (as well as to other destinations) and this the ideal solution for the less experienced helmsman.

from the City Airport to the Canary Wharf development. New housing and new industry have been drafted in, often with scant regard for established communities and cultures. In converting redundant warehouses the value of these solid symbols of a previous prosperity and optimism has at least been recognised.

St Katharine Dock E1W 1TW (www.skdocks.co.uk). St Katharine Dock was the first of the docks to be rejuvenated. Built on 23 acres in 1828, from a design by Thomas Telford, the original docks were closed down in 1968. Five years later an £80 million building scheme was begun which included the Tower Thistle Hotel and the World Trade Centre. The magnificent warehouses have been restored and now house shops, apartments, offices, restaurants, a yacht club and marina. Visiting cruisers nestle alongside resident yachts and barges.

Tobacco Dock Pennington Street E1. Designed by Terry Farrell in 1989, this 19th-C former warehouse has been converted into a shopping and leisure complex. Development work was carried out using original suppliers of materials wherever possible.

Butler's Wharf SE1 (www.london-se1.co.uk/areas/butlers.html). Transformed from narrow alleys, where Oliver Twist's Bill Sikes met his end, into a smart restaurant, shopping and office complex including the Conran restaurants and the Butler's Wharf Chop House.

The Design Museum Butler's Wharf, Shad Thames SE1 2YD (020 7403 6933; www.designmuseum.org). A fascinating introduction to 20th- and 21st-C design, technology and consumer culture. Shop and café. Opening hours vary so telephone for details.

Cherry Garden Pier SE16. Where ships sound their signal if they want Tower Bridge to be raised. Turner sat here to paint *The Fighting Temeraire* as she was being towed to be broken up.

Rotherhithe Tunnel SE16. Built 1904–8 by Sir Maurice Fitzmarice, the tunnel is still used as a thoroughfare between Rotherhithe and Stepney. The top of the tunnel is 48ft below the high-water mark to allow for large ships passing above.

YHA London Thameside 20 Salter Road SE16 5PR (0845 371 9756; www.yha.org.uk). This prominent landmark on the south bank of the river is a luxurious youth hostel catering for families, groups and individual travellers.

Limehouse Basin E14. This used to be called the Regent's Canal Dock, and forms part of the Grand Union Canal system, which was opened in 1820 to allow barges to trade between London and Birmingham. The Limehouse Cut also provides access to the River Lea.

Royal Naval Victualling Yard Grove Street SE8. Founded in 1513 as the Royal Dock for Henry VIII's navy, the yard became the principal naval dockyard in the kingdom, rivalling Woolwich. Sir Francis Drake was knighted here after his world voyage on the *Golden Hind*, and it was from this yard that Captain Cook's *Discovery* set sail.

Docklands Stretching from Tower Pier to Beckton is London's Docklands. The area has undergone massive change from a thriving, commercial port through closure to regeneration. The London Docklands Development Corporation (LDDC) was set up in 1981 to create a new city for the 21st C incorporating riverside apartments, shops, restaurants and offices.

Canary Wharf Tower One Canada Square, Canary Wharf E14. Designed by Cesar Pelli, 1988–90, this 800ft building is the tallest in the UK. Clad in stainless steel and topped with a pyramid, the 50-storey building boasts a magnificent lobby finished in Italian and Guatemalan marble. Thirty-two passenger lifts operate from the lobby and are the fastest in the country. Canary Wharf itself is full of elegant architecture, stately streets, well-planted squares and outdoor spaces.

Isle of Dogs E14. Until the industrialisation of the early 19th C, the Isle of Dogs was mainly pastureland and marshes. Windmills stood by the river. By 1799 the Port of London had become so overcrowded that Parliament authorised the building of a new dock on the Isle of Dogs, under the auspices of the West India Company. Built by William Jessop, the two West India Docks were opened in 1802. In 1870 the South Dock was added. It was built on the site of the City Canal which had connected Limehouse Reach and Blackwall Reach between 1805 and 1829. The Millwall Docks, the most southern, were completed in 1864. The West India Docks are also the site of Billingsgate Fish Market, which was moved here from its old site near London Bridge in 1982.

Island Gardens Saunders Ness Road E14. This small park at the south tip of the Isle of Dogs was opened in 1895 to commemorate the spot which Wren considered had the best view of Greenwich Palace across the water.

Greenwich Tunnel E14. The Blackwall Tunnel, opened in 1897, was designed as a road traffic tunnel. In 1902 it was decided to build a pedestrian subway to link Greenwich with the Isle of Dogs. There was opposition from the watermen and lightermen who, rightly, feared for their jobs. The southern entrance to the footway is in Cutty Sark Gardens, Greenwich, and the northern entrance is in Island Gardens, Isle of Dogs.

Greenwich SE10. Once a small fishing village, the historic town of Greenwich marks the eastern approach to London. Its royal and naval past is illustrated by the magnificent riverside grouping of the Queen's House, the Royal Naval College, the National Maritime Museum and the Old Royal Observatory. From the Observatory the views are magnificent, spanning Docklands and the City right through to Westminster. Museums, bookshops, antique shops, and a daily street market make for a bustling village atmosphere away from the industrialisation of the Docklands area.

The Cutty Sark King William Walk SE10 (www.cuttysark.org.uk). One of the great 19th-C tea and wool sailing clippers, stands in dry dock. There is no public access unti the ship re-opens in spring 2012. Close by stands *Gipsy Moth IV*, the yacht in which Sir Francis Chichester made his solo circumnavigation of the world in 1966.

Greenwich Park SE10 (www.royalparks.org.uk/parks/greenwich_park/). The park, laid out for Charles II by the French royal landscape gardener André Le Nôtre, commands a magnificent view of the Royal Naval College and of the river. It contains 13 acres of woodland and deer park, a bird sanctuary and archaeological sites. Crooms Hill lies to the west of the park, lined with a wealth of 17th-, 18th- and 19th-C houses, the oldest being at the southern end near Blackheath. Greenwich Theatre stands at the foot of the hill.

National Maritime Museum Park Row, Greenwich SE10 9NF (020 8858 4422; www.rmg.co.uk). At the heart of the Greenwich World Heritage Site, comprising three sites: the Maritime Galleries, the Royal Observatory and the Queen's House. The Maritime Galleries cover the country's encounters with the world at sea from the 16th to the early 20th centuries. The original observatory, still standing, was built by Wren for Flamsteed, first Astronomer Royal, in the 17th C. Astronomical instruments and exhibits relating to the history of astronomy, planetarium shows and the time ball which provided the first public time signal in 1833 still operates. Home to the Meridian Line, interactive science stations and the largest refracting telescope in the UK. The Queen's House is a delightful white house in the Palladian style, built for Queen Anne of Denmark by Inigo Jones, 1618. It showcases the museums's fine-art collection. *Open daily, 10.00–17.00.*

Royal Naval College 2 Cutty Sark Gardens, Greenwich SE10 9LW (020 8269 4747;

www.ornc.org). Mary II commissioned Wren to rebuild the palace as a hospital for aged and disabled seamen. Designed in the Baroque style, it was completed in 1705. The Painted Hall, or Dining Hall, has a swirling Baroque ceiling by Thornhill, one of the finest of its period. The neo-classical chapel dates from 1789. In 1873 the hospital became the Royal Naval College to provide for the higher education of naval officers. The *Painted Hall, Chapel and Visitor Centre are open to the public, daily 10.00–17.00.* Varied events programme.

Execution Dock SE16. At the entrance to Blackwall Tunnel. This is where, until the late 19th C, the bodies of convicted pirates were hung in iron cages until three tides had washed over them.

O2 Arena Peninsula Square SE10 0DX (020 8463 2000; www.theo2.co.uk). Once the Millennium Dome, now home to concerts, sports, cinema, exhibitions, special events, bars and restaurants. The structure is enormous: it is as high as Nelson's Column and the Eiffel Tower would fit inside it, lying on its side!

Blackwall Tunnel SE16. Built in 1897 by Sir Alexander Binnie. There are now two tunnels; the second opened in 1967. One is for northbound traffic, the other for southbound.

Thames Flood Barrier Unit Way, Woolich SE18 5NJ (020 8305 4188; www.environment-agency.gov.uk). The Flood Barrier is best seen from the river. As you round the bend, the steel fins rise up from the water. Completed in 1982, it is the world's largest movable flood barrier and is designed to swing up from the river bed and create a stainless steel barrage to stem periodically dangerous high tides. Each gate weighs 3000 tonnes and is the equivalent of a five-storey building in height. The structures housing the machines which operate the gates seem to have been inspired by the sails of Sydney Opera House. Blackwall Reach, on the way to the Flood Barrier, was where, in 1606, Captain John Smith and the Virginia Settlers left on their journey to found the first permanent colony in America.

LONDON RIVER SERVICES

Since Roman times the importance of the Thames has been recognised as a highway for both commerce and passenger carrying alike, with ferries and their attendant piers developing where necessary. In the latter half of the 20th C there was a move away from the river to buses, tubes and taxis, the river piers largely reduced to serving pleasure traffic. However, as part of the Thames 2000 initiative and funded by the Millennium Commission, five new piers were built at strategic points along the river: Blackfriars, Tate Britain, Waterloo, Westminster and the Tower of London. Forming part of an integrated transport strategy for the Thames, new vessels, services and upgraded piers have meant new links along and across the Thames. A series of central London fast ferry services operate alongside shuttle services to Greenwich, and pleasure and sightseeing cruises. Visit the Transport for London website (www.tfl.gov.uk) and select 'river' for details of ferry services, river timetables and maps.

Coxes Mill and Coxes Lock, Weybridge (see page 189)

WEY & GODALMING NAVIGATIONS

MAXIMUM DIMENSIONS

Length: 71' 6"
Beam: 13' 10"
Draught: 3' to Guildford
2' 6" above Guildford
Headroom: 7' to Guildford
6' to Godalming (at normal levels)

MILEAGES

THAMES LOCK (junction with River Thames) *to*:
Woodham Junction: 3 miles
Cartbridge: 9 miles
Guildford: 15 miles
Guns Mouth: 17¼ miles
Godalming: 19½ miles

Locks: 16 (including Worsfold and Walsham Flood Gates)

Navigation Authority:
The National Trust
River Wey Navigations
Dapdune Wharf
Wharf Road
Guildford GU1 4RR
Visitor Services Manager: 01483 561389
riverwey@nationaltrust.org.uk

Annual or visitor's licences are issued at Dapdune Wharf, or at Thames Lock. A copy of *Information for Boat Users* is supplied with each licence and can also be downloaded at www.nationaltrust.org.uk/river-wey-godalming-navigations-and-dapdune-wharf. It is essential reading for all those navigating this waterway.

The speed limit is 4 knots – in practice, slower. Watch your wash. Use only the correct Wey Navigation lock handle, available from Thames Lock, the NT Navigation Office or Guildford and Farncombe Boat Houses. When leaving locks, exit gates should be left open, but with all the paddles *down*.

As a river navigation, the Wey is subject to flooding, increasing the speed of the current and pull of the weirs. Under certain conditions, locks may be padlocked and craft should moor up in a sheltered place and seek advice. Water points on this navigation can be difficult to identify as they are not standard. The towpath side of the navigation is available for mooring.

Boats have used the River Wey since medieval times, but the present navigation dates from the 17th C. In 1651 authorisation was given to make the river navigable for 15 miles from Weybridge to Guildford. This involved the building of 12 locks and 10 miles of artificial cut. This early navigation had the usual battles with mill owners, but gradually trade developed, predominantly local and agricultural in character. More unusual were the extensive Farnham Potteries, who shipped their wares to London along the Wey. In 1763 the Godalming Navigation was opened, adding another four miles to the waterway, and by the end of the 18th C considerable barge traffic was using the river. This was greatly increased by the building of the Basingstoke Canal in 1796, and the Wey & Arun Junction Canal in 1816; the latter offered a direct route from London to Portsmouth and the south coast. This canal closed in 1871, but trade continued to thrive on the Wey and as late as 1960 barges were still carrying timber to Guildford. Grain traffic to Coxes Mill continued until 1968, with a brief revival in the early 1980s. There is now no commercial carrying on the navigation. In 1964 the Wey Navigation was given to the National Trust by Harry Stevens, its last private owner. In 1968 the Godalming Navigation Commissioners passed their section to Guildford Corporation, who in turn passed it on to the National Trust. It remains an artery of peace and tranquillity amidst the noise and bustle of Surrey, and will amply repay a visit.

Weybridge

The River Wey Navigation joins the Thames below Shepperton Lock where the correct channel is clearly signposted. Just around the corner is the Pound Gate used only when the water level is low or when a deep draughted vessel is passing through. Thames Lock is in an attractive wooded setting beside a smart new apartment conversion, and the keeper here is available to advise you. An informative display can be seen in the stable by the lock. Just above, beyond the weirs, smart houses and gardens line the east bank; the west is wooded. There is a sharp westward turn (*see* Navigational Notes) followed immediately by Weybridge Town Lock, where Addlestone Road flanks the navigation on its way to Ham Moor. Note the towline roller on the corner, installed to allow towed craft to negotiate the bend. Just below the railway bridge at Coxes Mill, the water point is hidden behind the wall of the old stable block. The large mill pond to the west is owned and managed as a wildlife habitat. Beyond Parvis Bridge the towpath skirts the old grist mill (NT), where all kinds of cattle and poultry food were produced. At New Haw lock there is *a useful newsagent and Chinese takeaway.* Much of New Haw consists of 20th-C Georgian-style commuter housing. Moored craft line the east bank above New Haw Lock (with its pretty lock cottage) as the cut makes a beeline for Byfleet, cowering under the massive concrete structures and earth embankments of the M25 motorway – there is no longer any peace to be had here. The Basingstoke Canal (*see* page 15) leaves the Wey Navigation in the midst of a flurry of bridges. Beyond Parvis Bridge, where rowing boats can be hired during the summer months, the Wey Navigation becomes more rural.

NAVIGATIONAL NOTES

1 Thames Lock (01932 843106). Attended. Licences, free *Information for Boat Users*, plus visitor passes. Lock handles for sale or hire. All those wishing to enter the lock should consult the lock keeper. Craft with draught deeper than 1ft 9in coming up from the Thames should advise the lock keeper – who may then use the pound gate to increase the water level before they enter the lock. *Open 09.00–13.00 and 14.00–18.30 or sunset.*
2 Weybridge Old Bridge – the navigation channel is clearly marked, and is the most westerly bridge-hole (furthest right) when coming upstream. The lock is immediately above the bridge and there is a winding hole below the lock..

● **Weybridge**
Surrey. All services. A commuter town in the stockbroker belt, built around the confluence of the rivers Wey and Thames – the junction is marked by a pretty iron bridge dated 1865. Weybridge represents the frontier of the suburbia which now spreads almost unbroken to London. Behind the town lie the remains of Brooklands, the doyen of motor racing circuits in the early 20th C (*see below*).
Coxes Mill *Surrey.* Overlooking Coxes Lock is a magnificent group of mostly 19th-C mill buildings, partly brick, partly concrete and partly weather-board, the best industrial architecture on the river.
Brooklands Museum Brooklands Road, Weybridge KT13 0QN (01932 857381; www. brooklandsmuseum.com). Assembled within what remains of the Brooklands race track, the world's first purpose-built motor racing circuit, constructed by wealthy landowner Hugh Locke King in 1907. Its heyday was in the 1920s and 30s, when records were being set by the likes of Malcolm Campbell and John Cobb, driving vehicles with evocative names, such as the Delage, Bentley and Bugatti. It became very fashionable, and was known as the Ascot of Motorsport. It was also an aerodrome and an aircraft factory, and it was here that A. V. Roe made the first flight in a British aeroplane. The Sopwith Pup and Camel were developed here, and later the Hawker Hurricane and the Vickers Wellington were built here – the only Wellington that saw war time service, salvaged in 1985 from Loch Ness and restored, is on display. The outbreak of war in 1939 brought an end to racing, and aircraft production ceased in 1987. Now you can walk on part of the legendary circuit, and see historic racing cars and aircraft, including a *Concorde*, in the museum. The clubhouse is a listed building. You can also visit the Raleigh Cycle Exhibition, a reminder that cycle races were also held at Brooklands. Special events are staged throughout the year. *Open 10.00–17.00 (16.00 winter). Closed Xmas.* Charge.
● **Byfleet**
Surrey. PO, shops. Although buried by modern commuter housing, parts of the old village can be found. The church with its bellcote is mostly late 13th-C, and the 17th-C brick manor house is an elegant delight in the midst of so much dreariness.

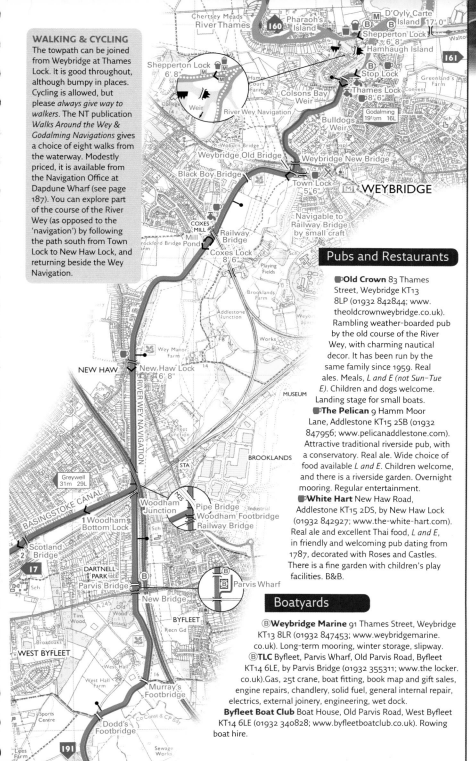

WALKING & CYCLING

The towpath can be joined from Weybridge at Thames Lock. It is good throughout, although bumpy in places. Cycling is allowed, but please *always give way to walkers*. The NT publication *Walks Around the Wey & Godalming Navigations* gives a choice of eight walks from the waterway. Modestly priced, it is available from the Navigation Office at Dapdune Wharf (see page 187). You can explore part of the course of the River Wey (as opposed to the 'navigation') by following the path south from Town Lock to New Haw Lock, and returning beside the Wey Navigation.

Map labels

Chertsey Meads
River Thames
Pharaoh's Island
D'Oyly Carte Island 17' 0"
160
Shepperton Lock
6' 8"
Walton
161
Hamhaugh Island
Shepperton Lock 6' 8"
Hampton Court Farm
Hamm
Weir
College
River Wey Navigation
Stop Lock
Colsons Bay Weir
Thames Lock 8' 6"
Greenland's Farm
Convent
Godalming 19½m 16L
Bulldogs Weir
Woburn Bridge
Weybridge Old Bridge
Weybridge New Bridge
Black Boy Bridge
Town Lock 5' 6"
WEYBRIDGE
COXES MILL
Railway Mill Bridge Pond
Brockford Bridge Farm
Railway Bridge
Navigable to Railway Bridge by small craft
Coxes Lock 8' 6"
Playing Fields
Brooklands Farm
Addlestone Junction
FB
Works
Weybridge Junction
Wey Manor Farm
MUSEUM
NEW HAW
New Haw Lock 6' 8"
RIVER WEY NAVIGATION
Byfleet Junction
BROOKLANDS
STA
M25
Greywell 31m 29L
BASINGSTOKE CANAL
Woodham Junction
Pipe Bridge
Woodham Footbridge
Woodham Bottom Lock
Woodham Railway Bridge
Industrial
Scotland Bridge
17
2
DARTNELL PARK
Parvis Bridge
New Bridge
Parvis Wharf
BYFLEET
Recn Gd
Old Wood
A245
Tins Wood
WEST BYFLEET
West Hall
West Hall Farm
Murray's Footbridge
Sports Centre
Dodd's Footbridge
Coconut & CP Bdy
Lees Farm
191
Sewage Works

Pubs and Restaurants

Old Crown 83 Thames Street, Weybridge KT13 8LP (01932 842844; www.theoldcrownweybridge.co.uk). Rambling weather-boarded pub by the old course of the River Wey, with charming nautical decor. It has been run by the same family since 1959. Real ales. Meals, *L and E (not Sun–Tue E)*. Children and dogs welcome. Landing stage for small boats.

The Pelican 9 Hamm Moor Lane, Addlestone KT15 2SB (01932 847956; www.pelicanaddlestone.com). Attractive traditional riverside pub, with a conservatory. Real ale. Wide choice of food available *L and E*. Children welcome, and there is a riverside garden. Overnight mooring. Regular entertainment.

White Hart New Haw Road, Addlestone KT15 2DS, by New Haw Lock (01932 842927; www.the-white-hart.com). Real ale and excellent Thai food, *L and E*, in friendly and welcoming pub dating from 1787, decorated with Roses and Castles. There is a fine garden with children's play facilities. B&B.

Boatyards

Ⓑ **Weybridge Marine** 91 Thames Street, Weybridge KT13 8LR (01932 847453; www.weybridgemarine.co.uk). Long-term mooring, winter storage, slipway.
Ⓑ **TLC** Byfleet, Parvis Wharf, Old Parvis Road, Byfleet KT14 6LE, by Parvis Bridge (01932 355311; www.the.locker.co.uk).Gas, 25t crane, boat fitting, book map and gift sales, engine repairs, chandlery, solid fuel, general internal repair, electrics, external joinery, engineering, wet dock.
Byfleet Boat Club Boat House, Old Parvis Road, West Byfleet KT14 6LE (01932 340828; www.byfleetboatclub.co.uk). Rowing boat hire.

Pyrford

The popular Anchor pub is close to the bridge at Pyrford, with Pyrford Marina opposite; just beyond is Pyrford Lock and many colourful moored craft. The old sanitary station still retains a manual water pump which you can use only for rinsing (it is NOT drinking water). The navigation then passes Pyrford Place, with its lovely old Elizabethan summerhouse with a pagoda roof, beside a charming little riverside terrace. Except in times of flood you may pass uninterrupted through Walsham Flood Gates, the last remaining turf-sided lock on the navigation, with old style vertical paddles, overlooked by the quaintly business-like lock cottage. The large weir is to the east. The river then becomes wider and strewn with lily pads, before it splits to form a trio of islands at Newark, where the remains of Newark Priory can be seen at the water's edge. The lock cut continues to Newark Lock – above here the river winds towards Papercourt Lock, arguably the prettiest on the river, with its stepped weir and charming garden. Factories and offices line the south bank as the navigation passes under High Bridge and approaches Cart Bridge, to the west of Send. It is, surprisingly, quite peaceful – a relief considering the boundless activity all around. The restored National Trust Workshop is by the lock, often with a few sturdy barges moored opposite. Then once again the Wey resumes its rural course, passing Triggs Lock, with another attractive lock cottage, this one dating from 1770. At one time it had a blacksmith's shop attached, and to the north there used to be a small wharf. William Stevens became lock keeper here in 1812 – it was one of his descendants, Harry Stevens, who was to give the navigation to the National Trust in 1964.

Pyrford Village
Surrey. Tel. Surrounded by water meadows and trees, Pyrford remains a 'real' village. Brick cottages overlook the church, an almost intact Norman building 'built of puddingstone, dressed with clunch'; such a thing is rare in the Home Counties and is thus an even greater pleasure. The north porch is half-timbered and dates from the 16th C. Inside are wall paintings depicting scenes from the flagellation and the Passion, c.1200: the pulpit is 17th-C. There are many attractive 18th-C houses.

The Summerhouse of Pyrford Place Canalside above Walsham Footbridge. Built at the end of the 17th C. The estate was inherited by Francis Egerton, who became Lord Chancellor. His son, Thomas Egerton had a secretary, John Donne, who wooed Anne More, a lonely heiress, in this summerhouse. They later married and lived at Pyrford Place. *Strictly private - NO landing.*

Royal Horticultural Society's Gardens Wisley GU23 6QB (0845 260 9000; www.rhs.org.uk). By footpath south east of Pigeon House Bridge to Ockham Mill, then north east towards Wisley, or by footpath from Pyrford Lock. A 200-acre botanic garden acquired by the RHS in 1904 and famous for its trials and improvements of new varieties. Notable collections of old-fashioned and new roses, rhododendrons, camellias, heathers and rock garden plants. Walled garden with tender perennial shrubs and climbers, Country Garden, Temperate Glasshouse and Garden of the Senses. *Open Mar-Oct, Mon-Fri 10.00-18.00, Sat, Sun 09.00-18.00, and Nov-Feb, Mon-Fri 10.00- 14.30, Sat, Sun 09.00-16.30.* Members only *on Sun.* Charge.

Newark Priory Near Pyrford Green. The tall broken flint of this 12th-C Augustinian priory stand in a meadow at the river's edge, an enticing and romantic ruin. Unfortunately there is no right of navigation up to the walls.

Send
Surrey. PO, stores, butcher, off-licence, takeaway, café. The church lies close to the River Wey and well to the south west of the main centre. Although nicely sited amongst trees and 18th-C houses, the village looks at its best from the river.

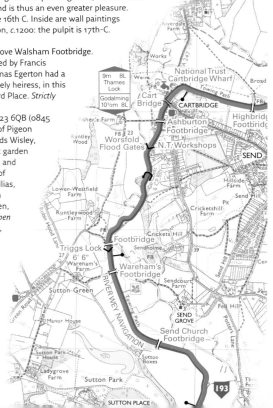

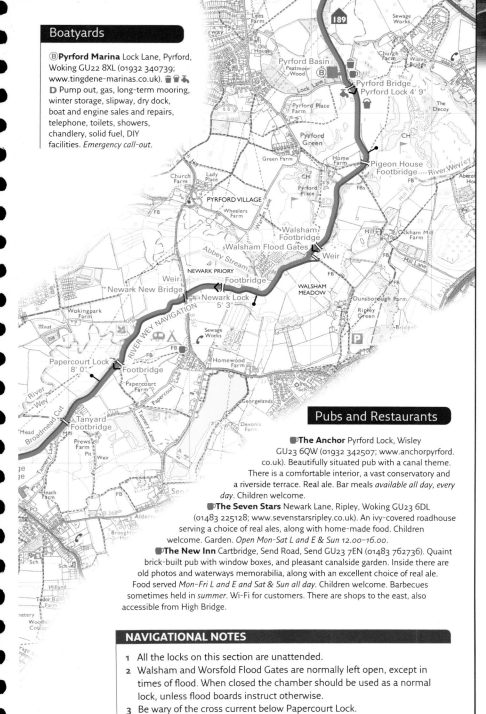

Boatyards

Ⓑ**Pyrford Marina** Lock Lane, Pyrford, Woking GU22 8XL (01932 340739; www.tingdene-marinas.co.uk). 📞🚻♿ **D** Pump out, gas, long-term mooring, winter storage, slipway, dry dock, boat and engine sales and repairs, telephone, toilets, showers, chandlery, solid fuel, DIY facilities. *Emergency call-out.*

Pubs and Restaurants

🍺**The Anchor** Pyrford Lock, Wisley GU23 6QW (01932 342507; www.anchorpyrford. co.uk). Beautifully situated pub with a canal theme. There is a comfortable interior, a vast conservatory and a riverside terrace. Real ale. Bar meals *available all day, every day*. Children welcome.

🍺**The Seven Stars** Newark Lane, Ripley, Woking GU23 6DL (01483 225128; www.sevenstarsripley.co.uk). An ivy-covered roadhouse serving a choice of real ales, along with home-made food. Children welcome. Garden. *Open Mon-Sat L and E & Sun 12.00-16.00.*

🍺**The New Inn** Cartbridge, Send Road, Send GU23 7EN (01483 762736). Quaint brick-built pub with window boxes, and pleasant canalside garden. Inside there are old photos and waterways memorabilia, along with an excellent choice of real ale. Food served *Mon-Fri L and E and Sat & Sun all day*. Children welcome. Barbecues sometimes held in *summer*. Wi-Fi for customers. There are shops to the east, also accessible from High Bridge.

NAVIGATIONAL NOTES

1. All the locks on this section are unattended.
2. Walsham and Worsfold Flood Gates are normally left open, except in times of flood. When closed the chamber should be used as a normal lock, unless flood boards instruct otherwise.
3. Be wary of the cross current below Papercourt Lock.

Guildford

The navigation now begins to sweep around Sutton Place, and comes very close to the A3, with its constant rumble of traffic. Care should be exercised at Broadoak Bridge (note the towline roller on the corner) and Bower's Lock (*see* below). The approach to Stoke Lock is tree-lined, but it is now very clear that Guildford is being approached and the scene is becoming increasingly urban. A few willows overhang by Stoke Bridge, but soon all is back gardens, roads and factories. The scene gradually improves, and at Dapdune Wharf, the National Trust has established a visitor centre, with a fine restored Wey barge amongst other exhibits. At Walnut Footbridge the Odeon Cinema is riverside. At Onslow Bridge the change of scene is completed: the town turns to face the water – and what a jolly scene it is – with riverside walks, a handsome mill, the theatre, a busy boatyard, pubs and restaurants, all overlooked by the castle. Note especially the rare treadwheel crane standing on what was the old Guildford Town Wharf: from here the Wey Navigation becomes the Godalming Navigation and leaves Guildford in an ideal setting, with parkland to the east and pleasant private gardens glimpsed over high walls to the west. A footbridge marks the site of the old St Catherine's Ferry on the Pilgrims' Way, and a small stream spills into the river here below a pretty grotto, where those who pass are 'treading the path trod by Geoffrey Chaucer's Canterbury Pilgrims in the reign of King Edward the Third'. Just beyond is St Catherine's Sands, a favourite haunt of the local children during warm school holidays. Guildford Boat House is a charming Victorian building.

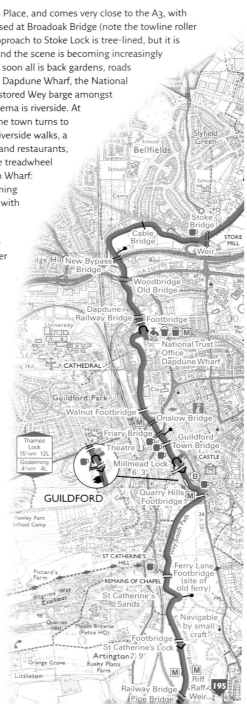

NAVIGATIONAL NOTES

1. At Broadoak Bridge pass through the arch closest to the towing path.
2. When approached from downstream Bower's Lock is to the left before the footbridge. When locking down, take the sharp blind turn to the right with care.
3. Keep clear of the weir above St Catherine's Lock.

BOAT TRIPS

Guildford Boat House Millbrook, Guildford GU1 3XJ (01483 504494; www.guildfordboats. co.uk). Regular trips on the *Harry Stevens* for up to 60 passengers, departing from Guildford Boat House or the Town Quay, from *Easter–end Oct*. Restaurant cruises on the *Alfred Leroy*, from *May–Oct*. Also private charter, narrowboat and rowing boat hire.

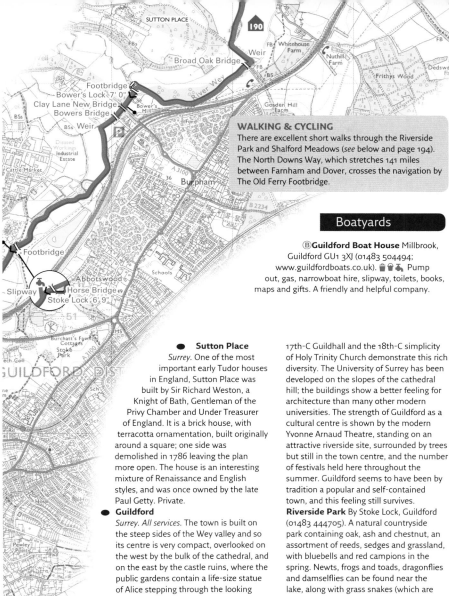

WALKING & CYCLING

There are excellent short walks through the Riverside Park and Shalford Meadows (*see* below and page 194). The North Downs Way, which stretches 141 miles between Farnham and Dover, crosses the navigation by The Old Ferry Footbridge.

Boatyards

Ⓑ**Guildford Boat House** Millbrook, Guildford GU1 3XJ (01483 504494; www.guildfordboats.co.uk). 🎁🎁⛽ Pump out, gas, narrowboat hire, slipway, toilets, books, maps and gifts. A friendly and helpful company.

● **Sutton Place**

Surrey. One of the most important early Tudor houses in England, Sutton Place was built by Sir Richard Weston, a Knight of Bath, Gentleman of the Privy Chamber and Under Treasurer of England. It is a brick house, with terracotta ornamentation, built originally around a square; one side was demolished in 1786 leaving the plan more open. The house is an interesting mixture of Renaissance and English styles, and was once owned by the late Paul Getty. Private.

● **Guildford**

Surrey. All services. The town is built on the steep sides of the Wey valley and so its centre is very compact, overlooked on the west by the bulk of the cathedral, and on the east by the castle ruins, where the public gardens contain a life-size statue of Alice stepping through the looking glass, celebrating the town's association with Lewis Carroll (*see* below). The castle grounds continue as Castle Cliffe Gardens: 'The Chestnuts', where the author once lived, is close by. The best parts of the town are around the traffic-free cobbled High Street, which leads steeply down to the river, where there are interesting mill and wharf buildings, including the last tread wheel operated crane in existence. The High Street is rich with good buildings of all periods; facing each other at the top, the Baroque splendour of the

17th-C Guildhall and the 18th-C simplicity of Holy Trinity Church demonstrate this rich diversity. The University of Surrey has been developed on the slopes of the cathedral hill; the buildings show a better feeling for architecture than many other modern universities. The strength of Guildford as a cultural centre is shown by the modern Yvonne Arnaud Theatre, standing on an attractive riverside site, surrounded by trees but still in the town centre, and the number of festivals held here throughout the summer. Guildford seems to have been by tradition a popular and self-contained town, and this feeling still survives.

Riverside Park By Stoke Lock, Guildford (01483 444705). A natural countryside park containing oak, ash and chestnut, an assortment of reeds, sedges and grassland, with bluebells and red campions in the spring. Newts, frogs and toads, dragonflies and damselflies can be found near the lake, along with grass snakes (which are harmless), all managed with conservation in mind.

Guildford Cathedral Stag Hill, Guildford GU2 7UP (01483 547860; www.guildford-cathedral.org.uk) The brick mass of the cathedral overlooks the town – it is an uncompromising and unsubtle thing, the last fling of the Gothic revival. Designed by Edward Maufe in 1932, it was only completed in 1961, and sadly reveals its period all too clearly. From the outside it is a mixture of cinema, power station and church; the inside is a complete contrast

– a wealth of detail, and delicate use of shape and form, far more genuinely Gothic in feeling. Interesting furniture, fittings, glass and statuary. *Open daily 08.30–17.30*. Gift shop, book shop and café.

Guildford House Gallery 155 High Street, Guidlford GU1 3AJ (01483 444751; www.guildford.gov.uk). The building dates from 1660, and contains fine decorative plasterwork, and a fine carved staircase. Permanent and visiting exhibitions. *Open Mon–Sat 10.00–16.45 & Summer Sun 11.00–16.00*. Free. Tea room *open Tue–Sat 10.00–16.15*. Craft shop.

Guildford Castle Castle Street, Guildford GU1 3UQ The huge motte dates from the 11th C, topped by a tower keep c.1170. It remains an imposing ruin.

Guildford Museum Castle Arch, Quarry Street, Guildford GU1 3SX (01483 444751; www.guildford.gov.uk/museum). Prehistoric, Roman and Saxon exhibits along with displays of Victorian life. Space is also devoted to Lewis Carroll. *Open Mon–Sat 11.00–17.00*. Free. Shop.

The Undercroft 72 High Street, Guildford GU1 3HE (01483 444751; www.guildford.gov.uk/undercroft). A vaulted medieval basement 13 x 19ft with a rib-vaulted ceiling, dating from the 13th C, with an exhibition illustrating life in medieval Guildford. *Open May–Sep Wed 14.00–16.00 & Sun 12.00–16.00*. Free.

Lewis Carroll's Grave You can find the grave of this Victorian author, who was born Charles Lutwidge Dodgson in Daresbury (*see Book 5*), near the chapel in the Mount Cemetery, which is to the south west of Onslow Bridge. *Open 09.00–20.00 (16.30 winter)*. Visit www.lewiscarrollsociety.org.uk for further details

Guided Walks Contact the TIC (*across*). Topics include Historic and Unknown Guildford, plus Ghosts and Legends, and Lewis Carroll. *May–Sep Sun, Mon and Wed 14.30 and Thu 19.30*.

Shalford Meadows East of St Catherine's Sands. There are rich plant communities in this riverside water-meadow.

Dapdune Wharf Visitor Centre Wharf Road, Guildford GU1 4RR (01483 561389/07900 137780; riverway@ nationaltrust.org.uk; www.nationaltrust.org.uk). Towpath access is via the footbridge beside the railway bridge. This was once the barge building centre of the River Wey Navigation, and has been tastefully restored with a stable, smithy, barge building shed and old cottages. Displays tell the story of the people who lived and worked here. Some handsome restored craft can be seen outside, including the barge *Reliance*, built 1931–2, one of 11 Wey barges built here by the Stevens family. It traded between the Wey and London Docks until it hit Cannon Street Bridge, in London, and sank. It languished on the mud flats at Leigh-on-Sea in Essex, to be later salvaged and returned to Dapdune for restoration. *Open Mar–Oct, Thu–Mon, 11.00–1700*. Charge. 40-minute boat trips to Town Wharf (no landing).

Tourist Information Centre 155 High Street, Guildford GU1 3AJ (01483 444333; www.guildford.gov.uk/visitguildford). *Open Mon–Sat 09.30–17.00 & summer Sun 11.00–16.00*.

● **Shalford**
Surrey. PO. A meandering village built along the main road. It is at its best by the river, which is flanked by old wharf and warehouse buildings.

Shalford Mill NT. Shalford, near Guildford GU4 8BS (01483 561389; www.nationaltrust.org.uk). Opposite the Seahorse pub. An early 19th-C tile-fronted water mill, containing some of the finest early 19th-C mill machinery in the country. It has remained unaltered since it went out of use in 1914. *Open Wed and Sun 11.00–17.00*. Charge.

Pubs and Restaurants

There are lots of pubs, restaurants and tearooms to choose from in Guildford. The following are all close to the navigation.

The Rowbarge 7 Riverside, Guildford GU1 1LW (01483 573358; www.rowbargeguildford.com). By Stoke Bridge. Pleasant garden and moorings, close to the Guildford Waterside Centre. Real ale. Coffee and bar food *Mon–Sat 12.00–19.00 & Sun 12.30–17.00*. Regular live music.

The White House 8 High Street, Guildford GU2 4AJ (01483 302006; www.whitehouseguildford.co.uk). A smart pub in an attractive riverside building, with a shady terrace by the water and the largest pub garden in Guildford. Real ale. Meals served *all day*. Children welcome.

Brittannia 9 Millmead, Guildford GU2 4BE (01483 572160; www.britanniaguildford.co.uk). Overlooking the lock, this is a handsome red brick pub. Real ale. Food served *all day, every day*. Live music *Thur*. Outside seating. Children welcome *during the day*.

The Boatman Shalford Road, Millbrook, Guildford GU1 3XJ (01483 568024; www.boatman-guildford.co.uk). Large riverside pub with a garden, conservatory and terrace. Real ale. Meals available *all day, every day*. Children welcome.

Ye Olde Ship Inn Portsmouth Road, Guildford GU2 4EB (01483 575731; www.yeoldeshipinn.com). Up the old Pilgrims' Way, this friendly pub serves real ale, cider and interesting food cooked using a wood-burning oven. Children welcome in the saloon. Garden. Takeaway food. *Open Mon–Fri L and E & all day Sat & Sun*.

WALKING & CYCLING
Stretches of the towpath approaching Godalming consist of very soft sand, which is not very kind to bicycles! Be warned. You can explore a section of the Wey & Arun Canal on foot by following the path south east from Broadford Bridge and then returning across Bramley Common to the Godalming Navigation, where you cross Unstead Bridge and head north along the towpath.

Godalming

The river passes Shalford through flat meadow land, and by former riverside mills above the low Broadford Bridge. There are craft moored here and at Guns Mouth, the entrance to the unnavigable Wey & Arun Canal. A fine wooded stretch below Unstead Lock ends abruptly, an indication that the main roads are closer than you might think. The gardens of very smart residences line the Farncombe bank as the river approaches Catteshall Lock, the highest on the river and the furthest south on the linked navigable system. There are good moorings at Lammas Lands on the towpath side above here, and it is only a short walk to Town Bridge, the usual

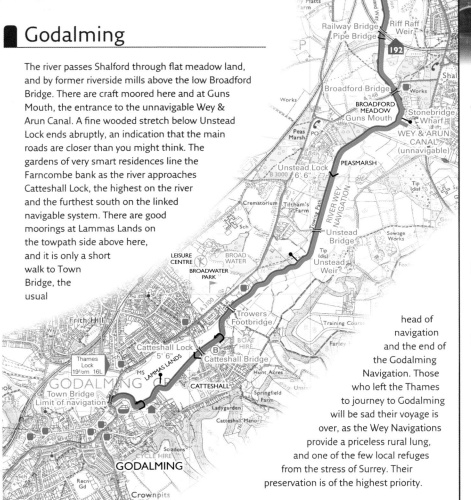

head of navigation and the end of the Godalming Navigation. Those who left the Thames to journey to Godalming will be sad their voyage is over, as the Wey Navigations provide a priceless rural lung, and one of the few local refuges from the stress of Surrey. Their preservation is of the highest priority.

BOAT TRIPS

Nb Iona The Packet Boat Company (01483 414938; www.horseboat. org.uk). A horse drawn narrowboat based at Godalming Wharf (GU7 1JL), available for public trips *daily Easter to Sep, usually starting at 14.00*, but dependant on the state of the river. Also private charter. The boat can carry up to 48 passengers. Shop and tea bar on board. Telephone for details.

Boatyards

Ⓑ**Farncombe Boat House** Catteshall Lock, Godalming GU7 1NH (01483 421306; www. farncombeboats. co.uk). ⚓D Pump out, gas, narrowboat hire, day-boat hire, rowing boats, long-term mooring, boat building, boat and engine sales and repairs, toilets, books and maps. Riverside bistro (*open Wed–Sun*).

1 Broadford Bridge is low, with only 6ft 4in maximum headroom.
2 In Godalming, at the last winding hole, navigators are advised to wind with their bows to the towpath side of the navigation.
3 Small, shallow draught craft may be able to pass under Town Bridge to reach Boarden Bridge – but note that it is beyond the navigable limit, and there is a weir just above the railway bridge.
4 A horse-drawn boat operates between Godalming Wharf and Unstead Bridge *from Easter–Sep*. Do not moor on bends in this area, and keep your cabin top clear.

Wey & Arun Canal

This navigation, built between 1816 and 1817, linked London with the south coast at Littlehampton, and Portsmouth, and has been romanticised as London's lost route to the sea. The first 100yds or so is still in water and used for moorings, but there is no turning space. A low bridge presently impedes further progress. Much of the rest of the route is still intact and the Wey & Arun Canal Trust (www.weyandarun.co.uk) is working towards full restoration having rebuilt a number of locks and bridges along its length, allowing completed sections of the waterway to be re-opened.. Meanwhile the canal makes a very attractive walk, linking the North and South Downs Way.

Godalming

Surrey. All services. The head of navigation is near the heavy stone bridge to the north east of the town centre. By tradition a cloth-making town, Godalming has developed in a haphazard way over the years, but its busy streets have plenty to offer. At its centre, The Town Hall, known as 'the Pepperpot', was built in 1814 by John Perry, a local man. It is a modestly handsome building with an open ground floor, and is ideally situated. The area around it was the first in the world to benefit from electric street lighting. The church of St Peter and St Paul, with its rare and tall leaded 13th-C spire, gives the town a dramatic skyline.

Pubs and Restaurants

The Parrot Inn Broadford Road, Shalford GU4 8DW (01483 561400; www.parrotinn.co.uk). East of Broadford Bridge. Victorian pub by the green, which has been a winner of the Guildford in Bloom Pub of the Year award. Real ales. Meals available *L and E*. Attractive walled garden. Well-behaved children welcome *until 20.00*. Occasional theme nights, such as lobster, Greek or French. B&B.

The Manor Inn Guildford Road, Godalming GU7 3BX (01483 427134). Riverside hotel with garden. Real ale. Bar and restaurant meals, including breakfast, *all day*. Garden and children's play area. B&B.

The Leathern Bottle 77 Meadrow, Godalming GU7 3JG (01483 425642). Small locals' pub serving real ale. Meals, such as steak and chips and *Sunday* roasts, *L and E*. Children welcome. Garden with a pool. Darts, cards and dominoes are played.

The Godalming Arms 1 Meadrow, Godalming GU7 3HJ (01483 416680). North of Town Bridge, and once called The Railway. A welcoming and friendly pub serving a range of real ales. Meals. *L and E (not Sun)* Children welcome. Skittle alley, games room and a garden.

The King's Arms and Royal Hotel 22-25 High Street, Godalming GU7 1EB (01483 421545; www.royalhotelgodalming.co.uk). Traditional coaching inn which was visited by Peter the Great in 1698. Real ale. Food including an all-day breakfast, *L and E*. Children welcome, and there is a garden. B&B.

Piazza Firenze 28 High Street, Godalming, GU7 1DZ (01483 418 675; www.piazzafirenze.com/godalming). Friendly, welcoming establishment serving delicious, authentic Italian food from a reasonably priced menu. Attentive staff. Child friendly. *Open daily 12.00–23.00 (Sun 22.30).*

Bel & The Dragon Old Church, Bridge Street, Godalming GU7 1HY (01483 527333; www.belandthedragon-godalming.co.uk). Describing itself as an all day Kitchen, bar and restaurant, this establishment is housed in a converted Congregational chapel – complete with gallery - close to the head of the navigation at Town Bridge. Real ales, a wide ranging wine selection and varied cocktails vie with appetising snacks and meals. Traditional afternoon teas, pastries and cakes, together with coffee, are also popular. Meals available *L and E. Open all day.*

The Sun Inn 1 Wharf Street, Godalming GU7 1NN (01483 415505; www.thesuninn-godalming.com). Popular pub majoring on sports TV and live *weekend* music. Traditional, home-made pub meals are served *12.00–18.00 (Sun 16.00)* daily. (Also *all day* breakfasts and *Sunday* roasts). Real ales. Patio. B&B. *Open all day.*

INDEX